Καλλίμαχος ὁ γραμματικὸς τὸ μέγα βιβλίον ἴσον ἔλεγεν εἶναι τῷ μεγάλῳ κακῷ.

Athenaeus, *Deipnosophistae* 3.1.1
(fragment 465, Pfeiffer)

D1214538

A Primer of
Biblical Greek

N. Clayton Croy

WILLIAM B. EERDMANS PUBLISHING COMPANY
GRAND RAPIDS, MICHIGAN / CAMBRIDGE, U.K.

© 1999 Wm. B. Eerdmans Publishing Co.

255 Jefferson Ave. S.E., Grand Rapids, Michigan 49503 /

P.O. Box 163, Cambridge CB3 9PU U.K.

All rights reserved

Printed in the United States of America

04 03 02 01 00 99   7 6 5 4 3 2 1

Library of Congress Cataloging-in-Publication Data

Croy, N. Clayton.

A primer of Biblical Greek / N. Clayton Croy.

p.   cm.

Includes Greek-English and English-Greek vocabulary sections.

Includes bibliographical references and index.

ISBN 0-8028-4628-9 (alk. paper)

1. Greek language, Biblical — Grammar Problems, exercises, etc.

2. Bible. N.T.—Language, style Problems, exercises, etc.

I. Title.

PA817.C76   1999

487′.4 — dc21

99-34385

CIP

Dedicated to my Greek teachers,
chief among whom were
William D. Blake,
Robert W. Lyon,
and
Robert Renehan

Contents

Contents

Contents

Contents

Contents

Contents

Contents

Introduction

A Primer of Biblical Greek is an introductory textbook aimed at college and seminary students. Inasmuch as several such texts already exist, a rationale for this *Primer* is needed. My own experience in teaching Greek and my conversations with other teachers suggest that most of the texts in print are flawed in various ways: faulty or inadequate grammatical explanations, excessive detail, inadequate exercises, unidiomatic exercises, pedagogical quirks or gimmicks, typographical errors, excessively high prices, and noninclusive language. While the present volume is certainly not beyond improvement, it has been written with these concerns in mind and has undergone much peer review and classroom testing prior to publication. I believe that its chief strengths are fourfold.

(1) There is an abundance of exercises. Every lesson from Lesson 2 on has four sets of exercises. A section entitled "Practice and Review" contains Greek sentences composed for intensive practice with material just introduced in that lesson. A second section has sentences drawn from the Septuagint. The third section consists of New Testament sentences. (A special vocabulary list follows the LXX and NT sentences to enable students to translate unfamiliar words and constructions. As a general rule, students should *not* try to acquire these words as part of their growing vocabulary. That is the function of the vocabulary sections at the beginning of each lesson.) The fourth section contains a small number of English to Greek exercises.

Some Greek textbooks use only sentences taken from the Bible, usually meaning the New Testament. Such exercises are useful for inductive learning, for insuring idiomatic style, and for maintaining student morale. After all, one learns biblical Greek in order to read and interpret the Bible, not the author's exercises. On the other hand, the Bible was not written for language students working progressively through syntax and slowly acquiring vocabulary. "Artificial" sentences have the advantage of providing intensive practice and review by using words and constructions the student has just learned. Moreover, familiarity with the Bible can sometimes short-circuit learning when only biblical sentences are used. Composed exercises, simply by being unfamiliar, require students to read more carefully. Thus, *A Primer of Biblical Greek* offers the best of both worlds: both composed and biblical exercises. In particular, I hope that the inclusion of sentences from the Septuagint will spark greater interest in that immensely important collection of writings. Finally, although the student's primary purpose will be to read rather than to write biblical Greek, the value of composition in building a more active knowledge of the language justifies the inclusion of a small number of English to Greek exercises.

(2) I have tried to keep grammatical explanations concise without thereby sacrificing clarity or accuracy. Some of the existing textbooks err in the direction of excessive detail; wary of this danger, others present oversimplified treatments. The reader will have to judge whether I have succeeded in finding the golden mean. On such matters as accentuation and contraction, in which the technicalities can be overwhelming, especially to the beginner, I have tried to offer explanations that are correct and adequate but usually qualified by statements of the *relative* value of such knowledge. Language study is incremental, inductive, and "circular." Concepts that are partially understood at one point will usually be reinforced by further study. It is generally counterproductive to insist that all technical details be mastered at one level before one moves to the next level. In some cases, this *Primer* offers technical information for reference rather than for mastery.

In particular, I have tried to give a fuller and more accurate treatment of the Greek participle than is found in some textbooks. The periphrastic participle and the nuances of the adverbial participle are sometimes omitted in introductory texts. I have also tried to be clear about the significance of tense in Greek, particularly the aorist, so as not to imply more than the language itself does.

(3) I have aimed for a natural order of presentation, one that takes full advantage of both the natural structure of the language and the traditional terminology of grammarians. Thus, declensions and principal parts are presented in numerical order. Similarities between different paradigms are pointed out, and naturally sequential material is juxtaposed to facilitate learning.

(4) Inclusive language for human beings is used throughout the text. This is accomplished in three ways. First, all grammar portions of the book use inclusive language in references to the student. Secondly, examples of Greek or English syntax involve female as well as male subjects. Third, the exercises also include female subjects as well as male, particularly the "Practice and Review" sentences, but also the LXX and NT exercises when possible. This may strike some users of the *Primer* as a relatively unimportant feature, but inasmuch as our use of language and our choice of examples can subtly imply things about how we conceive of ourselves and others, it a step forward to acknowledge intentionally the presence of women as well as men both in our classrooms and in the biblical tradition.

A Primer of Biblical Greek should be adaptable for use in full-year courses, semester long courses, and summer intensive courses, chiefly by selective assignment of exercises. Students who complete all the lessons with due diligence will be able to advance to the study of the biblical text with the help of resources listed in the bibliography. Indeed, most students should have dabbled in "real" Greek prior to completing all the lessons, either by way of the LXX and NT exercises or by their own ventures into favorite passages.

I must acknowledge my debt to several colleagues who have provided valuable feedback in the writing and editing of this book. Several instructors and professors of biblical Greek dared to use the *Primer* in its prepublication form. These include David Rensberger (Interdenominational Theological Center), Robert Lyon (Asbury Theological Seminary), Colleen Grant (Methodist Theological School in Ohio), Brian Whitfield (Candler School of Theology), Melissa Archer (Ashland Theological Seminary), and Brian Blount, Michael Daise, and Bill Pinches (all of Princeton Theological Seminary). Special thanks are due David A. de Silva (Ashland Theological Seminary), who was the first to make classroom use of the *Primer,* then in a rather primitive form, and was gracious enough both to recognize the grain of its pedagogical value and to help remove some of the chaff of its errors, shortcomings, and infelicitous style. Lastly, I thank John Simpson and his colleagues at Eerdmans for accepting the text for publication and contributing to its refinement. Whatever inadequacies remain are solely my responsibility. I offer *A Primer of Biblical Greek* in the hope that it will aid teachers in teaching and students in acquiring the basic language skills prerequisite to precise, disciplined, creative, and faithful interpretation of the Greek Bible.

Lesson 1

1. The Greek Alphabet

The Greek alphabet has twenty-four letters. The respective columns below show the small forms, capital forms, names, transliterations (English equivalents), and the approximate sounds of the letters.

α	A	alpha	a	father
β	B	beta	b	big
γ	Γ	gamma	g, n	God, ankle *(double gamma)*
δ	Δ	delta	d	door
ε	E	epsilon	e	met
ζ	Z	zeta	z, dz	zeal, kudzu
η	H	eta	e	obey
θ	Θ	theta	th	thing
ι	I	iota	i	pit, police
κ	K	kappa	k	keep
λ	Λ	lambda	l	law
μ	M	mu	m	mother
ν	N	nu	n	number
ξ	Ξ	xi	x	fox
ο	O	omicron — *small "o"*	o	not
π	Π	pi	p	poor
ρ	P	rho	r, rh	rod
σ, ς	Σ	sigma	s	save
τ	T	tau	t	time
υ	Y	upsilon	u, y	French u or German ü
φ	Φ	phi	ph	phone
χ	X	chi	ch	German ich
ψ	Ψ	psi	ps	tipsy
ω	Ω	omega	o	vote *"saw"*

within a word — σ, ς — *end of word*

omega "big o"

1

2. Remarks on Pronunciation

Gamma normally corresponds to English "g," but before another γ or before κ, χ, or ξ it has the nasal sound of "n" as in "thing" or "thank." *Zeta* has the sound of the letter "z" at the beginning of a word. Within a word, the conventional pronunciation combines the sounds of "d" and "z." *Iota* may be either short or long. Some people make a distinction between the sound of short iota (like "i" in "pit") and long iota (like "i" in "police"). *Rho* is transliterated with "r" within a word. At the beginning of a word, rho is aspirated (adding the sound of "h"), in which case the transliteration is "rh." *Sigma* has two forms. At the end of a word (final sigma), it is written "ς." Elsewhere "σ," the regular form, is used. For example, ἀπόστολος. The sounds of *upsilon* and *chi* are, strictly speaking, not used in English. Persons unfamiliar with French or German can approximate these sounds by pronouncing them like the "u" in "rude" and a hard "k" respectively.

Even though biblical Greek is no longer a spoken language, there is much value in reading it aloud. Reading in antiquity was often done aloud, and certain rhetorical qualities of texts are better appreciated when heard. Careful pronunciation will also help the student acquire vocabulary faster since words can be recognized by both sight and sound. Finally, since word meanings may differ significantly with the change of a single letter, a certain amount of precision in pronunciation is necessary. The student is advised to read the exercises aloud whenever possible.

3. Vowels, Diphthongs, and Breathing Marks

The seven Greek vowels are α, ε, η, ι, o, υ, and ω. Epsilon (ε) and omicron (o) are always short. Their counterparts, eta (η) and omega (ω), are always long. The difference in pronunciation between epsilon and eta and between omicron and omega should be carefully observed. The other vowels, alpha (α), iota (ι), and upsilon (υ), may be short or long. Nothing in the way they are written distinguishes the short version from the long. The difference in pronunciation between the short and the long versions has to do primarily with the length the sound is prolonged, in other words, a difference of quantity, not quality. As was mentioned above, some scholars suggest that short and long *iota* also differ qualitatively.

A diphthong is a combination of two vowel sounds in one syllable. The second letter of a Greek diphthong is always iota or upsilon. The common diphthongs and their pronunciations are:

αι	ai as in aisle
ει	ei as in neighbor
οι	oi as in oil
υι	uee as in queen

2

αυ	ow as in cow
ου	oo as in food
ευ	e as in met + u as in rude
ηυ	e as in obey + u as in rude

There are also three so-called improper diphthongs. These consist of the vowels (long) α, η, and ω with an iota written beneath them, which is called an iota subscript. Thus: ᾳ, ῃ, and ῳ. An iota subscript does not affect the pronunciation of the long vowel, but it often determines the form of the word.

In terms of vowel quantity, both common and improper diphthongs are long. The exceptions to this are few. Final οι and αι, that is, οι and αι at the very end of a word, are short. Elsewhere in a word they are long.

All words that begin with a vowel or diphthong have a breathing mark, either smooth (') or rough ('). The breathing mark is written over the vowel; in the case of diphthongs, it stands over the second vowel. A smooth breathing mark has no effect on pronunciation. Thus ἐν is pronounced "en." A rough breathing mark is equivalent to an "h" sound and is transliterated with "h." Thus ἑν is pronounced "hen." Finally, when the letters rho and upsilon stand in initial position, they have the rough breathing mark. Thus ῥητωρ = rhetor (speaker, orator); ὕβρις = hybris (arrogance).

4. Syllables

A Greek word has as many syllables as it has vowels or diphthongs. Thus, the word ἀπόστολος (apostle) is divided in this way: ἀ-πό-στο-λος. If a syllable contains a long vowel or a diphthong, it is long. If a syllable contains a short vowel (or final οι or αι; see §3 above), it is short. The quantity of a syllable is critical to the matter of accenting.

The final three syllables of a Greek word have special names. The last syllable is called the *ultima;* the second to last the *penult;* the third from last the *antepenult.* These syllables are the only ones that may receive an accent mark.

5. Accents

Accents in Greek were originally tonal, indicating pitch. For our purposes, accent simply identifies emphasis. The accented syllable is the one stressed in pronunciation. There are three accent marks in Greek, acute ('), circumflex (˜), and grave (`). No distinction in pronunciation is made among the three kinds of accents. Accents are placed over vowels and diphthongs. In the case of diphthongs, accents are written over the second of the two vowels. If the vowel or diphthong also has a breathing mark, an acute or grave accent is placed after the breathing mark, a circumflex accent over the breathing mark (thus: ἄνθρωπος, ὧραι.)

The basic rules of accent are as follows:

1. The acute accent can appear on any of the last three syllables: the ultima, the penult, or the antepenult. The circumflex accent will only appear on the last two; the grave accent only on the ultima. Thus: ἀπόστολος, πιστεύων, ἀδελφός, δοῦλος, γραφῆς, and καὶ. . . .
2. The circumflex accent can only stand over a long syllable.
3. If the ultima of a word is long, there are two results. First, the antepenult cannot be accented. Second, if the penult is accented, it must have the acute. Note the change from ἄνθρωπος to ἀνθρώπου.
4. If the ultima of a word is short, there are two results. First, the antepenult *may* receive an accent, which by rule 1 above would have to be acute. Second, a long penult, if accented, must take the circumflex. Thus, ἀπόστολος and προφῆται.
5. The grave accent is, in effect, a substitute for a final acute. An acute accent on the ultima is changed to a grave when the word is immediately followed (i.e., without intervening punctuation) by another word. Thus, ἀδελφός, but ἀδελφὸς καὶ ἀδελφή.

There are other rules for accenting Greek words. On the one hand, these rules should not be ignored, because in some cases accent reveals the form of a word and, consequently, its meaning. For example, κρίνω = I judge; κρινῶ = I *will* judge. On the other hand, because of their number, the rules are probably best learned gradually as the various instances are encountered. Only the basic information has been given here. The above rules set certain limits for accenting, but in most cases they do not determine what accent must be used. Additional rules, which help fix the accent precisely, will be introduced in subsequent lessons.

Again, the student is advised to learn Greek words by pronouncing them aloud, being sure to stress the accented syllable.

6. Punctuation

Greek has four punctuation marks. As in English, a minor pause is indicated by a comma (,) and a full stop by a period (.). A major pause, equivalent to our colon or semicolon, is indicated by a dot above the line of writing (·). The Greek question mark is identical in form to our semicolon (;).

7. Exercises

1. Practice writing the Greek alphabet until you can do so from memory.
2. Divide the following words into syllables. Identify each syllable as either short or long. ἄνθρωπος, βάλλομεν, ἐλυόμην, διδασκόμεθα, κῶμαι, ἀδελφαῖς, ἀπόστολοι, εἰρήνη, πνεύματος, οὐρανοῖς.
3. Use the following biblical passages to practice writing, transliteration, and pronunciation. First, simply transcribe the Greek for practice in writing Greek characters. Second, transliterate each passage into English characters. Lastly, read the passages several times out loud in Greek for practice in pronunciation.

LXX

Ἐν ἀρχῇ ἐποίησεν ὁ θεὸς τὸν οὐρανὸν καὶ τὴν γῆν. ἡ δὲ γῆ ἦν ἀόρατος καὶ ἀκατασκεύαστος, καὶ σκότος ἐπάνω τῆς ἀβύσσου, καὶ πνεῦμα θεοῦ ἐπεφέρετο ἐπάνω τοῦ ὕδατος. καὶ εἶπεν ὁ θεός Γενηθήτω φῶς. καὶ ἐγένετο φῶς. καὶ εἶδεν ὁ θεὸς τὸ φῶς ὅτι καλόν. (Genesis 1:1-4a)

NT

Ἐν ἀρχῇ ἦν ὁ λόγος, καὶ ὁ λόγος ἦν πρὸς τὸν θεόν, καὶ θεὸς ἦν ὁ λόγος. οὗτος ἦν ἐν ἀρχῇ πρὸς τὸν θεόν. πάντα δι’ αὐτοῦ ἐγένετο, καὶ χωρὶς αὐτοῦ ἐγένετο οὐδὲ ἕν. ὃ γέγονεν ἐν αὐτῷ ζωὴ ἦν, καὶ ἡ ζωὴ ἦν τὸ φῶς τῶν ἀνθρώπων· (John 1:1-4)

8. A Brief Introduction to the Septuagint (LXX)

The exercises in this book include sentences from the Septuagint, the Greek translation of the Hebrew Bible (along with a few additions to some biblical books as well as certain other books not belonging to the Hebrew scriptures). The name comes from the Latin word *septuaginta* meaning "seventy," thus the common abbreviation "LXX." According to tradition, seventy (some sources say seventy-two) elders from Jerusalem were sent to Alexandria, Egypt, in the middle of the third century BC to translate the first five books of the Hebrew Bible for the library of an Egyptian king. The translation and collection of the remaining books of the Septuagint no doubt took place in phases over many years.

The Septuagint was of immense importance in ancient Judaism and early Christianity. In the Hellenistic era (from the beginning of the third century BC on) more and more Jews lived outside Palestine, and few of them would have read Hebrew with ease. For these Jews and for most early Christians, the Septuagint was the Bible.

The Septuagint remains very important today for several reasons. First, as the earliest translation of the Hebrew Bible, it is extremely valuable in determining the original text of that document. When the Hebrew text is damaged or its meaning is uncertain, the Septuagint may shed light on the problem. Second, the Septuagint is one of the best sources for constructing the semantic and theological environment of early Christianity. When the authors of the New Testament cite authoritative scripture, they are, for the most part, citing the Septuagint. They use its language and interpret its texts. Third, and most important, the Septuagint reveals the theological understanding and interpretive strategies of Hellenistic Judaism. Translation inevitably involves some interpretation, so by comparing the Septuagint and the Hebrew text, we can gain insight into how the translators used their ancient traditions in new situations. In addition, the several books of the Septuagint that are *not* translated from the Hebrew Bible provide further windows into the diversity of Jewish thought in that era.

Students translating LXX exercises in this book need to be aware of certain peculiarities of the LXX. First, as mentioned above, there are several books in the LXX that are not found in the Hebrew Bible or Old Testament. Different Christian traditions call these books "deutero-canonical" or "apocryphal." Some of the exercises are drawn from these books. Thus, you will encounter sentences from 1 Esdras, Judith, 1-4 Maccabees, Sirach, Tobit, and Wisdom. The abbreviations for these books are easily recognized.

Second, you should be aware that the names of a few books in the LXX differ from their English counterparts. The Song of Solomon is called Canticum and is abbreviated "Cant." The books of 1-2 Samuel and 1-2 Kings are called 1-4 Kingdoms and are abbreviated "1-4 Kgdms."

Third, the LXX does not always have a fixed text. In some cases there are varying manuscript traditions for the same book. Occasionally the reference for an exercise might read "Tobit, codex S." This means that the various ancient manuscripts present different readings, and the exercise is drawn from the one scholars have designated "S" (Sinaiticus).

Finally, the content of some LXX books differs significantly from their Hebrew (and English) counterparts. Job and Jeremiah are shorter in the LXX; Esther is longer; and Daniel has three major additions. Because of these and other differences, the enumeration of verses in the LXX does not always correspond to that of English Bibles. For example, Jeremiah 38:8 in the LXX corresponds to 31:8 in English Bibles. For most of the Psalms, the LXX chapter number is one less than the corresponding English text. But this problem only arises in a few books. Whenever the LXX reference differs from the reference for the English text, both will be given, as follows: (Jeremiah 38:8, ET 31:8). When translating LXX exercises in this book, students should bear in mind that, strictly speaking, their English "Old Testament" is *not* a translation of the Septuagint, but rather of the Hebrew Bible. Sometimes the Septuagint is a rather free translation; sometimes it seems to have misunderstood the Hebrew; sometimes it makes deliberate changes, clarifying or modifying the meaning. Be aware that such differences may occur between the meaning of the Greek in the exercises and the English translation found at the reference given.

Lesson 2

9. Vocabulary

In each Greek vocabulary list, English words that in some way derive from the Greek entry will be given in parentheses. Usually the connection is obvious; other times only the root of the Greek word is involved or only part of the English word is related to the Greek.

ἀκούω, I hear (acoustics)

βλέπω, I see

γινώσκω, I know (agnostic)

γράφω, I write (graph)

διδάσκω, I teach (didactic)

θέλω, I wish, will, desire

καί, and

λέγω, I say, speak, tell (dialogue)

λύω, I loosen, destroy (analyze)

ὅτι, that, because

οὐ, οὐκ, οὐχ, not

πιστεύω, I believe

For the sake of greater variety, two additional words will appear in the exercises for this lesson: ἀδελφός (a brother) and ἀδελφή (a sister). You will not learn the forms and syntax of these nouns until lessons 3 and 4. For the time being, they will be used only in the singular and as the subjects of verbs.

The negative οὐ stands in front of the word it negates. The οὐκ form is used before a word beginning with a vowel having smooth breathing, the οὐχ form before rough breathing.

10. Characteristics of Greek Verbs

The Greek verbal system shares many characteristics with that of English, but it has some additional qualities that enable it to express finer nuances with greater economy of words. To be a competent reader of biblical Greek, it is essential that you learn the endings of the more common verbal forms.

Greek verbs have tense, voice, and mood (or mode). (1) The tense of a verb denotes the *time* and the *kind* of action. The time of action may be past, present, or future. The kind of action expressed by Greek verbs may be continuing, completed (with a result), or simple (an affirmation of action without regard to its duration or completion). English examples would be: "I am reading a book" (continuing action); "You have broken the window" (completed action); and "She painted a picture." (simple action). Tense in English has to do primarily with the *time* of action; Greek emphasizes the *kind* of action. (2) The voice of a verb indicates how the subject is related to the action. The subject may perform the action (active voice): "We ate the bread." Or the subject may be acted upon (passive voice): "The bread was eaten." In Greek there is a third alternative. The subject may perform action in a way that refers back to the subject (middle voice): "I wash myself." (3) The mood of a verb pertains to the manner in which the action is regarded by the speaker. The action may be simply asserted as a fact (indicative mood). It may be commanded (imperative mood). It may be expressed as a hope (optative mood). Or the action may be hypothetical or probable given the fulfillment of other conditions (subjunctive mood). In an inflected language like Greek, mood is indicated by changes in the form of the verb. English indicates mood in other ways, for example, by auxiliary words such as "may," "might," "should," and "would." Two other verb-related forms in Greek, the infinitive and the participle, are perhaps better referred to as modes. Unlike the four moods just described, the infinitive and participle lack the characteristic of "person."

Finally, Greek verb forms other than the infinitive and participle also have person — first, second, or third, corresponding to I/we, you, and he/she/it/they — and number (singular or plural).

11. The Present Active Indicative

The present active indicative of λύω is given below. This verb will be used as an example throughout the book since it is short and entirely regular in its conjugation.

Singular	Plural
1. λύω, I loosen or am loosening.	1. λύομεν, we loosen or are loosening.
2. λύεις, you (sing.) loosen or are loosening.	2. λύετε, you (pl.) loosen or are loosening.
3. λύει, he, she, or it loosens or is loosening.	3. λύουσι(ν), they loosen or are loosening.

(The original endings for the present active indicative were -μι, -ς, -σι, for the singular, and -μεν, -τε, -νσι, for the plural. In some cases, however, the original endings have undergone such changes that it is best simply to learn the resultant forms rather than the process by which they came about. The original endings are preserved in another conjugation to be learned later.)

A few basic observations should be made about the forms of the Greek verb. (1) Part of the verb (the stem) remains constant while part (the ending) changes. The stem of a Greek verb may be found by removing the "ω" from the first person singular form. Sometimes, between the stem and the ending, a "variable vowel" (either omicron or epsilon) is inserted. (Some grammars refer to this as a "connecting vowel" or "thematic vowel.") In the form λύομεν, strictly speaking, the ending is -μεν. This ending is connected to the verb stem by the variable vowel "o." The ending of the second person plural is -τε, and the variable vowel is "ε." The significance of this fact will become clear when other verb forms are encountered. (2) In Greek, unlike English, there is a different form for every person/number combination in the present active indicative. This means that the subject is adequately conveyed by the verb ending and that the pronouns that English must use are unnecessary in Greek. (The Greek third person singular does, however, remain ambiguous with regard to gender.) Thus, to say "we loosen" in Greek, it is sufficient to say λύομεν. Generally, the Greek pronoun is only added if the subject is emphasized. (3) Greek, unlike English, has different forms for second person singular and plural. (4) The letter "ν," called "movable ν," is sometimes attached to the third person plural form (λύουσι). The movable ν is added to certain verb forms when followed by a mark of punctuation or by a word beginning with a vowel. The purpose of this addition was to prevent "hiatus," or the succession of two vowels in adjacent words (cf. the use of the English article "an" before words beginning with a vowel). But this was not carried out consistently. Sometimes movable ν occurs in biblical Greek even when the following word begins with a consonant.

The above paradigm shows that the present tense in Greek does double duty for two kinds of action: simple and continuing. Thus, λύει can be translated either "she loosens" or "she is loosening." Only the nature of the verbal idea and contextual factors will determine which is better.

12. The Present Active Infinitive

The present active infinitive is formed by adding the suffix -ειν to the verb stem. Thus, λύειν = to loosen, to destroy. The forms of the infinitive will be given as the corresponding forms of the indicative are introduced. The full syntax of the infinitive is postponed until a later lesson, at which point all forms of the infinitive will be repeated. In the meantime, simply translate the Greek infinitive with the English infinitive "to ———."

13. Accentuation of Verbs

It was noted in §5 that the basic rules of accenting do not fix the precise accent of a word, but only set certain limits. Additional rules are necessary to fix the accent. Different kinds of words follow different rules.

Verb accent is *recessive*. This means that the accent on a Greek verb recedes, that is, moves back from the ultima toward the beginning of the word as far as the basic rules will allow. This one additional rule enables you to accent any verb form. For example, according to the basic rules διδάσκετε might be accented with an acute on any of the last three syllables (or with a grave on the ultima given the right conditions). Knowing that verb accent is recessive, we can fix the accent on the antepenult:

9

διδάσκετε. Similarly, γινωσκεις would be accented γινώσκεις, and ἠθρον (a verb form you have not yet learned) would be accented ἦρον.

14. Exercises

When translating the exercises in this book, the student should be aware that Greek word order often differs from that of English. Pay careful attention to the form of each word, determine its function in the sentence or clause, and translate according to normal English word order. One possible plan of attack, especially in the early stages of learning Greek, is to identify the main verb first and then the subject. Remember, however, that the subject may be a pronoun (I, we, you, he, she, etc.) only implied by the verb form.

Practice and Review
1. γινώσκομεν ὅτι πιστεύετε καὶ θέλετε διδάσκειν.
2. ἀκούω καὶ βλέπω ὅτι ἀδελφὴ γράφει.
3. λέγεις ὅτι ἀδελφὸς λύει· οὐ πιστεύομεν.
4. θέλει ἀδελφὴ ἀκούειν; οὐ γινώσκω.
5. λύουσι καὶ οὐ θέλομεν βλέπειν.
6. ἀδελφὸς λέγει ὅτι θέλει γράφειν καὶ διδάσκειν.
7. πιστεύεις ὅτι ἀδελφὸς καὶ ἀδελφὴ βλέπουσιν;
8. γινώσκω ὅτι ἀδελφὸς λέγει καὶ οὐκ ἀκούεις.
9. ἀδελφὴ διδάσκει καὶ θέλομεν ἀκούειν.
10. οὐ θέλω λύειν· θέλω γινώσκειν ὅτι ἀδελφὸς πιστεύει.

LXX
1. Ποῦ ἐστιν Αβελ ὁ ἀδελφός σου; . . . εἶπεν Οὐ γινώσκω· (Genesis 4:9)
2. φωνὴν ἀνθρώπων ἀκούω καὶ αὐτοὺς οὐ βλέπω. (Tobit 5:10, codex S)
3. γινώσκω ἐγὼ καὶ πιστεύω ὅτι πάντα . . . ἔσται (Tobit 14:4, codex S)
4. ἔχουσιν ὀφθαλμοὺς . . . βλέπειν καὶ οὐ βλέπουσιν καὶ ὦτα ἔχουσιν . . . ἀκούειν καὶ οὐκ ἀκούουσιν. (Ezek 12:2)
5. (concerning idols) οὐ βλέπουσιν καὶ οὐκ ἀκούουσιν καὶ οὐ γινώσκουσιν. (Dan 5:23)

NT
1. ὀφθαλμοὺς ἔχοντες οὐ βλέπετε καὶ ὦτα ἔχοντες οὐκ ἀκούετε; (Mark 8:18)
2. οἴδαμεν ὅτι ὀρθῶς λέγεις καὶ διδάσκεις (Luke 20:21)
3. ὅτι τὴν ἀλήθειαν λέγω, οὐ πιστεύετέ μοι. (John 8:45)
4. καὶ λέγει αὐτῷ, Κύριε . . . , σὺ γινώσκεις ὅτι φιλῶ σε. (John 21:17)
5. οὐ θέλω διὰ μέλανος καὶ καλάμου σοι γράφειν· (3 John 13)

English to Greek

1. We hear that a brother wishes to believe.
2. Do you (pl.) know that they are not writing?
3. I say that you (sing.) are destroying and you do not see.
4. Does a sister see and believe? She believes because she sees.

Vocabulary for LXX and NT Sentences

Note: Names will generally *not* be translated in these vocabulary lists.

ἀλήθειαν, truth (direct object)
ἀνθρώπων, of men, of people
αὐτῷ, to him
αὐτούς, them (direct object)
διά, through, by means of
ἐγώ, I
εἶπεν, he said
ἔσται, will be, will come about
ἐστιν, is
ἔχοντες, having
ἔχουσιν, they have
καλάμου, pen
Κύριε, Lord
μέλανος, ink

μοι, me (indirect object)
ὁ, the
οἴδαμεν = γινώσκομεν
ὀρθῶς, rightly
ὀφθαλμούς, eyes (direct object)
πάντα, all things
Ποῦ, Where?
σε, you (object)
σοι, to you
σου, of you, your
συ, you (subject)
τὴν, the
φιλῶ, I love
φωνήν, (the) voice (direct object)

Lesson 3

15. Vocabulary

ἀδελφή, ἡ, sister

ἀλήθεια, ἡ, truth (Alethea)

βασιλεία, ἡ, kingdom, reign, rule (basilica)

γῆ, ἡ, earth, soil, land (geology)

δόξα, ἡ, glory, honor (doxology)

ἐκκλησία, ἡ, assembly, church (ecclesiastic)

ἔχω, I have

ζωή, ἡ, life (protozoa)

ἡμέρα, ἡ, day (ephemeral)

θάλασσα, ἡ, sea, lake (thalassic)

καρδία, ἡ, heart (cardiac)

φωνή, ἡ, voice, sound (phone)

ὥρα, ἡ, hour, time (horoscope)

16. The First Declension

A declension is a group of nouns (or pronouns or adjectives) that have similar inflectional forms to show their function in a sentence. Nouns in English have different forms to show number (singular or plural), but grammatical function in English must be indicated by word order or by additional words such as prepositions. Because Greek is an inflected language, it can express grammatical relationships simply by the forms of nouns. Word order is therefore freer in Greek. This allows for subtle shifts of emphasis that English may only be able to express periphrastically or by intonation.

There are three declensions in Greek. The first declension contains a large group of feminine nouns (see §17 on gender of Greek nouns) ending in alpha (α) or eta (η). A smaller group of first declension nouns that are masculine in gender will be considered in a later lesson.

17. Characteristics of Greek Nouns

Greek nouns have three characteristics: case, number, and gender. As in English, there are two numbers in biblical Greek: singular and plural. There are three genders in Greek: masculine, feminine, and neuter. In English, only third person singular pronouns (he, she, it) and certain other nouns referring to persons (man, woman, actor, actress) have gender. Most English nouns are regarded as neuter or simply lacking in gender. In contrast, all Greek nouns have gender. Most Greek nouns referring to persons have the grammatical gender that corresponds to their sex. The Greek words for "woman," "sister," and "queen" are feminine; those for "man," "brother," and "king" are masculine. But abstract nouns and those referring to inanimate objects also have

12

grammatical gender in Greek. Thus, the Greek word for "land" is feminine, but the word for "world" is masculine, and nothing regarding the meanings of these words is conveyed by their genders. The gender of such nouns can seldom be predicted and must be learned by observation. It will be helpful to remember that gender is a *grammatical* category, not a biological one.

Case is the characteristic of greatest importance for syntax. Greek has five cases: nominative, genitive, dative, accusative, and vocative. Greek can convey a variety of syntactical relationships by means of the cases. For now we will consider the most basic functions of the five cases.

The basic function of the *nominative* case is to name or point out. It is used for the subject of a finite verb and for the predicate nominative. A predicate nominative is a noun that completes the meaning of a linking verb such as "to be," "to become," etc. Consider these sentences: "A woman buys the cloth." "The buyer is a woman." In the first sentence, "woman" would be in the nominative case as the subject; in the second sentence, "woman" is the predicate nominative. Examples: ἀδελφὴ γράφει. "A sister writes." ἡ γῆ [ἐστιν] βασιλεία. "The earth is a kingdom." In the second example, "earth" is the subject nominative; "kingdom" is the predicate nominative. (See §43 for a fuller explanation of this construction.)

The basic function of the *genitive* case is to describe or define, as an adjective does. This descriptive function can often be conveyed by the English word "of." Thus, βασιλεία δόξης could be translated, "a kingdom of glory," and would mean about the same as "a glorious kingdom." A specific and very common use of the genitive is to show possession. Example: φωνὴ ἀδελφῆς, "a voice of a sister" or "a sister's voice."

The *dative* case functions in many ways, usually to express personal interest or relationship; for example, as an indirect object. An indirect object is that person or thing to or for whom the action of the verb is performed. Indirect objects are common with verbs of saying, speaking, writing, giving, and the like. Examples: λέγω ἀλήθειαν ἐκκλησίᾳ, "I speak truth to an assembly/a church." γράφετε ἀδελφῇ, "You are writing to a sister."

The *accusative* case usually limits or qualifies the action of a verb. Its most common use is as the direct object. A direct object receives the action of a transitive verb. Examples: βλέπομεν γῆν. "We see land." ἔχουσι καρδίαν;, "Do they have a heart?"

The *vocative* case has a single function: direct address. Occasionally the vocative has its own distinct form, but often its form will be identical to that of the nominative. Example: ὦ ἀδελφή, βλέπεις; "O sister, do you see?" In this sentence the function of ἀδελφή shows that the form is vocative.

The nominative singular form of a noun is its "lexical form," that is, the form under which it is listed in the dictionary or lexicon.

18. Forms of the First Declension

There are three types of first declension nouns ending in -α or -η. We will call them "pure α," "pure η," and "mixed." A paradigm of each type is given below using ὥρα, φωνή, and δόξα.

"Pure Alpha" ὥρα

	Singular		Plural
Nom.	ὥρα	Nom.	ὧραι
Gen.	ὥρας	Gen.	ὡρῶν
Dat.	ὥρᾳ	Dat.	ὥραις
Acc.	ὥραν	Acc.	ὥρας
Voc.	ὥρα	Voc.	ὧραι

(SAME; CAN ONLY TELL BY CONTEXT)

"Pure Eta" φωνή

	Singular		Plural
Nom.	φωνή	Nom.	φωναί
Gen.	φωνῆς	Gen.	φωνῶν
Dat.	φωνῇ	Dat.	φωναῖς
Acc.	φωνήν	Acc.	φωνάς
Voc.	φωνή	Voc.	φωναί

"Mixed" δόξα

	Singular		Plural
Nom.	δόξα	Nom.	δόξαι
Gen.	δόξης	Gen.	δοξῶν
Dat.	δόξῃ	Dat.	δόξαις
Acc.	δόξαν	Acc.	δόξας
Voc.	δόξα	Voc.	δόξαι

In biblical Greek the plural endings of first declension nouns are the same throughout the declension; the singular endings distinguish the types. Whether or not first declension nouns ending in alpha will retain the alpha throughout the paradigm (as ὥρα does) or will be of the "mixed" type (like δόξα or θάλασσα) depends on the letter preceding the alpha. If that letter is a vowel (usually ε or ι) or rho (ρ), the noun will be a "pure alpha" type. If any other letter precedes the alpha (as ξ does in δόξα, or σ in θάλασσα), the noun will be of the "mixed" type. First declension nouns ending in eta will be of the "pure eta" type. Note that for each of these types, the vocative form is identical to the nominative.

14

19. The Definite Article

When a noun is given in the vocabulary list, it will be followed by the appropriate form of the definite article, which reveals the gender of the word (ἡ is feminine). The use of the definite article in Greek corresponds in many ways to its use in English. Thus, ἡ θάλασσα generally means "the sea." Greek does not have an indefinite article corresponding to English "a, an." When a Greek noun lacks the definite article, it normally will be translated as indefinite. Thus, θάλασσα would mean "a sea." The inflectional forms of the definite article and further syntax of the article will be learned in later lessons.

20. Accentuation of Nouns

In Lesson 2 you learned that verb accent is *recessive,* meaning that the accent of a verb recedes as far as the general rules permit. Noun accent, on the other hand, is *persistent* (or *retentive*). This means that as the noun goes through its various inflections, the accent persists, or is retained, on the same syllable on which the lexical form was accented, as far as the general rules permit. Thus, if a noun is accented on the ultima or penult, its accent will not move back on the word further than that syllable. To apply this rule, one must know where the accent falls in the nominative singular form. This must be learned or looked up in the dictionary. It is important, therefore, to learn the proper pronunciation of a word from the outset.

Three special observations about the accent of first declension nouns are in order here. (1) First declension nouns always have a circumflex on the ultima in the genitive plural (-ῶν) regardless of where the accent stood in the lexical form. (2) When the ultima of a first declension noun is accented, it receives the circumflex in the genitive and dative of both numbers; elsewhere it receives the acute (or grave, as required). Note how the accent of φωνή changes in the paradigm above. The noun γῆ is an exception to this rule. Because contraction has occurred in the formation of this word, it has the circumflex throughout. (3) If the nominative singular form of a first declension noun ends in a long alpha (as does ὥρα), the alpha is long throughout the paradigm (except for -αι in the nominative plural, which must be short). If the nominative singular ends in short alpha (as does ἀλήθεια or θάλασσα), then the alpha is also short in the accusative singular (ἀλήθειαν, θάλασσαν). Elsewhere (except for -αι in the nominative plural), the ending is long.

21. Exercises

Practice and Review

1. ἔχομεν βασιλείαν δόξης καὶ ἀκούομεν φωνὴν ἀληθείας.
2. γινώσκουσιν ὅτι βλέπει ἀδελφὸς θάλασσαν.

3. καρδία ἀδελφῆς οὐ θέλει πιστεύειν ὅτι ἔχετε ζωήν.
4. ἐκκλησία γινώσκει ὥραν δόξης καὶ ἡμέραν ἀληθείας.
5. θέλετε λέγειν ἀλήθειαν βασιλείᾳ;
6. ἔχουσιν ἀδελφὸς καὶ ἀδελφὴ γῆν καὶ θέλουσιν ἔχειν βασιλείας.
7. οὐ διδάσκομεν ἀδελφὴν λύειν· διδάσκομεν καρδίαν πιστεύειν.
8. γράφω ἐκκλησίᾳ ὅτι οὐ γινώσκει ἀλήθειαν.
9. θέλεις γινώσκειν ζωὴν καὶ βλέπειν ἡμέραν δόξης;
10. γῆ καὶ θάλασσα γινώσκουσιν ὅτι καρδίαι οὐ πιστεύουσιν.
11. ἀδελφαὶ λέγουσιν ἐκκλησίαις ὅτι οὐ βλέπουσιν ὥραν ἀληθείας. ἐκκλησίαι ἀκούουσιν;
12. λέγει φωνὴ ὅτι ἔχομεν ὥραν ζωῆς.

LXX

1. καὶ ἔσῃ ἐν διασπορᾷ ἐν πάσαις ταῖς βασιλείαις τῆς γῆς. (Deut 28:25)
2. ἐδίκαζεν Σαμουηλ . . . Ισραηλ πάσας τὰς ἡμέρας τῆς ζωῆς αὐτοῦ· (1 Kgdms 7:15)
3. δουλεύσατε αὐτῷ ἐν ἀληθείᾳ καὶ ἐν ὅλῃ καρδίᾳ ὑμῶν. (1 Kgdms 12:24)
4. καὶ γνώσονται πᾶσαι αἱ βασιλεῖαι τῆς γῆς ὅτι σὺ κύριος ὁ θεὸς μόνος. (4 Kgdms 19:19)
5. ἀλήθεια ἐκ τῆς γῆς ἀνέτειλεν. (Ps 84:12, ET 85:11)
6. ἐξομολογήσονται οἱ οὐρανοὶ . . . τὴν ἀλήθειάν σου ἐν ἐκκλησίᾳ ἁγίων. (Ps 88:6, ET 89:5)
7. καὶ βοήσει . . . ἐν τῇ ἡμέρᾳ ἐκείνῃ ὡς φωνὴ θαλάσσης· (Isa 5:30)

NT

1. ὅτι τὴν ἀλήθειαν λέγω, οὐ πιστεύετέ μοι. (John 8:45)
2. τὰ πρόβατα . . . ἀκούει . . . ὅτι οἴδασιν τὴν φωνὴν αὐτοῦ· (John 10:3-4)
3. λέγει αὐτῷ . . . Ἰησοῦς, Ἐγώ εἰμι ἡ ὁδὸς καὶ ἡ ἀλήθεια καὶ ἡ ζωή· (John 14:6)
4. [God] ἐποίησεν τὸν οὐρανὸν καὶ τὴν γῆν καὶ τὴν θάλασσαν . . . · (Acts 14:15)
5. (To God be) ἡ δόξα ἐν τῇ ἐκκλησίᾳ καὶ ἐν Χριστῷ Ἰησοῦ . . . ἀμήν. (Eph 3:21)
6. ἐγὼ . . . λέγω εἰς Χριστὸν καὶ εἰς τὴν ἐκκλησίαν. (Eph 5:32)
7. βλέπετε ἐγγίζουσαν τὴν ἡμέραν. (Heb 10:25)

English to Greek

1. Do they wish to hear a sound of a sea?
2. A land does not know an hour of truth and a kingdom does not have life.
3. A sister sees a day of glory and believes.
4. Does an assembly know that a heart wishes to believe?

Vocabulary for LXX and NT Sentences

Note: The forms of the Greek definite article are not given below. Try to recognize them in the exercises above. They are short, usually begin with "τ," and often have the same ending as the noun they go with.

ἁγίων, of [the] saints
ἀμήν, amen
ἀνέτειλεν, has risen
αὐτοῦ, of him, his
αὐτῷ, him, to him
βοήσει, he will cry out
γνώσονται, future of γινώσκουσι
δέ, and, but
διασπορᾷ, diaspora, dispersion
δουλεύσατε, serve!
ἐγγίζουσαν, drawing near
ἐγώ, I
ἐδίκαζεν, judged
εἰμι, am
εἰς, about
ἐκ, from, out of
ἐκείνῃ, that (do *not* translate the
    definite article in this sentence)
ἐν, in, with
ἐξομολογήσονται, will praise

ἐποίησεν, made, created
ἔσῃ, you will be
θεός, God
Ισραηλ, Israel (direct object)
κύριος, Lord
μοι, me
μόνος, alone
ὁδός, way
οἴδασιν = γινώσκουσι
ὅλῃ, whole, entire
οὐρανόν, (οὐρανοί) heaven(s)
πᾶσαι, πάσαις, πάσας, all
πρόβατα, sheep (uses a singular verb
    form here)
σου, of you, your
σύ, you
τέλος, end
ὑμῶν, of you (pl.), your
ὡς, as

17

Lesson 4

22. Vocabulary

ἀδελφός, ὁ, brother (Philadelphia)
ἀλλά, but
ἄνθρωπος, ὁ, human being, person,
   man (anthropology)
δέ, but, and
δοῦλος, ὁ, slave, servant
ἔργον, τό, deed, work (energy)
θάνατος, ὁ, death (euthanasia)

θεός, ὁ, God, god (theology)
κύριος, ὁ, Lord, master, owner
λόγος, ὁ, word (logic, logo)
νόμος, ὁ, law (economy)
οἶκος, ὁ, house (economy)
οὐρανός, ὁ, heaven, sky (Uranus)
τέκνον, τό, child
υἱός, ὁ, son

ERGONOM.L
Law of work

Again, the appropriate form of the definite article is given with the noun. The masculine (nominative singular) form of the article is ὁ; the corresponding neuter form is τό.

The word δέ is postpositive, meaning that it never comes first in its clause. Its usual position is second, but it may come later. The English translation of δέ will usually begin the clause.

23. The Second Declension

The second declension contains nouns ending in -ος and nouns ending in -ον. Most of those ending in -ος are masculine. (Feminine nouns ending in -ος, a relatively small group, will be introduced in a later lesson.) All second declension nouns ending in -ον are neuter and use the same form in the nominative, vocative, and accusative singular (-ον); the plural number of these cases also has a uniform ending (-α).

24. Forms of the Second Declension

The following are typical second declension forms.

Masculine Nouns

	Singular			Plural
Nom.	λόγος		Nom.	λόγοι
Gen.	λόγου		Gen.	λόγων
Dat.	λόγῳ		Dat.	λόγοις
Acc.	λόγον		Acc.	λόγους
Voc.	λόγε		Voc.	λόγοι

Nom.	ἀδελφός		Nom.	ἀδελφοί
Gen.	ἀδελφοῦ		Gen.	ἀδελφῶν
Dat.	ἀδελφῷ		Dat.	ἀδελφοῖς
Acc.	ἀδελφόν		Acc.	ἀδελφούς
Voc.	ἀδελφέ		Voc.	ἀδελφοί

Neuter Nouns

	Singular			Plural
Nom.	ἔργον		Nom.	ἔργα
Gen.	ἔργου		Gen.	ἔργων
Dat.	ἔργῳ		Dat.	ἔργοις
Acc.	ἔργον		Acc.	ἔργα
Voc.	ἔργον		Voc.	ἔργα

Nom.	τέκνον		Nom.	τέκνα
Gen.	τέκνου		Gen.	τέκνων
Dat.	τέκνῳ		Dat.	τέκνοις
Acc.	τέκνον		Acc.	τέκνα
Voc.	τέκνον		Voc.	τέκνα

25. Accentuation of Second Declension Nouns

The accent of second declension nouns, in accordance with the special rule of noun accent, is *persistent* (see §20). Just as in the first declension, when the ultima of a second declension noun is accented, it takes the circumflex in the genitive and dative of both numbers; elsewhere it receives the acute (or grave, as required). See the accentuation of ἀδελφός above. Note that the accent of the genitive plural varies in the second declension. The special rule mentioned in connection with the first declension (§20.1) does *not* apply here.

19

Lesson 4

26. Exercises

Practice and Review

1. γράφει ἄνθρωπος λόγους ζωῆς ἀδελφῇ.
2. θέλομεν διδάσκειν τέκνα, ἀλλὰ οὐ θέλουσι γινώσκειν ἀλήθειαν.
3. διδάσκει νόμος θεοῦ ὅτι οὐρανὸς ἔχει δόξαν.
4. λέγει ἀδελφὸς ἐκκλησίᾳ καὶ λέγουσιν υἱοὶ δούλῳ.
5. οὐ βλέπομεν γῆν θανάτου, πιστεύομεν δὲ ὅτι ζωὴν ἔχει οἶκος θεοῦ.
6. ἀδελφὸς καὶ ἀδελφὴ λέγουσιν, Κύριε, θέλομεν βλέπειν θεοῦ ἔργα.
7. τέκνα ἀδελφῆς θέλουσι βλέπειν οὐρανόν, τέκνα δὲ γῆς οὐ βλέπουσιν οἶκον θεοῦ.
8. διδάσκει κύριος δούλους γράφειν λόγους καὶ δοῦλοι διδάσκουσιν τέκνα.
9. ἔχετε ἔργα νόμου, γινώσκω δὲ ὅτι θεός βλέπει καρδίαν ἀνθρώπου.
10. υἱοῦ θάνατος λύει καρδίαν ἀνθρώπου, ἀλλὰ γινώσκομεν καὶ πιστεύομεν ὅτι βασιλεία θεοῦ ἔχει ζωήν.

LXX

1. ὁ οὐρανὸς καὶ ὁ οὐρανὸς τοῦ οὐρανοῦ οὐ φέρουσιν αὐτοῦ τὴν δόξαν. (2 Chron 2:5, ET 2:6)
2. καὶ εἶπεν Εὐλογητὸς κύριος ὁ θεὸς τοῦ κυρίου μου Αβρααμ, . . . ἐμὲ εὐόδωκεν κύριος εἰς οἶκον τοῦ ἀδελφοῦ τοῦ κυρίου μου. (Gen 24:27)
3. καὶ εἶπας Θεός εἰμι . . . σὺ δὲ εἶ ἄνθρωπος καὶ οὐ θεός. (Ezek 28:2)
4. δοῦλος κυρίου . . . εἰμι καὶ τὸν κύριον θεὸν τοῦ οὐρανοῦ . . . σέβομαι. (Jon 1:9)
5. σὺ εἶ κύριος ὁ θεὸς Ισραηλ κἀγὼ δοῦλός σου καὶ διὰ σὲ πεποίηκα τὰ ἔργα ταῦτα. (3 Kgdms 18:36)
6. Τὴν ζωὴν καὶ τὸν θάνατον δέδωκα πρὸ προσώπου ὑμῶν, . . . ἔκλεξαι τὴν ζωήν. (Deut 30:19)
7. Μωυσῆς . . . ἐλάλησεν πάντας τοὺς λόγους τοῦ νόμου τούτου εἰς τὰ ὦτα τοῦ λαοῦ. (Deut 32:44)
8. καὶ ἐκάλεσεν τὸν υἱὸν αὐτοῦ καὶ τοὺς υἱοὺς αὐτοῦ καὶ εἶπεν αὐτῷ Τέκνον, λαβὲ τοὺς υἱούς σου· (Tobit 14:3)

NT

1. Οὐ πᾶς ὁ λέγων μοι, Κύριε κύριε, εἰσελεύσεται εἰς τὴν βασιλείαν τῶν οὐρανῶν (Matt 7:21)
2. ἔσται ὁ υἱὸς τοῦ ἀνθρώπου ἐν τῇ καρδίᾳ τῆς γῆς τρεῖς ἡμέρας καὶ τρεῖς νύκτας. (Matt 12:40. Note: the acc. may express extent of time.)
3. καὶ λέγει αὐτοῖς . . . Ὁ οἶκός μου οἶκος προσευχῆς κληθήσεται (Matt 21:13)
4. παραδώσει ἀδελφὸς ἀδελφὸν εἰς θάνατον καὶ πατὴρ τέκνον (Mark 13:12)
5. λέγει αὐτοῖς ὁ Ἰησοῦς, Εἰ τέκνα τοῦ Ἀβραάμ ἐστε, τὰ ἔργα τοῦ Ἀβραὰμ ἐποιεῖτε· (John 8:39)

6. οὐ δικαιοῦται ἄνθρωπος ἐξ ἔργων νόμου (Gal 2:16)
7. Ἐν ἀρχῇ ἦν ὁ λόγος, καὶ ὁ λόγος ἦν πρὸς τὸν θεόν, καὶ θεὸς ἦν ὁ λόγος. (John 1:1)
8. καὶ λέγει μοι, . . . σύνδουλός σού εἰμι καὶ τῶν ἀδελφῶν σου (Rev 19:10)

English to Greek

1. A sister's children hear a slave's voice.
2. Human beings do not see God, but (the) Lord of heaven sees a brother's deeds.
3. A son speaks words of life to an assembly.
4. A house of death does not have laws.

Vocabulary for LXX and NT Sentences

Again, proper nouns and forms of the article are not given below.

ἀρχῇ, (the) beginning	κἀγώ = καὶ ἐγώ, and I
αὐτοῖς, to them	κληθήσεται, shall be called
αὐτοῦ, of him, his	λαβέ, take!
αὐτῷ, to him	λαοῦ, people
δέδωκα, I have set	λέγων, see πᾶς below
διά, because of	μοι, to me
δικαιοῦται, is justified	μου, of me, my
εἰ, if	νύκτας, nights
εἶ, you (sing.) are	πάντας, all
εἰμι, I am	παραδώσει, will hand over
εἶπας, you said	πᾶς ὁ λέγων, everyone who says
εἶπεν, he said	πατὴρ, father
εἰς, to, into	πεποίηκα, I have done
εἰσελεύσεται, will enter	πρὸ προσώπου ὑμῶν, before you
ἐκάλεσεν, he called	πρός, with
ἔκλεξαι, choose!	προσευχῆς, of prayer
ἐλάλησεν, spoke	σε, you
ἐμε, me	σέβομαι, I worship
ἐν, in	σου, of you, your
ἐξ, by	σύ, you
ἐποιεῖτε, you (pl.) would do	σύν-, fellow-
ἔσται, will be	ταῦτα, these
ἐστε, you (pl.) are	τούτου, this
εὐλογητός, blessed (be)	τρεῖς, three
εὐόδωκεν, has helped along the way	φέρουσιν, hold, contain
ἦν, was	ὦτα, ears

Lesson 5

27. Vocabulary

ἀγαθός, ή, όν, good, noble (Agatha)
ἅγιος, α, ον, holy, consecrated (hagio-)
γάρ, for (postpositive, see §22)
δίκαιος, α, ον, righteous, just
ἔσχατος, η, ον, last (eschatology)
κακός, ή, όν, bad, evil (cacophony)
καλός, ή, όν, good, beautiful
  (kaleidoscope)

λαμβάνω, I take, receive (epilepsy)
μικρός, ά, όν, small, little (micro-)
νεκρός, ά, όν, dead (necromancy)
ὁ, ἡ, τό, the
πιστός, ή, όν, faithful, believing
πονηρός, ά, όν, wicked, evil
πρῶτος, η, ον, first (prototype)

28. Forms and Syntax of the Definite Article

The definite article ὁ, ἡ, τό is declined as follows.

	Singular				Plural		
	Masc.	Fem.	Neut.		Masc.	Fem.	Neut.
N.	ὁ	ἡ	τό	N.	οἱ	αἱ	τά
G.	τοῦ	τῆς	τοῦ	G.	τῶν	τῶν	τῶν
D.	τῷ	τῇ	τῷ	D.	τοῖς	ταῖς	τοῖς
A.	τόν	τήν	τό	A.	τούς	τάς	τά

The syntax of the article in Greek is similar in many ways to that of English. In general, the definite article identifies, limits, or defines. A few of the differences in the use of the article between English and Greek can be noted here. (1) Biblical Greek sometimes uses the definite article with proper names. For example, one frequently finds the article with "Jesus" in the Gospels and occasionally with "Moses" and "David" in the LXX. In such cases, the article is not translated. (2) Abstract nouns (such as life, love, peace, and truth) often have the article in Greek where they would not in English. Thus, in Greek "the word of truth" might be written, ὁ λόγος τῆς ἀληθείας. (3) Sometimes Greek uses the article with monadic nouns where English would omit it. Monadic nouns refer to things for which there is generally thought to be only one corresponding reality. Thus, "the Lord of heaven and earth" might be written, ὁ κύριος τοῦ οὐρανοῦ καὶ τῆς γῆς. But neither Greek nor English is entirely consistent on this point. The translator must use the appropriate English idiom in each case.

Most forms of the article are similar to the corresponding forms of first and second declension nouns. Note, however, that the nominative singular and accusative

22

singular forms of the neuter do not end in "ν" as the corresponding forms of the neuter noun do (e.g., ἔργον). Four other forms of the article require comment. The masculine and feminine forms of both the nominative singular and the nominative plural (ὁ, ἡ, οἱ, αἱ) are called proclitics. Proclitics are monosyllabic words so closely associated with the following word that they have no accent of their own.

Note that there is no vocative form of the definite article.

29. Forms of First and Second Declension Adjectives

The adjective καλός, ή, όν is declined as follows.

	Singular				Plural		
	Masc.	Fem.	Neut.		Masc.	Fem.	Neut.
N.	καλός	καλή	καλόν	N.V.	καλοί	καλαί	καλά
G.	καλοῦ	καλῆς	καλοῦ	G.	καλῶν	καλῶν	καλῶν
D.	καλῷ	καλῇ	καλῷ	D.	καλοῖς	καλαῖς	καλοῖς
A.	καλόν	καλήν	καλόν	A.	καλούς	καλάς	καλά
V.	καλέ	καλή	καλόν				

Adjectives of the first and second declension are so named because their feminine forms are declined according to the first declension and their masculine and neuter forms according to the second declension. The ending in the feminine singular varies between eta (η) and long alpha (α) according to a rule similar to the one learned for first declension nouns (see §18). When the -ος ending of the lexical form is preceded by epsilon, iota, or rho, the feminine ends in long α. Examples: δίκαιος, μικρός. (See §244 for full declension of μικρός.) When any other letter precedes -ος, the feminine ends in η. Examples: ἔσχατος, καλός. (Note: the accent of the genitive plural feminine form of the adjective is recessive; that is, the special rule for first declension nouns (§20.1) does not apply to the adjective. Thus, δικαίων, *not* δικαιῶν.)

30. Syntax of Adjectives

Adjectives (including the article) agree in case, number, and gender with the nouns they modify. Examples: καλὸς λόγος, a good word; καλὴ γῆ, a good land; καλὸν ἔργον, a good deed.

There are three types of adjectives. *Attributive* adjectives identify or describe a noun by attributing some quality to it. In the phrase, "the good deed," "good" is an attributive adjective. *Predicate* adjectives are used with a linking verb ("to be," "to become," etc.) to assert something about the noun rather than simply identifying it. In the sentence "The deed is good," "good" is a predicate adjective. This distinction, which seems minor in English, is quite important in Greek. Attributive and predicate constructions will play a crucial role in the interpretation of Greek participles.

In Greek, attributive adjectives typically appear in one of two possible constructions. They may appear between the noun and its article: τὸ καλὸν ἔργον. Otherwise, the adjective will follow the noun and have its own article: τὸ ἔργον τὸ καλόν. These phrases have roughly the same meaning: "the good deed." The first construction puts a slight emphasis on the adjective; the second, on the noun. Predicate adjectives appear in different constructions. A predicate adjective will either precede a noun and its article (καλὸν τὸ ἔργον) or follow the noun with no repetition of the article (τὸ ἔργον καλόν). These sentences have roughly the same meaning: "The deed is good." Again, a slight emphasis falls on the component that comes first. (Note that the verb is implied by the construction and may be omitted.)

The easiest way to distinguish between attributive and predicate constructions is by the presence or absence of the article immediately before the adjective. Sometimes, however, there is no article at all, even with the noun. In such cases, only context will determine whether the adjective is attributive or predicate. Thus, καλὸν ἔργον could mean either "a good deed" or "a deed is good."

Lastly, there are *substantive* adjectives. In this case, the noun is omitted, and the adjective itself functions as a noun. This is done in English when we speak of "the poor," "the rich," and so on. Whereas in English, substantive adjectives almost always refer to a plural number of persons, in Greek they may be singular or plural and refer to persons or things. Thus, both the number and the gender of a substantive adjective are important in translation. For example, a substantive adjective that is plural and feminine might call for the translator to supply the word "women" in the English translation. (A substantive adjective that is plural and masculine might refer to a group of men, but the masculine also was the gender used in Greek to refer to a mixed group.) The definite article frequently accompanies a substantive adjective in Greek, but it may be lacking. Thus, either τὰ ἀγαθά or ἀγαθά might mean "(the) goods, good things, possessions."

Several examples of all three types of adjectives are given below.

Attributive
ὁ ἀγαθὸς δοῦλος or ὁ δοῦλος ὁ ἀγαθός = the good slave
ἡ πιστὴ καρδία or ἡ καρδία ἡ πιστή = the faithful heart
τὸ πρῶτον τέκνον or τὸ τέκνον τὸ πρῶτον = the first child
βλέπω τὸν οἶκον τὸν ἔσχατον = I see the last house
βασιλεία καλὴ ἔχει νόμους καλούς = a good kingdom has good laws

Predicate
ἡ ἀδελφὴ δικαία or δικαία ἡ ἀδελφή = the sister is righteous
ὁ κύριος ἅγιος or ἅγιος ὁ κύριος = the Lord is holy
τὸ ἔργον κακόν or κακὸν τὸ ἔργον = the work is evil
τὸ τέκνον νεκρόν or νεκρὸν τὸ τέκνον = the child is dead

Substantive

οἱ πιστοί = the faithful (ones, people, men, etc.)
αἱ πισταί = the faithful women
οἱ ἅγιοι = the holy ones, the saints
ὁ πονηρός = the evil one
τὸ δίκαιον = that which is right, just
γινώσκομεν καλὸν καὶ κακόν = we know good and evil

31. Cases with Special Verbs

Sometimes a Greek verb takes the genitive or dative case to complete its meaning where the equivalent English verb takes a direct object. An English speaker might expect such verbs to take the accusative, but the Greek idiom may simply differ from the English. Among the verbs already introduced, there are two noteworthy instances of this. First, ἀκούω may take either the genitive or the accusative. Thus, either ἀκούω τῆς φωνῆς or ἀκούω τὴν φωνήν, "I hear the sound." Secondly, πιστεύω usually takes a dative object: πιστεύω τῷ λόγῳ, "I believe the word"; πιστεύω τῷ θεῷ, "I trust God." But it occasionally takes an accusative, and the expression "believe in" often involves a Greek preposition just as the English does.

32. Exercises

Practice and Review
1. δίκαιος καὶ ἅγιος ὁ κύριος τοῦ οὐρανοῦ.
2. λέγουσιν ὅτι πιστεύουσι τῷ λόγῳ τοῦ θεοῦ, ἔργα δὲ καλὰ οὐκ ἔχουσιν.
3. ἡ γῆ ἀγαθὴ ὅτι ὁ κύριος τῆς γῆς ἔχει δούλους ἀγαθούς.
4. ὁ υἱὸς ὁ πρῶτος διδάσκει τὰ μικρὰ τέκνα γράφειν;
5. πιστὴ ἡ καρδία τοῦ μικροῦ δούλου, ἀλλὰ κακὰ τὰ ἔργα τοῦ κυρίου τοῦ οἴκου.
6. δικαία ἡ βασιλεία καὶ πιστοὶ οἱ ἄνθρωποι τῆς βασιλείας.
7. οἱ νεκροὶ οὐκ ἔχουσιν δόξαν, οὐ γὰρ βλέπουσι τὰ ἀγαθὰ τῆς ζωῆς.
8. ὁ πρῶτος ἄνθρωπος λέγει τῇ ἐκκλησίᾳ, ἀλλὰ ἡ ἐκκλησία θέλει ἀκούειν τῆς φωνῆς τοῦ ἐσχάτου ἀνθρώπου.
9. οἱ ἀδελφοὶ οἱ πονηροὶ οὐ λαμβάνουσι τὴν ἀλήθειαν τοῦ θεοῦ.
10. αἱ ἡμέραι πονηραὶ ἀλλὰ ὁ οἶκος τοῦ κυρίου ἅγιος.
11. ἡ ἐσχάτη βασιλεία οὐκ ἔχει νόμους κακούς.
12. ἡ μικρὰ ἀδελφὴ οὐ θέλει βλέπειν τὸ τέκνον τὸ νεκρόν, ὁ γὰρ θάνατος οὐ καλός.

LXX

1. καὶ εἶπεν Ιακωβ τῷ Φαραω . . . μικραὶ καὶ πονηραὶ γεγόνασιν αἱ ἡμέραι τῶν ἐτῶν τῆς ζωῆς μου. (Gen 47:9)
2. ἅγιοι ἔσεσθε, ὅτι ἐγὼ ἅγιος, κύριος ὁ θεὸς ὑμῶν. (Lev 19:2)
3. καὶ εἶπεν Εζεκιας πρὸς Ησαιαν Ἀγαθὸς ὁ λόγος κυρίου. (4 Kgdms 20:19)
4. καὶ οἱ λόγοι αὐτοῦ οἱ πρῶτοι καὶ οἱ ἔσχατοι ἰδοὺ γεγραμμένοι ἐπὶ βιβλίῳ βασιλέων Ισραηλ καὶ Ιουδα. (2 Chron 35:27)
5. (Gabael blesses Tobias) Καλὲ καὶ ἀγαθέ, ἀνδρὸς καλοῦ καὶ ἀγαθοῦ, δικαίου καὶ ἐλεημοποιοῦ, δῴη σοι κύριος εὐλογίαν οὐρανοῦ (Tobit 9:6, codex S)
6. ἀγαθὰ καὶ κακά, ζωὴ καὶ θάνατος . . . παρὰ κυρίου ἐστίν. (Sirach 11:14)
7. πιστὸς κύριος ἐν τοῖς λόγοις αὐτοῦ καὶ ὅσιος ἐν πᾶσι τοῖς ἔργοις αὐτοῦ. (Psalm 144:13, ET 145:13)
8. ἄνθρωπος οὐκ ἔστιν δίκαιος ἐν τῇ γῇ, ὃς ποιήσει ἀγαθόν . . . (Eccl 7:20)
9. οἱ δὲ νεκροὶ ζωὴν οὐ μὴ ἴδωσιν (Isaiah 26:14)

NT

1. ἔφη αὐτῷ ὁ κύριος αὐτοῦ, Εὖ, δοῦλε ἀγαθὲ καὶ πιστέ (Matt 25:21)
2. πολλοὶ δὲ ἔσονται πρῶτοι ἔσχατοι καὶ [οἱ] ἔσχατοι πρῶτοι. (Mark 10:31)
3. ὁ ἀγαθὸς ἄνθρωπος ἐκ τοῦ ἀγαθοῦ θησαυροῦ τῆς καρδίας προφέρει τὸ ἀγαθόν, καὶ ὁ πονηρὸς ἐκ τοῦ πονηροῦ προφέρει τὸ πονηρόν· (Luke 6:45)
4. πεπιστεύκαμεν καὶ ἐγνώκαμεν ὅτι σὺ εἶ ὁ ἅγιος τοῦ θεοῦ. (John 6:69)
5. ἐγώ εἰμι ὁ ποιμὴν ὁ καλός καὶ γινώσκω τὰ ἐμὰ καὶ γινώσκουσί με τὰ ἐμά. (John 10:14)
6. ὥστε ὁ . . . νόμος ἅγιος καὶ ἡ ἐντολὴ ἁγία καὶ δικαία καὶ ἀγαθή. (Rom 7:12)
7. ἀγαπητέ, μὴ μιμοῦ τὸ κακὸν ἀλλὰ τὸ ἀγαθόν. (3 John 11)
8. καὶ εἶδον τοὺς νεκρούς, τοὺς μεγάλους καὶ τοὺς μικρούς (Rev 20:12)

English to Greek

1. Are the holy men receiving the good things of the land?
2. The house is beautiful, but the heart of the master of the house is wicked.
3. The dead do not know the truth, for they do not hear God's voice.
4. The evil one wishes to destroy the faithful [women], but they trust God.

Vocabulary for LXX and NT Sentences

ἀγαπητέ, beloved

ἀνδρός, of a man

αὐτοῦ, of him, his

αὐτῷ, to him

βασιλέων, of (the) kings

βιβλίῳ, (the) book

γεγόνασιν, have been

γεγραμμένοι, are written

δῴη, may he give

ἐλεημοποιοῦ, giving alms

ἐγνώκαμεν, we have come to know

ἐγώ, I

εἶ, are

εἶδον, I saw

εἰμι, am

εἶπεν, he said

ἐκ, out of

ἐμά, my own

ἐν, in

ἐντολή, commandment

ἐπί, in

ἔσεσθε, you shall be

ἔσονται, will be

ἐστίν, is, are

ἐτῶν, of (the) years

Εὖ, well done!

εὐλογίαν, a blessing

ἔφη, said

θησαυροῦ, treasury, storehouse

ἰδού, behold

ἴδωσιν, they see

με, me

μεγάλους, great

μή, not

μιμοῦ, imitate!

μου, of me, my

ὅς, who

ὅσιος, holy

παρά, from

πᾶσι, all

πεπιστεύκαμεν, we have believed

ποιήσει, will do

ποιμήν, shepherd

πολλοί, many

πρός, to

προφέρει, brings forth

σοι, to you

σύ, you

ὑμῶν, of you (pl.), your

ὥστε, so, therefore

Lesson 6

33. Vocabulary

ἄγγελος, ὁ, angel, messenger (angel)

ἀπό, (+ gen.) from (apostasy)

βάλλω, I throw, put, place (ballistic)

διά, (+ gen.) through; (+ acc.) for the sake of, because of (diameter)

εἰς, (+ acc.) into, to, against (eisegesis)

ἐκ, ἐξ (+ gen.) out of, by (exodus)

ἐν, (+ dat.) in (endemic, enthusiast)

ἔρημος, ἡ, desert (hermit)

κόσμος, ὁ, world (cosmic)

λίθος, ὁ, stone (monolith)

μαθητής, ὁ, disciple (mathematics)

μένω, I remain, stay (cf. permanent)

μετά, (+ gen.) with; (+ acc.) after, behind (metaphysics)

ὁδός, ἡ, way, road (odometer)

πέμπω, I send

περί, (+ gen.) about, concerning; (+ acc.) around (perimeter)

πρός, (+ acc.) to, toward, with (proselyte)

προφήτης, ὁ, prophet (prophet)

Before vowels ἐκ is written ἐξ. Note that εἰς, ἐκ, and ἐν are proclitics (§28).

34. Feminine Nouns of the Second Declension

Most nouns of the second declension are masculine (e.g., ὁ λόγος) or neuter (e.g., τὸ τέκνον). A few second declension nouns ending in -ος are feminine. The most common of these in biblical Greek are ἡ ἔρημος (desert) and ἡ ὁδός (way). All such words are declined according to the pattern for masculine nouns of the second declension, but any articles, adjectives, or other modifiers associated with them will be feminine. See §240 for the declension of ὁδός.

35. Masculine Nouns of the First Declension

Most nouns of the first declension are feminine (e.g., ὥρα, φωνή, and δόξα), but those ending in -ης are masculine. Examples of such nouns from the above vocabulary are ὁ μαθητής (disciple) and ὁ προφήτης (prophet). The declension of προφήτης is as follows:

Singular		Plural	
Nom.	προφήτης	Nom. Voc.	προφῆται
Gen.	προφήτου	Gen.	προφητῶν
Dat.	προφήτῃ	Dat.	προφήταις
Acc.	προφήτην	Acc.	προφήτας
Voc.	προφῆτα		

The endings of masculine nouns of the first declension differ from the "pure eta" type only in the nominative, genitive, and vocative singular. Note that the vocative singular of these nouns has a distinctive form. For the declension of μαθητής, see §239.

36. Syntax of Prepositions

A preposition expresses a relationship between a noun or pronoun and some other part of the sentence. In English, the object of a preposition takes the objective case: "She walked toward *him*." "They spoke to *me*." In Greek, the object of a preposition may be in any of the oblique cases (genitive, dative, or accusative), but certain prepositions take certain cases. Some Greek prepositions are used exclusively with one case; others with two; a few with three. Most importantly, the prepositions that are used with more than one case may have very different meanings with different cases. It is essential, therefore, that the meanings of these prepositions be learned in conjunction with the particular cases. In other words, it is not sufficient to learn that διά means "through" or "for the sake of." You must learn that διά means "through" with the genitive case and "for the sake of" with the accusative case. To assist in this process, it is advisable that you learn the meanings of two and three case prepositions in a fixed order, for example, first the meaning with the genitive, then with the dative (if the preposition is so used), and lastly with the accusative.

Prepositions used exclusively with one case include ἀπό, (+ gen.) "from"; εἰς, (+ acc.) "into"; ἐκ, (+ gen.) "out of"; and ἐν, (+ dat.) "in." The preposition πρός, "to, toward, with," is rarely used with any case other than the accusative in biblical Greek. Prepositions used with two cases include: διά, (+ gen.) "through," (+ acc.) "for the sake of"; μετά, (+ gen.) "with," (+ acc.) "after, behind"; and περί, (+ gen.) "about, concerning," (+ acc.) "around." Prepositions used with all three cases will be introduced in future lessons. Here are examples of each of the prepositions in this lesson's vocabulary:

ἀπὸ τῆς ἐρήμου, from the desert

ἀπὸ τῆς καρδίας, from the heart

εἰς τὸν οἶκον, into the house

εἰς τὴν γῆν, into the land

ἐκ τῆς γῆς, out of the land

ἐκ τῶν οὐρανῶν, out of the heavens

ἐν τῇ ὁδῷ, in the way

ἐν τῇ ἡμέρᾳ, in the day

πρὸς τὴν θάλασσαν, to the sea

πρὸς τὸν οἶκον, to the house

διὰ τῆς ἐρήμου, through the desert

διὰ τὴν γῆν, because of the land

μετὰ τῶν τέκνων, with the children

μετὰ τὴν ἡμέραν, after the day

περὶ τοῦ μαθητοῦ, about the disciple

περὶ τὸν οἶκον, around the house

37. Special Constructions with Prepositions

In Lesson 5 you learned that attributive adjectives may occur in either of two constructions: between a noun and its article or after a noun with the article repeated. A prepositional phrase may be used in the same constructions. The English translation may use a relative clause.

> ὁ ἄνθρωπος ὁ ἐν τῷ οἴκῳ, the man (who is) in the house
> οἱ ἀπὸ τῶν οὐρανῶν ἄγγελοι, the angels (who are) from heaven
> βλέπω τοὺς λίθους τοὺς ἐν τῇ ἐρήμῳ, I see the stones (that are) in the desert

Prepositions in every language tend to be highly idiomatic. In actual practice, a variety of English words might be used to translate a Greek preposition, and English might employ a different preposition from the one used in Greek for a particular idiom. The Greek verb πιστεύω is found with several different constructions, sometimes simply with the dative case, sometimes with a preposition. A very common expression in the New Testament is πιστεύω εἰς + the accusative. Example: πιστεύετε εἰς τὸν θεόν, "You believe in God." English speakers do not think of "believing into." The equivalent idiom in English simply uses a different preposition. For now, learn the basic meanings given in the vocabulary lists. As you begin to read the Bible in Greek, it should not be difficult to add the less common nuances of the prepositions.

38. Elision and Aspiration

Greek generally tried to avoid hiatus: the succession of two vowels in adjacent words. We saw earlier that movable ν was one way that this was achieved (see §11.4). Another instance in which hiatus was avoided was between prepositions ending with a vowel and prepositional objects beginning with a vowel. When this would occur, the practice was to elide or drop the final vowel of the preposition. Thus, ἀπ' οὐρανοῦ, "from heaven"; μετ' ἀγγέλου, "with an angel"; and δι' οἴκου, "through a house." (Note that in the last example hiatus is not avoided even with elision.) Sometimes the word follow-ing one of these prepositions began with rough breathing. When this was the case, the final consonant of the preposition (after elision) was usually aspirated to make the two sounds more harmonious. Tau became theta, pi became phi, etc. Thus, μεθ' ἡμέραν, "after an hour"; ἀφ' ὁδοῦ, "from a road." Elision and aspiration are not car-ried out consistently though.

39. Neuter Plural Subjects with Singular Verbs

Generally, in Greek just as in English, subject and verb will agree in number. A partial exception to this is the neuter plural subject, which in biblical Greek *sometimes* had a singular verb. Example: τὰ τέκνα οὐ γινώσκει τὴν ἀλήθειαν, "The children do not know the truth."

40. Exercises

Practice and Review

1. πέμπομεν τοὺς ἀδελφοὺς τοὺς κακοὺς ἐκ τῆς ἐκκλησίας καὶ εἰς τὴν ἔρημον.
2. ὁ θεὸς μένει ἐν τοῖς οὐρανοῖς, βάλλει δὲ τοὺς πονηροὺς ἀγγέλους εἰς τὴν γῆν.
3. ἐν τῇ ὥρᾳ τῆς δόξης λέγει ὁ κύριος πρὸς τὰς καρδίας τῶν τέκνων.
4. οἱ ἀγαθοὶ προφῆται γινώσκουσι τὴν ἀλήθειαν περὶ τῆς ζωῆς καὶ τοῦ θανάτου;
5. διὰ τοῦ ἀγγέλου τοῦ κυρίου ἀκούετε περὶ τῆς ὁδοῦ τῆς ζωῆς.
6. μετὰ τῶν τέκνων αἱ ἀδελφαὶ βάλλουσι λίθους εἰς τὴν θάλασσαν.
7. προφῆτα, ἔχεις καλοὺς λόγους ἀπὸ θεοῦ καὶ βλέπεις τὴν δόξαν τῆς βασιλείας;
8. ἐν τῇ ἐσχάτῃ ἡμέρᾳ πέμπει ὁ κύριος τοὺς ἀγγέλους ἀπ' οὐρανοῦ καὶ οἱ ἄγγελοι λαμβάνουσι τοὺς πιστοὺς ἐκ τοῦ κόσμου.
9. ἐν τῇ ἐρήμῳ διδάσκει ὁ υἱὸς τοῦ ἁγίου τὰς ἀδελφὰς περὶ τοῦ νόμου.
10. οἱ περὶ τὸν προφήτην ἄνθρωποι μένουσι μετὰ τῶν μαθητῶν.
11. μετὰ τὸν νόμον καὶ τοὺς προφήτας θέλομεν ἀκούειν τοῦ λόγου τοῦ ἀδελφοῦ.
12. οὐ γινώσκομεν τὰς ὁδοὺς τοῦ θεοῦ ἐν τῷ κόσμῳ ἀλλὰ πιστεύομεν τῷ θεῷ.
13. οὐκ ἐξ ἔργων τοῦ νόμου λαμβάνει ἄνθρωπος ζωὴν ἀπ' οὐρανοῦ.
14. δι' ἀνθρώπους κακοὺς λέγομεν πρὸς τὸν θεόν.

LXX

1. καὶ συνετέλεσεν ὁ θεὸς ἐν τῇ ἡμέρᾳ τῇ ἕκτῃ τὰ ἔργα αὐτοῦ, . . . καὶ κατέπαυσεν τῇ ἡμέρᾳ τῇ ἑβδόμῃ ἀπὸ πάντων τῶν ἔργων αὐτοῦ (Gen 2:2)
2. Καὶ εἶπεν κύριος τῷ Αβραμ Ἔξελθε ἐκ τῆς γῆς σου καὶ ἐκ τῆς συγγενείας σου καὶ ἐκ τοῦ οἴκου τοῦ πατρός σου εἰς τὴν γῆν . . . (Gen 12:1)
3. καὶ εἶπεν ὁ θεός Τί ἐποίησας; φωνὴ αἵματος τοῦ ἀδελφοῦ σου βοᾷ πρός με ἐκ τῆς γῆς. καὶ νῦν ἐπικατάρατος σὺ ἀπὸ τῆς γῆς (Gen 4:10-11)

4. μετὰ δὲ τὰς ἡμέρας . . . ἐκείνας ἐτελεύτησεν ὁ βασιλεὺς Αἰγύπτου. εἶπεν δὲ κύριος πρὸς Μωυσῆν ἐν Μαδιαμ . . . ἄπελθε εἰς Αἴγυπτον· (Ex 4:19)

5. καὶ ἐξαπέστειλεν Ισραηλ ἀγγέλους πρὸς βασιλέα Εδωμ λέγων Παρελεύσομαι διὰ τῆς γῆς σου· (Judges 11:17, codex A)

6. καὶ ἠλέησεν κύριος αὐτοὺς καὶ . . . ἐπέβλεψεν πρὸς αὐτοὺς διὰ τὴν διαθήκην αὐτοῦ τὴν μετὰ Αβρααμ καὶ Ισαακ καὶ Ιακωβ (4 Kgdms 13:23)

7. Ἀληθινὸς ὁ λόγος, ὃν ἤκουσα ἐν τῇ γῇ μου περὶ τῶν λόγων σου καὶ περὶ τῆς σοφίας σου (2 Chr 9:5)

NT

1. πολλοὶ . . . ἀνακλιθήσονται μετὰ Ἀβραὰμ καὶ Ἰσαὰκ καὶ Ἰακὼβ ἐν τῇ βασιλείᾳ τῶν οὐρανῶν (Matt 8:11)

2. Περὶ δὲ τῆς ἡμέρας ἐκείνης καὶ ὥρας οὐδεὶς οἶδεν, οὐδὲ οἱ ἄγγελοι τῶν οὐρανῶν οὐδὲ ὁ υἱός (Matt 24:36)

3. Τὸ σάββατον διὰ τὸν ἄνθρωπον ἐγένετο καὶ οὐχ ὁ ἄνθρωπος διὰ τὸ σάββατον· (Mark 2:27)

4. Καὶ ὁ Ἰησοῦς μετὰ τῶν μαθητῶν αὐτοῦ ἀνεχώρησεν πρὸς τὴν θάλασσαν (Mark 3:7)

5. ἐξελθὼν ἐκ τῶν ὁρίων Τύρου ἦλθεν διὰ Σιδῶνος εἰς τὴν θάλασσαν τῆς Γαλιλαίας (Mark 7:31)

6. ἀπεστάλη ὁ ἄγγελος Γαβριὴλ ἀπὸ τοῦ θεοῦ εἰς πόλιν τῆς Γαλιλαίας (Luke 1:26)

7. ἤρξατο λέγειν πρὸς τοὺς ὄχλους περὶ Ἰωάννου, Τί ἐξήλθατε εἰς τὴν ἔρημον θεάσασθαι; (Luke 7:24)

8. Παῦλος ἀπόστολος οὐκ ἀπ' ἀνθρώπων οὐδὲ δι' ἀνθρώπου ἀλλὰ διὰ Ἰησοῦ Χριστοῦ καὶ θεοῦ πατρὸς τοῦ ἐγείραντος αὐτὸν ἐκ νεκρῶν (Gal 1:1)

English to Greek

1. Do the men in the assembly know that the prophet is teaching the slaves about the law?
2. The Lord of glory sends messengers from heaven to the children of earth.
3. For the sake of the kingdom of God we remain in the world with the faithful ones.
4. You (sing.) speak beautiful things out of a good heart, but you do not know the way into life.

Lesson 6

Vocabulary for LXX and NT Sentences

αἵματος, of (the) blood
ἀληθινός, true
ἀνακλιθήσονται, will recline
ἀνεχώρησεν, departed
ἄπελθε, go back!
ἀπεστάλη, was sent
ἀπόστολος, apostle
αὐτόν, him
αὐτοῦ, of him, his
αὐτούς, them
βασιλέα, king
βασιλεύς, king
βοᾷ, cries out
διαθήκην, covenant
ἑβδόμη, seventh
ἐγείραντος, (the one) having raised
ἐγένετο, was made
εἶπεν, said
ἐκείνας, those
ἐκείνης, that
ἕκτῃ, sixth
ἐξαπέστειλεν, sent out
ἔξελθε, go forth!
ἐξελθών, going forth
ἐξήλθατε, you went out
ἐπέβλεψεν, looked compassionately
ἐπικατάρατος, cursed
ἐποίησας, you have done
ἐτελεύτησεν, died

ἤκουσα, I heard
ἠλέησεν, had mercy on
ἦλθεν, (he) went
ἤρξατο, he began
θεάσασθαι, to see, behold
κατέπαυσεν, rested
λέγων, saying
με, me
μου, of me, my
νῦν, now
οἶδεν = γινώσκει
ὅν, that, which
ὁρίων, region, district
οὐδέ, and not, nor, not even
οὐδείς, no one
ὄχλους, crowds, multitudes
πάντων, all
παρελεύσομαι, I will pass through
πατρός, father
πόλιν, city
πολλοί, many
σάββατον, Sabbath
σου, of you, your
σοφίας, wisdom
σύ, you (sing.)
συγγενείας, relatives
συνετέλεσεν, finished
Τί, What?

Lesson 7

41. Vocabulary

ἀγάπη, ἡ, love
ἁμαρτία, ἡ, sin (hamartiology)
ἄρτος, ὁ, bread, loaf
αὐτός, ἡ, ό, he, she, it
δῶρον, τό, gift
ἐγώ, I (ego)
εἰμί, I am
ἐσθίω, I eat

κατά, (+ gen.) against, (+ acc.)
   according to (catastrophe)
ὄχλος, ὁ, crowd, multitude
   (ochlocracy)
πλοῖον, τό, boat
σύ, you (sing.)
σῴζω, I save (soteriology)
ψυχή, ἡ, soul, life (psycho-)

42. Enclitics

Enclitics are words that are so closely related to the preceding words that they often require no accent of their own. Remember that *proclitics* were similarly related to the words that *follow* them (See §28). Enclitics in biblical Greek include several forms of the personal pronouns, most forms of the verb εἰμί, and a few other words. When enclitic forms are given in this and later lessons, they will be identified as such.

A major difference between enclitics and proclitics is that enclitics give rise to a number of special rules of accenting. Due to the complexity of these rules, the best way to familiarize oneself with enclitic accenting is through reading Greek texts and seeing them in application. The rules are given here to provide an overview and for future reference.

The word preceding an enclitic is affected in the following ways:

(1) An acute accent on the ultima may remain. That is, it does not switch to a grave accent. Examples: ἡ ἀδελφή μου, "my sister"; ὁ υἱός σου, "your son." (2) A word with an acute accent on the antepenult or a circumflex on the penult receives an additional acute accent on the ultima. Examples: ὁ ἄγγελός σου, "your messenger"; ὁ δοῦλός μου, "my slave." (3) If the word before an enclitic is itself an enclitic or a proclitic, it receives an acute accent on the ultima. Examples: ἐγώ εἰμι ὁ κύριος, "I am the Lord"; ὁ ἄγγελός σού ἐστι πιστός, "Your messenger is faithful."

The enclitic itself will be accented in the following circumstances:

(4) An enclitic of two syllables retains its accent when it follows a word having an acute on the penult. Example: ὁ ἄρτος ἐστὶν ἅγιος, "The bread is holy." (5) An enclitic receives an acute on the ultima when it is emphatic, such as in contrasts or at the beginning of a sentence or clause. Examples: λέγω τὴν ἀλήθειαν, εἰμὶ γὰρ

34

προφήτης, "I speak the truth, for <u>I am</u> a prophet"; ἐγὼ διδάσκω ἐν τῇ ἐκκλησίᾳ, σὺ δὲ οὐ θέλεις ἀκούειν, "<u>I</u> am teaching in the church, but <u>you</u> do not wish to listen."

An enclitic forms a phonetic unit with the preceding word. Without these special rules of accenting, therefore, the result would in many cases be a long series of unaccented syllables. In general, the aim of these rules is to avoid such a series, either by adding an additional accent to the word preceding the enclitic or by accenting the enclitic itself.

43. Present Indicative of εἰμί

The present indicative of εἰμί is given below. Note that the third person forms, both singular and plural, may have movable ν. (See §11.4.)

Singular	Plural
1. εἰμί, I am	1. ἐσμέν, we are
2. εἶ, you (sing.) are	2. ἐστέ, you (pl.) are
3. ἐστί(ν), he, she, or it is	3. εἰσί(ν), they are

Like other linking verbs, εἰμί takes a predicate nominative to complete its meaning (see §17). A predicate nominative may be a noun or an adjective. Examples: (1) ὁ θεὸς ἀγάπη ἐστίν, "God is love"; (2) προφήτης ἐστὶν ὁ ἄνθρωπος, "The man is a prophet"; (3) ἡ ἀδελφή ἐστι πιστή, "The sister is faithful." The verb in each case could be omitted since the construction alone is adequate to show predication. Note that the presence of the article will usually distinguish the subject from the predicate nominative when the latter is a noun. Greek word order is flexible. The subject will not necessarily precede the predicate nominative.

All the above forms of εἰμί are enclitic except for the second person singular (εἶ), which always has the accent shown. The other forms take the indicated accents only when required by the above rules.

44. Accentuation of ἔστι(ν)

The third person singular form of εἰμί is accented on the penult when it stands first in its clause or sentence, or when it follows certain words such as οὐκ, καί, and ἀλλά. Example: ὁ δὲ ἄνθρωπος οὐκ ἔστιν δοῦλος, "But the man is not a slave."

45. Forms of Personal Pronouns

(1) First person pronoun:

	Singular			Plural
Nom.	ἐγώ, I		Nom.	ἡμεῖς, we
Gen.	ἐμοῦ, or μου, of me		Gen.	ἡμῶν, of us
Dat.	ἐμοί or μοι, to/for me		Dat.	ἡμῖν, to/for us
Acc.	ἐμέ or με, me		Acc.	ἡμᾶς, us

[handwritten annotation: ONES BEGINNING WITH ε ARE EMPHATIC]

The forms ἐμοῦ, ἐμοί, ἐμέ are emphatic and are always accented. The forms μου, μοι, and με are enclitic and only receive an accent when required by the special rules of enclitic accent.

(2) Second person pronoun:

	Singular		Plural
Nom.	σύ, you	Nom.	ὑμεῖς, you
Gen.	σοῦ, or σου, of you	Gen.	ὑμῶν, of you
Dat.	σοί or σοι, to/for you	Dat.	ὑμῖν, to/for you
Acc.	σέ or σε, you	Acc.	ὑμᾶς, you

The oblique cases of the singular second person pronoun also have both emphatic and enclitic forms. Unlike the corresponding forms of the first person pronoun, however, they are only distinguished by accent, not by spelling: σοῦ, σοί, and σέ are emphatic; σου, σοι, and σε are enclitic.

(3) Third person pronoun:

Singular

	Masc.	Fem.	Neut.
N.	αὐτός, he	αὐτή, she	αὐτό, it
G.	αὐτοῦ, of him	αὐτῆς, of her	αὐτοῦ, of it
D.	αὐτῷ, to/for him	αὐτῇ, to/for her	αὐτῷ, to/for it
A.	αὐτόν, him	αὐτήν, her	αὐτό, it

Plural

	Masc.	Fem.	Neut.
N.	αὐτοί, they	αὐταί, they	αὐτά, they
G.	αὐτῶν, of them	αὐτῶν, of them	αὐτῶν, of them
D.	αὐτοῖς, to/for them	αὐταῖς, to/for them	αὐτοῖς, to/for them
A.	αὐτούς, them	αὐτάς, them	αὐτά, them

36

αὐτός is a very versatile word. In addition to its pronominal use, it has other special uses which will be introduced in the next lesson.

46. Syntax of Personal Pronouns

Pronouns are words that take the place of nouns. The noun to which a pronoun refers is called its antecedent. In the sentence "After the woman addressed the students, they asked her questions," "they" is a pronoun whose antecedent is "students," and "her" is a pronoun whose antecedent is "woman."

A pronoun agrees with its antecedent in gender and number. In the above example, the feminine singular pronoun "her" is used because it refers to a feminine singular noun, "woman." The plural pronoun "they" refers to the plural noun "students." Although the word "they" in English does not have gender, it would in Greek, and its gender would agree with its antecedent. (Note that a pronoun does not necessarily agree with its antecedent in case, though it may by chance.) Examples:

βλέπομεν τοὺς <u>ἀδελφοὺς</u> καὶ λέγομεν <u>αὐτοῖς</u>.
"We see the <u>brothers</u> and we speak to <u>them</u>." (masculine, plural)

γινώσκω τὴν <u>ἀδελφήν</u> σου καὶ διδάσκω <u>αὐτήν</u>.
"I know your <u>sister</u> and I teach <u>her</u>." (feminine singular)

τὸ <u>πλοῖόν</u> ἐστιν ἐν τῇ θαλάσσῃ, ἀλλ' οὐ βλέπομεν <u>αὐτό</u>.
"The <u>boat</u> is on the lake, but we do not see <u>it</u>." (neuter singular)

In English, nouns that denote inanimate objects are usually regarded as neuter and referred to with the neuter pronoun "it." In Greek, however, such nouns may be masculine, feminine, or neuter. Pronouns referring to these nouns will use the appropriate gender in Greek, but will normally be translated "it" in English. Examples: (1) ὁ λίθος ἐστὶ καλός. βλέπεις <u>αὐτόν</u>; "The stone is beautiful. Do you see <u>it</u>?" (2) οἱ δοῦλοι ἔχουσι τὴν ζωήν, ὑμεῖς δὲ οὐκ ἔχετε <u>αὐτήν</u>, "The slaves have life, but you do not have <u>it</u>."

It is not necessary in Greek to use a pronoun to express the subject of a verb. Because Greek verbs are highly inflected, the verbal form alone, together with the context, is sufficient to indicate the subject. Thus, given a certain context, ἀκούει with no explicit subject pronoun will mean either "he hears" or "she hears." When a nominative case pronoun is added, there may be emphasis on the subject, perhaps due to contrast. Example: αὐτὴ ἀκούει τῆς φωνῆς, αὐτὸς δὲ οὐκ ἀκούει. "She hears the sound, but he does not hear (it)." But emphasis is not always evident; the nominative case sometimes functions as a simple pronoun.

The genitive case of personal pronouns is the most common way to express possession in biblical Greek, whereas English uses a possessive *adjective*. The unemphatic forms (in the first and second person singular) are used for this purpose. Examples: (1) βλέπω τὸν ἀδελφόν σου. "I see your brother." (2) ἐσθίετε τὸν ἄρτον μου; "Are you (pl.) eating my bread?" The Greek expressions "the brother of you," "the bread of me" obviously must be rendered according to English idiom: "your brother," "my bread."

Following prepositions, the emphatic or accented forms of the first and second person singular personal pronouns are generally used. Thus: (1) ἡ ἀλήθεια μένει ἐν ἐμοί, "The truth abides in me." (2) διὰ σοῦ ἀκούομεν τὸν λόγον, "Through you we are hearing the word." (3) ὁ ὄχλος λαμβάνει τὸ πλοῖον ἀπ' ἐμοῦ, "The crowd is taking the boat from me." (Remember that elision and aspiration sometimes occur with prepositions. See §38.) The preposition πρός is an exception to this rule. It commonly uses the enclitic forms of these pronouns: (1) φωνὴ λέγει πρός με, "A voice speaks to me"; (2) πέμπω τέκνον πρός σε, "I am sending a child to you."

47. Exercises

Practice and Review

1. λέγετε λόγον κατὰ τοῦ κυρίου τοῦ οὐρανοῦ;
2. αἱ ψυχαὶ ὑμῶν ἔχουσιν ἁμαρτίαν ὅτι ἐσθίετε τὸν ἄρτον τῶν τέκνων.
3. ἡ ἀδελφή σου καὶ τὸ τέκνον αὐτῆς εἰσιν ἐν τῷ πλοίῳ ἀλλὰ οὐκ ἔχουσιν ἄρτον.
4. ἡ ἀγάπη τοῦ θεοῦ σῴζει ὑμᾶς ἀπὸ τῆς ἁμαρτίας ὑμῶν.
5. προφήτης πιστὸς οὐ διδάσκει κατὰ τοῦ νόμου.

6. ἡ ἀγάπη τῆς ἁμαρτίας μένει ἐν σοί, ἐγὼ δὲ πιστεύω ὅτι ὁ κύριος θέλει σῴζειν σε.
7. ἐσθίει ὁ ὄχλος τὸν ἄρτον τῆς γῆς, ἀλλὰ οὐκ ἔχουσι τὰ δῶρα τοῦ οὐρανοῦ.
8. οὐ λαμβάνομεν δῶρα ἀπὸ τοῦ θεοῦ κατὰ τὰ ἔργα ἡμῶν ἀλλὰ κατὰ τὴν ἀγάπην αὐτοῦ.
9. οἱ δοῦλοι ἡμῶν βάλλουσι λίθους εἰς τὸ πλοῖον ὅτι αὐτὸ θέλουσι λύειν.
10. ἡ δίκαια ἀκούει τῆς φωνῆς τῆς ἀληθείας καὶ σῴζει τὴν ψυχὴν αὐτῆς ἐκ θανάτου.
11. γινώσκομεν ὅτι σὺ εἶ ὁ ἄγγελος τῆς ζωῆς. μετὰ σοῦ οἱ υἱοὶ τῆς βασιλείας εἰσίν;
12. ὁ μαθητὴς οὐκ ἔχει τὴν ἁμαρτίαν, διδάσκει γὰρ κατὰ τὸν νόμον τοῦ θεοῦ.
13. διὰ τὸν ὄχλον τὸν πονηρὸν πέμπει ὁ θεὸς τοὺς δούλους αὐτοῦ εἰς τὸν οἶκον.
14. λέγεις ὅτι ἐγὼ εἰμι ὁ ἅγιος, σὺ δὲ οὐ βλέπεις τὴν βασιλείαν μου.

LXX

1. οὐ γὰρ καθ' ἡμῶν ὁ γογγυσμὸς ὑμῶν ἐστιν, ἀλλ' ἢ κατὰ τοῦ θεοῦ. (Exod 16:8)
2. καὶ νῦν ἡ βασιλεία σου οὐ στήσεται, καὶ ζητήσει κύριος ... ἄνθρωπον κατὰ τὴν καρδίαν αὐτοῦ (1 Kgdms 13:14)

3. καὶ ἵνα τί οὐκ ἐσθίεις; καὶ ἵνα τί τύπτει σε ἡ καρδία σου; οὐκ ἀγαθὸς ἐγώ σοι ὑπὲρ δέκα τέκνα; (1 Kgdms 1:8)
4. καὶ οἱ πιστοὶ ἐν ἀγάπῃ προσμενοῦσιν αὐτῷ· (Wis 3:9)
5. καὶ αὐτοὶ ἤνεγκαν τὸ δῶρον αὐτῶν . . . κυρίῳ περὶ τῆς ἁμαρτίας αὐτῶν (Num 15:25)
6. οἱ καταβαίνοντες εἰς τὴν θάλασσαν ἐν πλοίοις . . . αὐτοὶ εἴδοσαν τὰ ἔργα κυρίου (Ps 106:23-4, ET 107:23-4)
7. καὶ ἀγαπήσεις κύριον τὸν θεόν σου ἐξ ὅλης τῆς καρδίας σου καὶ ἐξ ὅλης τῆς ψυχῆς σου (Deut 6:5)
8. εἶπεν δὲ κύριος πρὸς Μωυσῆν Ἰδοὺ ἐγὼ ὕω ὑμῖν ἄρτους ἐκ τοῦ οὐρανοῦ (Exod 16:4)
9. ὁ κύριος . . . ἀφίησιν ἁμαρτίας καὶ σῴζει ἐν καιρῷ θλίψεως. (Sir 2:11)

NT

1. καὶ ἔδωκεν ἡ θάλασσα τοὺς νεκροὺς τοὺς ἐν αὐτῇ καὶ ὁ θάνατος καὶ ὁ ᾅδης ἔδωκαν τοὺς νεκροὺς τοὺς ἐν αὐτοῖς, καὶ ἐκρίθησαν ἕκαστος κατὰ τὰ ἔργα αὐτῶν. (Rev 20:13)
2. αὐτὸς γὰρ σώσει τὸν λαὸν αὐτοῦ ἀπὸ τῶν ἁμαρτιῶν αὐτῶν. (Matt 1:21)
3. ἀμὴν ἀμὴν λέγω ὑμῖν, ὁ πιστεύων ἔχει ζωὴν αἰώνιον. ἐγώ εἰμι ὁ ἄρτος τῆς ζωῆς. (John 6:47-8)
4. οἱ Φαρισαῖοι ἔλεγον τοῖς μαθηταῖς αὐτοῦ, Διὰ τί μετὰ τῶν τελωνῶν καὶ ἁμαρτωλῶν ἐσθίει ὁ διδάσκαλος ὑμῶν; (Matt 9:11)
5. καθίσας δὲ ἐκ τοῦ πλοίου ἐδίδασκεν τοὺς ὄχλους. (Luke 5:3)
6. (re: salvation) καὶ τοῦτο οὐκ ἐξ ὑμῶν, θεοῦ τὸ δῶρον· οὐκ ἐξ ἔργων (Eph. 2:8-9)
7. καὶ ἐρῶ τῇ ψυχῇ μου, Ψυχή, ἔχεις πολλὰ ἀγαθὰ κείμενα (Luke 12:19)
8. ἐν τούτῳ ἐστὶν ἡ ἀγάπη, οὐχ ὅτι ἡμεῖς ἠγαπήκαμεν τὸν θεόν ἀλλ᾽ ὅτι αὐτὸς ἠγάπησεν ἡμᾶς (1 John 4:10)

English to Greek

1. We have your (pl.) bread, but we do not wish to eat it.
2. The crowds are speaking against the prophet because the prophet does not have gifts for them.
3. A good boat saves souls in the sea, but the Lord saves from sin.
4. According to the law, love is the way of truth.
5. I see you (sing.), but you do not see me.

Vocabulary for LXX and NT Sentences

ἀγαπήσεις, you will love

ᾅδης, Hades

αἰώνιον, eternal

ἁμαρτωλῶν, sinners

ἀμήν, amen, truly

ἀφίησιν, forgives

γογγυσμός, complaining

δέκα, ten

Διὰ τί, Why?

διδάσκαλος, teacher

ἐδίδασκεν, past of διδάσκει

ἔδωκαν, (they) gave up, yielded

ἔδωκεν, (it) gave up, yielded

εἴδοσαν, they saw

εἶπεν, said

ἕκαστος, each

ἐκρίθησαν, they were judged

ἔλεγον, said

ἐρῶ, I will say

ζητήσει, will seek

ἤ, rather

ἠγαπήκαμεν, we have loved

ἠγάπησεν, he loved

ἤνεγκαν, they offered

θλίψεως, of trouble, tribulation

Ἰδού, Behold!

ἵνα τί, why?

καθίσας, having sat down

καιρῷ, time

καταβαίνοντες, going down

κείμενα, laid up, stored up

λαὸν, people

νῦν, now

ὅλης, whole, entire

πιστεύων, believing, who believes

πολλά, many

προσμενοῦσιν, will abide with

στήσεται, it will stand

σώσει, future of σῴζει

τελωνῶν, tax collectors

τοῦτο, this

τούτῳ, this

τύπτει, strike, trouble

ὑπὲρ, above, beyond

ὕω, rain, cause to rain

Lesson 8

48. Vocabulary

ἄλλος, η, ο, other (allomorph)

ἀποστέλλω, I send (apostle)

αὐτός, ή, ό, same, -self (automatic)

βαπτίζω, I baptize (baptize)

ἐγείρω, I raise up

εἰρήνη, ἡ, peace (irenic)

ἐκεῖνος, η, ο, that

ἐξουσία, ἡ, authority

εὑρίσκω, I find (heuristic)

κρίνω, I judge (critic)

λαός, ὁ, people (laity)

οὖν, therefore, consequently
    (postpositive, see §22)

οὗτος, αὕτη, τοῦτο, this

οὕτως, thus, so

πρόσωπον, τό, face

49. Forms of the Demonstratives *- USUALLY COMES BEFORE THE WORD IT MODIFIES (PREDICATE)*

The forms of the demonstrative οὗτος, "this," are as follows:

Singular

Masc.	Fem.	Neut.
N. οὗτος	αὕτη	τοῦτο
G. τούτου	ταύτης	τούτου
D. τούτῳ	ταύτῃ	τούτῳ
A. τοῦτον	ταύτην	τοῦτο

SAME AS 3RD PERSON PRONOUN EXCEPT FOR ROUGH BREATHING

Plural

Masc.	Fem.	Neut.
N. οὗτοι	αὗται	ταῦτα
G. τούτων	τούτων	τούτων
D. τούτοις	ταύταις	τούτοις
A. τούτους	ταύτας	ταῦτα

The forms of the demonstrative ἐκεῖνος, "that," are as follows:

- TOTALLY FOLLOWS BASIC ADJECTIVE FORMS

Singular

Masc.	Fem.	Neut.
N. ἐκεῖνος	ἐκείνη	ἐκεῖνο
G. ἐκείνου	ἐκείνης	ἐκείνου
D. ἐκείνῳ	ἐκείνῃ	ἐκείνῳ
A. ἐκεῖνον	ἐκείνην	ἐκεῖνο

41

	Masc.	Plural Fem.	Neut.
N.	ἐκεῖνοι	ἐκεῖναι	ἐκεῖνα
G.	ἐκείνων	ἐκείνων	ἐκείνων
D.	ἐκείνοις	ἐκείναις	ἐκείνοις
A.	ἐκείνους	ἐκείνας	ἐκεῖνα

Certain forms of the demonstrative οὗτος are very similar to the corresponding forms of the third person pronoun αὐτός. To distinguish them from one another, remember that forms of οὗτος are always accented on the first syllable and always begin with a "τ" or with rough breathing.

As for the curious variation of the diphthong in the first syllable (between ου and αυ), note that when an "a-type" vowel (α or η) occurs in the ending, the αυ diphthong is found in the first syllable. When an "o-type" vowel (o or ω) occurs in the ending, the ου diphthong is found in the first syllable.

The endings of ἐκεῖνος are identical to those of αὐτός except for accent. Note that there is no "ν" on the end of the nominative and accusative neuter singular forms. (This is also true of the adjective ἄλλος introduced in this lesson.)

50. Syntax of the Demonstratives

Demonstratives are words that specify or "point out" a person or thing. They may be used with nouns as adjectives or by themselves as pronouns. Biblical Greek, like English, has a "near" demonstrative, οὗτος, for something relatively close in time, space, or thought, and a "far" demonstrative, ἐκεῖνος, for something relatively distant.

When a Greek demonstrative is used with a noun, it regularly stands in the predicate position, and the noun it modifies has the article (see §30). A demonstrative adjective will agree in case, number, and gender with its noun. Thus: οὗτος ὁ λίθος (or ὁ λίθος οὗτος), "this stone"; αὕτη ἡ ἀδελφή (or ἡ ἀδελφὴ αὕτη), "this sister"; τοῦτο τὸ δῶρον, "this gift"; ὁ δοῦλος ἐκεῖνος, "that slave"; ἐκεῖναι αἱ ψυχαί, "those souls"; τὰ πλοῖα ἐκεῖνα, "those boats." Note that the English translation in each case omits the definite article.

When a demonstrative stands alone, it is a pronoun. It will agree in gender and number with its antecedent; its function in the sentence will determine its case. English idiom will sometimes require the expression of the implied noun. Examples: (1) οὗτος γινώσκει τὸν κύριον, "This man knows the Lord"; (2) βλέπομεν ταύτην, "We see this woman"; (3) οὗτοι πιστεύουσιν, "These men/persons believe"; (4) ἐκεῖναι διδάσκουσι τὸ τέκνον, "Those women are teaching the child"; (5) μετὰ ταῦτα πέμπει ἐκεῖνος ἄγγελον, "After these things, that man sends a messenger." The gender and number of the demonstrative pronoun determine what noun must be added to the translation: "man," "woman," "persons," "things," etc.

51. Special Uses of αὐτός *(review §30)*

The word αὐτός is quite versatile. We saw in §46 that it functions as a third person pronoun (especially in the oblique cases). In the nominative case it may be emphatic. These functions it shares with the other personal pronouns.

Regular   διδάσκω αὐτόν. "I teach him."
Emphatic   διδάσκω, αὐτὸς δὲ οὐκ ἀκούει. "I teach, but *he* does not listen."

But in conjunction with nouns, αὐτός has special adjectival uses. One of these is the *intensive* use. In this use αὐτός stands in the *predicate* position with a noun and is translated "-self" or "-selves." The number and gender of the accompanying noun determine the exact translation. Thus: αὐτὸς ὁ ἄνθρωπος, "the man himself"; αὐτὴ ἡ ἀδελφή, "the sister herself"; αὐτὸ τὸ ἔργον, "the deed itself"; οἱ υἱοὶ αὐτοί, "the sons themselves." In some constructions the translation "very" or "that very" may be suitable: ἐν αὐτῇ τῇ ὥρᾳ, "in that very hour." *or "in that hour itself."*

The intensive use of αὐτός also occurs with pronouns and even with the unexpressed subjects of verbs. Gender and number are determined by the pronoun or implied subject. Thus: αὐτὸς σὺ λέγεις, "You yourself (addressing a man) say"; αὐτός ἐγὼ κρίνω, "I myself (a man speaking) judge"; αὐταὶ ὑμεῖς ἀκούετε τὸν λόγον, "You (women) yourselves hear the word"; αὐτὸς ἔχω τὴν ἐξουσίαν, "I myself (a man speaking) have the authority"; αὐτὴ σὺ πιστεύεις, "You yourself (addressing a woman) believe." Note that as an intensive adjective αὐτός is by no means limited to the third person. It may intensify first, second, or third person subjects. Only in its pronominal use does αὐτός denote the third person.

A second special use of αὐτός is the *identical* use. In this use αὐτός stands in the *attributive* position with a noun and is translated "same." Thus: ὁ αὐτὸς λόγος or ὁ λόγος ὁ αὐτός, "the same word"; ἡ αὐτὴ ἀγάπη or ἡ ἀγάπη ἡ αὐτή, "the same love"; τὰ αὐτὰ δῶρα, etc., "the same gifts."

The identical use of αὐτός also occurs without a noun. The context will supply a noun if English idiom requires one. Examples: (1) πιστεύομεν τὰ αὐτά, "We believe the same (things)"; (2) ὁ αὐτὸς σῴζει καὶ λύει, "The same (man, person) saves and destroys."

As opposed to
αὐτὸς ὁ λόγος
"the word itself"

Lesson 8

Here is a summary of several of the constructions learned to this point.

Attributive Adjective	ὁ ἅγιος ἄρτος	or	ὁ ἄρτος ὁ ἅγιος	The holy bread
Predicate Adjective	ἅγιος ὁ ἄρτος	or	ὁ ἄρτος ἅγιος	The bread is holy
"Near" Demonstrative	οὗτος ὁ ἄρτος	or	ὁ ἄρτος οὗτος	This bread
"Far" Demonstrative	ἐκεῖνος ὁ ἄρτος	or	ὁ ἄρτος ἐκεῖνος	That bread
Intensive αὐτός	αὐτὸς ὁ ἄρτος	or	ὁ ἄρτος αὐτός	The bread itself
Identical αὐτός	ὁ αὐτὸς ἄρτος	or	ὁ ἄρτος ὁ αὐτός	The same bread
Possessive	ὁ ἄρτος αὐτοῦ	or	αὐτοῦ ὁ ἄρτος	His bread
	ὁ ἄρτος αὐτῆς	or	αὐτῆς ὁ ἄρτος	Her bread

(Note: The special uses of αὐτός learned in this lesson are common in the NT but rare in the LXX.)

52. Exercises

Practice and Review
1. ὁ θεὸς ἀποστέλλει τοῦτον τὸν προφήτην εἰς τὸν λαόν.
2. ἡμεῖς ἔχομεν ἐξουσίαν βαπτίζειν, ὑμεῖς δὲ οὐκ ἔχετε ἐξουσίαν κρίνειν ἡμᾶς.
3. ἔχομεν τὴν ἀγάπην τὴν αὐτὴν ἐν ταῖς καρδίαις ἡμῶν καὶ αὐτὸς ὁ προφήτης γινώσκει τοῦτο.
4. τὰ τέκνα τῆς γῆς ἐκείνης οὐχ εὑρίσκουσιν τὴν εἰρήνην ὅτι ἡ καρδία τοῦ λαοῦ ἐστι κακή.
5. ἐν τῇ ὥρᾳ ἐκείνῃ ὁ κύριος πέμπει τοὺς ἀγγέλους αὐτοῦ εἰς τὸν κόσμον εὑρίσκειν τὴν ἁγίαν ἀδελφήν.
6. οὕτως λέγει ὁ κύριος, Ἐγείρω ἄγγελον θανάτου διὰ τοὺς κακοὺς ἀλλὰ πέμπω ζωὴν τοῖς πιστοῖς.
7. ἐν τῇ ἡμέρᾳ ἐκείνῃ ὁ θεὸς αὐτὸς ἐγείρει τοὺς νεκροὺς καὶ οἱ ὄχλοι τῆς γῆς ἀκούουσι τὴν αὐτὴν φωνήν.
8. ἀποστέλλω τούτους τοὺς μαθητὰς βαπτίζειν τὰ τέκνα τὰ μικρά.
9. οὐ βλέπετε ἡμᾶς πρόσωπον πρὸς πρόσωπον ἀλλὰ γράφετε τοὺς λόγους τούτους ἡμῖν.
10. διδάσκομεν καὶ πιστεύομεν τὰ αὐτά, ἐκεῖνοι δὲ οἱ ἀδελφοὶ οὐ μένουσιν ἐν τῇ ἐκκλησίᾳ τῆς ἀληθείας.
11. οὗτος ὁ κόσμος μένει ἐν ἁμαρτίᾳ, ἡμεῖς δὲ βλέπομεν τὴν δόξαν ἄλλου κόσμου ἐν τοῖς οὐρανοῖς.
12. δίκαιος ὁ κύριος· κρίνει οὖν τὴν βασιλείαν ἐκείνην κατὰ τὴν ἀλήθειαν.
13. οὐ θέλετε ἀκούειν ἡμῶν τῆς φωνῆς· ἡμεῖς οὖν λέγομεν τούτους τοὺς λόγους ἄλλοις.
14. γινώσκομεν τὴν εἰρήνην τοῦ θεοῦ· ἐσθίομεν οὖν τὸν αὐτὸν ἄρτον ἐν τῷ αὐτῷ οἴκῳ.

LXX

1. ἐν τῇ ἡμέρᾳ ἐκείνῃ διέθετο κύριος τῷ Αβραμ διαθήκην λέγων Τῷ σπέρματί σου δώσω τὴν γῆν ταύτην (Gen 15:18)
2. καὶ πᾶσα ψυχή, ἥτις ποιήσει ἔργον ἐν αὐτῇ τῇ ἡμέρᾳ ταύτῃ, ἀπολεῖται ἡ ψυχὴ ἐκείνη ἐκ τοῦ λαοῦ αὐτῆς. (Lev 23:30)
3. ἀλλὰ αὐτὸς ὁ κύριος δίδωσιν πάντα τὰ ἀγαθά (Tob 4:19)
4. Καὶ ἰδοὺ ἐγὼ ἀποστέλλω τὸν ἄγγελόν μου πρὸ προσώπου σου (Exod 23:20)
5. καὶ οὐχ εὑρίσκομεν ἄλλον ὅμοιον τῇ ἰσχύι αὐτοῦ· (Job 37:23)
6. κύριος ἰσχὺν τῷ λαῷ αὐτοῦ δώσει, κύριος εὐλογήσει τὸν λαὸν αὐτοῦ ἐν εἰρήνῃ. (Ps 28:11, ET 29:11)
7. υἱὸς καὶ πατὴρ αὐτοῦ εἰσεπορεύοντο πρὸς τὴν αὐτὴν παιδίσκην (Amos 2:7)
8. σὺ γὰρ ζωῆς καὶ θανάτου ἐξουσίαν ἔχεις (Wis 16:13)
9. ἐπάραι κύριος τὸ πρόσωπον αὐτοῦ ἐπὶ σὲ καὶ δῴη σοι εἰρήνην. (Num 6:26)

NT

1. Ἐν δὲ ταῖς ἡμέραις ἐκείναις παραγίνεται Ἰωάννης ὁ βαπτιστὴς κηρύσσων ἐν τῇ ἐρήμῳ τῆς Ἰουδαίας. (Matt 3:1)
2. οἱ δὲ ὄχλοι ἔλεγον, Οὗτός ἐστιν ὁ προφήτης Ἰησοῦς ὁ ἀπὸ Ναζαρὲθ τῆς Γαλιλαίας. (Matt 21:11)
3. Καὶ οἱ κύριοι, τὰ αὐτὰ ποιεῖτε πρὸς [τοὺς δούλους ὑμῶν], . . . εἰδότες ὅτι . . . αὐτῶν καὶ ὑμῶν ὁ κύριός ἐστιν ἐν οὐρανοῖς. (Eph 6:9)
4. ζωὴν αἰώνιον ἔδωκεν ἡμῖν ὁ θεός, καὶ αὕτη ἡ ζωὴ ἐν τῷ υἱῷ αὐτοῦ ἐστιν. (1 John 5:11)
5. Αὐτὸς δὲ ὁ θεός . . . καὶ ὁ κύριος ἡμῶν Ἰησοῦς κατευθύναι τὴν ὁδὸν ἡμῶν πρὸς ὑμᾶς· (1 Thess 3:11)
6. Ἰδοὺ ἐγὼ ἀποστέλλω τὸν ἄγγελόν μου πρὸ προσώπου σου. (Matt 11:10)
7. καὶ εἶπαν αὐτῷ, Τί οὖν βαπτίζεις εἰ σὺ οὐκ εἶ ὁ Χριστὸς οὐδὲ Ἠλίας οὐδὲ ὁ προφήτης; (John 1:25)
8. ἐξουσίαν ἔχει ὁ υἱὸς τοῦ ἀνθρώπου ἐπὶ τῆς γῆς ἀφιέναι ἁμαρτίας. (Matt 9:6)
9. ὁ δὲ Πιλᾶτος εἶπεν πρὸς . . . τοὺς ὄχλους, Οὐδὲν εὑρίσκω αἴτιον ἐν τῷ ἀνθρώπῳ τούτῳ. (Luke 23:4)

English to Greek

1. The people do not have authority to take these stones.
2. The prophet himself is judging the assembly because those brothers are not abiding in peace.
3. The same Lord is sending the sisters and the brothers to baptize the children and to raise the dead.
4. We do not find the glory of God in this kingdom; therefore, we wish to have a house in another land.

Vocabulary for LXX and NT Sentences

αἴτιον, guilt
αἰώνιον, eternal
ἀπολεῖται, will perish
ἀφιέναι, to forgive
δίδωσιν, gives
διέθετο . . . διαθήκην, made a covenant
δῴη, may (he) give!
δώσει, will give
δώσω, I will give
ἔδωκεν, gave
εἰ, if
εἰδότες, knowing
εἶπαν, they said
εἶπεν, said
εἰσεπορεύοντο, go into
ἔλεγον, said
ἐπάραι, may (he) lift up!
ἐπὶ, on, upon
εὐλογήσει, will bless
ἥτις, which

Ἰδοὺ, behold!
ἰσχύι, strength
ἰσχὺν, strength
κατευθύναι, may (he) direct!
κηρύσσων, preaching
λέγων, saying
ὅμοιον, similar to, equal to
οὐδὲ, and not, nor
Οὐδὲν, no, nothing
παιδίσκην, maid, servant-girl
πάντα, all
παραγίνεται, appeared
πᾶσα, every
πατὴρ, father
ποιεῖτε, do!
ποιήσει, shall do
πρὸ, before (+ genitive)
σπέρματι, seed (dative)
Τί, Why?

Lesson 9

53. Vocabulary

ἁμαρτωλός, ὁ, sinner

ἀποκρίνομαι, I answer (+ dat.)

ἄρχω, (active voice) I rule (+ gen.);
(middle voice) I begin (monarch,
archetype)

γίνομαι, become, be, happen, arise,
come, appear (+ nom.)

διέρχομαι, I go through

δύναμαι, I can, am able

εἰσέρχομαι, I go in, I enter

ἐξέρχομαι, I go out

ἔρχομαι, I come, I go

οὐδέ, and not, nor, not even

πορεύομαι, I go, walk, travel, live

σύν, (+ dat.) with (symphony)

54. Middle and Passive Voices

Voice is that characteristic of a verb which indicates the relationship between the subject and the verbal action (see §10). In the active voice, the subject performs the action: "The disciple is teaching." In the passive voice, the subject is acted upon: "The disciple is being taught." English has active and passive voices, so they should pose no problem. But in addition to these, Greek had a middle voice. The middle voice was not as common in biblical Greek as it was in classical, but it had by no means disappeared. The sense of the middle voice is that the subject acts, not on a separate object, but with reference to itself, either directly or indirectly. Certain verbal ideas are especially well-suited to the middle voice: λούομαι, "I wash myself"; ἀλείφομαι, "I anoint myself"; θερμαίνομαι, "I warm myself." The point is that Greek could express these ideas by a single word with the appropriate ending and without the reflexive pronoun "myself." But since the middle voice is *relatively* infrequent in biblical Greek and since many of its forms are identical to the corresponding passive forms, the nuances of the middle voice should be learned as they are encountered in the Bible. For now, forms in the exercises that could be either middle or passive should be regarded as passive.

55. Forms of the Present Middle Indicative

The forms of the present middle indicative are as follows:

Singular	Plural
1. λύομαι, I loosen (for myself)	1. λυόμεθα, we loosen (for ourselves)
2. λύῃ, you (sing.) loosen (for yourself)	2. λύεσθε, you (pl.) loosen (for yourselves)
3. λύεται, he, she, or it loosens (for himself, herself, etc.)	3. λύονται, they loosen (for themselves)

The translations given in the paradigm attempt to express the idea of the middle voice, although λύω is not so used in biblical Greek. The original middle and passive endings for the primary tenses were -μαι, -σαι, -ται, for the singular, and -μεθα, -σθε, -νται, for the plural. (These endings are preserved in certain other tenses and in another conjugation.) They are joined to the verb stem by a variable vowel (ο or ε). The second person singular form was originally λύεσαι. The sigma dropped out, and the diphthong of the ending contracted with the variable vowel to produce λύῃ. A less common alternative ending for the second person singular is λύει.

56. Forms of the Present Passive Indicative

The forms of the present passive indicative are as follows:

Singular	Plural
1. λύομαι, I am being loosened	1. λυόμεθα, we are being loosened
2. λύῃ, you (sing.) are being loosened	2. λύεσθε, you (pl.) are being loosened
3. λύεται, he, she or it is being loosened	3. λύονται, they are being loosened

The forms of the present passive indicative are clearly identical to those of the present middle indicative. This is the case with some, but not all, of the other tenses. The translations reflect *continuous* action, one of the nuances of the present tense. For now, such translations are preferable to the simpler rendering "I am loosened," "you are loosened," etc. The latter might be understood as indicating *completed* action, that is, "I am now in a state of having been loosened." But this idea is conveyed by the Greek perfect tense, not the present.

57. The Present Middle/Passive Infinitive

The form of the present middle/passive infinitive is λύεσθαι. It is used the same way the present active infinitive is used. Examples: θέλω διδάσκεσθαι, "I wish to be taught"; οἱ νεκροὶ δύνανται ἐγείρεσθαι;, "Can the dead be raised?"

58. Personal Agent with ὑπό

When the passive voice is used, the performer of the action is not identified: "Mistakes were made." One way to supply this information is by a phrase expressing the agent: "Mistakes were made by the president." In Greek, this construction often involves the preposition ὑπό followed by a noun in the genitive case. The noun usually denotes a person, although in rare cases it may refer to a thing or an impersonal force.

 Examples: ὁ δοῦλος πέμπεται ὑπὸ τοῦ προφήτου, "The slave is being sent by the prophet"; οἱ νεκροὶ ἐγείρονται ὑπὸ τοῦ θεοῦ, "The dead are being raised by God"; διδασκόμεθα ὑπὸ τῆς ἀδελφῆς ἡμῶν, "We are being taught by our sister."

59. Impersonal Dative of Means

In contrast to the above construction denoting personal agent, Greek usually expressed the (impersonal) instrument or means of an action by the dative case. No preposition was needed to convey this idea. "Means" is simply one of the functions of the dative case. Occasionally this usage is found with active verbs.

 Examples: διδασκόμεθα τῷ λόγῳ τοῦ θεοῦ, "We are being taught by the word of God"; ὁ οἶκος τοῦ ἁμαρτωλοῦ λύεται τοῖς λίθοις, "The house of the sinner is being destroyed with stones."

60. Deponent Verbs

Several important verbs in biblical Greek do not have active forms. Instead, they have middle and passive forms with active meanings. These verbs are called deponent because they "lay aside" (Latin *depono*) the active forms. Deponent verbs will appear in the vocabulary lists with the -ομαι ending. Examples: γίνομαι, ἔρχομαι, and πορεύομαι.

61. Comments on Certain Verbs in This Lesson

The verb δύναμαι is a somewhat irregular deponent verb. Its present tense forms have an alpha "connecting vowel" where regular verbs have ο or ε. In addition, the second person singular form δύνῃ has an alternative: δύνασαι.

Several verbs introduced in this lesson have a prefixed preposition that changes the basic meaning of the word. The new meaning of such "compound" verbs is usually clear: ἔρχομαι = I go; εἰσέρχομαι = I go *in*. But sometimes the meaning cannot be predicted: ἀποκρίνομαι = I answer.

The Greek equivalents of most verbs that take a direct object in English will take an accusative, but this is not always so (see §31). In this lesson's vocabulary list ἀποκρίνομαι (I answer) takes the dative to complete its meaning, and ἄρχω (I rule) takes the genitive. It is a good idea to learn such characteristics as part of your vocabulary work.

62. Exercises

Practice and Review

1. οἱ πονηροὶ ἁμαρτωλοὶ οὗτοι ἐξέρχονται εἰς τὸν προφήτην. αὐτοὶ δύνανται σῴζεσθαι;
2. ὑμεῖς ἀκούετε τῆς φωνῆς ἀγγέλου, ἡμεῖς δὲ διδασκόμεθα ὑπὸ τοῦ θεοῦ αὐτοῦ.
3. ἄνθρωπος οὐ γίνεται δίκαιος ἐξ ἔργων. ἡ εἰρήνη πρὸς τὸν θεόν ἐστι δῶρον.
4. διερχόμεθα διὰ τῆς ἐρήμου ἀλλὰ οὐκ ἔχομεν ἄρτον οὐδὲ βλέπομεν τὴν θάλασσαν.
5. μετὰ ταῦτα ἔρχεται ὁ ἄγγελος τοῦ κυρίου καὶ οἱ νεκροὶ ἐγείρονται.
6. εἰσέρχονται τὰ τέκνα εἰς τὸν οἶκον σὺν τοῖς μαθηταῖς.
7. ἡ ἀδελφὴ ἡμῶν θέλει γινώσκειν τὴν ἀλήθειαν περὶ τοῦ υἱοῦ αὐτῆς, ὑμεῖς δὲ οὐκ ἀποκρίνεσθε αὐτῇ.
8. οὐ θέλω ἄρχειν τῆς βασιλείας ταύτης· πορεύομαι οὖν πρὸς ἄλλην γῆν.
9. ἐν τῇ ἡμέρᾳ ἐκείνῃ πλοῖα λύονται καὶ ἡ θάλασσα οὐ δύναται εὑρίσκεσθαι.
10. ὁ ὄχλος γίνεται μικρὸς ὅτι κακοὶ ἁμαρτωλοὶ εἰσέρχονται εἰς τὴν ἐκκλησίαν.
11. ἄρχεσθε πιστεύειν ἐν ταῖς καρδίαις ὑμῶν, ἀλλὰ οὐκ ἐξέρχεσθε ἐκ τῆς ὁδοῦ τῆς ἁμαρτίας.
12. σὺν τῇ ἀδελφῇ σου ἔρχῃ πρὸς τὸν προφήτην βαπτίζεσθαι ὑπ' αὐτοῦ.
13. ὁ ἀδελφὸς ὑμῶν οὐκ ἀποκρίνεται τῷ λαῷ μετ' ἀγάπης· κρίνεται οὖν ὑπὸ τοῦ λαοῦ.
14. πορευόμεθα πρὸς τὴν θάλασσαν, ἀλλὰ οὐ θέλομεν διέρχεσθαι ταύτην τὴν γῆν.

LXX

1. καὶ ἀποκρίνεται Δωηκ ὁ Σύρος . . . Ἑόρακα τὸν υἱὸν Ιεσσαι (1 Kgdms 22:9)
2. Ὁ υἱός σου Ιωσηφ ζῇ, καὶ αὐτὸς ἄρχει πάσης γῆς Αἰγύπτου. (Gen 45:26)

3. δεκταὶ παρὰ κυρίῳ ὁδοὶ ἀνθρώπων δικαίων, διὰ δὲ αὐτῶν καὶ οἱ ἐχθροὶ φίλοι γίνονται. (Prov 15:28a, ET 16:7)

4. καὶ οὐ δύνανται οἱ ἄνθρωποι εἶναι χωρὶς τῶν γυναικῶν. (1 Esdr 4:17)

5. γενεὰ πορεύεται καὶ γενεὰ ἔρχεται, καὶ ἡ γῆ εἰς τὸν αἰῶνα ἕστηκεν. (Eccl 1:4)

6. καὶ εἶπαν αὐτῷ Ἰδοὺ σὺ γεγήρακας, καὶ οἱ υἱοί σου οὐ πορεύονται ἐν τῇ ὁδῷ σου· (1 Kgdms 8:5)

7. εἶπεν κύριος πρὸς Ἰησοῦν Ἐν τῇ ἡμέρᾳ ταύτῃ ἄρχομαι ὑψῶσαί σε (Josh 3:7)

8. ἡ σοφία . . . εὑρίσκεται ὑπὸ τῶν ζητούντων αὐτήν (Wis 6:12)

9. οὐ γὰρ δύναται πάντα εἶναι ἐν ἀνθρώποις, ὅτι οὐκ ἀθάνατος υἱὸς ἀνθρώπου. (Sir 17:30)

10. Τέκνα βδελυρὰ γίνεται [τὰ] τέκνα ἁμαρτωλῶν (Sir 41:5)

NT

1. καὶ ἐβαπτίζοντο ὑπ' αὐτοῦ ἐν τῷ Ἰορδάνῃ ποταμῷ ἐξομολογούμενοι τὰς ἁμαρτίας αὐτῶν. (Mark 1:5)

2. λέγω γὰρ ὑμῖν ὅτι δύναται ὁ θεὸς ἐκ τῶν λίθων τούτων ἐγεῖραι τέκνα τῷ Ἀβραάμ. (Luke 3:8)

3. μέλλει γὰρ ὁ υἱὸς τοῦ ἀνθρώπου ἔρχεσθαι ἐν τῇ δόξῃ τοῦ πατρὸς αὐτοῦ μετὰ τῶν ἀγγέλων αὐτοῦ (Matt 16:27)

4. ὁ δὲ Ἰησοῦς ἀποκρίνεται αὐτοῖς λέγων, Ἐλήλυθεν ἡ ὥρα (John 12:23)

5. λέγει αὐτοῖς Σίμων Πέτρος, Ὑπάγω ἁλιεύειν. λέγουσιν αὐτῷ, Ἐρχόμεθα καὶ ἡμεῖς σὺν σοί. (John 21:3)

6. γίνεται τὰ ἔσχατα τοῦ ἀνθρώπου ἐκείνου χείρονα τῶν πρώτων. (Matt 12:45)

7. καὶ ἐν τῇ Βεροίᾳ κατηγγέλη ὑπὸ τοῦ Παύλου ὁ λόγος τοῦ θεοῦ (Acts 17:13)

8. ἡμεῖς οἴδαμεν ὅτι οὗτος ὁ ἄνθρωπος ἁμαρτωλός ἐστιν. (John 9:24)

9. ἁμαρτία γὰρ ὑμῶν οὐ κυριεύσει· οὐ γάρ ἐστε ὑπὸ νόμον ἀλλὰ ὑπὸ χάριν. (Rom 6:14)

10. νυνὶ δὲ πορεύομαι εἰς Ἰερουσαλὴμ διακονῶν τοῖς ἁγίοις. (Rom 15:25)

English to Greek

1. We are walking with you (pl.) in the way of peace and are being saved by the word of life.
2. *You* (pl.) are beginning to teach us, but *we* do not wish to be taught by you.
3. The prophet answers the sinners, "You can become disciples of the Lord."
4. The child goes out to the lake and is baptized by the slave.

Lesson 9

Vocabulary for LXX and NT Sentences

ἀθάνατος, immortal
(εἰς τὸν) αἰῶνα, forever
ἀλιεύειν, to fish, fishing
βδελυρά, abominable, loathsome
γεγήρακας, have grown old
γενεά, generation
γυναικῶν, women
δεκταὶ, acceptable
διακονῶν, serving, in order to serve
ἐβαπτίζοντο, past of βαπτίζονται
ἐγεῖραι, an infinitive of ἐγείρω
εἶναι, to be, be
εἶπαν, they said
εἶπεν, said
Ἐλήλυθεν, has come
ἐξομολογούμενοι, confessing
ἑόρακα, I have seen
ἕστηκεν, stands
ἐχθροὶ, enemies
ζῇ, lives, is alive

ζητούντων, seeking, who seek
Ἰδοὺ, behold!
κατηγγέλη, was proclaimed
κυριεύσει, will rule over (+ gen.)
λέγων, saying
μέλλει, is about to
νυνί, now
οἴδαμεν = γινώσκομεν
πάντα, all things
παρὰ, with, in the presence of
πάσης, all
πατρὸς, father
ποταμῷ, river
σοφία, wisdom
Ὑπάγω, I am going
ὑψῶσαί, to exalt
φίλοι, friends
χάριν, grace
χείρονα, worse than (+ gen.)
χωρὶς, without

Lesson 10

63. Vocabulary

ἄγω, I lead
αἴρω, I take up, take away, lift up
ἀναβαίνω, I go up (Anabasis)
ἀπέρχομαι, I depart, go away, go
ἀποθνῄσκω, I die
ἀποκτείνω, I kill
ἀπόστολος, ὁ, apostle
ἱερόν, τό, temple (hierarchy)
καταβαίνω, I go down

μέλλω, I am about to, am going to
ὀφείλω, I owe, ought, must
παρά, (+ gen.) from; (+ dat.) beside,
with, among; (+ acc.) by, along
(parallel, paralegal)
συνάγω, I gather together (synagogue)
ὑπέρ, (+ gen.) in behalf of; (+ acc.)
above (hyperactive)

64. Primary and Secondary Tenses

Up to this point in the book, you have worked exclusively with the present tense. Since this lesson introduces a new tense, the imperfect, it is appropriate to comment briefly on the verbal system in Greek. Biblical Greek has six tenses — three primary tenses (present, future, perfect), and three secondary tenses (aorist, imperfect, pluperfect). (Strictly speaking Greek also had a future perfect, but it was uncommon even in the classical era and quite rare in biblical Greek.) The primary tenses refer to present and future time; the secondary tenses to past time. The endings of the secondary tenses are different from those of the primary tenses, although several similarities will be observed. In addition, secondary tense forms are identified by a certain prefix and, in some cases, other markers.

It was noted in Lesson 2 that the *kind* of action is the most important thing indicated by the tense of a Greek verb. Tense also relates to *time* of action, but contextual factors contribute heavily too. It was seen that the Greek present tense could denote either continuous or undefined action (see §11). The tense you will learn in this lesson, the imperfect, denotes *continuous* (or repeated, or attempted) action in *past* time. Undefined or simple action in past time is the function of a tense you will learn later.

65. The Imperfect Active Indicative

The forms of the imperfect active indicative are the following:

Singular	Plural
1. ἔλυον, I was loosening	1. ἐλύομεν, we were loosening
2. ἔλυες, you (sing.) were loosening	2. ἐλύετε, you (pl.) were loosening
3. ἔλυε(ν), he, she, it was loosening	3. ἔλυον, they were loosening

The imperfect tense is built on the same verb stem as the present tense: λυ- in the case of λύω. But a prefix known as an *augment* has been added, and the endings differ slightly from those of the present tense. The augment is simply an epsilon (ἐ-) for verbs that begin with a consonant. Other forms of the augment are discussed below. The endings for the active voice of the secondary tenses are -ν, -ς, and -none for the singular, and -μεν, -τε, and -ν (or -σαν) for the plural. In the imperfect these endings are joined to the verb stem by a variable vowel, either ο or ε. Note that the third person singular sometimes takes the "movable ν" (see §11.4).

The imperfect tense is limited to the indicative mood. There is, therefore, no infinitive for this tense.

66. Forms of the Augment

Although the augment is an epsilon for verbs beginning with a consonant, it takes a different form for verbs beginning with a vowel or diphthong. The initial vowel of a verb lengthens: alpha becomes eta; epsilon becomes eta; omicron becomes omega. The first vowel of a diphthong usually undergoes a similar lengthening. Examples:

Present	Imperfect
ἄγω, I lead	ἦγον, I was leading
ἀκούω, I hear	ἤκουον, I was hearing
ἐγείρω, I raise up	ἤγειρον, I was raising up
ὀφείλω, I am obligated	ὤφειλον, I was obligated
αἴρω, I take up	ἦρον, I was taking up
εὑρίσκω, I find	ηὕρισκον, I was finding (but also εὕρισκον)

Compound verbs (see §61) require a special comment. When one of these verbs is augmented, the augment will appear *between* the prefixed preposition and the verb stem. If the preposition ends in a vowel, that vowel is usually dropped before the augment. Examples:

54

ἀποθνήσκω, I die   ἀπέθνησκον, I was dying
ἀποκτείνω, I kill   ἀπέκτεινον, I was killing
καταβαίνω, I go down   κατέβαινον, I was going down

A few verbs beginning with consonants have alternate imperfect forms, being augmented either with epsilon or eta. Examples:

θέλω, I wish   ἔθελον or ἤθελον, I was wishing
μέλλω, I am about to   ἔμελλον or ἤμελλον, I was about to

In the case of θέλω this variation exists because there was an alternate form for the *present* tense: ἐθέλω. This form, when augmented, would obviously begin with eta. The same variation in μέλλω and similar "modal" verbs may be in imitation of θέλω. A final note: the accent on a past tense, compound verb does *not* recede past the augment, even if the rules of accent would permit it. Thus:

συνάγω, I gather together   συνῆγον, I was gathering together

67. The Imperfect Indicative of εἰμί

The imperfect tense of εἰμί is as follows:

Singular	Plural
1. ἤμην, I was	1. ἦμεν, we were
2. ἦς, you (sing.) were	2. ἦτε, you (pl.) were
3. ἦν, he, she, or it was	3. ἦσαν, they were

(Less common alternate forms are ἦσθα for 2nd person singular and ἤμεθα for 1st person plural.)

68. Exercises

Practice and Review

1. ἡ δόξα τοῦ θεοῦ ἀπέρχεται ἀπὸ τῆς ἐκκλησίας ὅτι ὁ προφήτης ἀποθνήσκει.
2. οὗτος ὁ ἄνθρωπος ἀπέθνησκεν ὑπὲρ τοῦ ἀδελφοῦ αὐτοῦ καὶ ἐδίδασκε τὸν λαὸν περὶ ἀγάπης.
3. Πρὸς θάνατον ἄγει ἡ ὁδὸς τῆς ἁμαρτίας, ὑμεῖς δὲ ἠμέλλετε πορεύεσθαι ἐν αὐτῇ.
4. ὁ ἀπόστολος ἦγεν τὰ τέκνα ἀπὸ τοῦ ἱεροῦ εἰς τὴν ἔρημον.
5. συνῆγον οἱ μαθηταὶ οἱ πιστοὶ ἄρτους, οἱ δὲ ἄρτοι ἦσαν μικροὶ καὶ κακοί.

6. ἤθελεν ὁ πονηρὸς ἄνθρωπος ἀποκτείνειν τὸν δοῦλον αὐτοῦ, ἡ δὲ ἀδελφὴ τοῦ ἀνθρώπου ἤθελε σῴζειν αὐτόν.

7. ἡμεῖς ἀνεβαίνομεν πρὸς τὴν καλὴν γῆν, ὑμεῖς δὲ κατεβαίνετε παρὰ τὴν θάλασσαν.

8. ἐν τῇ ὥρᾳ ἐκείνῃ ἤρετε τὴν φωνὴν ὑμῶν πρὸς τὸν κύριον ζωῆς ὅτι ἐμέλλετε ἀποθνήσκειν.

9. οὗτοι οἱ ἁμαρτωλοί εἰσιν πονηροί, ἀλλὰ οὐκ ὀφείλομεν ἀποκτείνειν αὐτούς.

10. αἴρεις τὸ πλοῖον παρὰ τοῦ ἀποστόλου ὅτι ὀφείλεις καταβαίνειν εἰς τὴν θάλασσαν.

11. ἐν τῇ ἡμέρᾳ ἐκείνῃ ἀνέβαινες εἰς τὸ ἱερὸν μετὰ δώρων ταῖς ἐξουσίαις.

12. ἀπέρχεσθε πρὸς ἄλλους θεούς, ὀφείλετε δὲ πιστεύειν εἰς τὸν θεὸν τοῦ οὐρανοῦ.

13. ὁ προφήτης συνάγει τὸν ὄχλον εἰς τὸν οἶκον καὶ λέγει αὐτοῖς ὑπὲρ τοῦ θεοῦ.

14. ἐγὼ ἤμην ἐν τῷ ἱερῷ, ὑμεῖς δὲ ἦτε ἐν τῇ ἐρήμῳ.

LXX

1. κύριος μόνος ἦγεν αὐτούς, καὶ οὐκ ἦν μετ᾽ αὐτῶν θεὸς ἀλλότριος (Deut 32:12)

2. καὶ ἰδοὺ κλίμαξ . . . καὶ οἱ ἄγγελοι τοῦ θεοῦ ἀνέβαινον καὶ κατέβαινον ἐπ᾽ αὐτῆς. (Gen 28:12)

3. αἴρεται ἀπὸ τῆς γῆς ἡ ζωὴ αὐτοῦ, ἀπὸ τῶν ἀνομιῶν τοῦ λαοῦ μου ἤχθη εἰς θάνατον (Isa 53:8)

4. εἶπεν δὲ Ισραηλ τῷ Ιωσηφ Ἰδοὺ ἐγὼ ἀποθνήσκω, καὶ ἔσται ὁ θεὸς μεθ᾽ ὑμῶν (Gen 48:21)

5. ἐγὼ ἄγω αὐτοὺς ἀπὸ βορρᾶ καὶ συνάξω αὐτοὺς ἀπ᾽ ἐσχάτου τῆς γῆς (Jer 38:8, ET 31:8)

6. ἐγὼ γὰρ ἀποθνήσκω ἐν τῇ γῇ ταύτῃ καὶ οὐ διαβαίνω τὸν Ιορδάνην τοῦτον (Deut 4:22)

7. διὰ τοῦτο ὀφείλετε πάντα πόνον ὑπομένειν διὰ τὸν θεόν (4 Macc 16:19)

8. Ἰδοὺ ἐγὼ συνάγω αὐτοὺς ἐκ πάσης τῆς γῆς (Jer 39:37, ET 32:37)

9. Οὐκ ἀποθανοῦνται πατέρες ὑπὲρ τέκνων, καὶ υἱοὶ οὐκ ἀποθανοῦνται ὑπὲρ πατέρων· ἕκαστος τῇ ἑαυτοῦ ἁμαρτίᾳ ἀποθανεῖται. (Deut 24:16)

10. ἡ βοήθειά μου παρὰ κυρίου τοῦ ποιήσαντος τὸν οὐρανὸν καὶ τὴν γῆν. (Ps 120:2, ET 121:2)

11. Ισραηλ, τί κύριος ὁ θεός σου αἰτεῖται παρὰ σοῦ ἀλλ᾽ ἢ φοβεῖσθαι κύριον τὸν θεόν σου πορεύεσθαι ἐν πάσαις ταῖς ὁδοῖς αὐτοῦ . . . ; (Deut 10:12)

NT

1. Οὐκ ἔστιν μαθητὴς ὑπὲρ τὸν διδάσκαλον οὐδὲ δοῦλος ὑπὲρ τὸν κύριον αὐτοῦ. (Matt 10:24)

2. ἐκεῖνος ὑπὲρ ἡμῶν τὴν ψυχὴν αὐτοῦ ἔθηκεν· καὶ ἡμεῖς ὀφείλομεν ὑπὲρ τῶν ἀδελφῶν τὰς ψυχὰς θεῖναι. (1 John 3:16)

3. ὁ Ἰησοῦς εἶπεν, Ἄνθρωπός τις κατέβαινεν ἀπὸ Ἰερουσαλὴμ εἰς Ἰεριχω (Luke 10:30)

4. Πέτρος . . . καὶ Ἰωάννης ἀνέβαινον εἰς τὸ ἱερὸν ἐπὶ τὴν ὥραν τῆς προσευχῆς (Acts 3:1)

5. Καὶ πάλιν ἤρξατο διδάσκειν παρὰ τὴν θάλασσαν· καὶ συνάγεται πρὸς αὐτὸν ὄχλος (Mark 4:1)

6. τοῦτο δὲ ἔλεγεν σημαίνων ποίῳ θανάτῳ ἤμελλεν ἀποθνήσκειν. (John 12:33)

7. μέλλει γὰρ ὁ υἱὸς τοῦ ἀνθρώπου ἔρχεσθαι ἐν τῇ δόξῃ τοῦ πατρὸς αὐτοῦ μετὰ τῶν ἀγγέλων αὐτοῦ (Matt 16:27)

8. ἀπεκρίθησαν αὐτῷ οἱ Ἰουδαῖοι, Ἡμεῖς νόμον ἔχομεν καὶ κατὰ τὸν νόμον ὀφείλει ἀποθανεῖν (John 19:7)

9. Ἄγουσιν αὐτὸν πρὸς τοὺς Φαρισαίους τόν ποτε τυφλόν. (John 9:13)

10. εἶτα ἔρχεται ὁ διάβολος καὶ αἴρει τὸν λόγον ἀπὸ τῆς καρδίας αὐτῶν (Luke 8:12)

English to Greek

1. We were lifting up our voice in behalf of our sister and were going down along the sea to find her.
2. We ought to go up to the temple and die with the prophets of God.
3. We are not going to kill the evil slaves, but they must depart to another land.
4. The apostle was about to gather together the children and lead them to the house.

Vocabulary for LXX and NT Sentences

αἰτεῖται, ask, require
ἀλλ’ ἤ, other than, but
ἀλλότριος, foreign, strange
ἀνομιῶν, transgressions
ἀπεκρίθησαν, past of ἀποκρίνονται
ἀποθανεῖν, an inf. of ἀποθνήσκω
ἀποθανεῖται, fut. of ἀποθνήσκει
ἀποθανοῦνται, fut. of ἀποθνήσκουσι
βοήθεια, help
βορρᾶ, the north
διαβαίνω, go through, cross
διάβολος, devil
διδάσκαλον, teacher
ἑαυτοῦ, of himself, herself
ἔθηκεν, laid down
εἶπεν, said
εἶτα, then
ἕκαστος, each person
ἐπὶ, at, on
ἔσται, will be
ἤρξατο, simple past of ἄρχομαι
ἤχθη, he was led

θεῖναι, to lay down
ἰδού, behold!
κλίμαξ, ladder, stairway
μόνος, alone, only
πάλιν, again
πάντα, every
πάσαις, all
πάσης, all
πατρὸς, father
πατέρες, πατέρων, fathers
ποιήσαντος, who made
ποίῳ, by what sort of
πόνον, pain, hardship
ποτε, formerly
προσευχῆς, of prayer
σημαίνων, showing, indicating
συνάξω, gather together
τί, what?
τις, a certain
τυφλόν, blind
ὑπομένειν, endure
φοβεῖσθαι, to fear

Lesson 11

69. Vocabulary

ἀμήν, amen, truly
βιβλίον, τό, book
δαιμόνιον, τό, demon
δέχομαι, I receive, accept
ἐπί, (+ gen.) on, upon, over; (+ dat.) on, at, in addition to; (+ acc.) on, over, toward, for (epidermis, epitaph)
ἔτι, yet, still
θεραπεύω, I heal, serve (therapy)
ἰδού, behold! see!

μέν . . . δέ, on the one hand . . . on the other (or leave μέν untranslated) . . . but . . .
οὔτε, neither, nor
ὀφθαλμός, ὁ, eye (ophthalmology)
πάλιν, again (palimpsest)
τέ, and (a weak conjunction, often correlated with another τέ or καί)
τόπος, ὁ, place (topography, topic)
τότε, then

70. The Imperfect Middle/Passive Indicative

The forms of the imperfect middle/passive indicative are as follows:

Singular	Plural
1. ἐλυόμην, I was being loosened	1. ἐλυόμεθα, we were being loosened
2. ἐλύου, you (sing.) were being loosened	2. ἐλύεσθε, you (pl.) were being loosened
3. ἐλύετο, he, she, it was being loosened	3. ἐλύοντο, they were being loosened

The imperfect middle and passive use the very same forms. As before, forms in the exercises that could be translated either middle or passive should be regarded as passive. Remember that the imperfect expresses linear (or continuous, repeated, etc.) action in past time. Again, the augment indicates that the imperfect is a secondary or past tense.

The middle/passive endings for the secondary tenses were originally -μην, -σο, and -το for the singular and -μεθα, -σθε, and -ντο for the plural. Most of these endings are simply connected to the verb stem by the variable vowel (ε or ο). The second person singular form requires special comment. The original form was ἐλύεσο. The sigma of the ending dropped out, however, and the vowels epsilon and omicron contracted to the diphthong -ου.

Verbs that are deponent in the present tense will also be deponent in the imperfect tense. Thus: πορεύομαι, I am going; ἐπορευόμην, I was going; δύναμαι, I am able; ἐδυνάμην (but also ἠδυνάμην), I was able.

59

71. Adverbial καί

In addition to its regular use as a conjunction to join two elements, καί may be used with a single element as an adverb. In such cases it will usually be translated "also" or "even." Examples:

ἐγὼ βλέπω τὴν ἀδελφήν σου. καὶ σὺ βλέπεις αὐτήν;
"I see your sister. Do you *also* see her?"

σὺ πιστεύεις εἰς τὸν θεόν· τοῦτ᾽ ἀγαθόν. ἀλλὰ καὶ τὰ δαιμόνια πιστεύουσιν.
"You believe in God. This is good. But *even* the demons believe."

72. Correlative Constructions

Certain conjunctions in biblical Greek sometimes occur in pairs and are correlated with one another. The most common of these constructions is καὶ . . . καί. Its meaning is "both . . . and." The enclitic particle τε also occurs in correlative constructions, sometimes as τε . . . τε, sometimes as τε . . . καί. Τε is postpositive, occurring *after* the word to which it is related. One might think of τε after a word as approximately equal (though slightly weaker) to καί before a word. Τε . . . τε may be translated "as . . . so," "not only . . . but also," or simply "and." Τε . . . καί is best translated "and." Examples:

καὶ οἱ ἀγαθοὶ καὶ οἱ κακοὶ ἐσθίουσι τὸν ἄρτον τῆς γῆς.
"*Both* the good *and* the evil are eating the bread of the land."

ἡμᾶς τε ὁ ἀδελφὸς διδάσκει, ὑμᾶς τε ἡ ἀδελφὴ διδάσκει.
"*As* the brother is teaching us, *so* the sister is teaching you."

λόγοι τε καὶ ἔργα κρίνονται ὑπὸ τοῦ κυρίου τοῦ οὐρανοῦ.
"Words *and* deeds are judged by the Lord of heaven."

The negative counterpart to τε . . . τε is οὔτε . . . οὔτε. (The word οὔτε is, in fact, no more than the Greek negative with a suffixed τε.) The meaning of this construction is "neither . . . nor." Thus:

θεοὶ λίθου οὔτε ἀκούουσιν οὔτε λέγουσιν.
"Gods of stone neither hear nor speak."

73. Exercises

Practice and Review

1. οἱ ὀφθαλμοὶ τοῦ τέκνου ἐθεραπεύοντο τῷ λόγῳ τοῦ προφήτου.
2. ἐν τῷ ἱερῷ ἠκούομεν τούτους τοὺς λόγους παρὰ σοῦ, ἀλλ' οὐκ ἠθέλομεν δέχεσθαι αὐτούς.
3. ταῦτα ἐγράφοντο ἐν τῷ βιβλίῳ τοῦ νόμου, ὑμεῖς δὲ οὐκ ἐδύνασθε βλέπειν αὐτά.
4. τὰ μὲν δαιμόνια ἐξήρχοντο ἀπὸ τοῦ τέκνου, αὐτὸ δὲ ἔτι ἀπέθνῃσκεν.
5. ἐκείνη ἡ βασιλεία ἦν πονηρά, ἀλλὰ καὶ πρὸς τὸν τόπον ἐκεῖνον ὁ μαθητὴς ἀπεστέλλετο.
6. ἐπέμποντο βιβλία τε καὶ δῶρα πρὸς τοὺς ἁμαρτωλούς, αὐτοὶ δὲ οὔτε ἤθελον οὔτε ἐδέχοντο αὐτά.
7. ᾖρον καὶ τὰ τέκνα τὴν φωνὴν αὐτῶν καὶ ἔλεγον, Τὸν αὐτὸν ἄρτον ὀφείλομεν ἐσθίειν πάλιν;
8. καὶ ἐπορεύεσθε ἐν τῇ ὁδῷ τῆς ἀγάπης καὶ ἐδιδάσκεσθε τὸν νόμον τῆς ἀγάπης.
9. σὺ ἔλεγες τότε ὅτι θεὸς ἐθεράπευε τοὺς ὀφθαλμούς σου, ἀμὴν δὲ λέγω σοι, Θεὸς μέλλει θεραπεύειν τὴν καρδίαν σου.
10. ὁ κύριος ἡμῶν μὲν ἦν πρῶτος ἐν τῇ γῇ, αὐτὸς δὲ ἐλύετο ταῖς ἁμαρτίαις αὐτοῦ.
11. κακὰ δαιμόνια διήρχοντο τὴν γῆν, ἀλλὰ οὔτε ἔμενον ἐν τῷ τόπῳ ἐκείνῳ οὔτε ἤθελον ἀποκτείνειν τὸν λαόν.
12. ἰδοὺ ἡ βασιλεία τοῦ οὐρανοῦ ἔρχεται· ἡ δόξα τῷ θεῷ καὶ ἡ εἰρήνη τοῖς δούλοις αὐτοῦ. ἀμήν.
13. ὑμεῖς ἦτε πιστοὶ τῷ κυρίῳ ἔν τε τῷ ἱερῷ καὶ ἐν τῷ ὁδῷ, ἀλλὰ ἐν τοῖς οἴκοις ὑμῶν οὐκ ἐπορεύεσθε ἐν τῇ ἀληθείᾳ.
14. θέλομεν βλέπειν τὸ πρόσωπον τοῦ θεοῦ ἐπὶ τῆς γῆς καὶ πάλιν ἐν οὐρανῷ.

LXX

1. ἐν παντὶ τόπῳ ὀφθαλμοὶ κυρίου, σκοπεύουσιν κακούς τε καὶ ἀγαθούς. (Prov 15:3)
2. Ισμαηλῖται ἤρχοντο ἐκ Γαλααδ . . . ἐπορεύοντο δὲ . . . εἰς Αἴγυπτον. (Gen 37:25)
3. πολλοὶ θεραπεύουσιν πρόσωπα ἡγουμένων, παρὰ δὲ κυρίου γίνεται τὸ δίκαιον ἀνδρί. (Prov 29:26)
4. Καὶ ἔγραψεν Μωυσῆς τὰ ῥήματα τοῦ νόμου τούτου εἰς βιβλίον (Deut 31:9)
5. οὐκ ἰδοὺ ταῦτα γέγραπται ἐν βιβλίῳ λόγων τῶν ἡμερῶν τῶν βασιλέων Ισραηλ; (3 Kgdms 22:39)
6. καὶ Ασμοδαυς τὸ πονηρὸν δαιμόνιον ἀπέκτεινεν αὐτούς (Tob 3:8 BA)
7. οἱ θεοὶ τῶν ἐθνῶν δαιμόνια, ὁ δὲ κύριος τοὺς οὐρανοὺς ἐποίησεν· (Ps 95:5, ET 96:5)

8. ἰδοὺ οἱ ὀφθαλμοὶ ὑμῶν βλέπουσιν καὶ οἱ ὀφθαλμοὶ Βενιαμιν τοῦ ἀδελφοῦ μου ὅτι τὸ στόμα μου τὸ λαλοῦν πρὸς ὑμᾶς. (Gen 45:12)

9. καὶ ὅταν ἤρχετο ὁ λέων . . . καὶ ἐλάμβανεν πρόβατον . . . καὶ ἐξεπορευόμην ὀπίσω αὐτοῦ (1 Kdgms 17:34-35)

10. καὶ ἐπορευόμην πρὸς τοὺς ἰατροὺς θεραπευθῆναι, . . . καὶ ἤμην ἀδύνατος τοῖς ὀφθαλμοῖς (Tob 2:10 S)

NT

1. μετὰ χαρᾶς δέχονται τὸν λόγον, καὶ οὗτοι ῥίζαν οὐκ ἔχουσιν (Luke 8:13)

2. οἱ λοιποὶ . . . ἔχοντες ἀσθενείας προσήρχοντο καὶ ἐθεραπεύοντο (Acts 28:9)

3. (an unclean spirit) διέρχεται δι' ἀνύδρων τόπων ζητοῦν ἀνάπαυσιν καὶ οὐχ εὑρίσκει. τότε λέγει, Εἰς τὸν οἶκόν μου ἐπιστρέψω (Matt 12:43-44)

4. ἐξήρχετο δὲ καὶ δαιμόνια ἀπὸ πολλῶν . . . λέγοντα . . . Σὺ εἶ ὁ υἱὸς τοῦ θεοῦ. (Luke 4:41)

5. καὶ οὐδεὶς ἐδύνατο ἐν τῷ οὐρανῷ οὐδὲ ἐπὶ τῆς γῆς . . . ἀνοῖξαι τὸ βιβλίον οὔτε βλέπειν αὐτό. (Rev 5:3)

6. ὁ δὲ τελώνης . . . οὐκ ἤθελεν οὐδὲ τοὺς ὀφθαλμοὺς ἐπᾶραι εἰς τὸν οὐρανόν (Luke 18:13)

7. Καὶ ἐξῆλθεν πάλιν παρὰ τὴν θάλασσαν· καὶ πᾶς ὁ ὄχλος ἤρχετο πρὸς αὐτόν, καὶ ἐδίδασκεν αὐτούς. (Mark 2:13)

8. οὕτως καὶ ὑμεῖς λογίζεσθε ἑαυτοὺς . . . νεκροὺς μὲν τῇ ἁμαρτίᾳ ζῶντας δὲ τῷ θεῷ ἐν Χριστῷ Ἰησοῦ. (Rom 6:11)

9. Ἕλλησίν τε καὶ βαρβάροις, σοφοῖς τε καὶ ἀνοήτοις ὀφειλέτης εἰμί (Rom 1:14)

10. Καὶ εἶδον οὐρανὸν καινὸν καὶ γῆν καινήν. ὁ γὰρ πρῶτος οὐρανὸς καὶ ἡ πρώτη γῆ ἀπῆλθαν, καὶ ἡ θάλασσα οὐκ ἔστιν ἔτι. (Rev 21:1)

English to Greek

1. Both eyes and hearts were being healed in that holy place.
2. Truly I tell you (sing.) again, the angels of God were coming down to the temple.
3. The demons were accepting neither the books of the prophets nor the gifts of the son.
4. On earth we still have death, but, behold, life rules in heaven!

Vocabulary for LXX and NT Sentences

ἀδύνατος, powerless (cf. δύναμαι)
ἀνάπαυσιν, resting place
ἀνδρὶ, to a man
ἀνοήτοις, foolish
ἀνοῖξαι, to open
ἀνύδρων, waterless, dry
ἀπῆλθαν, simple past of ἀπέρχονται
ἀσθενείας, illnesses, diseases
βαρβάροις, barbarians
βασιλέων, kings
γέγραπται, are written
ἑαυτοὺς, yourselves
ἔγραψεν, simple past of γράφει
ἐθνῶν, nations, Gentiles
εἶδον, I saw
Ἕλλησίν, to Greeks
ἐξεπορευόμην, ἐκ + πορεύομαι
ἐξῆλθεν, he went out
ἐπᾶραι, to raise
ἐπιστρέψω, I will return
ἐποίησεν, made
ἔχοντες, having
ζητοῦν, seeking
ζῶντας, living, alive
ἡγουμένων, of governors

θεραπευθῆναι, a passive infinitive
ἰατροὺς, doctors, physicians
καινὸν, καινήν, new
λαλοῦν, speaking, one that speaks
λέγοντα, saying
λέων, lion
λογίζεσθε, reckon, consider
λοιποὶ, the rest, the others
ὀπίσω, after, in pursuit of
ὅταν, whenever
οὐδεὶς, no one
ὀφειλέτης, debtor (cf. ὀφείλω)
παντὶ, every
πᾶς, all, entire
πολλοὶ, πολλῶν, many (people)
πρόβατον, sheep
προσήρχοντο, from προς + ἔρχομαι
ῥήματα, words
ῥίζαν, root
σκοπεύουσιν, examine, consider
σοφοῖς, wise
στόμα, mouth
τελώνης, tax collector
χαρᾶς, joy

Lesson 12

74. Vocabulary

ἀνοίγω, I open

γενήσομαι, I will become (deponent
  fut. of γίνομαι)

γνώσομαι, I will know (deponent fut.
  of γινώσκω)

διδάξω, I will teach

διδάσκαλος, ὁ, teacher

δοξάζω, I glorify

εἰ, if, whether (usually followed by an
  indicative mood verb)

ἐλεύσομαι, I will come (deponent fut.
  of ἔρχομαι)

θαυμάζω, I marvel, wonder
  (thaumaturge)

κηρύσσω, I preach, proclaim

λήμψομαι, I will take, receive (deponent
  fut. of λαμβάνω)

νῦν, now

προσεύχομαι, I pray

φέρω, I bring, bear, carry (Christopher,
  pheresis)

75. Principal Parts of Verbs

The following tense/voice combinations have been introduced up to this point: present active, present middle, present passive, imperfect active, imperfect middle, and imperfect passive. All of these verb forms are constructed on what is called the first *principal part* of the Greek verb. Principal parts are the basic inflected forms of a verb from which all other forms can be derived. An English verb has three principal parts: the present infinitive, the simple past, and the past participle. For a regular verb such as "walk," those forms are: walk, walked, and walked. For an irregular verb such as "go," the forms are: go, went, and gone. As is apparent from the example "go," the formation of principal parts is sometimes unpredictable. This is precisely what makes learning principal parts so important. Once you know the principal parts of a given verb, it is usually rather easy to generate any particular form needed.

Greek verbs have six principal parts, although not every verb has all six and some verbs may be commonly used in only two or three parts. The first principal part is the present active indicative with the first person singular ending (except for deponent verbs, in which case the deponent form substitutes for the nonexistent active form). Thus the first principal part is the "dictionary form" of the word. On this principal part are built the above mentioned conjugations. The second principal part of a Greek verb is the future active (or deponent) indicative with the first person singular ending. The second principal part of λύω is λύσω. On this principal part are built the future active indicative and the future middle indicative. Remember that λύω is an entirely regular verb, and, therefore, its stem is always easily recognizable. You will learn, however, that the formation of principal parts may involve major changes in the verb stem. These changes sometimes follow certain predictable patterns, but in other cases they are utterly unpredictable and can only be memorized or looked up.

76. Forms of the Future Active Indicative

The forms of the future active indicative are as follows:

Singular	Plural
1. λύσω, I will loosen	1. λύσομεν, we will loosen
2. λύσεις, you (sing.) will loosen	2. λύσετε, you (pl.) will loosen
3. λύσει, he, she or it will loosen	3. λύσουσι(ν), they will loosen

For regular verbs, the future tense is formed by adding a sigma (σ) to the verb stem and then suffixing the primary active endings. This simple process applies to verbs whose stems end with certain vowels or diphthongs: ἀκούω, θεραπεύω, λύω, πιστεύω, πορεύομαι, etc. But many Greek verbs do not fall into this category. Some of them will be discussed below.

Remember that the Greek present tense could convey either linear or simple action. Thus λύω could be translated "I am loosening" or "I loosen." The future tense must also do "double duty." Therefore, λύσω could mean either "I will loosen" or "I will be loosening." However, since simple action predominates in the future, only that translation has been given above.

77. Forms of the Future Middle Indicative

The forms of the future middle indicative are as follows:

Singular	Plural
1. λύσομαι, I will loosen (for myself)	1. λυσόμεθα, we will loosen (for ourselves)
2. λύσῃ, you (sing.) will loosen (for yourself)	2. λύσεσθε, you (pl.) will loosen (for yourselves)
3. λύσεται, he, she, it will loosen (for himself, herself, etc.)	3. λύσονται, they will loosen (for themselves)

You may remember that the Greek present and imperfect tenses used the very same forms for the middle and passive voice. In contrast, the future has distinct forms for the middle voice. Future *passive* forms are different from those shown above and are built on a principal part to be learned later. The middle voice has various nuances that are not always easily expressed in English (see §54). However, future middle forms will be encountered most often as *deponent* futures, in which case they are only middle *in form* and will be translated with active meanings.

Like the active, the future middle is formed by adding sigma to the stem. Then the primary middle/passive endings are added (see §55).

Note: the future active infinitive and future middle infinitive exist but are so rare in biblical Greek that they need not be learned. For the sake of reference, the forms are: λύσειν (active) and λύσεσθαι (middle).

78. Formation of the Future Tense

It was noted above that the future tense of verbs whose stems end in certain vowels or diphthongs is formed simply by suffixing a sigma to the stem. The stems of many Greek verbs, however, end in consonants. Sometimes these consonants interact with the sigma of the future tense and are altered in more-or-less predictable ways. How they are altered depends on the consonant. It may be helpful to categorize them.

	Voiceless	Voiced	Aspirate
1. Labial stops	π	β	φ
2. Palatal stops	κ	γ	χ
3. Dental stops	τ	δ	θ

Labial stops (or mutes) are sounds produced by closing the breath stream with the lips; palatal stops do the same with the palate; dental (or lingual) stops are pronounced by positioning the tongue behind the upper teeth. A voiceless stop involves a burst of air but not the vocal chords; a voiced stop involves both; an aspirated stop allows some breath to escape but creates a hissing sound through friction.

These groups of consonants react in certain ways to the sigma of the future tense. When the sigma is added to a labial stop, a psi (ψ) usually results. When added to a palatal stop, the letter xi (ξ) usually results. Dental stops, on the other hand, usually drop out, leaving only the sigma. Here are some examples drawn from verbs you have already learned.

πέμπω, I send	πέμψω, I will send
βλέπω, I see	βλέψω, I will see
γράφω, I write	γράψω, I will write
ἄρχομαι, I begin	ἄρξομαι, I will begin
ἄγω, I lead	ἄξω, I will lead

Many Greek verbs do not fall neatly into these categories, however, and some that would seem to fit nevertheless have irregular future forms. The verb κηρύσσω actually belongs in the category of palatal stops since its true stem is κηρυκ-. Its future form is κηρύξω. Many verbs whose stems end in zeta (ζ) fall into the dental category (βαπτίζω — βαπτίσω; σῴζω — σώσω), but some have irregular futures. Thus, one sees the importance of learning principal parts. If the second principal part of a verb is known, it is relatively easy to conjugate it in the future active and middle. But the principal part itself cannot always be predicted.

79. Irregular Futures

A few common verbs that are regular in the present have deponent futures. Some verbs that are deponent in the present tense will also be deponent in the future, but their future forms may have undergone major stem changes. These forms simply must be learned or looked up in the dictionary. Here are some of the more important verbs in this category along with others that have unusual future tense forms.

Present	Future
γίνομαι, I become	γενήσομαι, I will become
γινώσκω, I know	γνώσομαι, I will know
δύναμαι, I am able	δυνήσομαι, I will be able
ἔρχομαι, I go	ἐλεύσομαι, I will go
ἐσθίω, I eat	φάγομαι, I will eat (also ἔδομαι, LXX)
εὑρίσκω, I find	εὑρήσω, I will find
ἔχω, I have	ἕξω, I will have (note the breathing)
θαυμάζω, I marvel	θαυμάσομαι or θαυμάσω, I will marvel
λαμβάνω, I take	λήμψομαι, I will take
φέρω, I bring	οἴσω, I will bring

80. Future Indicative of εἰμί

The forms of the future indicative of εἰμί are as follows:

Singular	Plural
1. ἔσομαι, I will be	1. ἐσόμεθα, we will be
2. ἔσῃ, you (sing.) will be	2. ἔσεσθε, you (pl.) will be
3. ἔσται, he, she, it will be	3. ἔσονται, they will be

81. Exercises

Practice and Review

1. ἐθαυμάζομεν ἐν τοῖς ἔργοις τοῦ διδασκάλου ἡμῶν, καὶ ὑμεῖς δὲ θαυμάσεσθε ἐν τῇ ἡμέρᾳ ἐκείνῃ.

2. τότε μὲν οὐκ ἐγινώσκομεν τὰς ὁδοὺς τῆς εἰρήνης, νῦν δὲ ἐλεύσεται ὁ προφήτης καὶ ἀνοίξει τὴν καρδίαν ἡμῶν.

3. προσεύχονται τὰ τέκνα ὑπὲρ τῆς ἀδελφῆς αὐτῶν, ἀλλ' οὐ πιστεύουσιν εἰς τὸν κύριον καὶ θεοὶ τοῦ λίθου οὐκ ἀποκρίνονται.

4. εἰ δοξάζετε τὸ ἔργον ἁμαρτωλῶν, οὐ λήμψεσθε τὸ δῶρον ζωῆς ἐν ταῖς ἡμέραις ταῖς ἐσχάταις.

5. ὁ διδάσκαλος λέγει τῷ πονηρῷ ὄχλῳ, Κηρύσσω ὑμῖν τὸν λόγον τῆς ἀληθείας ἀλλὰ οὐ λήμψεσθε αὐτόν.

6. τὰς ἁμαρτίας μου οὐκ ἐδυνάμην φέρειν, ὁ δὲ κύριος οἴσει αὐτὰς ὑπὲρ ἐμοῦ.

7. ἰδοὺ ἡ ὥρα τοῦ θανάτου ἐλεύσεται καὶ αἱ κακαὶ ἐξουσίαι τούτου τοῦ κόσμου γνώσονται ὅτι θεός ἐστιν ὁ κυρίος.

8. οἱ δοῦλοι αὐτοὶ γενήσονται μαθηταὶ τοῦ ἀποστόλου καὶ διδάξουσιν ἄλλους.

9. ἀνοίξω τὸ ἱερὸν τῷ λαῷ καὶ τότε ἀκούσουσι καὶ γνώσονται τὸν νόμον τοῦ οὐρανοῦ.

10. τὰ τέκνα θεοῦ ἔσονται φωνὴ ἀληθείας ἐν τῷ κόσμῳ, διδάξουσιν οὖν ἡμᾶς προσεύχεσθαι.

11. εἰ θεὸς νῦν δοξάζεται ὑπὸ τοῦ ἀδελφοῦ μου, καὶ ἐγὼ γενήσομαι ἄγγελος καὶ ἄξω τὸν υἱόν μου πρὸς δόξαν.

12. εἰ κηρύσσεται ὅτι δαιμόνια ἄρξεται κρίνειν τὸν κόσμον, οὐ πιστεύσομεν τοῦτο οὐδὲ κηρύξομεν ἄλλοις.

13. ἡμεῖς μὲν ἐσόμεθα ἐν τῷ οἴκῳ καὶ φαγόμεθα τὸν ἄρτον τῆς γῆς, ὑμεῖς δὲ ἔσεσθε ἐν τῇ ἐκκλησίᾳ καὶ φάγεσθε τὸν ἄρτον τοῦ οὐρανοῦ.

14. ὁ υἱός μου οὔτε πέμψει ἀγγέλους οὔτε γράψει μοι ἀπ' ἄλλης γῆς.

LXX

1. ἀνοίξεις τὰς χεῖράς σου τῷ ἀδελφῷ σου . . . καὶ τῷ ἐπιδεομένῳ τῷ ἐπὶ τῆς γῆς σου. (Deut 15:11)

2. καὶ λήμψομαι ἐμαυτῷ ὑμᾶς λαὸν ἐμοὶ καὶ ἔσομαι ὑμῶν θεός, καὶ γνώσεσθε ὅτι ἐγὼ κύριος ὁ θεὸς ὑμῶν (Exod 6:7)

3. καὶ εἶπεν Μωυσῆς πρὸς τὸν θεόν, Ἰδοὺ ἐγὼ ἐλεύσομαι πρὸς τοὺς υἱοὺς Ισραηλ (Exod 3:13)

4. οὐ λήμψῃ πρόσωπον πτωχοῦ οὐδὲ θαυμάσεις πρόσωπον δυνάστου (Lev 19:15)

5. ἀλλὰ εἰς τὴν γῆν μου . . . πορεύσῃ καὶ εἰς τὴν φυλήν μου καὶ λήμψῃ γυναῖκα τῷ υἱῷ μου Ισαακ (Gen 24:4)

6. καὶ ἐμβαλεῖτε τὰ ῥήματα ταῦτα εἰς τὴν καρδίαν ὑμῶν . . . καὶ διδάξετε αὐτὰ τὰ τέκνα ὑμῶν (Deut 11:18-9)

7. καὶ ἔσται ἐν ἐκείνῃ τῇ ἡμέρᾳ, λέγει κύριος, ἀπολεῖται ἡ καρδία τοῦ βασιλέως
   . . . καὶ οἱ προφῆται θαυμάσονται. (Jer 4:9)

8. ἐκεῖθεν συνάξει σε κύριος ὁ θεός σου, καὶ ἐκεῖθεν λήμψεταί σε κύριος ὁ θεός
   σου· (Deut 30:4)

9. καὶ προσεύξονται εἰς τὸν τόπον τοῦτον . . . καὶ ἀπὸ τῶν ἁμαρτιῶν αὐτῶν
   ἀποστρέψουσιν (3 Kgdms 8:35)

10. κἀγὼ καὶ οἱ υἱοί μου καὶ οἱ ἀδελφοί μου πορευσόμεθα ἐν διαθήκῃ πατέρων
    ἡμῶν· (1 Macc 2:20)

NT

1. καὶ γνώσεσθε τὴν ἀλήθειαν, καὶ ἡ ἀλήθεια ἐλευθερώσει ὑμᾶς. (John 8:32)

2. Διδάσκαλε, οἴδαμεν ὅτι ἀληθὴς εἶ καὶ τὴν ὁδὸν τοῦ θεοῦ ἐν ἀληθείᾳ
   διδάσκεις, (Matt 22:16)

3. ἐλεύσομαι δὲ . . . πρὸς ὑμᾶς . . . καὶ γνώσομαι οὐ τὸν λόγον τῶν
   πεφυσιωμένων ἀλλὰ τὴν δύναμιν· οὐ γὰρ ἐν λόγῳ ἡ βασιλεία τοῦ θεοῦ ἀλλ' ἐν
   δυνάμει. (1 Cor 4:19-20)

4. οὐ γὰρ ἑαυτοὺς κηρύσσομεν ἀλλὰ Ἰησοῦν Χριστὸν κύριον, ἑαυτοὺς δὲ
   δούλους ὑμῶν διὰ Ἰησοῦν. (2 Cor 4:5)

5. προσεύξομαι τῷ πνεύματι, προσεύξομαι δὲ καὶ τῷ νοΐ· (1 Cor 14:15)

6. Ἐνοικήσω ἐν αὐτοῖς . . . καὶ ἔσομαι αὐτῶν θεός, καὶ αὐτοὶ ἔσονταί μου λαός.
   (2 Cor 6:16)

7. οὐδεὶς ἄξιος εὑρέθη ἀνοῖξαι τὸ βιβλίον οὔτε βλέπειν αὐτό. (Rev 5:4)

8. ἐν ἐκείνῃ τῇ ἡμέρᾳ γνώσεσθε ὑμεῖς ὅτι ἐγὼ ἐν τῷ πατρί μου (John 14:20)

9. ῥύσεταί με ὁ κύριος ἀπὸ παντὸς ἔργου πονηροῦ καὶ σώσει εἰς τὴν βασιλείαν
   αὐτοῦ τὴν ἐπουράνιον· (2 Tim 4:18)

10. καὶ ἐν ταῖς ἡμέραις ἐκείναις ζητήσουσιν οἱ ἄνθρωποι τὸν θάνατον καὶ οὐ μὴ
    εὑρήσουσιν αὐτόν (Rev 9:6)

English to Greek

1. If you (pl.) will preach about heaven and will glorify God, we will come to
   hear you.
2. The teacher will teach us, but we will not become disciples.
3. The Lord will open heaven to sinners if they will receive the gift of life.
4. I marvel that you (sing.) are bringing boats into the temple and I will pray
   for you.
5. I will be your (pl.) sister's messenger, and these men will be her servants.

Vocabulary for LXX and NT Sentences

ἀληθής, true
ἀνοῖξαι, an infinitive of ἀνοίγω
ἄξιος, worthy
ἀπολεῖται, will perish
ἀποστρέψουσιν, they will turn away
βασιλέως, of a king
γυναῖκα, wife
διαθήκη, covenant
δυνάμει, δύναμιν, power
δυνάστου, of a ruler
ἑαυτοὺς, ourselves
εἶπεν, said
ἐκεῖθεν, from there
ἐλευθερώσει, will set free
ἐμαυτῷ, to myself
ἐμβαλεῖτε, you will put in
Ἐνοικήσω, I will dwell in
ἐπιδεομένῳ, one lacking, needing

ἐπουράνιον, heavenly
εὑρέθη, was found
ζητήσουσιν, will seek
κἀγὼ = καὶ ἐγώ
μὴ, not (with οὐ, emphatic)
νοΐ, (with/by the) mind
οἴδαμεν = γινώσκομεν
οὐδεὶς, no one
παντὸς, every
πατέρων, of fathers
πατρί, father
πεφυσιωμένων, arrogant persons
πνεύματι, (with/by the) spirit
πτωχοῦ, of a poor person
ῥήματα, words
ῥύσεται, will rescue
φυλήν, tribe
χεῖρας, hands

Lesson 13

82. Vocabulary

ἀπολύω, I release, dismiss

δεῖ, it is necessary (+ infinitive)

δικαιοσύνη, ἡ, righteousness

ἐκεῖ, there, to that place

ἐπιστρέφω, I turn, I return (strophe)

ἑτοιμάζω, I prepare

ἤδη, already

θρόνος, ὁ, throne

ἴδιος, -α, -ον, one's own (idiosyncrasy, idiom)

ἱμάτιον, τό, garment

κεφαλή, ἡ, head (cephalic)

κράζω, I cry out, call out

ὅλος, -η, -ον, whole (predicate position) (holocaust)

πείθω, I persuade

ὑποστρέφω, I return (strophe)

83. The Third Principal Part

You have learned that the first principal part of a Greek verb is the present active (or deponent) indicative, which is the basis for the present active, middle, and passive forms and the imperfect active, middle, and passive forms. The second principal part is the future active indicative, which is the basis for the future active and middle forms. In this lesson the third principal part is introduced: the aorist active indicative (with the first person singular ending). This part serves as the basis for the aorist active and middle forms. Like the future tense, the aorist has different forms for the passive voice, based on a principal part to be learned later.

There are two groups of aorist verbs. In this lesson you will learn the *first* aorist forms. The second aorist, introduced in the next lesson, uses different *forms,* but is not a different tense. The time and kind of action signified by an aorist tense verb are the same whether it belongs to the first or second aorist group. The only difference is in how the word is formed. Consider the English verbs "walk" and "go." The past tense of these words is formed differently — "walked" and "went" — but both make a simple statement of action in past time. Most Greek verbs will have *either* a first aorist *or* a second aorist form; only rarely will a verb have both.

84. Significance of the Aorist Tense

The aorist, like the imperfect, is a secondary tense. This means that an aorist indicative verb (1) signifies action in past time, and (2) will have an augment. Unlike the imperfect, however, the aorist denotes simple or undefined action. In fact, "aorist" means

71

"not defined" (ἀ + ὅριστος, from ὁρίζω, "define, determine"). Thus, an aorist tense verb does not suggest that the action it signifies is ongoing or repetitive or completed. Neither does it suggest that the action is instantaneous or of short duration. Such information can sometimes be gleaned from the context or the verbal idea, but the aorist tense itself only affirms the occurrence of the action. It does *not* describe the action. Whereas the imperfect, ἔλυον, might have meant "I was loosening," "I used to loosen," or "I loosened (again and again)," the aorist, ἔλυσα, is best translated simply "I loosened." (Occasionally the aorist tense may be translated with the English perfect "I *have* loosened," but only when this refers to indefinite action in past time. Similarly, the English pluperfect, "I *had* loosened," might be required as a translation when the aorist expresses indefinite action prior to a point already in past time. In neither of these cases does the aorist imply completed action. These translations, when necessary, are only concessions to English idiom.)

85. Forms of the First Aorist Active Indicative

The forms of the aorist active indicative are as follows:

Singular	Plural
1. ἔλυσα, I loosened	1. ἐλύσαμεν, we loosened
2. ἔλυσας, you (sing.) loosened	2. ἐλύσατε, you (pl.) loosened
3. ἔλυσε(ν), he, she, or it loosened	3. ἔλυσαν, they loosened

The rules for the augment in the aorist tense are the same as those for the imperfect (see §66). The endings are the regular active endings for the secondary tenses (see §65), with the exception of the first person singular which lacks the normal "ν." Note that the third person singular may have the movable ν. The chief indicator of the first aorist is the suffix -σα. Since this suffix itself ends in a vowel, there is no need for the variable vowel (ο or ε) and the endings may be attached directly. Note that in one instance (the third person singular) the -σα suffix is changed to -σε.

86. Forms of the First Aorist Middle Indicative

The forms of the aorist middle indicative are given below. Remember that the aorist *passive* indicative uses entirely different forms.

Singular	Plural
1. ἐλυσάμην, I loosened (for myself)	1. ἐλυσάμεθα, we loosened (for ourselves)
2. ἐλύσω, you (sing.) loosened (for yourself)	2. ἐλύσασθε, you (pl.) loosened (for yourselves)
3. ἐλύσατο, he, she, or it loosened (for himself, herself, etc.)	3. ἐλύσαντο, they loosened (for themselves)

The only form that requires comment is the second person singular. The original ending was -σο (see §70). The original form, ἐλύσασο, was shortened to ἐλύσω by the loss of the σ and the contraction of the α and o.

87. First Aorist Infinitives

The first aorist active infinitive is λῦσαι. The first aorist middle infinitive is λύσασθαι. Note that there is no augment. The augment occurs *only in the indicative mood*. A minor note: the accent on the first aorist active infinitive is *not* recessive; it will always be on the penult. Thus, ἐπιστρέψαι, ἑτοιμάσαι, θεραπεῦσαι, πιστεῦσαι, etc.

88. Formation of the First Aorist

The formation of the first aorist is regular for verbs whose stems end with certain vowels or diphthongs: ἀκούω, ἀπολύω, θεραπεύω, πιστεύω, etc. For verbs whose stems end in certain consonants, various changes occur when the first aorist tense suffix -σα is added. As one might expect, these changes are similar to those occurring before the future tense suffix -σ. Certain final stem consonants will act in certain ways that have already been described (see §78). Here we need only give examples. (Note that verbs whose stems end in ζ, the fourth group below, usually form the aorist like verbs in the "dental stop" group, that is, by dropping the ζ.)

πέμπω, I send	ἔπεμψα, I sent
βλέπω, I see	ἔβλεψα, I saw (usually in compounds)
γράφω, I write	ἔγραψα, I wrote
ἀνοίγω, I open	ἤνοιξα, I opened
ἄρχομαι, I begin	ἠρξάμην, I began
δέχομαι, I receive	ἐδεξάμην, I received
κηρύσσω, I preach	ἐκήρυξα, I preached
λέγω, I say	ἔλεξα (only in compounds)
πείθω, I persuade	ἔπεισα, I persuaded

βαπτίζω, I baptize   ἐβάπτισα, I baptized
δοξάζω, I glorify   ἐδόξασα, I glorified
θαυμάζω, I marvel   ἐθαύμασα, I marveled
σῴζω, I save   ἔσωσα, I saved

κράζω, I cry out   ἔκραξα, or ἐκέκραξα (esp. LXX), I cried out

There is no way to predict if a particular Greek verb will have a first or second aorist form. One might think, for example, since the verb ἄγω has as its future tense form, ἄξω, that the aorist would be formed similarly. But, in fact, ἄγω has a *second* aorist form that could not be predicted. To be able to read biblical Greek with any fluency, one must be able to recognize the principal parts of the more common verbs.

89. Exercises

Practice and Review

1. τότε ὁ διδάσκαλος ἀπέλυσε τὸν ὄχλον καὶ ὑπέστρεψεν εἰς τὸν οἶκον αὐτοῦ.
2. ἐκεῖνοι οἱ ἁμαρτωλοὶ ἐπέστρεψαν πρὸς τὸν κύριον, καὶ νῦν ἑτοιμάζει ἐν οὐρανοῖς τόπον αὐτοῖς.
3. ἔθελον πεῖσαι τὴν ἀδελφήν μου τὰ ἱμάτια τὰ καλὰ δέξασθαι, αὐτὴ δὲ οὐκ ἐπίστευσεν ὅτι δεῖ αὐτὰ δέξασθαι.
4. σὺ ἡτοίμασας ἄρτον τῷ ἀποστόλῳ, αὐτὸς δὲ ἤδη ἤσθιεν τὸν ἴδιον ἄρτον.
5. ἐπέμψατε τὰ τέκνα εἰς τὴν ἔρημον ἀποθνήσκειν καὶ οὐκ ἐσώσατε αὐτά· τοῦτο ἔσται ἐπὶ τὴν κεφαλὴν ὑμῶν.
6. ἐγὼ ἔκραζον ἐν τῇ ἁμαρτίᾳ μου, αὐτὴ δὲ ἔπεισέ με πορεύεσθαι ἐν τῇ ὁδῷ τῆς δικαιοσύνης.
7. ἠκούσατε τὸν λόγον τῆς ζωῆς καὶ ἠνοίξατε τὴν καρδίαν ὑμῶν καὶ ἐπεστρέψατε ἐπὶ τὸν θεόν.
8. ὁ ἄγγελος τοῦ θανάτου ἔρχεται κρίνειν τὸν κόσμον, ἤδη δὲ κράζουσιν οἱ θρόνοι βασιλειῶν πονηρῶν.
9. οὐκ ἔχει προφήτης δόξαν ἐν τῇ ἰδίᾳ γῇ, ὁ δὲ κόσμος ὅλος λέγει κατὰ τῆς φωνῆς τοῦ ἀγγέλου τοῦ θεοῦ.
10. οἱ μαθηταὶ οὐκ ἐδύναντο ἐκεῖ θεραπεῦσαι τὰ τέκνα ὅτι οὐκ ἐπίστευσαν οἱ ὄχλοι.
11. αἱ ἐξουσίαι αἱ κακαὶ ἤμελλον ἀποκτείνειν τὸν διδάσκαλον τῆς δικαιοσύνης καὶ φέρειν τὴν κεφαλὴν αὐτοῦ εἰς τὴν ἐκκλησίαν.
12. δεῖ τοὺς δούλους ἀπολῦσαι καὶ τὸν θεὸν δοξάζειν, αὕτη γὰρ ἡμέρα εἰρήνης ἐν ὅλῃ τῇ γῇ.
13. οὐκ ἔχω τὸ δῶρον ἱματίων καλῶν, φέρω δὲ πρὸς τὸ ἱερὸν καρδίαν ἀγάπης.
14. ὁ θρόνος τοῦ θεοῦ ἐστιν ἐν τῷ οὐρανῷ καὶ αἱ ψυχαὶ τῶν ἁγίων ὑποστρέφουσιν ἐκεῖ.

LXX

1. καὶ διέρρηξεν Ματταθιας καὶ οἱ υἱοὶ αὐτοῦ τὰ ἱμάτια αὐτῶν (1 Macc 2:14)
2. ἐδίδαξας δέ σου τὸν λαὸν διὰ τῶν τοιούτων ἔργων ὅτι δεῖ . . . εἶναι φιλάνθρωπον (Wis 12:19)
3. κύριος ἐν τῷ οὐρανῷ ἡτοίμασεν τὸν θρόνον αὐτοῦ (Ps 102:19, ET 103:19)
4. καὶ [Ορφα] ἐπέστρεψεν εἰς τὸν λαὸν αὐτῆς, Ρουθ δὲ ἠκολούθησεν αὐτῇ [Νωεμιν]. (Ruth 1:14)
5. [Ιωσιας] ἐπέστρεψεν πρὸς κύριον ἐν ὅλῃ καρδίᾳ αὐτοῦ καὶ ἐν ὅλῃ ψυχῇ αὐτοῦ (4 Kgdms 23:25)
6. Ἐγὼ Τωβιτ ὁδοῖς ἀληθείας ἐπορευόμην καὶ δικαιοσύνης πάσας τὰς ἡμέρας τῆς ζωῆς μου (Tob 1:3 BA)
7. ἐπέστρεψεν δὲ ὁ Μαρδοχαῖος εἰς τὴν αὐλήν, Αμαν δὲ ὑπέστρεψεν εἰς τὰ ἴδια (Esth 6:12)
8. πάντες οὗτοι συνῴκισαν γυναῖκας ἀλλογενεῖς· καὶ ἀπέλυσαν αὐτὰς σὺν τέκνοις. (1 Esdras 9:36)
9. καὶ ἰδοὺ ἀνὴρ ἦλθεν . . . ἐκ τοῦ λαοῦ Σαουλ, καὶ τὰ ἱμάτια αὐτοῦ διερρωγότα, καὶ γῆ ἐπὶ τῆς κεφαλῆς αὐτοῦ (2 Kgdms 1:2)
10. ἡτοίμασαν . . . τὰ δῶρα . . . ἤκουσαν γὰρ ὅτι ἐκεῖ μέλλει ἀριστᾶν. (Gen 43:25)
11. καὶ πρὸς τὸν θεόν μου ἐκέκραξα· ἤκουσεν ἐκ ναοῦ ἁγίου αὐτοῦ φωνῆς μου (Ps 17:7, ET 18:6)

NT

1. λέγει οὖν αὐτῷ ὁ Πιλᾶτος, Ἐμοὶ οὐ λαλεῖς; οὐκ οἶδας ὅτι ἐξουσίαν ἔχω ἀπολῦσαί σε καὶ ἐξουσίαν ἔχω σταυρῶσαί σε; (John 19:10)
2. Ἀγαπήσεις κύριον τὸν θεόν σου ἐξ ὅλης [τῆς] καρδίας σου καὶ ἐν ὅλῃ τῇ ψυχῇ σου (Luke 10:27)
3. Μετὰ ταῦτα εἶδον ἄλλον ἄγγελον καταβαίνοντα ἐκ τοῦ οὐρανοῦ ἔχοντα ἐξουσίαν μεγάλην, . . . καὶ ἔκραξεν ἐν ἰσχυρᾷ φωνῇ (Rev 18:1-2)
4. Ἔμεινεν δὲ Μαριὰμ σὺν αὐτῇ ὡς μῆνας τρεῖς, καὶ ὑπέστρεψεν εἰς τὸν οἶκον αὐτῆς. (Luke 1:56)
5. καὶ ἐν δικαιοσύνῃ κρίνει καὶ πολεμεῖ. οἱ δὲ ὀφθαλμοὶ αὐτοῦ [ὡς] φλὸξ πυρός, καὶ ἐπὶ τὴν κεφαλὴν αὐτοῦ διαδήματα πολλά (Rev 19:11-12)
6. φέρουσιν τὸν πῶλον πρὸς . . . Ἰησοῦν καὶ ἐπιβάλλουσιν αὐτῷ τὰ ἱμάτια αὐτῶν . . . καὶ πολλοὶ τὰ ἱμάτια αὐτῶν ἔστρωσαν εἰς τὴν ὁδόν (Mark 11:7)
7. καὶ αὐτὸς προελεύσεται ἐνώπιον αὐτοῦ . . . ἐπιστρέψαι καρδίας πατέρων ἐπὶ τέκνα . . . ἑτοιμάσαι κυρίῳ λαόν (Luke 1:17)
8. καὶ ἤκουσα φωνῆς μεγάλης ἐκ τοῦ θρόνου λεγούσης, Ἰδοὺ ἡ σκηνὴ τοῦ θεοῦ μετὰ τῶν ἀνθρώπων (Rev 21:3)
9. Καὶ ἤρξατο διδάσκειν αὐτοὺς ὅτι δεῖ τὸν υἱὸν τοῦ ἀνθρώπου πολλὰ παθεῖν (Mark 8:31)
10. ἕκαστος δὲ τὸν ἴδιον μισθὸν λήμψεται κατὰ τὸν ἴδιον κόπον· (1 Cor 3:8)

English to Greek

1. The master returned and cried out because the slaves had not prepared the garments.
2. It is necessary to dismiss the people and destroy the whole house, for righteousness is not there.
3. By his own authority the prophet persuaded the man to release his slaves and to send them to another place.
4. Because of my sins I was not able to raise up my head to see the throne of glory.

Vocabulary for LXX and NT Sentences

ἀγαπήσεις, you (sing.) will love
ἀνὴρ, a man
ἀριστᾶν, eat a meal, dine
αὐλήν, courtyard, palace
γυναῖκας ἀλλογενεῖς, foreign women
διαδήματα, crowns
διέρρηξεν, tore, rent
διερρωγότα, (were) torn
εἶναι, to be (infinitive of εἰμί)
ἕκαστος, each person
Ἔμεινεν, aorist of μένω
ἐνώπιον, before
ἐπιβάλλουσιν, ἐπί + βάλλω (+ dat.)
ἔστρωσαν, spread out
ἔχοντα, having
ἠκολούθησεν, accompanied
ἦλθεν, came (2nd aorist of ἔρχομαι)
ἰσχυρᾷ, strong, loud
καταβαίνοντα, coming down
κόπον, labor, toil
λαλεῖς, you are speaking
λεγούσης, saying

μεγάλης, μεγάλην, great, loud
μῆνας τρεῖς, three months
μισθὸν, reward
ναοῦ, temple
οἶδας = γινώσκεις
παθεῖν, to suffer (subject = υἱὸν)
πάντες, all
πάσας, all
πατέρων, of fathers
πολεμεῖ, wage war
πολλὰ, many (things)
πολλοὶ, many (people)
προελεύσεται, will go before
πῶλον, young donkey
σκηνὴ, dwelling
σταυρῶσαι, to crucify
συνῴκισαν, (had) married
τοιούτων, such
φιλάνθρωπον, kind, benevolent
φλὸξ πυρός, a flame of fire
ὡς, like, about

Lesson 14

90. Vocabulary

εἶδον, I saw (serves as the 2nd aorist of βλέπω) (idea)

εἶπον, I said (serves as the 2nd aorist of λέγω) (epic)

ἦλθον, I came, went (serves as the 2nd aorist of ἔρχομαι)

ἤνεγκα, I brought, bore, carried (irregular 1st aorist of φέρω, conjugated with -κα, not -σα)

οἶνος, ὁ, wine (oenophile)

ὄψομαι, I will see (serves as the deponent future of βλέπω)

πίνω, πίομαι, ἔπιον, I drink, I will drink, I drank (pinocytosis)

πίπτω, ἔπεσον, I fall, I fell

προσέρχομαι, I come to, approach (usually + dative)

προσφέρω, I offer, present

σημεῖον, τό, sign, miracle, portent (semaphore)

φάγομαι, ἔφαγον, I will eat, I ate (deponent future, 2nd aor. of ἐσθίω)

φεύγω, φεύξομαι, ἔφυγον, I flee, I will flee, I fled (fugitive)

91. The Second Aorist

As you learned in the previous lesson, the second aorist is not a different tense from the first aorist, but simply a different way of forming the tense. The chief difference is that the second aorist is formed, not by adding a -σα suffix, but by making changes in the stem of the verb. The second aorist stem generally reflects a more primitive form of the verb than the present tense stem does. Often the second aorist stem is shorter than the present, but this is not always the case. Examples: βάλλω, I throw; ἔβαλον, I threw; λαμβάνω, I take; ἔλαβον, I took.

Sometimes a verb will have a second aorist form that bears no resemblance to its present tense form. Some of the most common of these are included in the vocabulary list above. These words differ so radically from their corresponding present tense forms that they may need to be learned as separate words. They differ so radically because, in fact, they *are* separate words! Strictly speaking, εἶδον, I saw, is not a form of βλέπω, but is the aorist tense of a different verb whose present tense became obsolete. This use of unrelated forms to make a complete verbal paradigm, technically known as suppletion, is seen in the English verb "go, went, gone." "Went" is actually the past tense of the archaic verb "wend," but for all practical purposes it is the past tense of "go." Similarly, the student may regard εἶδον as the second aorist of βλέπω, understanding that this is a "functional" description, not a strict morphological one.

92. Forms of the Second Aorist Active Indicative

The forms of the second aorist active indicative are given below. Since λύω has a first aorist, it cannot be used for this paradigm. Ἔλαβον, the second aorist of λαμβάνω, is used instead.

Singular	Plural
1. ἔλαβον, I took	1. ἐλάβομεν, we took
2. ἔλαβες, you (sing.) took	2. ἐλάβετε, you (pl.) took
3. ἔλαβε(ν), he, she, it took	3. ἔλαβον, they took

Some observations: (1) the augment occurs as one would expect in the aorist indicative; (2) since there is no -σα suffix in the second aorist, the secondary active endings are joined to the stem by means of a variable vowel (ο or ε); (3) the result is that second aorist endings are similar to those of the imperfect; and (4) the third singular may have movable ν.

93. Forms of the Second Aorist Middle Indicative

The forms of the second aorist middle are given below. Remember that middle and passive forms are *not* the same in the aorist tense. The second aorist form of λαμβάνω is again used although this word does not occur in the aorist middle. For that reason, translations are omitted.

Singular	Plural
1. ἐλαβόμην	1. ἐλαβόμεθα
2. ἐλάβου	2. ἐλάβεσθε
3. ἐλάβετο	3. ἐλάβοντο

Note the similarity between the second aorist middle endings and those of the imperfect middle/passive. The original second person singular ending -σο has been altered to -ου as the corresponding imperfect form was (§70).

94. Second Aorist Infinitives

The second aorist active infinitive is λαβεῖν; the second aorist middle infinitive is λαβέσθαι. The accent of both forms is irregular, not receding fully as one might expect. Cf. §87. There is no augment because the augment only occurs in the indicative mood. For second aorist stems that begin with a vowel, the "loss" of the augment in the infinitive will usually shorten the initial vowel to its original form. Examples:

(1) ἦλθον, I came; ἐλθεῖν, to come; (2) εἶδον, I saw; ἰδεῖν, to see (the iota having been lengthened irregularly to ει); but, (3) εἶπον, I said; εἰπεῖν, to say (because the initial diphthong of the stem εἰπ- was not lengthened for the aorist).

95. Some Common Second Aorist Forms

For the sake of reference, here is a list of several of the verbs you have learned to this point that have second aorists. It includes both functional second aorists and "true" second aorists.

ἄγω, I lead	ἤγαγον, I led
ἀποθνῄσκω, I die	ἀπέθανον, I died
βάλλω, I throw	ἔβαλον, I threw
βλέπω, I see	εἶδον, I saw
γίνομαι, I become	ἐγενόμην, I became
ἔρχομαι, I go	ἦλθον, I went
ἐσθίω, I eat	ἔφαγον, I ate
εὑρίσκω, I find	εὗρον, I found
ἔχω, I have	ἔσχον, I had
λαμβάνω, I take	ἔλαβον, I took
λέγω, I say	εἶπον, I said
πίνω, I drink	ἔπιον, I drank
πίπτω, I fall	ἔπεσον, I fell
φεύγω, I flee	ἔφυγον, I fled

A final note: During the Koine period the distinction between first and second aorist endings was not strictly maintained. (This began in classical Greek; modern Greek abandons the distinction entirely.) It is not unusual, therefore, to find second aorist stems with first aorist endings in biblical Greek. For example, εἶπαν (with alpha) is commonly used instead of εἶπον (with omicron) for the third person plural. For now, the student is advised to learn the second aorist endings and associate them with second aorist stems. When mixed forms are encountered in the Bible, they should be recognized without too much difficulty.

96. Exercises

Practice and Review

1. ἐν ἐκείνῃ τῇ ἡμέρᾳ ἡμεῖς ἐπίομεν οἶνον καὶ ἐφάγομεν ἄρτον, ἀλλὰ ὑμεῖς ἐφύγετε εἰς τὴν ἔρημον καὶ προσηύξασθε.

2. ὁ προφήτης εἶδεν τὸν κύριον ἐπὶ τοῦ θρόνου καὶ εἶπεν πρὸς αὐτὸν περὶ τῆς βασιλείας τοῦ θεοῦ.

3. οἱ μαθηταὶ εἶδον τὰ σημεῖα τοῦ οὐρανοῦ καὶ ἔπεσαν ἐπὶ πρόσωπον αὐτῶν.

4. εὗρες τὴν ὁδὸν ἀληθείας ἐν τῷ ἱερῷ καὶ ἐγένου δοῦλος δικαιοσύνης, ἐγὼ δὲ οὐκ ἤθελον ἀκοῦσαι.

5. αἱ ἀδελφαὶ προσῆλθον τῷ διδασκάλῳ καὶ προσήνεγκαν τὰ δῶρα αὐτῶν.

6. οἱ ὀφθαλμοὶ τοῦ κυρίου ὄψονται καὶ τὰ ἔργα σου καὶ τὴν καρδίαν σου.

7. εἴδομεν ὅτι ὁ ἀπόστολος ἐθεράπευεν ἐκεῖνα τὰ τέκνα, καὶ ὑμεῖς δὲ ὄψεσθε τὰ σημεῖα τὰ αὐτά.

8. οὐ φαγόμεθα ἐν τῷ οἴκῳ τῶν ἁμαρτωλῶν, ἄρτον δὲ καὶ οἶνον ἐν τῷ τόπῳ τῶν δικαίων ἐλάβομεν.

9. εἶπεν δὲ ὁ ἄνθρωπος, Λίθοι ἀπ᾽ οὐρανοῦ ἔπεσον, ἀλλὰ ὁ λαὸς οὐκ ἐπίστευσαν οὐδὲ συνήγαγον τὰ τέκνα εἰς τοὺς οἴκους.

10. ἀπελύσαμεν τὸν πονηρὸν ὄχλον, προσηρχόμεθα γὰρ τῷ θρόνῳ τῆς δόξης.

11. ὁ ἀδελφὸς ἡμῶν οὐκ ἔπιεν τὸν οἶνον, ἤθελε γὰρ αὐτὸν προσφέρειν ἐν τῷ ἱερῷ.

12. ἦλθεν ὁ υἱὸς ὑμῶν πρός με καὶ ἤνεγκε τὰ βιβλία τοῦ νόμου.

13. τὰ δαιμόνια ἔλαβον τὰ ἱμάτια τῶν ἀγγέλων καὶ ἔβαλον αὐτὰ εἰς τὴν θάλασσαν.

14. ἐγὼ αὐτὸς ἤγαγον τὰ τέκνα ἐκ τῆς ἐκκλησίας, σὺ γὰρ οὐκ ἔσχες τὴν ἐξουσίαν διδάσκειν αὐτά.

15. ἐν ἐκείνῃ τῇ ὥρᾳ ἐφύγομεν ἀπὸ τοῦ προσώπου τοῦ ἀγγέλου τοῦ θεοῦ, νῦν δὲ φεύγομεν ἀπὸ τῆς ἁμαρτίας.

LXX

1. καὶ ἔφαγον καὶ ἔπιον, αὐτὸς καὶ οἱ ἄνδρες οἱ μετ᾽ αὐτοῦ (Gen 24:54)

2. καὶ ἔλαβον τὸν Ιωναν καὶ ἐξέβαλον αὐτὸν εἰς τὴν θάλασσαν (Jon. 1:15)

3. εἶπεν δὲ κύριος πρὸς Μωυσῆν . . . εἶδον τὴν κάκωσιν τοῦ λαοῦ μου τοῦ ἐν Αἰγύπτῳ (Exod 3:7)

4. εἶπεν δὲ ὁ θεὸς Μωυσεῖ . . . Ἔσομαι μετὰ σοῦ, καὶ τοῦτό σοι τὸ σημεῖον ὅτι ἐγώ σε ἐξαποστέλλω· (Exod 3:12)

5. Καὶ μετὰ ταῦτα εἰσῆλθεν Μωυσῆς καὶ Ααρων πρὸς Φαραω καὶ εἶπαν αὐτῷ, Τάδε λέγει κύριος ὁ θεὸς Ισραηλ (Exod 5:1)

6. καὶ ἔπεσεν ἐπὶ πρόσωπον αὐτῆς καὶ . . . εἶπεν πρὸς αὐτόν, Τί ὅτι εὗρον χάριν ἐν ὀφθαλμοῖς σου (Ruth 2:10)

7. καὶ πάλιν [Ιωσηφ] προσῆλθεν πρὸς αὐτοὺς καὶ εἶπεν αὐτοῖς καὶ ἔλαβεν τὸν Συμεων ἀπ᾽ αὐτῶν καὶ ἔδησεν αὐτὸν ἐναντίον αὐτῶν. (Gen 42:24)

8. καὶ [θεὸς] ἤγαγεν ὑμᾶς τεσσαράκοντα ἔτη ἐν τῇ ἐρήμῳ· . . . ἄρτον οὐκ ἐφάγετε, οἶνον . . . οὐκ ἐπίετε (Deut 29:4-5, ET 29:5-6)

9. καὶ εἶδεν ὁ θεὸς ὅτι καλόν. καὶ ἐγένετο ἑσπέρα καὶ ἐγένετο πρωί, ἡμέρα δευτέρα. (Gen 1:8)

10. καὶ ἐγὼ εἰσελεύσομαι εἰς τὸν οἶκόν μου φαγεῖν καὶ πιεῖν καὶ κοιμηθῆναι μετὰ τῆς γυναικός μου; (2 Kgdms 11:11)

11. καὶ ἦλθεν Γοργίας εἰς τὴν παρεμβολήν Ιουδου νυκτὸς καὶ οὐδένα εὗρεν· καὶ
. . . εἶπεν, Φεύγουσιν οὗτοι ἀφ᾽ ἡμῶν. (1 Macc 4:5)

NT

1. εἶδεν αὐτὸν ἄλλη καὶ λέγει τοῖς ἐκεῖ, Οὗτος ἦν μετὰ Ἰησοῦ . . . (Matt 26:71)
2. εἰς τὰ ἴδια ἦλθεν, καὶ οἱ ἴδιοι αὐτὸν οὐ παρέλαβον. (John 1:11)
3. ἐξῆλθον δὲ ἰδεῖν . . . καὶ ἦλθον πρὸς τὸν Ἰησοῦν καὶ εὗρον . . . τὸν ἄνθρωπον
ἀφ᾽ οὗ τὰ δαιμόνια ἐξῆλθεν (Luke 8:35)
4. καὶ εἶπεν ὁ ἄγγελος αὐτῇ, Μὴ φοβοῦ, Μαριάμ, εὗρες γὰρ χάριν παρὰ τῷ
θεῷ. (Luke 1:30)
5. ὁ Ἰησοῦς . . . εἶπεν, Ἀμὴν ἀμὴν λέγω ὑμῖν, ζητεῖτέ με οὐχ ὅτι εἴδετε σημεῖα,
ἀλλ᾽ ὅτι ἐφάγετε ἐκ τῶν ἄρτων (John 6:26)
6. χειραγωγοῦντες δὲ αὐτὸν εἰσήγαγον εἰς Δαμασκόν . . . καὶ οὐκ ἔφαγεν οὐδὲ
ἔπιεν. (Acts 9:8-9)
7. Καὶ προσῆλθον αὐτῷ τυφλοὶ καὶ χωλοὶ ἐν τῷ ἱερῷ, καὶ ἐθεράπευσεν αὐτούς.
(Matt 21:14)
8. λέγει ἡ μήτηρ τοῦ Ἰησοῦ πρὸς αὐτόν, Οἶνον οὐκ ἔχουσιν. (John 2:3)
9. ἀκούσας δὲ ταῦτα ὁ Ἰησοῦς . . . εἶπεν, Λέγω ὑμῖν, οὐδὲ ἐν τῷ Ἰσραὴλ
τοσαύτην πίστιν εὗρον. (Luke 7:9)
10. Νῦν ἀπολύεις τὸν δοῦλόν σου, δέσποτα, κατὰ τὸ ῥῆμά σου ἐν εἰρήνῃ· ὅτι
εἶδον οἱ ὀφθαλμοί μου τὸ σωτήριόν σου (Luke 2:29-30)
11. καὶ εἶδον θρόνον μέγαν λευκόν καὶ τόν καθήμενον ἐπ᾽ αὐτόν, οὗ ἀπὸ τοῦ
προσώπου ἔφυγεν ἡ γῆ καὶ ὁ οὐρανός. (Rev 20:11)

English to Greek

1. We will not see death because we saw the signs and fled from our evil deeds.
2. You (pl.) brought bread to your sister and she ate in your house, but you did
not see her teacher.
3. The prophet went into the temple and offered gifts to God, but he did not
drink wine in the assembly.
4. In that day the same angels fell from heaven, for they had sin in their hearts.

Vocabulary for LXX and NT Sentences

ἀκούσας, hearing
ἄνδρες, men
γυναικός, wife
δέσποτα, Lord, Master
δευτέρα, second
ἔδησεν, bound, tied up
εἰσήγαγον, from εἰς + ἄγω
ἐναντίον, before, in the presence of
ἐξέβαλον, from ἐκ + βάλλω
ἑσπέρα, evening
ζητεῖτε, you seek
καθήμενον, [one who is] sitting
κάκωσιν, oppression, mistreatment
κοιμηθῆναι, sleep
λευκόν, white
μέγαν, great
Μὴ φοβοῦ, Do not be afraid!
μήτηρ, mother

νυκτὸς, at night
οὗ, whom, of whom, whose
οὐδένα, no one
παρέλαβον, accepted, received
παρεμβολήν, (military) camp
πίστιν, faith
πρωί, morning, in the morning
ῥῆμα, word
σωτήριον, salvation
Τάδε, these things, thus
τεσσαράκοντα ἔτη, forty years
Τί ὅτι, why?
τοσαύτην, such great
τυφλοί, blind (persons)
χάριν, favor
χειραγωγοῦντες, taking by the hand
χωλοί, lame

Lesson 15

97. Vocabulary

ἀκήκοα, I have heard (perfect of
    ἀκούω)
γέγονα, I have become, been (perfect
    of γίνομαι)
ἐγγίζω, I draw near (perfect = ἤγγικα)
ἐγήγερμαι, I have been raised, am risen
    (perf. pass. of ἐγείρω)
ἔγνωκα, I have come to know (perfect
    of γινώσκω)
εἴρηκα, I have said, spoken (serves as
    the perfect of λέγω)

ἐλήλυθα, I have come, gone (serves as
    the perfect of ἔρχομαι)
ἔτερος, -α, -ον, other, different
    (heterodoxy, heterosexual)
ἑώρακα, I have seen (serves as the
    perfect of βλέπω)
οὔπω, not yet
πέποιθα, I depend on, trust in (perfect
    active of πείθω)
πολλάκις, often, many times
τέθνηκα, I have died, I am dead
    (perfect of θνήσκω)

98. The Fourth and Fifth Principal Parts

The fourth principal part of a Greek verb is the perfect active indicative with the first person singular ending (λέλυκα). This principal part serves as the basis for perfect active forms in all moods and modes and the pluperfect active, which occurs only in the indicative.

The fifth principal part is the perfect middle/passive indicative with the first person singular ending (λέλυμαι). This principal part serves as the basis for perfect middle and passive forms in all moods and modes and the pluperfect middle and passive, which only occur in the indicative.

99. Significance of the Perfect Tense

The Greek perfect tense denotes an action completed in past time with an effect that continues into the present. The tense thus has two foci: a completed past action and a present effect. To say in the Greek perfect tense, "I have filled the cup," is equivalent to saying, "I filled the cup and it is now full." It is important to realize that the Greek perfect corresponds *only in part* to the English perfect tense. Consider these examples:

He has often gone into the temple.
He has gone into the temple. You cannot speak with him.

Both of these sentences use the English perfect form, "He has . . . ," but only the second corresponds to the idea of the Greek perfect tense. The first denotes action in past time (in this case, repeated action) with no particular reference to a continuing effect. Greek would express this with either the aorist or imperfect tense. The second sentence clearly implies that the action of "going to the temple" has a present result: He is not here. This is the sense of the Greek perfect. In Greek these sentences would be written:

πολλάκις [αὐτὸς] εἰσῆλθεν (or εἰσήρχετο) εἰς τὸ ἱερόν.
[αὐτὸς] εἰσελήλυθεν εἰς τὸ ἱερόν· οὐ δύνασθε λέγειν μετ' αὐτοῦ.

The perfect *passive* of certain Greek verbs may sometimes be translated by a present tense form of "to be" followed by a participle. Thus, one may translate γέγραπται, not only as "it has been written," but as "it is written." Similarly, ἐγήγερται may be rendered "he (or she) is risen." In each case, the translation captures the idea of a past completed action with a result that extends into the present.

100. Forms of the Perfect Active Indicative

The forms of the perfect active indicative are as follows:

Singular	Plural
1. λέλυκα, I have loosened	1. λελύκαμεν, we have loosened
2. λέλυκας, you have loosened	2. λελύκατε, you have loosened
3. λέλυκε(ν), he, she, it has loosened	3. λελύκασι(ν) or -καν, they have loosened

Two characteristics distinguish the perfect active: (1) reduplication, and (2) the tense suffix -κα. Reduplication is a prefix consisting of the first consonant of the verb followed by the letter epsilon. Various forms of the reduplication are discussed below. The tense suffix -κα is roughly parallel to the -σα of the aorist system except that the suffix -κα only appears in the active indicative. (The -κ by itself also appears in the other forms of the active voice: the infinitive and the participle.)

Although the perfect is a primary tense, its endings in the active voice are almost identical to the (secondary) endings of the aorist tense. Only the third person plural has a primary type ending (-σι) and even here the alternate form (-ν) resembles the aorist. As with the aorist, the perfect endings are attached directly to the tense suffix.

101. Forms of the Perfect Middle/Passive Indicative

The forms of the perfect middle/passive indicative are as follows:

Singular	Plural
1. λέλυμαι, I have been loosened	1. λελύμεθα, we have been loosened
2. λέλυσαι, you have been loosened	2. λέλυσθε, you have been loosened
3. λέλυται, he, she, it has been loosened	3. λέλυνται, they have been loosened

Middle and passive forms are identical in the perfect tense. Note that reduplication occurs, but the -κα suffix found in the active voice is lacking here. Note also that the normal primary middle/passive endings are joined *directly* to the verb stem. There is no variable vowel. This causes no problem with a verb whose stem ends in a vowel, such as λύω. But for many verbs whose stems end in a consonant, certain changes occur for the sake of euphony. The resultant forms will differ slightly from the ones in the paradigm above, but will usually be recognizable. For example: γέγραπται, "it has been written" (γεγραφ + ται); δεδίωγμαι, "I have been persecuted" (δεδιωκ + μαι); βεβάπτισμαι, "I have been baptized" (βεβαπτιζ + μαι); etc.

102. Perfect Infinitives

The perfect active infinitive is λελυκέναι, "to have loosened." The perfect middle/passive infinitive is λελύσθαι, "to have loosened for oneself" or "to have been loosened." Both forms have reduplication, but the -κ suffix only occurs in the active. Note that the accent is irregular in both forms. It does not recede fully, but goes only as far as the penult.

103. Various Forms of Perfect Tense Reduplication

With regular verbs reduplication consists of the first consonant of the verb stem followed by an ε. Examples: λύω (I loosen), λέλυκα (I have loosened); πιστεύω (I believe), πεπίστευκα (I have believed). But a number of variations occur, depending on the initial consonant of the verb. In the examples that follow, several verbs you have not learned are used in order to illustrate the various possibilities. In a few cases, passive forms are used where these are more common for the words involved.

1. Verbs beginning with a vowel or diphthong are reduplicated by lengthening the vowel or diphthong. The result is that reduplication is identical to augment. Examples: ἀγαπάω (I love), ἠγάπηκα (I have loved); ἑτοιμάζω (I prepare), ἡτοίμακα (I have prepared).

2. Verbs beginning with aspirated consonants (φ, θ, χ) are reduplicated with the corresponding unaspirated consonants (π, τ, κ). Examples: φιλέω (I love), πεφίληκα (I have loved); θεραπεύω (I heal), τεθεράπευκα (I have healed); χωρίζω (I separate), κεχώρικα (I have separated).

3. Verbs beginning with a double consonant (ψ, ζ, ξ) or with two consonants (unless the second consonant is λ or ρ) are reduplicated with epsilon. Again, reduplication is identical to augment. Examples: ζητέω (I seek), ἐζήτηκα (I have sought); ξηραίνω (I dry out), ἐξήραμμαι (I have been dried out); κτίζω (I create), ἔκτισμαι (I have been created); σταυρόω (I crucify), ἐσταύρωμαι (I have been crucified); but πληρόω (I fulfill), πεπλήρωκα (I have fulfilled).

4. Irregular verbs: a number of verbs form the perfect in a wholly unpredictable way. Examples: ἔρχομαι (I come), ἐλήλυθα (I have come); ἀκούω (I hear), ἀκήκοα (I have heard).

104. The Pluperfect in Biblical Greek

The pluperfect tense is not common in biblical Greek. Although its forms need not be memorized, the active voice is given here for the sake of reference. As a secondary tense, the pluperfect normally has an augment, but this is not carried out consistently in biblical Greek. The significance of the pluperfect is similar to that of the perfect, but is further back in time. That is, it denotes action completed *prior to* a point in past time, with an effect that continued up to that point in past time. Example: "She *had eaten* the bread before the man arrived."

Singular	Plural
1. ἐλελύκειν, I had loosened	1. ἐλελύκειμεν, we had loosened
2. ἐλελύκεις, you had loosened	2. ἐλελύκειτε, you had loosened
3. ἐλελύκει, he, she, it had loosened	3. ἐλελύκεισαν, they had loosened

105. Some Common Perfect Tense Forms

For reference, here is a list of the perfect forms of several verbs you have learned. A few of these forms are "functional" perfects, that is, forms not truly related to the present tense shown (see §90). The first group contains entirely regular verbs; the second group involves forms that are irregular to a greater or lesser extent.

θεραπεύω, I heal	τεθεράπευκα, I have healed
λύω, I loosen	λέλυκα, I have loosened
πιστεύω, I believe	πεπίστευκα, I have believed

ἀκούω, I hear	ἀκήκοα, I have heard
βάλλω, I throw	βέβληκα, I have thrown
βλέπω, I see	ἑώρακα, I have seen
γίνομαι, I become	γέγονα, I have become
γινώσκω, I know	ἔγνωκα, I have come to know
γράφω, I write	γέγραπται, It is written
ἐγείρω, I raise up	ἐγήγερται, He, she has been raised
ἔρχομαι, I go	ἐλήλυθα, I have gone
ἑτοιμάζω, I prepare	ἡτοίμακα, I have prepared
εὑρίσκω, I find	εὕρηκα, I have found
ἔχω, I have	ἔσχηκα, I had
θνήσκω, I die*	τέθνηκα, I have died, I am dead
λαμβάνω, I take	εἴληφα, I have taken
λέγω, I say	εἴρηκα, I have said
πείθω, I persuade	πέποιθα, (act.) I depend on, trust
	πέπεισμαι, (pass.) I am convinced
πίπτω, I fall	πέπτωκα, I have fallen

*θνήσκω is the simple form of the compound verb ἀποθνήσκω. In biblical Greek, the present tense of θνήσκω is replaced completely by the present tense of the compound verb. The future and the aorist are also supplied chiefly by the compound form. The simple verb, however, is used for the perfect tense forms: τέθνηκα, etc.

106. Exercises

Practice and Review

1. ἐν ταῖς ἡμέραις ἐκείναις ἦν ὁ υἱὸς αὐτῆς μικρός, νῦν δὲ γέγονεν ἄνθρωπος καὶ ἔχει αὐτὸς υἱόν.

2. ἀκηκόατε τοῦ προφήτου; ὁ λαὸς λέγει ὅτι ἐλήλυθεν ἀπὸ τοῦ οὐρανοῦ αὐτοῦ.

3. πολλάκις ἔπεσον ἐν τῷ οἴκῳ μου, νῦν δὲ πέπτωκα καὶ οὐ δύναμαι ἐγείρεσθαι.

4. αἱ ἐξουσίαι εἰρήκασιν καὶ οἱ δοῦλοι ἀπολέλυνται, αὐτοὶ γὰρ οὐκ ἔλαβον τὰ ἱμάτια οὐδὲ τὸν οἶνον.

5. πονηροὶ ἄνθρωποι λελύκασιν τὸ ἱερόν, καὶ νῦν ὀφείλομεν συναγαγεῖν καλοὺς λίθους καὶ ἑτοιμάσαι ἕτερον οἶκον τῷ θεῷ ἡμῶν.

6. εἰ οὔπω ἐγνώκατε τὴν ἀγάπην τοῦ θεοῦ, οὐδὲ ἑωράκατε τὰ σημεῖα τοῦ οὐρανοῦ, οὐ δύνασθε κηρύξαι τοῖς ὄχλοις.

7. ὁ δοῦλος τῆς ἀδελφῆς ἡμῶν εἴληφεν τὸν ἄρτον. οὐ δυνάμεθα ἐσθίειν.

8. οἱ ὀφθαλμοὶ τοῦ ἁμαρτωλοῦ τεθεράπευνται ὑπὸ τοῦ κυρίου, καὶ νῦν πέπεισμαι ὅτι γενήσεται μαθητής.

9. ὁ διδάσκαλος τῆς δικαιοσύνης ἐγήγερται ἐκ τῶν νεκρῶν; ἡ ὥρα τῆς βασιλείας ἤγγικεν;

10. τέθνηκεν ὁ ἀδελφός σου. προσευξόμεθα ὑπὲρ αὐτοῦ, ἡ γὰρ ψυχὴ αὐτοῦ ἐξελήλυθεν ἀπὸ τούτου τοῦ κόσμου;

11. ὁ ὄχλος ἐθαύμασεν καὶ εἶπεν, Ἑωράκαμεν τὸν ἄγγελον τοῦ κυρίου καὶ ἀκηκόαμεν τῆς φωνῆς αὐτοῦ.

12. τέκνον ἦλθεν εἰς τὴν ἐκκλησίαν καὶ ἔκραξεν, Εὕρηκα ἄνθρωπον νεκρὸν ἐν τῇ θαλάσσῃ.

13. ὁ θεὸς αὐτὸς εἴρηκεν, Οὐκ ἀπελεύσομαι ἀπὸ σοῦ, καὶ πεπείσμεθα ὅτι ὁ θεὸς ἡμῶν πιστός.

14. πολλάκις ἐξηρχόμεθα κατὰ ἑτέρων λαῶν καὶ ἀπεκτείνομεν, νῦν δὲ ἤγγικεν ἡ ἡμέρα τῆς εἰρήνης.

LXX

1. εἶπεν δὲ Φαραω τῷ Ιωσηφ, Ἐνύπνιον ἑώρακα, καὶ ὁ συγκρίνων οὐκ ἔστιν αὐτό· ἐγὼ δὲ ἀκήκοα περὶ σοῦ (Gen 41:15)

2. εἴρηκα τοῖς υἱοῖς Ισραηλ, Πᾶσα ψυχὴ ἐξ ὑμῶν οὐ φάγεται αἷμα (Lev 17:12)

3. καὶ εἶπεν αὐτῷ, Πόθεν εἶ, νεανίσκε; καὶ εἶπεν αὐτῷ, Ἐκ τῶν υἱῶν Ισραηλ τῶν ἀδελφῶν σου καὶ ἐλήλυθα ὧδε ἐργατεύεσθαι. (Tob 5:5 S)

4. εἶπεν δὲ κύριος πρὸς Μωυσῆν ἐν Μαδιαμ . . . ἄπελθε εἰς Αἴγυπτον· τεθνήκασιν γὰρ πάντες οἱ ζητοῦντές σου τὴν ψυχήν. (Exod 4:19)

5. ὁ γὰρ Μωυσῆς οὗτος ὁ ἄνθρωπος, ὃς ἐξήγαγεν ἡμᾶς ἐξ Αἰγύπτου, οὐκ οἴδαμεν, τί γέγονεν αὐτῷ. (Exod 32:1)

6. Καὶ εἶπεν κύριος πρὸς Μωυσῆν, Ἰδοὺ ἠγγίκασιν αἱ ἡμέραι τοῦ θανάτου σου· (Deut 31:14)

7. καὶ εἶπεν Ιωνας πρὸς αὐτούς . . . ἔγνωκα ἐγὼ ὅτι δι' ἐμὲ ὁ κλύδων ὁ μέγας οὗτος ἐφ' ὑμᾶς ἐστιν. (Jon 1:12)

8. οἱ ὀφθαλμοὶ ὑμῶν ἑώρακαν πάντα τὰ ἔργα κυρίου τὰ μεγάλα . . . (Deut 11:7)

9. Ἐγώ εἰμι κύριος ὁ θεός σου, ὅστις ἐξήγαγόν σε ἐκ γῆς Αἰγύπτου ἐξ οἴκου δουλείας. οὐκ ἔσονταί σοι θεοὶ ἕτεροι πλὴν ἐμοῦ. (Exod 20:2-3)

10. κύριε, ἐλέησον ἡμᾶς, ἐπὶ σοὶ γὰρ πεποίθαμεν· (Isa 33:2)

NT

1. πέπεισμαι γὰρ ὅτι οὔτε θάνατος οὔτε ζωὴ . . . οὔτε τις κτίσις ἑτέρα δυνήσεται ἡμᾶς χωρίσαι ἀπὸ τῆς ἀγάπης τοῦ θεοῦ τῆς ἐν Χριστῷ . . . (Rom 8:38-39)

2. οὔτε φωνὴν αὐτοῦ πώποτε ἀκηκόατε οὔτε εἶδος αὐτοῦ ἑωράκατε, καὶ τὸν λόγον αὐτοῦ οὐκ ἔχετε ἐν ὑμῖν (John 5:37-38)

3. εἰ ἐγνώκατέ με, καὶ τὸν πατέρα μου γνώσεσθε· καὶ ἀπ' ἄρτι γινώσκετε αὐτὸν καὶ ἑωράκατε αὐτόν. (John 14:7)

4. λέγει αὐτῷ [Θωμᾷ] ὁ Ἰησοῦς, Ὅτι ἑώρακάς με πεπίστευκας; (John 20:29)

5. Εἰ δὲ Χριστὸς κηρύσσεται ὅτι ἐκ νεκρῶν ἐγήγερται, πῶς λέγουσιν ἐν ὑμῖν τινες ὅτι ἀνάστασις νεκρῶν οὐκ ἔστιν; (1 Cor 15:12)

6. τότε λέγει αὐτῷ ὁ Ἰησοῦς, Ὕπαγε, Σατανᾶ· γέγραπται γάρ, Κύριον τὸν θεόν σου προσκυνήσεις (Matt 4:10)

7. Ἰησοῦς . . . εἶπεν, Οὐ δι' ἐμὲ ἡ φωνὴ αὕτη γέγονεν ἀλλὰ δι' ὑμᾶς. (John 12:30)
8. Ἀπὸ τότε ἤρξατο ὁ Ἰησοῦς κηρύσσειν καὶ λέγειν, Μετανοεῖτε· ἤγγικεν γὰρ ἡ βασιλεία τῶν οὐρανῶν. (Matt 4:17)
9. οὐκ ἐλήλυθα καλέσαι δικαίους ἀλλὰ ἁμαρτωλοὺς εἰς μετάνοιαν. (Luke 5:32)
10. εἶπεν αὐτῷ ὁ Ἰησοῦς ὅτι Εἴρηται, Οὐκ ἐκπειράσεις κύριον τὸν θεόν σου. (Luke 4:12)
11. ἤρχοντο πέραν τῆς θαλάσσης εἰς Καφαρναούμ. καὶ σκοτία ἤδη ἐγεγόνει καὶ οὔπω ἐληλύθει πρὸς αὐτοὺς ὁ Ἰησοῦς (John 6:17)

English to Greek

1. If you (pl.) have heard the words of the prophet and have come to know the truth, you will teach others.
2. This faithful messenger has come to us now because he has seen a different world.
3. We ourselves trust in God because the teacher of righteousness has spoken to us about God's love.
4. She has become a disciple because the hour of her death has drawn near.

Vocabulary for LXX and NT Sentences

αἷμα, blood
ἀνάστασις, resurrection
ἄπελθε, go!
ἄρτι, now
δουλείας, slavery, bondage
εἶδος, appearance, form
ἐκπειράσεις, you will tempt, test
ἐλέησον, have mercy on!
Ἐνύπνιον, a dream
ἐξήγαγεν, -ον, from ἐκ + ἄγω
ἐργατεύεσθαι, to work, labor
ζητοῦντές, (ones) seeking
καλέσαι, to call
κλύδων, storm
κτίσις, created thing, creature
μεγάλα, μέγας, great
Μετανοεῖτε, Repent!
μετάνοιαν, repentance
νεανίσκε, young man

οἴδαμεν = γινώσκομεν
ὅς, who
ὅστις, who
πάντα, πάντες, Πᾶσα, every, all
πατέρα, father
πέραν, across + gen.
πλὴν, except, apart from
Πόθεν, Whence? From where?
προσκυνήσεις, you will worship
πώποτε, ever, at any time
πῶς, how?
σκοτία, darkness
συγκρίνων, (one) interpreting
τί, what
τινες, some
τις, any
Ὕπαγε, go away!
χωρίσαι, to separate
ὧδε, here

Lesson 16

107. Vocabulary

ἀπεστάλην, I was sent (2nd aorist passive of ἀποστέλλω)

ἐβλήθην, I was thrown (aorist passive of βάλλω)

ἐγενήθην, I became (aorist passive deponent of γίνομαι)

ἐγνώσθην, I was known (aorist passive of γινώσκω)

ἐγράφην, I was written (2nd aorist passive of γράφω)

ἐκβάλλω, I cast out

ἐλήμφθην, I was taken (aorist passive of λαμβάνω)

εὑρέθην, I was found (aorist passive of εὑρίσκω)

ἠγέρθην, I was raised (aorist passive of ἐγείρω)

ἠνέχθην, I was brought (serves as the aorist passive of φέρω)

ἤχθην, I was led (aor. pass. of ἄγω)

πῶς, how?

ὤφθην, I was seen, I appeared (serves as the aorist passive of βλέπω)

108. The Sixth Principal Part

The sixth (and last) principal part is the aorist passive indicative with the first person singular ending (ἐλύθην). This part is the basis for the aorist passive in all moods and modes and for the future passive, which occurs almost exclusively in the indicative mood.

Remember that the aorist passive and future passive forms are quite different from the middle forms of the same tenses. This creates a special situation in the case of deponent verbs. A verb that is deponent in the present may have either a middle deponent form or a passive deponent form in the aorist and future tenses. With some verbs, both forms occur. Examples: πορεύομαι has an aorist passive form (ἐπορεύθην); δέχομαι has both an aorist middle (ἐδεξάμην) and an aorist passive (ἐδέχθην), but the middle is much more common; ἀποκρίνομαι has both forms, although the passive (ἀπεκρίθην) is much more common than the middle (ἀπεκρινάμην); γίνομαι has both middle (ἐγενόμην) and passive (ἐγενήθην) forms with the middle predominating. When both forms exist, it is usually difficult to detect any difference in meaning.

90

109. Forms of the Aorist Passive Indicative

The forms of the aorist passive indicative are as follows:

Singular	Plural
1. ἐλύθην, I was loosened	1. ἐλύθημεν, we were loosened
2. ἐλύθης, you (sing.) were loosened	2. ἐλύθητε, you (pl.) were loosened
3. ἐλύθη, he, she or it was loosened	3. ἐλύθησαν, they were loosened

The aorist passive is formed by adding the suffix -θη to the verb stem. The augment is to be expected since the aorist is a secondary tense. The endings, however, are unusual in that the secondary *active* endings are used (see §65). These endings are added directly to the -θη suffix without a connecting vowel.

110. The Second Aorist Passive

A small number of verbs in biblical Greek have what is called a second aorist passive. The second aorist passive differs from the regular form in that it lacks the -θ in the tense suffix, having only the -η. Of the verbs you have learned so far, three regularly have second aorist passives: ἀποστέλλω — ἀπεστάλην; γράφω — ἐγράφην; ἐπιστρέφω — ἐπεστράφην. Except for the absence of the -θ, the second aorist passive is conjugated exactly like the first aorist passive: ἐγράφην, ἐγράφης, ἐγράφη, ἐγράφημεν, etc. (The verb ἀνοίγω does have a second aorist form ἠνοίγην, but the first aorist passive form of this verb predominates. Other common verbs in biblical Greek with second aorist passive forms include: κρύπτω, I conceal; σπείρω, I sow; and χαίρω, I rejoice.) Note: there is *no* connection between second aorist *active* and second aorist *passive!* That is, a verb with a second aorist active does *not* necessarily have a second aorist passive.

111. Forms of the Future Passive Indicative

The forms of the future passive indicative are as follows:

Singular	Plural
1. λυθήσομαι, I will be loosened	1. λυθησόμεθα, we will be loosened
2. λυθήσῃ, you (sing.) will be loosened	2. λυθήσεσθε, you (pl.) will be loosened
3. λυθήσεται, he, she, or it will be loosened	3. λυθήσονται, they will be loosened

The future passive indicative is built on the aorist passive stem. A -σ is suffixed to the -θη; then the primary middle endings are attached by means of the variable vowel (o or ε). Since the future is a primary tense, there is no augment. Thus, the future passive indicative resembles the future middle indicative except that its stem is that of the sixth principal part rather than the second.

112. The Aorist Passive Infinitive

The form of the aorist passive infinitive is λυθῆναι. Again, there is no augment because the augment only occurs in the indicative mood. The accent is not recessive; it will always be a circumflex over the eta in the penult. The future passive infinitive is exceedingly rare in biblical Greek; its form need not be learned.

113. Formation of the Aorist Passive

The formation of the aorist passive in regular verbs was described above, but as in the formation of the other principal parts, the combination of the tense suffix -θη with certain final consonants in the verb stem creates special cases. Before the -θη suffix, a final π or β becomes φ; a final κ or γ becomes χ; and a final τ, δ, or θ becomes σ. Stems ending in φ or χ remain unchanged. These rules are helpful, but just as the other principal parts are sometimes irregular and unpredictable, so is the aorist passive. Below is a list of aorist passive forms for reference. The list includes deponent forms, "functional" aorist passives, and second aorist passives.

θεραπεύω, I heal	ἐθεραπεύθην, I was healed
λύω, I loosen	ἐλύθην, I was loosened
πιστεύω, I believe	ἐπιστεύθην, I was entrusted with
πορεύομαι, I go	ἐπορεύθην, I went
ἀκούω, I hear	ἠκούσθην, I was heard
πέμπω, I send	ἐπέμφθην, I was sent
ἄγω, I lead	ἤχθην, I was led
ἀνοίγω, I open	ἠνεῴχθην, I was opened
διδάσκω, I teach	ἐδιδάχθην, I was taught
κηρύσσω, I preach	ἐκηρύχθην, I was preached
βαπτίζω, I baptize	ἐβαπτίσθην, I was baptized
δοξάζω, I glorify	ἐδοξάσθην, I was glorified
ἑτοιμάζω, I prepare	ἡτοιμάσθην, I was prepared
πείθω, I persuade	ἐπείσθην, I was persuaded

ἀποκρίνομαι, I answer   ἀπεκρίθην, I answered
βάλλω, I throw   ἐβλήθην, I was thrown
βλέπω, I see   ὤφθην, I was seen, appeared

γίνομαι, I become   ἐγενήθην, I became
γινώσκω, I know   ἐγνώσθην, I was known
ἐγείρω, I raise up   ἠγέρθην, I was raised
εὑρίσκω, I find   εὑρέθην, I was found
λαμβάνω, I take   ἐλήμφθην, I was taken
σῴζω, I save   ἐσώθην, I was saved
φέρω, I bring   ἠνέχθην, I was brought

ἀποστέλλω, I send   ἀπεστάλην, I was sent
γράφω, I write   ἐγράφην, I was written
ἐπιστρέφω, I return   ἐπεστράφην, I was returned

114. Exercises

Practice and Review

1. ὁ δοῦλος ἀπεκρίθη τῷ ἀνθρώπῳ, Ἀπεστάλην πρός σε ὑπὸ τοῦ κυρίου μου, ἀλλὰ οὐκ ἐλήμφθην εἰς τὸν οἶκόν σου.
2. ἤχθημεν εἰς τὴν ἔρημον φωνῇ ἐκ τῶν οὐρανῶν καὶ ἐκεῖ ὤφθη ἡμῖν ἄγγελος θεοῦ.
3. πῶς ἐγερθήσονται οἱ νεκροὶ καὶ πῶς ἐκβληθήσεται τὰ δαιμόνια ἐκ τῆς γῆς ταύτης;
4. ἡ ἀδελφὴ ὑμῶν ἐπορεύθη πρὸς τὸν λαὸν κηρύξαι τὴν ἀλήθειαν καὶ οἱ λόγοι αὐτῆς ἐγράφησαν ἐν βιβλίῳ.
5. ἐν τῷ ἱερῷ τόπος οὐκ εὑρέθη τοῖς τέκνοις, ἐνεχθήσονται οὖν εἰς τὸν οἶκον τοῦ διδασκάλου.
6. οὐκ ἐγνώσθη ὁ κακὸς τῷ προσώπῳ ταῖς ἐξουσίαις, οὕτως ἠδυνήθη πάλιν ἀπολυθῆναι.
7. καλὰ δῶρα προσηνέχθησαν τῷ προφήτῃ, ἀλλὰ ἤθελεν αὐτὰ πεμφθῆναι τοῖς τέκνοις.
8. ἐν τῇ ὥρᾳ ἐκείνῃ οἱ ὀφθαλμοὶ τοῦ υἱοῦ ἡμῶν ἐθεραπεύθησαν καὶ ἐπορεύθη εἰς τὴν ἐκκλησίαν δοξάσαι τὸν θεόν.
9. λίθοι ἐβλήθησαν εἰς τὰ πλοῖα, καὶ οἱ ὄχλοι ἐθαύμασαν ὅτι αὐτὰ οὐκ ἐλύθη.
10. ἐβαπτίσθητε ἐν τῇ θαλάσσῃ καὶ ἐδιδάχθητε τὴν ὁδόν, οὕτως δὲ ἐγενήθητε πιστοὶ μαθηταί.
11. ἡ ἀδελφὴ ἡμῶν ἐκρίθη ὑπὸ τῶν ἐξουσιῶν καὶ εὑρέθη πιστὴ ἐν ὅλῳ τῷ οἴκῳ αὐτῆς.

12. οἱ ἁμαρτωλοὶ ἀχθήσονται πρὸς τὸν θρόνον τῆς δικαιοσύνης, καὶ τὰ ἔργα αὐτῶν κατὰ τοῦ νόμου γνωσθήσονται.

13. πῶς σωθήσονται αἱ βασιλεῖαι τοῦ κόσμου τούτου ἐν τῇ ἐσχάτῃ ἡμέρᾳ;

14. ἄρτος καὶ οἶνος ἡτοιμάσθησαν τῷ ἀποστόλῳ, ἀλλὰ ἰδοὺ οὔτε ἔφαγεν οὔτε ἔπιεν.

LXX

1. οἱ δὲ υἱοὶ Ισραηλ ἐπορεύθησαν διὰ ξηρᾶς ἐν μέσῳ τῆς θαλάσσης (Exod 14:29)

2. αὕτη κληθήσεται γυνή, ὅτι ἐκ τοῦ ἀνδρὸς αὐτῆς ἐλήμφθη αὕτη. (Gen 2:23)

3. Οὔτε ἐγενήθη οὔτε ὤφθη οὕτως ἀπὸ τῆς ἡμέρας ἀναβάσεως υἱῶν Ισραηλ ἐξ Αἰγύπτου ἕως τῆς ἡμέρας ταύτης. (Judg 19:30)

4. τέκνα, . . . ἰσχύσατε ἐν τῷ νόμῳ, ὅτι ἐν αὐτῷ δοξασθήσεσθε. (1 Macc 2:64)

5. καὶ ἀπεκρίθη καὶ εἶπεν πρός με . . . Οὗτος ὁ λόγος κυρίου . . . (Zech 4:6)

6. καὶ εἶπεν Ησαιας πρὸς Εζεκιαν . . . Ἰδοὺ ἡμέραι ἔρχονται καὶ λημφθήσεται πάντα τὰ ἐν τῷ οἴκῳ σου . . . εἰς Βαβυλῶνα· (4 Kgdms 20:16-7)

7. καὶ ὤφθη κύριος τῷ Αβραμ καὶ εἶπεν αὐτῷ, Ἐγώ εἰμι ὁ θεός σου· (Gen 17:1)

8. οὐχ εὑρέθη ρομφαία καὶ δόρυ ἐν χειρὶ παντὸς τοῦ λαοῦ τοῦ μετὰ Σαουλ . . . , καὶ εὑρέθη τῷ Σαουλ καὶ τῷ Ιωναθαν υἱῷ αὐτοῦ. (1 Kgdms 13:22)

9. καὶ Δανιηλ ὁ δίκαιος εἰς λέοντας ἐβλήθη, καὶ Ανανιας καὶ Αζαριας καὶ Μισαηλ εἰς κάμινον πυρὸς . . . καὶ ὑπέμειναν διὰ τὸν θεόν. (4 Macc 16:21)

10. Καὶ ἀπεστάλη Ησαιας υἱὸς Αμως πρὸς Εζεκιαν καὶ εἶπεν αὐτῷ, Τάδε λέγει κύριος ὁ θεὸς Ισραηλ (Isa 37:21)

11. καὶ ἐν τέκνοις αὐτοῦ γνωσθήσεται ἀνήρ. (Sir 11:28)

NT

1. καὶ ἐξῆλθεν ἀπ' αὐτοῦ τὸ δαιμόνιον καὶ ἐθεραπεύθη ὁ παῖς ἀπὸ τῆς ὥρας ἐκείνης. (Matt 17:18)

2. Καὶ ἐγένετο ἐν ἐκείναις ταῖς ἡμέραις ἦλθεν Ἰησοῦς ἀπὸ Ναζαρὲτ τῆς Γαλιλαίας καὶ ἐβαπτίσθη εἰς τὸν Ἰορδάνην ὑπὸ Ἰωάννου. (Mark 1:9)

3. ἀπεκρίθη αὐτῷ Ναθαναήλ, Ῥαββί, σὺ εἶ ὁ υἱὸς τοῦ θεοῦ . . . (John 1:49)

4. Τότε ἔλεγεν αὐτοῖς, Ἐγερθήσεται ἔθνος ἐπ' ἔθνος καὶ βασιλεία ἐπὶ βασιλείαν (Luke 21:10)

5. καὶ ὁ δράκων ἐπολέμησεν καὶ οἱ ἄγγελοι αὐτοῦ, καὶ οὐκ ἴσχυσεν οὐδὲ τόπος εὑρέθη αὐτῶν ἔτι ἐν τῷ οὐρανῷ. καὶ ἐβλήθη ὁ δράκων . . . εἰς τὴν γῆν, καὶ οἱ ἄγγελοι αὐτοῦ μετ' αὐτοῦ ἐβλήθησαν. (Rev 12:7-9)

6. ἔλεγον οὖν αὐτῷ, Πῶς [οὖν] ἠνεῴχθησάν σου οἱ ὀφθαλμοί; (John 9:10)

7. ὄντως ἠγέρθη ὁ κύριος καὶ ὤφθη Σίμωνι. καὶ αὐτοὶ ἐξηγοῦντο τὰ ἐν τῇ ὁδῷ καὶ ὡς ἐγνώσθη αὐτοῖς ἐν τῇ κλάσει τοῦ ἄρτου. (Luke 24:34-35)

8. ὑμεῖς γὰρ μιμηταὶ ἐγενήθητε, ἀδελφοί, τῶν ἐκκλησιῶν τοῦ θεοῦ . . . ἐν τῇ Ἰουδαίᾳ ἐν Χριστῷ Ἰησοῦ (1 Thess 2:14)

9. ὤφθη ἀγγέλοις, ἐκηρύχθη ἐν ἔθνεσιν, ἐπιστεύθη ἐν κόσμῳ, ἀνελήμφθη ἐν δόξῃ. (1 Tim 3:16)

10. ἔλεγεν αὐτοῖς, Πῶς δύναται Σατανᾶς Σατανᾶν ἐκβάλλειν; (Mark 3:23)
11. Ἥξει δὲ ἡμέρα κυρίου ὡς κλέπτης, . . . στοιχεῖα δέ . . . λυθήσεται καὶ γῆ καὶ τὰ ἐν αὐτῇ ἔργα εὑρεθήσεται. (2 Pet 3:10)

English to Greek

1. In the hour of my death angels will appear and I will be taken to the throne of God.
2. A beautiful stone was found in the desert and was brought into the temple.
3. The prophet answered, "I was sent to teach the disciples, but I was cast out of the land by the authorities."
4. How will we be raised by God in the last day? And how will we be led into glory?

Vocabulary for LXX and NT Sentences

ἀναβάσεως, going up, expedition
ἀνδρὸς, man, husband
ἀνελήμφθη, from ἀνα (up) + λαμβάνω
ἀνήρ, a man
γυνή, woman
δόρυ, spear
δράκων, dragon
ἔθνεσιν, nations
ἔθνος, nation
ἐξηγοῦντο, they told, reported
ἐπολέμησεν, made war
ἕως, until
Ἥξει, will come
ἰσχύσατε, Be strong!
ἴσχυσεν, were strong, prevailed
κάμινον πυρὸς, furnace of fire
κλάσει, breaking

κλέπτης, thief
κληθήσεται, shall be called
λέοντας, lions
μέσῳ, middle
μιμηταὶ, imitators
ξηρᾶς, dry ground
ὄντως, truly
παῖς, child
πάντα, all things
παντὸς, all
ρομφαία, sword
στοιχεῖα, elements
Τάδε, these things, thus
ὑπέμειναν, they endured
χειρὶ, hand
ὡς, how

Lesson 17

115. Vocabulary

αἷμα, -ατος, τό, blood (hemo-)

αἰών, αἰῶνος, ὁ, age, world (eon)

ἀνήρ, ἀνδρός, ὁ, man, husband
(android, androgynous)

ἄρχων, ἄρχοντος, ὁ, ruler (monarch)

γυνή, γυναικός, ἡ, woman, wife
(gynecology, androgynous)

ἕως, until; (+ gen.) to, as far as, to the
point of, until

θέλημα, -ατος, τό, will

νύξ, νυκτός, ἡ, night (nocturnal)

ὄνομα, -ατος, τό, name (anonymous,
pseudonym)

πνεῦμα, -ατος, τό, spirit, Spirit
(pneumatic, pneumonia)

ῥῆμα, -ατος, τό, word (rhetoric)

σάρξ, σαρκός, ἡ, flesh (sarcophagus,
sarcasm)

σπέρμα, -ατος, τό, seed, offspring,
children (sperm)

στόμα, -ατος, τό, mouth (stomach)

σῶμα, -ατος, τό, body (somatic)

Note -αἰών often occurs in idioms: εἰς τὸν αἰῶνα (or τοὺς αἰῶνας), "forever"; εἰς τοὺς αἰῶνας τῶν αἰώνων, "forever and ever"; ἕως τοῦ αἰῶνος, "forever" (LXX).

116. The Third Declension

So far you have learned the first and second declensions in Greek. The first declension consisted mostly of feminine nouns such as ὥρα, δόξα, and γραφή, but there was also a group of masculine first declension nouns ending in -της such as μαθητής. The second declension consisted chiefly of masculine and neuter nouns such as λόγος and δῶρον, but there was also a group of feminine nouns in the second declension such as ὁδός.

   The third declension is the most difficult since it contains nouns of all three genders and several different groups and, therefore, presents the greatest variety. In this lesson you will be introduced to the basic endings and to two special groups of third declension nouns.

117. Basic Third Declension Endings

The basic third declension endings are the following:

	Singular			Plural	
Nom.	-ς or none		Nom.		-ες
Gen.	-ος		Gen.		-ων
Dat.	-ι		Dat.		-σι
Acc.	-α		Acc.		-ας
Voc.	-ς or none		Voc.		-ες

These endings are added to the noun stem, but the stem of a third declension noun cannot be determined from its nominative singular form. The stem usually can be found by removing the -ος from the genitive singular form. The following noun, ἄρχων, "ruler," is a good illustration of the basic third declension endings.

	Singular		Plural	
Nom.	ἄρχων	Nom.	ἄρχοντες
Gen.	ἄρχοντος	Gen.	ἀρχόντων
Dat.	ἄρχοντι	Dat.	ἄρχουσι(ν)
Acc.	ἄρχοντα	Acc.	ἄρχοντας
Voc.	ἄρχων	Voc.	ἄρχοντες

The stem of ἄρχων is ἀρχοντ-. Most of the declension is formed by adding the basic endings to this stem. The nominative and vocative singular are shortened forms, however, and the dative plural in particular presents a special situation. The combination of the dative plural ending -σι with the final letter(s) of the noun stem produces changes that generally follow the rules in §78. Here the -ντ- of the stem drops out before the -σι, and the stem vowel -ο- is lengthened to -ου-. Otherwise, the endings are quite regular. Two minor notes: the dative plural ending may take the movable ν, and the alpha in both the accusative singular and accusative plural endings is short (allowing the accent to remain on the antepenult).

Thus, the third declension has three special characteristics that the student should keep in mind. (1) The gender of a third declension noun cannot necessarily be known from the lexical form. (2) The stem cannot be known from the nominative singular, as was the case with the first and second declensions. Therefore, the genitive singular of a third declension noun will always be given in the vocabulary lists in addition to the lexical form. (3) The form of the dative plural varies because the sigma of the ending often interacts with the final letter(s) of the noun stem.

118. Monosyllabic Nouns of the Third Declension

Third declension nouns of one syllable have an irregular accent. In the genitive and dative of both numbers, the accent falls on the ultima even when the rule of noun accent would dictate otherwise. In the genitive plural, this accent will be a circumflex.

	Singular			Plural	
Nom.	σάρξ		Nom.	σάρκες
Gen.	σαρκός		Gen.	σαρκῶν
Dat.	σαρκί		Dat.	σαρξί(ν)
Acc.	σάρκα		Acc.	σάρκας
Voc.	σάρξ		Voc.	σάρκες

✒ 119. Neuter Nouns in -μα

Third declension nouns ending in -μα (whose true stems end in -ματ) form a special group. These nouns are always neuter. Like other neuter nouns they have identical forms in the nominative, vocative, and accusative of each number. Moreover, the nominative, vocative, and accusative plural forms always end in short alpha. Several common nouns in biblical Greek fall into this group.

	Singular			Plural	
Nom. Voc.	σῶμα		Nom. Voc.	σώματα
Gen.	σώματος		Gen.	σωμάτων
Dat.	σώματι		Dat.	σώμασι(ν)
Acc.	σῶμα		Acc.	σώματα

120. Exercises

Practice and Review

1. ἐκ τοῦ στόματος τοῦ διδασκάλου ἡμῶν ἐξέρχονται ταῦτα τὰ ῥήματα τῆς ζωῆς.
2. οὐ γινώσκομεν τὸ ὄνομα τοῦ ἀνδρὸς ἐκείνου, ἡ δὲ γυνὴ αὐτοῦ μέλλει λέγειν ὑπὲρ αὐτοῦ τοῖς ἄρχουσιν.
3. ἕως τὸ πνεῦμα ἔρχεται ἀπ' οὐρανοῦ, δεῖ κηρύσσειν τὸ θέλημα τοῦ θεοῦ ἐν τούτῳ τῷ πονηρῷ αἰῶνι.
4. ἐν ἐκείνῃ τῇ νυκτὶ γνώσεσθε ὅτι σὰρξ καὶ αἷμα οὐ δύναται σῶσαι ἄνθρωπον ἀφ' ἁμαρτίας.
5. τὰ ἔργα τῆς σαρκὸς οὐ δοξασθήσεται οὐδὲ ῥήματα δαιμονίου ἀκουσθήσεται ἐν τῇ ἐκκλησίᾳ.

6. ἐν τῷ ὀνόματι τοῦ ἀνδρὸς τῆς εἰρήνης ἐθέλομεν ἐγείρειν λίθον παρὰ τὴν ὁδόν.

7. ὁ πιστὸς ἄρχων τῆς γῆς ἐκείνης μέλλει ἀποθνήσκειν καὶ οὐκ ἔχει σπέρμα. ἀχθήσεται ὁ λαὸς τῷ πνεύματι;

8. νὺξ οὐκ ἔσται ἐν τῇ βασιλείᾳ δόξης καὶ συναχθησόμεθα περὶ τὸν θρόνον τοῦ θεοῦ εἰς τοὺς αἰῶνας τῶν αἰώνων.

9. ἔπεσεν ὁ δοῦλος ἐκ τοῦ πλοίου εἰς τὸ στόμα τῆς θαλάσσης καὶ οὐ πάλιν ὤφθη τὸ σῶμα αὐτοῦ.

10. τὸ αἷμα τοῦ δικαίου προφήτου ἔσται σπέρμα, καὶ ἡ βασιλεία τῆς δικαιοσύνης ὀφθήσεται.

11. ἀπεκρίθησαν αἱ γυναῖκες, Τὰ σώματα ἡμῶν ἤγγισαν ἕως θανάτου, ἀλλὰ ἦν τὸ θέλημα τοῦ κυρίου θεραπεῦσαι ἡμᾶς.

12. οὐκ ἐπιστεύσαμεν τοῖς ῥήμασι τοῦ ἀγγέλου, ἡ γὰρ ἀλήθεια οὐκ ἦν ἐν τῷ στόματι αὐτοῦ ἀλλὰ οἶνος.

13. αἷμα εὑρέθη ἐν τῷ στόματι τοῦ ἀνδρός, εἶπεν δὲ ἡ γυνὴ αὐτοῦ τοῖς ἄρχουσιν ὅτι αὐτὸς ἀπέθανεν ἐν τῇ νυκτὶ καὶ αὐτὴ οὐκ ἦν ἐκεῖ.

14. ἑωράκαμεν τὸ σημεῖον τοῦ πνεύματος καὶ ἐγνώκαμεν τὸ ὄνομα τοῦ ἁγίου τοῦ θεοῦ.

LXX

1. καὶ εἶπα τοῖς υἱοῖς Ισραηλ, Αἷμα πάσης σαρκὸς οὐ φάγεσθε, ὅτι ἡ ψυχὴ πάσης σαρκὸς αἷμα αὐτοῦ ἐστιν· (Lev 17:14)

2. Γυναικὸς ἀγαθῆς μακάριος ὁ ἀνήρ, . . . γυνὴ ἀνδρεία εὐφραίνει τὸν ἄνδρα αὐτῆς (Sir 26:1-2)

3. καὶ ὤφθη αὐτῷ κύριος ἐν τῇ νυκτὶ ἐκείνῃ καὶ εἶπεν, Ἐγώ εἰμι ὁ θεὸς Αβρααμ τοῦ πατρός σου· (Gen 26:24)

4. ἐξομολογήσομαί σοι, κύριε ὁ θεός μου, ἐν ὅλῃ καρδίᾳ μου καὶ δοξάσω τὸ ὄνομά σου εἰς τὸν αἰῶνα (Ps 85:12, ET 86:12)

5. ἐγνώρισεν τὰς ὁδοὺς αὐτοῦ τῷ Μωυσῇ, τοῖς υἱοῖς Ισραηλ τὰ θελήματα αὐτοῦ. (Ps 102:7, ET 103:7)

6. καὶ ἤκουσεν τὰ ῥήματα τοῦ λαοῦ τὰ πονηρὰ ἐπὶ τὸν ἄρχοντα (Judith 8:9)

7. καὶ ἐπορεύθησαν ὅλην τὴν νύκτα καὶ ἔλαβον τὸ σῶμα Σαουλ καὶ τὸ σῶμα Ιωναθαν τοῦ υἱοῦ αὐτοῦ ἀπὸ τείχους Βαιθσαν (1 Kgdms 31:12)

8. καὶ ἐρεῖς πρὸς αὐτὸν καὶ δώσεις τὰ ῥήματά μου εἰς τὸ στόμα αὐτοῦ· καὶ ἐγὼ ἀνοίξω τὸ στόμα σου καὶ τὸ στόμα αὐτοῦ (Exod 4:15)

9. καὶ ὤφθη κύριος τῷ Αβραμ καὶ εἶπεν αὐτῷ, Τῷ σπέρματί σου δώσω τὴν γῆν ταύτην. (Gen 12:7)

10. καὶ ἔσονται οἱ λίθοι οὗτοι ὑμῖν μνημόσυνον τοῖς υἱοῖς Ισραηλ ἕως τοῦ αἰῶνος. (Josh 4:7)

11. ἐπιθήσω τὸ πνεῦμά μου ἐπὶ τὸ σπέρμα σου καὶ τὰς εὐλογίας μου ἐπὶ τὰ τέκνα σου (Isa 44:3)

NT

1. ὅτε . . . ἐπίστευσαν τῷ Φιλίππῳ . . . περὶ τῆς βασιλείας τοῦ θεοῦ καὶ τοῦ ὀνόματος Ἰησοῦ Χριστοῦ, ἐβαπτίζοντο ἄνδρες τε καὶ γυναῖκες. (Acts 8:12)
2. νῦν ὁ ἄρχων τοῦ κόσμου τούτου ἐκβληθήσεται ἔξω· (John 12:31)
3. πᾶσα σὰρξ ὡς χόρτος . . . τὸ δὲ ῥῆμα κυρίου μένει εἰς τὸν αἰῶνα. (1 Pet 1:24-5)
4. Τοῦτο δέ φημι, ἀδελφοί, ὅτι σὰρξ καὶ αἷμα βασιλείαν θεοῦ κληρονομῆσαι οὐ δύναται (1 Cor 15:50)
5. Ἐγγύς σου τὸ ῥῆμά ἐστιν ἐν τῷ στόματί σου καὶ ἐν τῇ καρδίᾳ σου, τοῦτ᾽ ἔστιν τὸ ῥῆμα τῆς πίστεως ὃ κηρύσσομεν. (Rom 10:8)
6. εἶπεν, Ὁ σπείρων τὸ καλὸν σπέρμα ἐστὶν ὁ υἱὸς τοῦ ἀνθρώπου, . . . τὸ δὲ καλὸν σπέρμα οὗτοί εἰσιν οἱ υἱοὶ τῆς βασιλείας· (Matt 13:37-38)
7. ὥσπερ γὰρ τὸ σῶμα χωρὶς πνεύματος νεκρόν ἐστιν, οὕτως καὶ ἡ πίστις χωρὶς ἔργων νεκρά ἐστιν. (Jas 2:26)
8. τὸ γὰρ φρόνημα τῆς σαρκὸς θάνατος, τὸ δὲ φρόνημα τοῦ πνεύματος ζωὴ καὶ εἰρήνη· . . . ὑμεῖς δὲ οὐκ ἐστὲ ἐν σαρκὶ ἀλλὰ ἐν πνεύματι, εἴπερ πνεῦμα θεοῦ οἰκεῖ ἐν ὑμῖν. εἰ δέ τις πνεῦμα Χριστοῦ οὐκ ἔχει, οὗτος οὐκ ἔστιν αὐτοῦ. εἰ δὲ Χριστὸς ἐν ὑμῖν, τὸ μὲν σῶμα νεκρὸν διὰ ἁμαρτίαν τὸ δὲ πνεῦμα ζωὴ διὰ δικαιοσύνην. (Rom 8:6, 9-10)
9. καὶ ὁ κόσμος παράγεται καὶ ἡ ἐπιθυμία αὐτοῦ, ὁ δὲ ποιῶν τὸ θέλημα τοῦ θεοῦ μένει εἰς τὸν αἰῶνα. (1 John 2:17)
10. καὶ ὁ διάβολος . . . καὶ τὸ θηρίον καὶ ὁ ψευδοπροφήτης . . . βασανισθήσονται ἡμέρας καὶ νυκτὸς εἰς τοὺς αἰῶνας τῶν αἰώνων. (Rev 20:10)

English to Greek

1. We are able to see flesh and blood, but we draw near to the Spirit in our hearts.
2. These men and these women do not know the will of God nor the name of his prophet.
3. The ruler said that you (pl.) ought to scatter (cast) seeds until the night comes.
4. The body of the child was healed, and now words of life come forth from her mouth.

Vocabulary for LXX and NT Sentences

(Beginning with this lesson, the lexical form of a word will usually be given in these lists instead of the exact form appearing in the above sentences. Moreover, words that you should be able to determine from context or other clues may be omitted.)

ἀνδρεία, courageous, strong
βασανίζω, torture, torment
γνωρίζω, make known
διάβολος, devil
δώσεις, you will give
δώσω, I will give
ἐγγύς, near
εἶπα = εἶπον
εἴπερ, if indeed
ἐξομολογέω, praise
ἔξω, out
ἐπιθήσω, I will put (on)
ἐπιθυμία, lust
ἐρεῖς, you will say
εὐλογία, blessing
εὐφραίνω, gladden, cheer
θηρίον, beast
κληρόνομέω, inherit
μακάριος, blessed, happy

μνημόσυνον, memorial
ὅ, which
οἰκέω, dwell
ὅτε, when
παράγεται, passes away
πᾶς, πάντος, etc., all
πατήρ, πατρός, father
πίστις, faith
ποιῶν, (one) doing
σπείρων, (one) sowing
τεῖχος, τείχους, wall
τις, someone, anyone
φημι = λέγω
φρόνημα, mind
χόρτος, grass
χωρὶς, without
ὡς, like
ὥσπερ, just as

Lesson 18

121. Vocabulary

ἁμαρτάνω, I sin (hamartiology)
βούλομαι, (dep.) I wish, want
διώκω, I persecute, pursue
ἐργάζομαι, (dep.) I work, do (energy)
εὐαγγελίζομαι, (usu. dep.) I bring good
   news, preach (evangelize)
κάθημαι, (dep.) I sit, live, stay

λογίζομαι, (dep.) I reckon, consider
μή, not (the usual negative for nonindicative moods)
ὑπάρχω, I am, exist (τὰ ὑπάρχοντα,
   possessions, belongings)
ὤν, οὖσα, ὄν, being (present participle
   of εἰμί) (ontology)

122. Introduction to Participles

A participle is a *verbal adjective.* As such, it has characteristics of both verbs and adjectives. Like a verb, a participle expresses an action (or a state of being) and has tense and voice. Like an adjective, a participle is related to a noun or pronoun, with which it agrees in case, number, and gender. In this lesson you will learn the forms of present tense participles. In later lessons you will be introduced to aorist and perfect participles.

    The participle's nature as a verbal adjective is also seen in its many functions. Sometimes its function is primarily *adverbial,* in which case the participle denotes action that is in some way related to the action of another verb. Example: "We removed the dead tree, cutting it down with a saw." In this case, the participle "cutting" expresses the means by which the tree was removed. But a participle's function may also be primarily *adjectival,* in which case it gives information about the noun or pronoun with which it agrees. Example: "Who is that person over there cutting down the dead tree?" In this sentence, "cutting" gives a verbal description of the person.

123. Forms of the Present Active Participle

Here are the forms of the present active participle of λύω, "loosening."

	Masculine	Singular Feminine	Neuter
Nom. Voc.	λύων	λύουσα	λῦον
Gen.	λύοντος	λυούσης	λύοντος
Dat.	λύοντι	λυούσῃ	λύοντι
Acc.	λύοντα	λύουσαν	λῦον

102

	Masculine	Plural Feminine	Neuter
Nom. Voc.	λύοντες	λύουσαι	λύοντα
Gen.	λυόντων	λυουσῶν	λυόντων
Dat.	λύουσι(ν)	λυούσαις	λύουσι(ν)
Acc.	λύοντας	λυούσας	λύοντα

The endings of the participle should be familiar. The masculine and neuter are declined according to the third declension; the feminine follows the pattern of the first declension noun δόξα. A few minor observations: (1) the masculine and neuter dative plural forms may take the movable ν, just as the dative plural of third declension nouns may; (2) the feminine genitive plural takes the circumflex accent on the ultima, just as the same form of a first declension noun does; and (3) the accent of participles, strictly speaking, is not recessive, but rather retentive. None of the forms of λύω makes this evident, but consider the nominative singular neuter participle of πιστεύω: πιστεῦον. The accent is retained on the syllable on which the lexical form is accented.

124. Forms of the Present Middle/Passive Participle

Here are the forms of the present middle/passive participle of λύω, "being loosened."

	Masculine	Singular Feminine	Neuter
Nom. Voc.	λυόμενος	λυομένη	λυόμενον
Gen.	λυομένου	λυομένης	λυομένου
Dat.	λυομένῳ	λυομένη	λυομένῳ
Acc.	λυόμενον	λυομένην	λυόμενον

	Masculine	Plural Feminine	Neuter
Nom. Voc.	λυόμενοι	λυόμεναι	λυόμενα
Gen.	λυομένων	λυομένων	λυομένων
Dat.	λυομένοις	λυομέναις	λυομένοις
Acc.	λυομένους	λυομένας	λυόμενα

Again, the endings should be familiar. The masculine and neuter are declined like second declension nouns; cf. λόγος and ἔργον. The feminine is declined according to the first declension; cf. ἀγάπη. Middle and passive participles use identical forms in the present tense. The chief indicator of a present middle/passive participle is the morpheme -μεν-.

125. Syntax of the Participle

A participle may occur in any of the positions described in §30: attributive, substantive, or predicate. The presence (or absence) and position of the definite article will usually make it clear which construction is being used. A participle in an attributive or substantive construction (indicated by a preceding definite article) will have an *adjectival* function in the sentence. A participle in a predicate construction (lacking the definite article) will usually have an *adverbial* function in the sentence.

Adjectival Participles. A participle in the *attributive* position will identify or describe the noun or pronoun with which it agrees in case, number, and gender. This construction may take the form of either of the two alternatives learned earlier for an attributive adjective. Examples:

ὁ πιστεύων ἀνήρ or ὁ ἀνὴρ ὁ πιστεύων = "The believing man"
ἡ προσευχομένη γυνή or ἡ γυνὴ ἡ προσευχομένη = "The praying woman"
τὸ ἐσθίον τέκνον or τὸ τέκνον τὸ ἐσθίον = "The eating child"

An English translation using the -ing form is only provisional. A smoother translation of an attributive participle will use a relative clause introduced with "who" or "that." For example, "the man who believes," "the woman who prays," and "the child who eats." Since the participle is based on a verb, it may have any kind of modifier that the corresponding verb in the indicative might have: an adverb, a prepositional phrase, a direct object, etc. Examples:

ὁ πιστεύων εἰς τὸν κύριον ἀνήρ = "The man who believes in the Lord"
ἡ πολλάκις προσευχομένη γυνή = "The woman who often prays"
τὸ ἐσθίον ἄρτον τέκνον = "The child who eats bread"

Another adjectival use of the participle is the *substantive* use. Here the participle does not modify a noun, but stands in the place of a noun. It functions as a substantive. A substantive participle will usually have the definite article. The presence of the article and the absence of a noun are clear indications of the substantive use, but in rare cases the article may be lacking. The number and gender of a substantive participle are clues to its translation. Examples:

οἱ πιστεύοντες = "The believing ones," "The men, the ones who believe"
ἡ βαπτιζομένη = "The woman who is being baptized"
τὰ μέλλοντα = "The things about to be," "Things to come"

Adverbial Participles. A participle in the *predicate* position will agree with the noun it modifies in case, number, and gender, but its chief function is to modify another verb in the sentence, usually the main verb. It does this by denoting some circumstance in relation to which the action of the main verb takes place. For example: λέγων τῷ ὄχλῳ ὁ προφήτης εἶδεν ἄγγελον, "Speaking to the crowd, the prophet saw an angel." Here the action of "speaking" modifies the action of the main verb "he saw." The function of this particular participle might be temporal, that is, it might answer the question, *When* did the prophet see an angel? If so, one could translate: "*While* he was speaking to the crowd, the prophet saw an angel." Translating a participle thus involves a certain amount of interpretation. In a later lesson you will learn some of the finer nuances of the adverbial participle. For now, you may use the provisional translation "Speaking to the crowd . . ." or, if it seems suitable, the temporal translation "While he was speaking. . . ." Here are further examples of adverbial participles.

καταβαίνων πρὸς τὴν θάλασσαν ὁ ἀνὴρ ἔφερεν πλοῖον.
"(While he was) going down to the sea, the man was carrying a boat."

εἴδομεν τὴν γυναῖκα ἐσθίουσαν ἄρτον μετὰ τῶν τέκνων.
"We saw the woman (as she was) eating bread with the children."

μὴ βλέποντα τοὺς λίθους τὰ τέκνα ἔπεσον εἰς τὴν ὁδόν.
"Not seeing the stones, the children fell on the road," or perhaps, "Because they did not see. . . ."

126. Tense and Time in the Participle

The tense of a participle has nothing to do with the time of the action, but only with the "kind" of action. A present tense participle does not necessarily denote action occurring in present time; it denotes linear or ongoing action. In actual practice, present participles *usually* denote action simultaneous with that of the main verb, but this tendency derives from context, not from the nature of the tense. The participle is fundamentally *non*temporal. *(IN PRACTICE, IT IS USUALLY TEMPORAL IN ENGLISH)*

127. The Present Participle of εἰμί

The forms of the present participle of εἰμί, "being," are as follows:

		Singular	
	Masculine	Feminine	Neuter
Nom. Voc.	ὤν	οὖσα	ὄν
Gen.	ὄντος	οὔσης	ὄντος
Dat.	ὄντι	οὔσῃ	ὄντι
Acc.	ὄντα	οὖσαν	ὄν

(SAME AS ENDINGS FOR PARTICIPLES)

Lesson 18

	Masculine	Plural Feminine	Neuter
Nom. Voc.	ὄντες	οὖσαι	ὄντα
Gen.	ὄντων	οὐσῶν	ὄντων
Dat.	οὖσι(ν)	οὔσαις	οὖσι(ν)
Acc.	ὄντας	οὔσας	ὄντα

Note that, except for accent and breathing marks, the forms of the participle of εἰμί are simply the endings of the present active participle.

128. Exercises

Practice and Review

1. πιστὸς μαθητὴς ὢν οὐκ ἁμαρτάνω εἰς τὸν κύριον οὐδὲ διώκω τοὺς δικαίους.
2. ὁ καθήμενος ἐπὶ τοῦ θρόνου γινώσκει τὰς καρδίας τῶν ἁμαρτωλῶν καὶ λογίζεται τὰς ἁμαρτίας αὐτοῖς.
3. τότε οἱ ἀπόστολοι διήρχοντο διὰ τῆς γῆς κηρύσσοντες καὶ εὐαγγελιζόμενοι τῷ λαῷ.
4. τὰ ὑπάρχοντά σου οὐκ ἔστιν ἡ ζωή σου, οὐ δεῖ οὖν ἔχειν οἴκους καλοὺς καὶ ἱμάτια καὶ δῶρα.
5. εἰ λέγομεν ὅτι οὐχ ἡμαρτήκαμεν, οὐ δυνησόμεθα ἐγγίσαι εἰς τὸν θρόνον τῆς ζωῆς, μὴ λέγοντες ῥήματα τῆς ἀληθείας.
6. καθήμενοι ἐπὶ λίθῳ παρὰ τὸν οἶκον ὑμῶν, πολλάκις ἠνοίγετε τὸ βιβλίον τοῦ νόμου.
7. ὁ πιστεύων θεῷ καὶ ἐργαζόμενος δικαιοσύνην ἀχθήσεται εἰς τὸν οὐρανόν.
8. ἀποθνῄσκουσα ἐν τῇ ἐρήμῳ ἡ γυνὴ ἔκραξε τῷ θεῷ τῷ βλέποντι καὶ θεραπεύοντι τὰ τέκνα αὐτοῦ.
9. ὁ κύριος τῆς δόξης οὐκ ἐγγίσει τῷ ἐργαζομένῳ ἔργα τοῦ νόμου ἀλλὰ τῷ πιστεύοντι εἰς τὸν θεὸν τὸν σῴζοντα ἁμαρτωλούς.
10. εἰ ὑμεῖς πονηροὶ ὄντες βούλεσθε πέμψαι ἀγαθὰ τοῖς τέκνοις ὑμῶν, ὁ θεὸς οὐ πέμψει ἀγαθὰ ὑμῖν;
11. οἱ βουλόμενοι εὑρίσκειν τὴν εἰρήνην ὀφείλουσι δέχεσθαι εἰς τοὺς οἴκους αὐτῶν τοὺς πορευομένους διὰ τῆς γῆς.
12. πῶς ἀγαθόν ἐστιν ἀκοῦσαι τοὺς λόγους τῶν εὐαγγελιζομένων προφητῶν.
13. ὑπάρχοντες ἄνθρωποι τοῦ πνεύματος ἐλογιζόμεθα ὅτι καὶ ἐκ νεκρῶν ἐγείρειν δύναται ὁ θεὸς ἡμᾶς.
14. ἄγγελοι ἤνεγκαν ἄρτον πρὸς τὰς διωκομένας ἀδελφὰς ὑπὸ τῶν ἐξουσιῶν.

LXX

1. ὁ ἐργαζόμενος τὴν . . . γῆν πλησθήσεται ἄρτων, ὁ δὲ διώκων σχολὴν πλησθήσεται πενίας. (Prov 28:19)

2. ἐπίστευσεν Αβραμ τῷ θεῷ, καὶ ἐλογίσθη αὐτῷ εἰς δικαιοσύνην. (Gen 15:6)

3. Κύριε ὁ θεός μου, ἐπὶ σοὶ ἤλπισα· σῶσόν με ἐκ πάντων τῶν διωκόντων με (Ps 7:2, ET 7:1)

4. ἡ δὲ ψυχὴ ἡ ἁμαρτάνουσα ἀποθανεῖται· ὁ δὲ υἱὸς οὐ λήμψεται τὴν ἀδικίαν τοῦ πατρὸς αὐτοῦ, οὐδὲ ὁ πατὴρ λήμψεται τὴν ἀδικίαν τοῦ υἱοῦ αὐτοῦ· (Ezek 18:20)

5. εἶπεν δέ . . . ἕξει υἱὸν Σαρρα ἡ γυνή σου. Σαρρα δὲ ἤκουσεν πρὸς τῇ θύρᾳ τῆς σκηνῆς, οὖσα ὄπισθεν αὐτοῦ. . . . ἐγέλασεν δὲ Σαρρα . . . λέγουσα, Οὔπω . . . μοι γέγονεν (Gen 18:10, 12)

6. Μακάριοι . . . οἱ πορευόμενοι ἐν νόμῳ κυρίου. . . . οὐ γὰρ οἱ ἐργαζόμενοι τὴν ἀνομίαν ἐν ταῖς ὁδοῖς αὐτοῦ ἐπορεύθησαν. (Ps 118:1, 3, ET 119:1, 3)

7. ἡμάρτοσαν αὐτῷ καὶ οὐκ ἐβούλοντο ἐν ταῖς ὁδοῖς αὐτοῦ πορεύεσθαι οὐδὲ ἀκούειν τοῦ νόμου αὐτοῦ (Isa 42:24)

8. τὸν ἁμαρτάνοντα εἰς τὴν ψυχὴν αὐτοῦ τίς δικαιώσει; καὶ τίς δοξάσει τὸν ἀτιμάζοντα τὴν ζωὴν αὐτοῦ; (Sir 10:29)

9. καὶ ἔλαβεν Αβραμ τὴν Σαραν γυναῖκα αὐτοῦ καὶ τὸν Λωτ υἱὸν τοῦ ἀδελφοῦ αὐτοῦ καὶ πάντα τὰ ὑπάρχοντα αὐτῶν (Gen 12:5)

10. Ἰδοὺ ἐπὶ τὰ ὄρη οἱ πόδες εὐαγγελιζομένου καὶ ἀπαγγέλλοντος εἰρήνην· (Nah 2:1, ET 1:15)

11. καὶ ἔσται τὰ ῥήματα ταῦτα . . . ἐν τῇ καρδίᾳ σου καὶ ἐν τῇ ψυχῇ σου· καὶ προβιβάσεις αὐτὰ τοὺς υἱούς σου . . . καθήμενος ἐν οἴκῳ καὶ πορευόμενος ἐν ὁδῷ (Deut 6:6-7)

NT

1. καὶ κράζουσιν φωνῇ μεγάλῃ λέγοντες, Ἡ σωτηρία τῷ θεῷ ἡμῶν τῷ καθημένῳ ἐπὶ τῷ θρόνῳ (Rev 7:10)

2. θεὸς ἦν ἐν Χριστῷ κόσμον καταλλάσσων ἑαυτῷ, μὴ λογιζόμενος αὐτοῖς τὰ παραπτώματα αὐτῶν (2 Cor 5:19)

3. Ἰωσὴφ δὲ ὁ ἀνὴρ αὐτῆς, δίκαιος ὢν καὶ μὴ θέλων αὐτὴν δειγματίσαι, ἐβουλήθη λάθρα ἀπολῦσαι αὐτήν. (Matt 1:19)

4. Καὶ ἰδοὺ ἀνὴρ ὀνόματι Ἰωσὴφ βουλευτὴς ὑπάρχων [καὶ] ἀνὴρ ἀγαθὸς καὶ δίκαιος . . . ᾐτήσατο τὸ σῶμα τοῦ Ἰησοῦ (Luke 23:50-52)

5. δόξα δὲ καὶ τιμὴ καὶ εἰρήνη παντὶ τῷ ἐργαζομένῳ τὸ ἀγαθόν, Ἰουδαίῳ τε πρῶτον καὶ Ἕλληνι· (Rom 2:10)

6. ἐξερχόμενοι δὲ διήρχοντο . . . τὰς κώμας εὐαγγελιζόμενοι καὶ θεραπεύοντες (Luke 9:6)

7. καὶ μὴ εὑροῦσαι τὸ σῶμα αὐτοῦ ἦλθον λέγουσαι καὶ ὀπτασίαν ἀγγέλων ἑωρακέναι (Luke 24:23)

8. οὗτός ἐστιν ὁ ἄρτος ὁ ἐκ τοῦ οὐρανοῦ καταβαίνων (John 6:50)

9. ἀκούοντες ἦσαν ὅτι Ὁ διώκων ἡμᾶς ποτε νῦν εὐαγγελίζεται τὴν πίστιν . . .
   καὶ ἐδόξαζον ἐν ἐμοὶ τὸν θεόν. (Gal 1:23-4)

10. Οἱ οὖν ἄνθρωποι . . . ἔλεγον . . . Οὗτός ἐστιν ἀληθῶς ὁ προφήτης ὁ
    ἐρχόμενος εἰς τὸν κόσμον. (John 6:14)

11. οὕτως δὲ ἁμαρτάνοντες εἰς τοὺς ἀδελφοὺς καὶ τύπτοντες αὐτῶν τὴν
    συνείδησιν . . . εἰς Χριστὸν ἁμαρτάνετε. (1 Cor 8:12)

English to Greek

1. Trusting in God, we are bringing good news to the sinners who are
   persecuting us.
2. Not wishing to hear the prophet's words, you (pl.) took your possessions and
   went to your house.
3. Those who sit in the house and pray must also do good works to their
   brothers and sisters.
4. (Since he was) not reckoning that God saw him, the man who was sinning
   against the law came into the temple.

Vocabulary for LXX and NT Sentences

ἀδικία, (penalty for the) wickedness

ἀληθῶς, truly

ἀνομία, lawlessness

ἀπαγγέλλω, announce

ἀποθανεῖται, fut. of ἀποθνήσκω

ἀτιμάζω, dishonor

βουλευτής, council member

γελάω, laugh

δειγματίζω, disgrace, expose

δικαιόω, justify

ἑαυτῷ, to himself

ἤλπισα, from ἐλπίζω, I hope

ᾐτήσατο, asked for

θύρα, door

καταλλάσσω, reconcile

κώμη, village

λάθρᾳ, secretly

ὄπισθεν, behind (+ genitive)

ὀπτασία, vision

ὄρη, mountains

μακάριος, blessed

μέγας, μεγάλη, μέγα, great, loud

παράπτωμα = ἁμαρτία

πᾶς, πᾶσα, πᾶν, all, every

πατήρ, πατρός, father

πενία, poverty

πίστις, faith

πλησθήσεται, will be filled with

πόδες, feet

ποτε, formerly

προβιβάζω = διδάσκω

σκηνή, tent

συνείδησις, conscience

σχολή, leisure

σῶσον, imperative of σῴζω

σωτηρία, salvation

τιμή, honor

τίς, who?

τύπτω, beat, wound

Lesson 19

129. Vocabulary

ἀσπάζομαι, I greet, salute
καθίζω, I sit; seat (trans.) (cathedral)
μήτηρ, μητρός, ἡ, mother (maternal)
παραγίνομαι, I come, arrive
παραλαμβάνω, I receive, take along

πατήρ, πατρός, ὁ, father (paternal)
πούς, ποδός, ὁ, foot (podiatry)
σάββατον, τό, Sabbath
συναγωγή, ἡ, synagogue, gathering
χείρ, χειρός, ἡ, hand (chiropractic)

130. Aorist Active Participles

The declension of the aorist active participle λύσας, λύσασα, λῦσαν, "having loosened," is as follows: *—ALPHA DOMINATES*

STEM — ADD SIGMA; FOLLOWS WEAK AORIST PARADIGM (BUT NO EPSILON)

Singular

	Masculine	Feminine	Neuter
Nom. Voc.	λύσας	λύσασα	λῦσαν
Gen.	λύσαντος	λυσάσης	λύσαντος
Dat.	λύσαντι	λυσάσῃ	λύσαντι
Acc.	λύσαντα	λύσασαν	λῦσαν

SAME AS MASC.

Plural

	Masculine	Feminine	Neuter
Nom. Voc.	λύσαντες	λύσασαι	λύσαντα
Gen.	λυσάντων	λυσασῶν	λυσάντων
Dat.	λύσασι(ν)	λυσάσαις	λύσασι(ν)
Acc.	λύσαντας	λυσάσας	λύσαντα

SAME AS MASC.

131. Aorist Middle Participles

The declension of the aorist middle participle λυσάμενος, λυσαμένη, λυσάμενον, is as follows:

	Singular		
	Masculine	Feminine	Neuter
Nom. Voc.	λυσάμενος	λυσαμένη	λυσάμενον
Gen.	λυσαμένου	λυσαμένης	λυσαμένου
Dat.	λυσαμένῳ	λυσαμένῃ	λυσαμένῳ
Acc.	λυσάμενον	λυσαμένην	λυσάμενον

	Plural		
	Masculine	Feminine	Neuter
Nom. Voc.	λυσάμενοι	λυσάμεναι	λυσάμενα
Gen.	λυσαμένων	λυσαμένων	λυσαμένων
Dat.	λυσαμένοις	λυσαμέναις	λυσαμένοις
Acc.	λυσαμένους	λυσαμένας	λυσάμενα

Aorist active and middle participles are built on the third principal part. The -σα-tense indicator is found throughout both declensions (for regular verbs). The aorist active participle is declined according to the third declension in the masculine and neuter, and according to the first declension in the feminine. The aorist middle participle has the morpheme -μεν- throughout. It is declined according to the second declension in the masculine and neuter, and according to the first declension in the feminine. Note that there is *no* augment; the augment only occurs in the indicative. Thus, when an aorist indicative form begins with a lengthened vowel or diphthong, the beginning of the corresponding aorist participle will revert to its original length. Example: ἀνοίγω, "I open"; ἤνοιξα, "I opened"; ἀνοίξας, "having opened."

132. Second Aorist Active Participles

The declension of the second aorist active participle ἰδών, ἰδοῦσα, ἰδόν, "having seen," (from εἶδον, the "functional" third principal part of βλέπω) is as follows:

	Singular		
	Masculine	Feminine	Neuter
Nom. Voc.	ἰδών	ἰδοῦσα	ἰδόν
Gen.	ἰδόντος	ἰδούσης	ἰδόντος
Dat.	ἰδόντι	ἰδούσῃ	ἰδόντι
Acc.	ἰδόντα	ἰδοῦσαν	ἰδόν

	Masculine	Plural Feminine	Neuter
Nom. Voc.	ἰδόντες	ἰδοῦσαι	ἰδόντα
Gen.	ἰδόντων	ἰδουσῶν	ἰδόντων
Dat.	ἰδοῦσι(ν)	ἰδούσαις	ἰδοῦσι(ν)
Acc.	ἰδόντας	ἰδούσας	ἰδόντα

Note that the endings of the second aorist participle are identical to those of the present participle, except for the accent. The accent of the second aorist active participle is *not* recessive. (Note its position in the nominative singular masculine.) Here are a few of the more common second aorist active participles with their first and third principal parts:

ἄγω, I lead	ἤγαγον, I led	ἀγαγών, having led
βλέπω, I see	εἶδον, I saw	ἰδών, having seen
ἔρχομαι, I come	ἦλθον, I came	ἐλθών, having come
λαμβάνω, I take	ἔλαβον, I took	λαβών, having taken
λέγω, I say	εἶπον, I said	εἰπών, having said

On the peculiar shortening of the augmented syllable εἶ- in the formation of the participles ἰδών and εἰπών, see §94.

133. Second Aorist Middle Participles

The forms of the second aorist middle (or deponent) participle are similar to the those of the present middle/passive participle. The only difference is the stem on which they are constructed. Example: γίνομαι, "I become"; ἐγενόμην, "I became"; γενόμενος, "having become." Note that this particular second aorist participle differs from the corresponding present participle by a single letter: γε̱νόμενος vs. γι̱νόμενος. The declension of the second aorist middle (deponent) participle of γίνομαι is as follows:

	Masculine	Singular Feminine	Neuter
Nom. Voc.	γενόμενος	γενομένη	γενόμενον
Gen.	γενομένου	γενομένης	γενομένου
Dat.	γενομένῳ	γενομένῃ	γενομένῳ
Acc.	γενόμενον	γενομένην	γενόμενον

	Masculine	Plural Feminine	Neuter
Nom. Voc.	γενόμενοι	γενόμεναι	γενόμενα
Gen.	γενομένων	γενομένων	γενομένων
Dat.	γενομένοις	γενομέναις	γενομένοις
Acc.	γενομένους	γενομένας	γενόμενα

134. Syntax of the Aorist Participle

The syntax of aorist tense participles is the same as that of present tense participles. They have the same adjectival and adverbial functions, and occur in the same attributive, substantive, and predicate constructions. Like all participles, the aorist participle does not denote any particular *time* of action. The tense denotes simple or undefined action. In actual practice, an aorist tense participle often expresses action that is *prior to* the action of the main verb. It is not unusual, however, for an aorist tense participle to denote action *simultaneous* with that of the main verb. For now, attributive and substantive participles should be translated with a relative clause ("the one who/the thing which did/had done, etc."), and adverbial participles either with a provisional English participle ("having done such and such") or a temporal clause if this seems suitable ("When or after he/she had done such and such"). Examples:

εἰπὼν ταῦτα τὰ ῥήματα ὁ προφήτης ἐξῆλθεν ἐκ τοῦ ἱεροῦ.
When he had said these words, the prophet went out of the temple.

ἐφύγομεν ἀπὸ τῶν ἀνδρῶν ἐκείνων λαβόντων πνεῦμα πονηρόν.
We fled from those men [for] they had received an evil spirit.

ἀσπασαμένη τὴν ἐκκλησίαν ἡ μήτηρ μου ἤρξατο εὐαγγελίσασθαι.
After she greeted the church, my mother began to preach good news.

ἡ γυνὴ ἡ διδάξασα τὰ τέκνα ἤγαγεν αὐτὰ εἰς τὸν οἶκον.
The woman who (had) taught the children led them into the house.

ὀφείλομεν προσεύχεσθαι ὑπὲρ τῶν ἁμαρτησάντων εἰς τὸν κύριον.
We ought to pray for those who have sinned against the Lord.

οἱ μαθηταὶ ἐθαύμασαν τὰ γενόμενα ἐν ἐκείνῃ τῇ ἡμέρᾳ.
The disciples marveled at the things that (had) happened in that day.

135. Genitive Absolute

Usually the case of a participle and its subject is determined by its relationship to the rest of the sentence. If the participle modifies the subject of the sentence, it will be in the nominative case; if it modifies the direct object of the main verb, it will be in the accusative case, etc. But sometimes the participle and its subject are grammatically independent of the rest of the sentence. An English example would be: "The weather being nice, we went to the park." In Greek such a construction is written in the genitive case and is called the genitive absolute. Examples:

λεγούσης τῆς γυναῖκος τὰ ῥήματα ταῦτα ἔκραξεν τὸ τέκνον.
While the woman was speaking these words, the child cried out.

καθίσαντος τοῦ ἄρχοντος ἐπὶ τὸν θρόνον οἱ δοῦλοι ἤνεγκαν ἄρτον καὶ οἶνον.
When the ruler had sat on the throne, the slaves brought bread and wine.

εἰσελθόντος τοῦ κυρίου εἰς τὸν οἶκον τὰ δαιμόνια ἔφυγεν.
When the Lord entered the house, the demons fled.

136. Exercises

Practice and Review
1. ἀσπασάμενοι τοὺς ἀδελφοὺς καὶ τὰς ἀδελφάς, ἀπῆλθον οἱ ἀπόστολοι εἰς ἑτέραν γῆν.
2. παραλαβὼν τὴν μητέρα αὐτοῦ ὁ ἀνὴρ ἐπορεύθη εἰς τὴν ἔρημον προσεύξασθαι.
3. ἡ ψυχὴ ἡ κράξασα ἐν τῇ συναγωγῇ γνώσεται τὴν εἰρήνην τοῦ θεοῦ.
4. καθίσαντος τοῦ διδασκάλου ἐπὶ λίθον ὁ ὄχλος ὁ πίνων οἶνον ἤρξατο ἀκοῦσαι αὐτοῦ.
5. παραγενόμενος δὲ καὶ συναγαγὼν τὰ τέκνα ὁ πατὴρ προσήνεγκε τὰ δῶρα.
6. καὶ οἱ μὴ ἔχοντες πόδας καὶ χεῖρας δύνανται ἐργάσασθαι ἔργα δικαιοσύνης.
7. οἱ μὴ λογισάμενοι τὴν θεοῦ ἀγάπην εἶπον ὑμῖν, Οὐκ ὀφείλετε θεραπεῦσαι ἐν τῷ σαββάτῳ.
8. ἐλθόντος τοῦ προφήτου εἰς τὴν συναγωγὴν αἱ γυναῖκες αἱ καθίζουσαι ἐν ἐκείνῳ τῷ τόπῳ εἶπον, Θέλομεν αἴρειν τὰς χεῖρας ἡμῶν καὶ δοξάζειν τὸν κύριον.
9. ἐφάγομεν καὶ ἐπίομεν μετὰ τοῦ πατρός σου ἀσπασαμένου τοὺς δούλους καὶ λύσαντος τὸ ἱμάτιον αὐτοῦ.
10. τῆς μητρός μου ἔτι ἑτοιμαζούσης ἄρτον παρεγένοντο οἱ ἄγγελοι.
11. ὁ ἄνθρωπος ὁ παραλαβόμενος βασιλείαν καὶ βουλόμενος γινώσκειν περὶ αὐτῆς ἔπεμψε δούλους βλέπειν αὐτήν.

12. γενομένου σαββάτου ὁ ἀναβαίνων πρὸς τὸ ἱερὸν ἔπεσεν πρὸς τοὺς πόδας τοῦ διδασκάλου.

13. τοῦ πνεύματος ἀγαγόντος τοὺς ἁμαρτωλοὺς εἰς τὴν ἐκκλησίαν, ἠνοίξαμεν τὸ στόμα ἡμῶν καὶ εὐηγγελισάμεθα.

14. ὁ κηρύξας ὑμῖν τὸν λόγον τῆς ἀληθείας ἑώρακε τὸ βιβλίον τῆς ζωῆς καὶ ἔγνωκε τὰ μέλλοντα.

LXX

1. Ἔτι τούτου λαλοῦντος ἦλθεν ἕτερος ἄγγελος καὶ εἶπεν πρὸς Ιωβ, Πῦρ ἔπεσεν ἐκ τοῦ οὐρανοῦ (Job 1:16)

2. καὶ εἰσελθὼν εἶπεν τῷ πατρί, Ἰδοὺ εὕρηκα ὃς συμπορεύσεταί μοι. . . . καὶ εἰσῆλθεν, καὶ ἠσπάσαντο ἀλλήλους. (Tob 5:9-10 BA)

3. καὶ καθίσαντες ἐκλαίετε ἔναντι κυρίου, καὶ οὐκ εἰσήκουσεν κύριος τῆς φωνῆς ὑμῶν (Deut 1:45)

4. ἔτι αὐτοῦ λαλοῦντος αὐτοῖς καὶ Ραχηλ . . . ἤρχετο μετὰ τῶν προβάτων τοῦ πατρὸς αὐτῆς· (Gen 29:9)

5. καὶ παραγενόμενος ὁ λαὸς πρὸς Μωυσῆν ἔλεγον ὅτι Ἡμάρτομεν ὅτι κατελαλήσαμεν κατὰ τοῦ κυρίου καὶ κατὰ σοῦ· (Num 21:7)

6. καὶ παραλαβόντες τὸν πατέρα ὑμῶν καὶ τὰ ὑπάρχοντα ὑμῶν ἥκετε πρός με, καὶ δώσω ὑμῖν πάντων τῶν ἀγαθῶν Αἰγύπτου (Gen 45:18)

7. καὶ [Ιωνας] προσεύξατο πρὸς κύριον καὶ εἶπεν, Ὦ κύριε, οὐχ οὗτοι οἱ λόγοι μου ἔτι ὄντος μου ἐν τῇ γῇ μου; (Jonah 4:2)

8. καὶ γνώσονται ὅτι ἐγώ εἰμι κύριος ὁ θεὸς αὐτῶν ὁ ἐξαγαγὼν αὐτοὺς ἐκ γῆς Αἰγύπτου (Exod 29:46)

9. Λαβοῦσα δὲ Μαριαμ ἡ προφῆτις ἡ ἀδελφὴ Ααρων τὸ τύμπανον ἐν τῇ χειρὶ αὐτῆς, καὶ ἐξήλθοσαν πᾶσαι αἱ γυναῖκες ὀπίσω αὐτῆς (Exod 15:20)

10. οἱ υἱοὶ Ισραηλ . . . εὗρον ἄνδρα συλλέγοντα ξύλα τῇ ἡμέρᾳ τῶν σαββάτων. καὶ προσήγαγον αὐτὸν οἱ εὑρόντες αὐτὸν . . . πρὸς Μωυσῆν καὶ Ααρων καὶ πρὸς πᾶσαν συναγωγὴν υἱῶν Ισραηλ. (Num 15:32-3)

11. γινώσκω γὰρ ἐγὼ ὅτι ὁ πατήρ μου καὶ ἡ μήτηρ μου οὐ πιστεύουσιν ὅτι ὄψονταί με ἔτι· (Tob 10:8 S, ET 10:7)

NT

1. εἰπὼν ταῦτα ἐπορεύετο ἔμπροσθεν ἀναβαίνων εἰς Ἱεροσόλυμα. (Luke 19:28)

2. καὶ καθίσαντος αὐτοῦ προσῆλθαν αὐτῷ οἱ μαθηταὶ αὐτοῦ· καὶ ἀνοίξας τὸ στόμα αὐτοῦ ἐδίδασκεν αὐτούς (Matt 5:1-2)

3. ὁ Παῦλος τοὺς μαθητὰς . . . ἀσπασάμενος ἐξῆλθεν πορεύεσθαι εἰς Μακεδονίαν. διελθὼν δὲ τὰ μέρη ἐκεῖνα . . . ἦλθεν εἰς τὴν Ἑλλάδα (Acts 20:1-2)

4. ἴδετε τὰς χεῖράς μου καὶ τοὺς πόδας μου ὅτι ἐγώ εἰμι αὐτός· . . . καὶ τοῦτο εἰπὼν ἔδειξεν αὐτοῖς τὰς χεῖρας καὶ τοὺς πόδας. (Luke 24:39-40)

5. καὶ παραλαβὼν πάλιν τοὺς δώδεκα ἤρξατο αὐτοῖς λέγειν τὰ μέλλοντα αὐτῷ συμβαίνειν (Mark 10:32)

6. καὶ γενομένου σαββάτου ἤρξατο διδάσκειν ἐν τῇ συναγωγῇ (Mark 6:2)

7. ἐκβαλὼν πάντας παραλαμβάνει τὸν πατέρα τοῦ παιδίου καὶ τὴν μητέρα καὶ τοὺς μετ' αὐτοῦ, καὶ εἰσπορεύεται ὅπου ἦν τὸ παιδίον. (Mark 5:40)

8. ὁ μὴ τιμῶν τὸν υἱὸν οὐ τιμᾷ τὸν πατέρα τὸν πέμψαντα αὐτόν. (John 5:23)

9. ἀλλὰ ὁ ὄχλος οὗτος ὁ μὴ γινώσκων τὸν νόμον ἐπάρατοί εἰσιν. (John 7:49)

10. παραγενόμενοι δὲ πρὸς αὐτὸν οἱ ἄνδρες εἶπαν, Ἰωάννης ὁ βαπτιστὴς ἀπέστειλεν ἡμᾶς πρὸς σέ (Luke 7:20)

11. Ἐσθιόντων δὲ αὐτῶν λαβὼν ὁ Ἰησοῦς ἄρτον . . . εἶπεν, . . . τοῦτό ἐστιν τὸ σῶμά μου. (Matt 26:26)

English to Greek

1. While we were still greeting your mother and father, you (pl.) and your sister arrived.

2. Having seen the man's hands and feet, the prophet came and healed him.

3. The sinners who have persecuted the righteous will come into the synagogue to pray, but they will not be heard by the Lord of the Sabbath.

4. God having sat on the throne in heaven, we know that the righteous will receive the kingdom in the last day.

Vocabulary for LXX and NT Sentences

ἀλλήλους, one another
ἀπέστειλεν, aorist of ἀποστέλλω
δώδεκα, twelve
δώσω, I will give
ἔδειξεν, he showed
εἰσακούω, hear
ἔμπροσθεν, on ahead
ἔναντι, before
ἐπάρατος, under a curse
ἥκω, have come
καταλαλέω, speak against
κλαίω, weep
λαλοῦντος = λέγοντος
μέρη, regions
ξύλον, piece of wood

ὀπίσω, after, behind
ὅπου, where
ὅς, one who
παιδίον, child
πᾶς, πᾶσα, πᾶν, all, every
προβάτον, sheep
προσήγαγον, from πρός + ἄγω
προφῆτις, cf. προφήτης
πῦρ, fire
συλλέγω, gather
συμβαίνω, happen
συμπορεύομαι, journey with
τιμάω, honor
τύμπανον, tamborine, drum

Lesson 20

137. Vocabulary

ἁγιάζω, I sanctify, consecrate
(hagiography)
γνωρίζω, I make known, reveal
εὐαγγέλιον, τό, good news, Gospel
(evangel)
θύρα, ἡ, door
κτίζω, I create

τυφλός, -ή, -όν, blind, blind person
φυλακή, ἡ, prison, watch, guard
(prophylactic)
χαρίζομαι, I graciously give, forgive
χάρις, χάριτος, ἡ, grace, favor
(charisma) Note: accusative singular
form usually = χάριν

138. Aorist Passive Participles

The declension of the aorist passive participle λυθείς, λυθεῖσα, λυθέν, "having been loosened," is as follows:

	Masculine	Singular Feminine	Neuter
Nom. Voc.	λυθείς	λυθεῖσα	λυθέν
Gen.	λυθέντος	λυθείσης	λυθέντος
Dat.	λυθέντι	λυθείσῃ	λυθέντι
Acc.	λυθέντα	λυθεῖσαν	λυθέν

	Masculine	Plural Feminine	Neuter
Nom. Voc.	λυθέντες	λυθεῖσαι	λυθέντα
Gen.	λυθέντων	λυθεισῶν	λυθέντων
Dat.	λυθεῖσι(ν)	λυθείσαις	λυθεῖσι(ν)
Acc.	λυθέντας	λυθείσας	λυθέντα

The aorist passive participle is built on the stem of the sixth principal part. The -θη morpheme of the aorist passive appears in its short form -θε throughout. The masculine and neuter are declined according to the third declension; the feminine according to the first. As with aorist active and middle participles, there is no augment. The accent is not recessive, but *retentive,* and the genitive plural feminine has a circumflex on the ultima. Finally, the dative plural masculine and neuter may take the movable ν.

The syntax of the aorist passive participle is the same as that of the other participles. The tense denotes the *kind* of action (undefined, simple), not necessarily the time of action. Although in practice the aorist passive participle often expresses action prior to that of the main verb, it may also express simultaneous action. Examples:

θεραπευθέντες ὑπὸ τοῦ προφήτου ἐδόξασαν οἱ ἄνθρωποι τὸν θεόν.
Having been healed by the prophet, the men glorified God.

ἡ βαπτισθεῖσα γυνὴ συνήγαγεν τὰς ἀδελφὰς αὐτῆς.
The woman who had been baptized gathered together her sisters.

ἠκούσαμεν τὰ κηρυχθέντα ἐν τῇ συναγωγῇ.
We heard the things that were proclaimed in the synagogue.

139. Perfect Active Participles

The declension of the perfect active participle is as follows:

	Singular		
	Masculine	Feminine	Neuter
Nom. Voc.	λελυκώς	λελυκυῖα	λελυκός
Gen.	λελυκότος	λελυκυίας	λελυκότος
Dat.	λελυκότι	λελυκυίᾳ	λελυκότι
Acc.	λελυκότα	λελυκυῖαν	λελυκός

	Plural		
	Masculine	Feminine	Neuter
Nom. Voc.	λελυκότες	λελυκυῖαι	λελυκότα
Gen.	λελυκότων	λελυκυιῶν	λελυκότων
Dat.	λελυκόσι(ν)	λελυκυίαις	λελυκόσι(ν)
Acc.	λελυκότας	λελυκυίας	λελυκότα

The perfect active participle has the characteristic reduplication and the -κ. It is declined according to the third declension in the masculine and neuter and according to the first declension in the feminine. The accent is retentive, the genitive plural feminine takes the circumflex on the ultima, and the dative plural masculine and neuter may take the movable ν.

140. Perfect Middle/Passive Participles

The declension of the perfect middle/passive participle is as follows:

	Singular		
	Masculine	Feminine	Neuter
Nom. Voc.	λελυμένος	λελυμένη	λελυμένον
Gen.	λελυμένου	λελυμένης	λελυμένου
Dat.	λελυμένῳ	λελυμένῃ	λελυμένῳ
Acc.	λελυμένον	λελυμένην	λελυμένον

	Plural		
	Masculine	Feminine	Neuter
Nom. Voc.	λελυμένοι	λελυμέναι	λελυμένα
Gen.	λελυμένων	λελυμένων	λελυμένων
Dat.	λελυμένοις	λελυμέναις	λελυμένοις
Acc.	λελυμένους	λελυμένας	λελυμένα

Perfect middle and passive participles use the same forms. Just as in the perfect middle/passive indicative, there is no kappa, but reduplication occurs throughout the declension. It is declined according to the second declension in the masculine and neuter, according to the first declension in the feminine. The accent is retentive.

The syntax of perfect participles is like that of the other participles. The tense denotes *completed* action with a continuing result. Examples:

ὁ τυφλὸς ὁ τεθεραπευμένος προσήνεγκε δῶρον ἐν τῷ ἱερῷ.
The blind man who had been healed presented a gift in the temple.

πεπιστευκυῖα εἰς θεὸν ἡ ἀδελφὴ ἡμῶν ἤρξατο κηρύσσειν τὸν λόγον.
Having come to believe in God, our sister began to preach the word.

οἱ ἀδελφοὶ αὐτοὶ θέλουσιν ἰδεῖν τὰ γεγραμμένα ἐν τῷ βιβλίῳ.
The brothers themselves want to see the things written in the book.

141. Periphrastic Participles

Occasionally in biblical Greek one will find a form of the verb εἰμί combined with a participle, producing a compound verbal expression. This construction should cause little difficulty since it is so similar to certain English constructions. For example, "I was teaching" can be expressed with the imperfect tense of διδάσκω: ἐδίδασκον. But it might also be expressed with the imperfect tense of εἰμί and a present participle: ἤμην διδάσκων. Such constructions are called periphrastic. Several different combinations of εἰμί and the participle are possible. Periphrastic participles are found most often as substitutes for the imperfect and perfect tenses. Examples:

ὁ διδάσκαλος τῆς δικαιοσύνης ἦν βαπτίζων ἐν τῇ ἐρήμῳ.
The teacher of righteousness was baptizing in the desert.

ταῦτά ἐστιν γεγραμμένα ἐν τῷ βιβλίῳ τοῦ νόμου.
These things are written in the book of the law.

142. Nuances of the Adverbial Participle

When adverbial participles were introduced (§125), you learned to use either a provisional translation ("Having said these things . . .") or a temporal translation ("After she had said these things . . ."). The temporal translation, when appropriate, derives from the context, not from the participle itself. Adverbial participles simply express some circumstance related to the main verb of the sentence. Various nuances are possible. Sometimes an accompanying adverb or particle will indicate what kind of circumstance is involved, but there will be cases in which a determination is difficult. Here are some common types.

Time
ἔτι λέγοντος αὐτοῦ ταῦτα, ἡ γυνὴ αὐτοῦ εἰσῆλθεν εἰς τὸν οἶκον.
While he was still saying these things, his wife entered the house.

Manner
ἔχων ἐξουσίαν ἐκήρυξεν ὁ ἀπόστολος ἐν τῇ συναγωγῇ.
The apostle preached with authority in the synagogue.

Means
ὁ ἄνθρωπος ἔσωσεν τὰ τέκνα ἐκεῖνα ἀποθνήσκων ὑπὲρ αὐτῶν.
The man saved those children (by) dying in their behalf.

Cause
βουλόμενοι γινώσκειν τὸ θέλημα τοῦ θεοῦ πολλάκις προσηυξάμεθα.
Because we wanted to know the will of God, we prayed often.

Condition
μὴ ἐργαζόμενοι ἔργα ἀγάπης πῶς γενησόμεθα ἀγαθοὶ μαθηταί;
If we do not do works of love, how will we become good disciples?

Concession

ὄντες υἱοὶ ὀφείλετε ἐργάζεσθαι τὴν γῆν μετὰ τῶν δούλων.
Although you are sons, you ought to work the land with the slaves.

143. Exercises

Practice and Review

1. ἐδεξάμην τὰ δῶρα τὰ ἁγιασθέντα καὶ ἤνεγκα αὐτὰ διὰ τῶν θύρων τοῦ ἱεροῦ.
2. ἦσαν καθήμενοι ἐν τῇ φυλακῇ καὶ θέλοντες ἀκοῦσαι τὸ εὐαγγέλιον.
3. διδαχθέντες ὑπὸ τοῦ διδασκάλου, καὶ γινώσκομεν τὴν χάριν τοῦ θεοῦ καὶ γνωρίζομεν ἄλλοις αὐτήν.
4. νῦν οἱ τυφλοὶ οὐ δύνανται ἰδεῖν τὰ κτισθέντα ὑπὸ θεοῦ, ἀλλὰ ἐν ἐκείνῃ τῇ ἡμέρᾳ θεὸς χαρίσεται ὀφθαλμοὺς αὐτοῖς βλέπειν.
5. πολλάκις ἁμαρτάνοντες εἰς τὸν νόμον πῶς λημψόμεθα τὴν ἡτοιμασμένην ἡμῖν ζωὴν ἐν οὐρανοῖς;
6. βλέποντες τοὺς καλοὺς οὐρανοὺς καὶ τὴν ἀγαθὴν γῆν πεπιστεύκαμεν ὅτι ὁ κόσμος ἐκτίσθη ὑπὸ τοῦ θεοῦ.
7. ἀποκριθεὶς τῷ πατρί μου εἶπον, Γνωρίσω τὸ εὐαγγέλιον τῷ λαῷ, ἐμοὶ γὰρ ἐχαρίσατο ὁ κύριος τὰς ἁμαρτίας.
8. ὑμεῖς αὐτοὶ ἀκούσαντες τὰ ῥήματα τῶν τεθεραπευμένων οὔπω πιστεύετε τούτοις τοῖς σημείοις.
9. οὗτοι οἱ μαθηταί εἰσιν ἡγιασμένοι ἐν τῷ πνεύματι τῷ ἁγίῳ καὶ αὐτῶν τὰ ὀνόματά ἐστι γεγραμμένα ἐν οὐρανῷ.
10. κράζουσα ἐν τῇ νυκτὶ ἡ γυνὴ ἐγνώρισεν ὅτι ἄνθρωπος πονηρὸς εἰσῆλθεν εἰς τὸν οἶκον αὐτῆς καὶ λαβὼν ἄρτον ἔφυγεν.
11. τὰ τέκνα τὰ ἐκβληθέντα ἐκ τοῦ οἴκου ὑποστρέψει, τῆς μητρὸς αὐτῶν θελούσης.
12. ἰδόντες ἀνεῳγμένας τὰς θύρας τῆς φυλακῆς ἐθαυμάσαμεν ἐπὶ τῇ χάριτι τοῦ θεοῦ.
13. πορευθέντες εἰς τὴν συναγωγὴν προσηύξασθε λέγοντες, Κύριε, ἑωράκαμεν τὸ αἷμα τῶν δεδιωγμένων τέκνων σου.
14. οὐκ ἔχεις βιβλία, τὰ δὲ γεγραμμένα ἐν τῇ καρδίᾳ σου γνωρίζει τὴν χάριν θεοῦ.

LXX

1. καὶ ἐπορεύθη . . . καὶ εὗρεν αὐτὸν καθήμενον ὑπὸ δρῦν καὶ εἶπεν αὐτῷ . . . σὺ εἶ ὁ ἄνθρωπος τοῦ θεοῦ ὁ ἐληλυθὼς ἐξ Ιουδα; (3 Kgdms 13:14)
2. εἰ μὲν ὁ ἀδελφὸς ἡμῶν ὁ νεώτερος καταβαίνει μεθ’ ἡμῶν, καταβησόμεθα· οὐ γὰρ δυνησόμεθα ἰδεῖν τὸ πρόσωπον τοῦ ἀνθρώπου, τοῦ ἀδελφοῦ τοῦ νεωτέρου μὴ ὄντος μεθ’ ἡμῶν. (Gen 44:26)
3. καὶ ἐρρύσατο κύριος τὸν Ισραηλ ἐν τῇ ἡμέρᾳ ἐκείνῃ ἐκ . . . τῶν Αἰγυπτίων·

καὶ εἶδεν Ισραηλ τοὺς Αἰγυπτίους τεθνηκότας παρὰ τὸ χεῖλος τῆς θαλάσσης. (Exod 14:30)

4. καὶ ἰδοὺ οὐκ ἦν ὁ ἀνοίγων τὰς θύρας . . . καὶ ἔλαβον τὴν κλεῖδα καὶ ἤνοιξαν, καὶ ἰδοὺ ὁ κύριος αὐτῶν πεπτωκὼς ἐπὶ τὴν γῆν τεθνηκώς. (Judg 3:25)

5. καὶ εἶπεν τῷ πατρὶ αὐτοῦ, Ἰδοὺ ὁ υἱός σου ἔρχεται καὶ ὁ ἄνθρωπος ὁ πορευθεὶς μετ' αὐτοῦ. (Tob 11:6 BA)

6. καὶ γάρ φησιν ὁ Μωυσῆς, Καὶ πάντες οἱ ἡγιασμένοι ὑπὸ τὰς χεῖράς σου. καὶ οὗτοι οὖν ἁγιασθέντες διὰ θεὸν τετίμηνται (4 Macc 17:19-20)

7. εἶπαν, Σέσωκας ἡμᾶς, εὕρομεν χάριν ἐναντίον τοῦ κυρίου ἡμῶν (Gen 47:25)

8. θοῦ, κύριε, φυλακὴν τῷ στόματί μου καὶ θύραν περιοχῆς περὶ τὰ χείλη μου. (Ps 140:3, ET 141:3)

9. τὸν τεθνηκότα . . . ἐν τῇ πόλει φάγονται οἱ κύνες, καὶ τὸν τεθνηκότα . . . ἐν τῷ πεδίῳ φάγονται τὰ πετεινὰ τοῦ οὐρανοῦ. (3 Kgdms 20:24, ET 21:24)

10. καὶ ἀποκριθεὶς Αβρααμ εἶπεν, Νῦν ἠρξάμην λαλῆσαι πρὸς τὸν κύριον, ἐγὼ δέ εἰμι γῆ (Gen 18:27)

NT

1. Ἦν δὲ διδάσκων ἐν μιᾷ τῶν συναγωγῶν ἐν τοῖς σάββασιν. (Luke 13:10)

2. Μετὰ ταῦτα εἶδον, καὶ ἰδοὺ θύρα ἠνεῳγμένη ἐν τῷ οὐρανῷ (Rev 4:1)

3. ἀπελθοῦσα εἰς τὸν οἶκον αὐτῆς [ἡ Συροφοινίκισσα γυνὴ] εὗρεν τὸ παιδίον βεβλημένον ἐπὶ τὴν κλίνην καὶ τὸ δαιμόνιον ἐξεληλυθός. (Mark 7:30)

4. Ἦν δὲ σάββατον ἐν ἐκείνῃ τῇ ἡμέρᾳ. ἔλεγον οὖν οἱ Ἰουδαῖοι τῷ τεθεραπευμένῳ, Σάββατόν ἐστιν (John 5:9-10)

5. ἀπεκρίθη οὖν ἐκεῖνος, Εἰ ἁμαρτωλός ἐστιν οὐκ οἶδα· ἓν οἶδα ὅτι τυφλὸς ὢν ἄρτι βλέπω. (John 9:25)

6. τῇ ἐκκλησίᾳ τοῦ θεοῦ τῇ οὔσῃ ἐν Κορίνθῳ, ἡγιασμένοις ἐν Χριστῷ Ἰησοῦ, . . . χάρις ὑμῖν καὶ εἰρήνη (1 Cor 1:2-3)

7. τῇ γὰρ χάριτί ἐστε σεσῳσμένοι διὰ πίστεως· . . . αὐτοῦ γάρ ἐσμεν ποίημα, κτισθέντες ἐν Χριστῷ Ἰησοῦ ἐπὶ ἔργοις ἀγαθοῖς (Eph 2:8, 10)

8. ἡμεῖς δὲ οὐ τὸ πνεῦμα τοῦ κόσμου ἐλάβομεν ἀλλὰ τὸ πνεῦμα τὸ ἐκ τοῦ θεοῦ, ἵνα εἰδῶμεν τὰ ὑπὸ τοῦ θεοῦ χαρισθέντα ἡμῖν· (1 Cor 2:12)

9. ἦν δὲ καὶ ὁ Ἰωάννης βαπτίζων ἐν Αἰνὼν . . . οὔπω γὰρ ἦν βεβλημένος εἰς τὴν φυλακὴν ὁ Ἰωάννης. (John 3:23-4)

10. Γνωρίζω γὰρ ὑμῖν, ἀδελφοί, τὸ εὐαγγέλιον τὸ εὐαγγελισθὲν ὑπ' ἐμοῦ ὅτι οὐκ ἔστιν κατὰ ἄνθρωπον· οὐδὲ γὰρ ἐγὼ παρὰ ἀνθρώπου παρέλαβον αὐτὸ οὔτε ἐδιδάχθην (Gal 1:11-12)

11. ἀποκριθεὶς δὲ Σίμων . . . εἶπεν, Σὺ εἶ ὁ Χριστὸς ὁ υἱὸς τοῦ θεοῦ (Matt 16:16)

English to Greek

1. Having been sanctified by the grace of God, we went into the prison and began to preach the gospel.
2. (Since there is) a door standing open for the apostles, they will make known to others that the Lord graciously forgives sinners.
3. The women who have come to believe are gathering the blind and leading them into the temple.
4. The apostles were teaching (use periphrastic) the disciples that the things created by God are good.

Vocabulary for LXX and NT Sentences

ἄρτι, now

δρῦς, oak tree

εἰδῶμεν, we may know

ἕν, one (thing)

ἐναντίον, before, in the presence of

ἐρρύσατο, rescued

θοῦ, Place! Put!

ἵνα, in order that

καταβησόμεθα, dep. fut. καταβαίνω

κλεῖς, κλεῖδος, ἡ, key

κλίνη, bed

κύνες, dogs

λαλῆσαι = λέγειν

μία, one

νεώτερος, younger

οἶδα = γινώσκω

παιδίον, child

πᾶς, πᾶσα, πᾶν, all, every

πεδίον, plain

περιοχή, containment

πετεινόν, bird

πίστις, faith

ποίημα, creation

πόλις, city

τιμάω, honor

φησιν = λέγει

χεῖλος, τό, shore, lip

Lesson 21

144. Vocabulary

ἀγαπάω, I love
αἰτέω, I ask, request (often mid. voice)
ἀκολουθέω, I follow (+ dat.) (acolyte)
γεννάω, I beget, bear
ἑαυτοῦ, of himself, herself, etc.
ἐμαυτοῦ, of myself
ζάω, I live (conjugated with η rather than α in the present tense)
ζητέω, I seek, ask for, deliberate
καλέω, I call, name, invite
λαλέω, I speak (glossolalia)

ὁράω, I see (panorama)
παρακαλέω, I exhort, encourage comfort (Paraclete)
πᾶς, πᾶσα, πᾶν, all, every; entire, whole (pantheism, panacea)
περιπατέω, I walk, live (peripatetic)
πληρόω, I fill, make full of, fulfill
ποιέω, I do, make (poem)   *IMPORTANT!*
σεαυτοῦ, of yourself
σταυρόω, I crucify
φοβέομαι, I fear (phobia)

145. Introduction to Contract Verbs

Many of the verbs you have learned so far have had stems ending in upsilon (λύω, πιστεύω, etc.) or one of the mute consonants (ἄγω, πέμπω, etc.). A new category of verbs consists of those whose stems end in the vowels alpha, epsilon, or omicron. These are called contract verbs because when they are conjugated, the final vowel of the verb stem contracts with the initial vowel or diphthong of the person/number ending. Contraction often yields a slightly different ending from the ones you are used to, but most forms of contract verbs can be easily recognized, especially in context. Contraction occurs *only in the first principal part,* that is, in the present tense in all moods and modes and in the imperfect indicative.

Most of the vocabulary words in this lesson are contract verbs. All three types are represented. The forms given above are the *uncontracted* forms. These forms are used in dictionaries and other reference tools because they immediately reveal which of the three types is involved. The uncontracted forms will only appear in such contexts, never in the Bible.

The rules of contraction are complex. The presentation here foregoes the rules and simply gives the resulting contractions in chart form.

146. Contraction Chart

	ε	ει	η	ῃ	ο	ου	ω
α	α	ᾳ	α	ᾳ	ω	ω	ω
ε	ει	ει	η	ῃ	ου	ου	ω
ο	ου	οι	ω	οι	ου	ου	ω

On the left side of the chart are the three vowels that constitute the types of contract verbs: α, ε, and ο. The top horizontal row of the chart shows the various vowels and diphthongs of the person/number endings. The rest of the chart gives the resulting contractions. Thus, in order to say "we make" from the verb ποιέω, one contracts ποιε + ομεν. The chart shows the contracted syllable would be ου, so the form is ποιοῦμεν.

If one does Greek composition, it is obviously helpful to know the above chart from memory. More important, however, is the ability to recognize contracted forms in context. The following observations may be helpful. (1) All contracted syllables are long. (2) An "o" type vowel is never lost in contraction. If ο, ου, or ω enters the contraction, an ο, ου, or ω (or οι) results. (3) Anything contracted with omega yields omega. (4) An epsilon contracted with a long vowel or diphthong yields that same long vowel or diphthong. (5) When an alpha contracts with an "e" type vowel (ε, ει, η, or ῃ), an alpha will appear in the result. But when an alpha contracts with an "o" type vowel, an omega results. (6) If an iota (subscript or full) enters the contraction, an iota (subscript or full) will appear in the result. (7) In biblical Greek there are more contract verbs in epsilon than of the other types. The contractions that you will encounter most often are ε + ε = ει and ε + ο = ου. (8) Finally, there are two exceptions to the above chart. Present active infinitives in -αω (for example, ἀγαπά + ειν) end in -ᾶν; and present active infinitives in -οω (πληρό + ειν) end in -οῦν.

147. Accentuation of Contract Verbs

Contraction slightly complicates accenting. To determine the accent of a contract verb, (1) first write out the word in its uncontracted form and accent it according to the recessive rule. (2) If either of the syllables entering the contraction is accented (which is usually the case), then the resulting contracted syllable will be accented. If that syllable is the penult or antepenult, follow the general rules. If the accented syllable is the ultima, use the circumflex. (3) If step one permits the accent to recede beyond the syllables entering the contraction, then the resulting contracted syllable will not be accented. Follow the general rules to accent the word. Examples: ποιέ + ομεν = ποιοῦμεν; ποιέ + ω = ποιῶ; ἐποίε + ον = ἐποίουν.

148. Principal Parts of Contract Verbs

As mentioned above, contraction only occurs in the first principal part. What typically happens in the formation of the other principal parts is the lengthening of the contract vowel before the addition of the various tense suffixes. Both alpha and epsilon lengthen to eta; omicron lengthens to omega. Thus the principal parts of λαλέω and πληρόω are as follows:

λαλέω	λαλήσω	ἐλάλησα	λελάληκα	λελάλημαι	ἐλαλήθην
πληρόω	πληρώσω	ἐπλήρωσα	πεπλήρωκα	πεπλήρωμαι	ἐπληρώθην

A partial exception to this rule is the verb καλέω, which does not lengthen its contract vowel in all of its principal parts. Thus:

καλέω	καλέσω	ἐκάλεσα	κέκληκα	κέκλημαι	ἐκλήθην

149. Reflexive Pronouns

Reflexive pronouns refer back to the subject of the sentence or clause in which they occur. By the nature of the case, they will never *be* the subject of a sentence or clause so there are no nominative forms.

The forms of the *first person* reflexive, "of myself," are as follows:

	Singular			Plural	
	Masc.	Fem.		Masc.	Fem.
G.	ἐμαυτοῦ	ἐμαυτῆς	G.	ἑαυτῶν	ἑαυτῶν
D.	ἐμαυτῷ	ἐμαυτῇ	D.	ἑαυτοῖς	ἑαυταῖς
A.	ἐμαυτόν	ἐμαυτήν	A.	ἑαυτούς	ἑαυτάς

The forms of the *second person* reflexive, "of yourself," are as follows:

	Singular			Plural	
	Masc.	Fem.		Masc.	Fem.
G.	σεαυτοῦ	σεαυτῆς	G.	ἑαυτῶν	ἑαυτῶν
D.	σεαυτῷ	σεαυτῇ	D.	ἑαυτοῖς	ἑαυταῖς
A.	σεαυτόν	σεαυτήν	A.	ἑαυτούς	ἑαυτάς

The forms of the *third person* reflexive, "of himself, herself, itself," are as follows:

	Singular				Plural		
	Masc.	Fem.	Neut.		Masc.	Fem.	Neut.
G.	ἑαυτοῦ	ἑαυτῆς	ἑαυτοῦ	G.	ἑαυτῶν	ἑαυτῶν	ἑαυτῶν
D.	ἑαυτῷ	ἑαυτῇ	ἑαυτῷ	D.	ἑαυτοῖς	ἑαυταῖς	ἑαυτοῖς
A.	ἑαυτόν	ἑαυτήν	ἑαυτό	A.	ἑαυτούς	ἑαυτάς	ἑαυτά

Note that the first and second person reflexives lack neuter forms. Presumably, someone who is speaking (first person) or someone who is being addressed (second person) can be designated masculine or feminine. More significant is the fact that the third person plural forms ἑαυτῶν, etc., do triple duty for all three persons. Thus, in a given context, ἑαυτῶν might mean "of ourselves," "of yourselves," or "of themselves."

A reflexive pronoun is used in such cases as when a direct object, an indirect object, an object of a preposition, or a possessive genitive refers back to the subject of the sentence or clause. Examples: (1) ποιήσω ἐμαυτῷ οἶκον, "I will make a house for myself"; (2) συνάξεις πρὸς σεαυτὴν τὸν λαόν, "You will gather the people to yourself"; (3) ἁμαρτωλοὶ οὐ δύνανται σῶσαι ἑαυτούς, "Sinners are not able to save themselves."

150. The Declension of πᾶς

πᾶς is a very common adjective in biblical Greek. Its declension is somewhat irregular in that a few of its forms are shortened. Otherwise, it should pose no special problems. The declension of πᾶς is like the aorist active participle λύσας, following the third declension in the masculine and neuter, the first declension in the feminine.

	Singular		
	Masculine	Feminine	Neuter
Nom.	πᾶς	πᾶσα	πᾶν
Gen.	παντός	πάσης	παντός
Dat.	παντί	πάσῃ	παντί
Acc.	πάντα	πᾶσαν	πᾶν

	Plural		
	Masculine	Feminine	Neuter
Nom.	πάντες	πᾶσαι	πάντα
Gen.	πάντων	πασῶν	πάντων
Dat.	πᾶσι(ν)	πάσαις	πᾶσι(ν)
Acc.	πάντας	πάσας	πάντα

151. Uses of πᾶς

The use of πᾶς requires brief comment because its syntax is so varied. Πᾶς occurs with singular and plural nouns, with and without the article, and in attributive, predicate, and substantive constructions.

(1) In the (very common) predicate position its meaning corresponds closely to English: ἑώρακα πάντα τὰ πλοῖα, "I have seen all the boats"; ἐλαλήσαμεν πρὸς τοὺς μαθητὰς πάντας, "We spoke to all the disciples."

(2) In the (less common) attributive position it refers to the whole, the collective sum of the individual parts: ὁ πᾶς νόμος διδάσκει ἀγάπην, "The whole law teaches love"; οἱ πάντες μαθηταὶ προσηύξαντο ὑπὲρ τοῦ τέκνου, "The whole body of disciples prayed for the child."

(3) Without the article πᾶς means "every" or each" with a singular noun; "all (conceivable)" with a plural noun: πᾶς λόγος πληρωθήσεται, "Every word will be fulfilled"; ἡ ἁμαρτία εἰσῆλθεν εἰς πάντας ἀνθρώπους, "Sin has entered into all persons."

(4) Πᾶς often occurs with personal pronouns, demonstratives, and participles: πάντες ὑμεῖς γινώσκετε τὴν ἀλήθειαν, "You all know the truth"; ἡ γυνὴ κηρύσσει πάντα ταῦτα, "The woman is proclaiming all these things"; πᾶς ὁ πιστεύων σωθήσεται, "Everyone who believes will be saved."

(5) Πᾶς is often used as a substantive, both with and without the article: εἶπεν ὁ διδάσκαλος αὐτοῖς τὰ πάντα ἐν παραβολαῖς, "The teacher told them all things in parables"; πάντες ἐθαύμασαν ἐπὶ τοῖς σημείοις, "Everyone marveled at the signs."

152. Exercises

Practice and Review

1. ἀγαπῶμεν δὲ πάντας τοὺς ἀδελφοὺς ἡμῶν καὶ πάσας τὰς ἀδελφὰς ἡμῶν καὶ παρακαλοῦμεν ζῆν μὴ ἑαυτοῖς ἀλλὰ τῷ κυρίῳ.

2. φοβεῖσθε τοὺς ἄρχοντας τοὺς σταυροῦντας τοὺς ἁγίους προφήτας καὶ διώκοντας τοὺς πιστούς;

3. τὰ τέκνα ἐκάλεσαν τὴν μητέρα αὐτῶν καὶ ᾔτησαν ἄρτον παρ' αὐτῆς, αὐτὴ δὲ οὐκ ἠδύνατο ἑτοιμάσαι αὐτόν.

4. ὁ διδάσκαλός μου ἐλάλει τοῖς ἁμαρτωλοῖς τούτοις, ἀλλ' οὐκ ἤθελον ἀκολουθεῖν αὐτῷ οὐδὲ περιπατεῖν ἐν τῇ ὁδῷ τοῦ πνεύματος.

5. οἱ τυφλοὶ οὐκ ὁρῶσι τὰ κτισθέντα ὑπὸ θεοῦ, οἱ δὲ ὀφθαλμοὶ τῆς καρδίας αὐτῶν βλέπουσι τὴν βασιλείαν τοῦ οὐρανοῦ.

6. πᾶσαι αἱ γυναῖκες ἐποίησαν ἑαυταῖς καλὰ ἱμάτια, ἀλλὰ πονηροὶ ἄνθρωποι ἔβαλον αὐτὰ εἰς τὴν θάλασσαν.

7. εἰ ζητῶ δοξάζειν ἐμαυτόν, οὔτε πληρώσω τὸν λόγον τοῦ θεοῦ οὔτε ποιήσω τὸ ἔργον πνεύματος.

8. ὁ ἀνὴρ ἐκεῖνος ἐλάλει περὶ ἑαυτοῦ καὶ οὐ περὶ τῆς χάριτος θεοῦ. σὺ οὖν οὐκ ἤκουσας αὐτοῦ οὐδὲ ἠκολούθησας.

9. ἐγὼ οὔπω λογίζομαι ἐμαυτὸν πεπληρωκέναι τὸν πάντα νόμον, ζητῶ δὲ ἀγαπᾶν πάντας τοὺς διώκοντάς με.

10. ὁ μὲν ἄνθρωπος ἐκεῖνος ἐγέννησέν με καὶ τὴν ἀδελφήν μου, ἡμεῖς δὲ οὐ ζῶμεν ἐν τῷ οἴκῳ αὐτοῦ οὐδὲ περιπατοῦμεν ἐν ταῖς ὁδοῖς αὐτοῦ.

11. ἐδίδαξας ἄλλους φοβεῖσθαι τὸν κύριον· ἐδίδαξας δὲ σεαυτὸν τὸ αὐτὸ ποιεῖν;

12. ὁρᾷ ὁ δοῦλος ἀπὸ τῆς γῆς πλοῖον ἐπὶ τῆς θαλάσσης καὶ καλεῖ τοῖς ἐργαζομένοις ἐν αὐτῷ.

13. ἡ μήτηρ μου παρεκάλει με καὶ τὴν γυναῖκά μου γεννῆσαι τέκνα, ἡμεῖς δὲ ἔτι ἡτοιμάζομεν ἑαυτούς.

14. ποιῶν σεαυτῷ θρόνον ἐβούλου ἄρχειν τῆς γῆς, ὁ δὲ ἄγγελος τοῦ θανάτου εἶπεν, Ἐν ταύτῃ τῇ νυκτὶ τὴν ψυχήν σου αἰτήσω ἀπὸ σοῦ·

15. σταυρωθέντος τοῦ κυρίου ὑπὸ τῶν ἐξουσιῶν καὶ ἀποθανόντος, ᾐτήσαντο πάντες οἱ ἀκολουθοῦντες αὐτῷ τὸ σῶμα αὐτοῦ.

LXX

1. ἐζήτησα ὃν ἠγάπησεν ἡ ψυχή μου, ἐζήτησα αὐτὸν καὶ οὐχ εὗρον αὐτόν, ἐκάλεσα αὐτόν, καὶ οὐχ ὑπήκουσέν μου. (Cant 3:1)

2. Καὶ νῦν, Ισραηλ, τί κύριος ὁ θεός σου αἰτεῖται παρὰ σοῦ ἀλλ᾽ ἢ φοβεῖσθαι κύριον τὸν θεόν σου πορεύεσθαι ἐν πάσαις ταῖς ὁδοῖς αὐτοῦ καὶ ἀγαπᾶν αὐτόν (Deut 10:12)

3. Κύριος εἶπεν πρός με, Υἱός μου εἶ σύ, ἐγὼ σήμερον γεγέννηκά σε· (Ps 2:7)

4. πᾶσαν τὴν γῆν, ἣν σὺ ὁρᾷς, σοὶ δώσω αὐτὴν καὶ τῷ σπέρματί σου ἕως τοῦ αἰῶνος. καὶ ποιήσω τὸ σπέρμα σου ὡς τὴν ἄμμον τῆς γῆς· (Gen 13:15-16)

5. καὶ [Ισαακ] ἔλαβεν τὴν Ρεβεκκαν, καὶ ἐγένετο αὐτοῦ γυνή, καὶ ἠγάπησεν αὐτήν· καὶ παρεκλήθη Ισαακ περὶ . . . τῆς μητρὸς αὐτοῦ. (Gen 24:67)

6. καὶ κατεφίλησεν Ορφα τὴν πενθερὰν αὐτῆς καὶ ἐπέστρεψεν εἰς τὸν λαὸν αὐτῆς, Ρουθ δὲ ἠκολούθησεν αὐτῇ. (Ruth 1:14)

7. καὶ ἐρεῖ πρὸς αὐτὸν ὁ πατὴρ αὐτοῦ καὶ ἡ μήτηρ αὐτοῦ οἱ γεννήσαντες αὐτόν, Οὐ ζήσῃ, ὅτι ψευδῆ ἐλάλησας ἐπ᾽ ὀνόματι κυρίου· (Zech 13:3)

8. ἐθεώρει αὐτοὺς ζῶντας, τότε Ναβουχοδονοσορ ὁ βασιλεὺς ἐθαύμασε καὶ . . . εἶπεν τοῖς φίλοις αὐτοῦ, Ἰδοὺ ἐγὼ ὁρῶ ἄνδρας τέσσαρας λελυμένους περιπατοῦντας ἐν τῷ πυρί (Dan 3:91-92, akin to ET 3:24-25)

9. [Ρουθ] εἶπεν Εὕροιμι χάριν ἐν ὀφθαλμοῖς σου, κύριε, ὅτι παρεκάλεσάς με καὶ ὅτι ἐλάλησας ἐπὶ καρδίαν τῆς δούλης σου (Ruth 2:13)

10. καὶ ἰδοὺ ἔτι λαλούσης σου ἐκεῖ μετὰ τοῦ βασιλέως καὶ ἐγὼ εἰσελεύσομαι ὀπίσω σου καὶ πληρώσω τοὺς λόγους σου. (3 Kgdms 1:14)

11. εἶπεν ἡ γυνή . . . εἰσελεύσομαι καὶ ποιήσω αὐτὸ ἐμαυτῇ καὶ τοῖς τέκνοις μου, καὶ φαγόμεθα καὶ ἀποθανούμεθα. καὶ εἶπεν πρὸς αὐτὴν Ηλιου . . . ποίησον κατὰ τὸ ῥῆμά σου· ἀλλὰ ποίησον ἐμοὶ . . . ἐν πρώτοις καὶ ἐξοίσεις μοι, σεαυτῇ δὲ καὶ τοῖς τέκνοις σου ποιήσεις ἐπ᾽ ἐσχάτου· (3 Kgdms 17:12-13)

NT

1. πᾶς γὰρ ὁ αἰτῶν λαμβάνει καὶ ὁ ζητῶν εὑρίσκει καὶ τῷ κρούοντι ἀνοιγήσεται. (Matt 7:8)

2. εἶπεν δὲ πρὸς αὐτὸν ὁ ἄγγελος, . . . καὶ ἡ γυνή σου Ἐλισάβετ γεννήσει υἱόν σοι καὶ καλέσεις τὸ ὄνομα αὐτοῦ Ἰωάννην. (Luke 1:13)

3. Πᾶς ὁ πιστεύων ὅτι Ἰησοῦς ἐστιν ὁ Χριστὸς ἐκ τοῦ θεοῦ γεγέννηται, καὶ πᾶς ὁ ἀγαπῶν τὸν γεννήσαντα ἀγαπᾷ [καὶ] τὸν γεγεννημένον ἐξ αὐτοῦ. (1 John 5:1)

4. λέγει οὖν αὐτῷ ὁ Πιλᾶτος, Ἐμοὶ οὐ λαλεῖς; οὐκ οἶδας ὅτι ἐξουσίαν ἔχω ἀπολῦσαί σε καὶ ἐξουσίαν ἔχω σταυρῶσαί σε; (John 19:10)

5. καὶ ἐπληρώθη ἡ γραφὴ ἡ λέγουσα, Ἐπίστευσεν δὲ Ἀβραὰμ τῷ θεῷ, καὶ ἐλογίσθη αὐτῷ εἰς δικαιοσύνην . . . ὁρᾶτε ὅτι ἐξ ἔργων δικαιοῦται ἄνθρωπος καὶ οὐκ ἐκ πίστεως μόνον. (Jas 2:23-24)

6. Οὐ δύναμαι ἐγὼ ποιεῖν ἀπ’ ἐμαυτοῦ οὐδέν· . . . οὐ ζητῶ τὸ θέλημα τὸ ἐμὸν ἀλλὰ τὸ θέλημα τοῦ πέμψαντός με. (John 5:30)

7. Πάλιν οὖν αὐτοῖς ἐλάλησεν ὁ Ἰησοῦς λέγων, Ἐγώ εἰμι τὸ φῶς τοῦ κόσμου· ὁ ἀκολουθῶν ἐμοὶ [οὐ περιπατήσει] ἐν τῇ σκοτίᾳ, ἀλλ’ ἕξει τὸ φῶς τῆς ζωῆς. (John 8:12)

8. [ἦμεν] παρακαλοῦντες ὑμᾶς . . . περιπατεῖν . . . ἀξίως τοῦ θεοῦ τοῦ καλοῦντος ὑμᾶς εἰς τὴν ἑαυτοῦ βασιλείαν καὶ δόξαν. (1 Thess 2:12)

9. εἶπαν . . . Τί ζητεῖτε τὸν ζῶντα μετὰ τῶν νεκρῶν· οὐκ ἔστιν ὧδε, ἀλλὰ ἠγέρθη. μνήσθητε ὡς ἐλάλησεν ὑμῖν ἔτι ὢν ἐν τῇ Γαλιλαίᾳ (Luke 24:5-6)

10. καὶ θέλων αὐτὸν ἀποκτεῖναι ἐφοβήθη τὸν ὄχλον (Matt 14:5)

11. ἔπεχε σεαυτῷ καὶ τῇ διδασκαλίᾳ, . . . τοῦτο γὰρ ποιῶν καὶ σεαυτὸν σώσεις καὶ τοὺς ἀκούοντάς σου. (1 Tim 4:16)

English to Greek

1. All the men who were living in the desert were seeking to fulfill the prophet's words.

2. If you (pl.) are not speaking the truth nor exhorting all sinners, you are neither walking in righteousness nor doing the work of heaven.

3. We do not fear those who crucify the body, for God is calling us to himself and we will follow the way of peace.

4. I do not glorify myself because I begat a son, but I ask for the heart of a father from God.

5. If you (sing.) love the Lord with (ἐκ) all your heart and if you love yourself, you will see the kingdom of glory.

Vocabulary for LXX and NT Sentences

ἀλλ' ἤ, but, other than
ἄμμος, sand
ἀξίως, worthily
ἀποθανούμεθα, future tense
βασιλεύς, king
διδασκαλία, teaching
δικαιόω, justify
δούλη, cf. δοῦλος
δώσω, I will give
ἐμόν, my
ἐξοίσεις, from ἐκφέρω
ἐπέχω, give attention to
ἐρεῖ, will say
εὕροιμι, may I find
ἥν, which, that
θεωρέω, behold, look on
καταφιλέω, kiss
κρούω, knock
μνήσθητε, remember! (impv.)

μόνον, alone
οἶδας = γινώσκεις
ὅν, (the one) whom
ὀπίσω, behind, after
οὐδέν, nothing
πενθερά, mother-in-law
πίστις, πίστεως, faith
ποίησον, make! do! (impv.)
πῦρ, πυρός, fire
σήμερον, today
σκοτία, darkness
τέσσαρας, four
τί, what? why?
ὑπακούω, respond, answer
φίλος, friend
φῶς, light
ψευδῆ, lies
ὧδε, here
ὡς, how

Lesson 22

153. Vocabulary

[handwritten: BOTH CONTRACT AND LIQUID]

ἀλλήλων, of each other, of one another

ἀπαγγέλλω, I report, announce, declare

δοκέω, think, seem, seem good
(Docetic)

ἕκαστος, η, ον, each, every

ἐμός, ἐμή, ἐμόν, my, mine

ἐντολή, ἡ, commandment

ἡμέτερος, α, ον, our

ὅπου, where, whither

πεσοῦμαι, I will fall (fut. of πίπτω)

προσκυνέω, I worship, bow down to
(usu. + dat, less often + acc.)

πῦρ, πυρός, τό, fire (pyro-)

σός, σή, σόν, your (sing.)

σπείρω, I sow

τηρέω, I keep, observe, obey

ὕδωρ, ὕδατος, τό, water (hydrant)

ὑμέτερος, α, ον, your (pl.)

φῶς, φωτός, τό, light (photo)

154. Introduction to Liquid Verbs

Liquid verbs are those whose stems end in the letters λ, μ, ν, and ρ. These consonants are called liquids (μ and ν are also called nasals) because their sounds are frictionless and can be prolonged like a vowel. Unlike mute consonants, liquid sounds "flow." Liquid verbs form a special group because they do not accept the direct attachment of the -σ of the future tense or the -σα of the first aorist. These tenses are formed in special ways.

155. Future of Liquid Verbs

The future of liquid verbs is formed by adding an epsilon suffix to the verb stem prior to the person/number endings. This epsilon contracts, however, with the variable vowel of the endings with the result that the future active and middle of a liquid verb resemble the present active and middle/passive of a contract verb in -εω. The future active of μένω, "I remain," is as follows:

Singular	Plural
1. μενῶ, I will remain	1. μενοῦμεν, we will remain
2. μενεῖς, you (sing.) will remain	2. μενεῖτε, you (pl.) will remain
3. μενεῖ, he, she, or it will remain	3. μενοῦσι(ν), they will remain

[handwritten: ONLY ONES THAT LOOK DIFFERENT FROM PRESENT]

131

The future middle of μένω is as follows:

Singular	Plural
1. μενοῦμαι	1. μενοῦμεθα
2. μενῇ	2. μενεῖσθε
3. μενεῖται	3. μενοῦνται

Several of the above forms cannot be distinguished from the corresponding present tense forms apart from accent. This is an instance in which accent is important for translation. μένω means "I remain." μενῶ means "I will remain."

Sometimes a liquid future will have a slightly different stem from the present tense. Example: βάλλω, "I throw"; βαλῶ, "I will throw." It is also sometimes the case that a verb whose lexical form does not appear to be a liquid will, nevertheless, have a liquid future or even a deponent liquid future. Thus, ἀποθνήσκω, "I die"; ἀποθανοῦμαι, "I will die." In this case, the present tense disguises the true stem (ἀποθαν-).

156. First Aorist of Liquid Verbs

Liquid verbs form the first aorist active and middle by adding -α to the verb stem rather than -σα. In addition, the verb stem changes, usually lengthening the stem vowel to compensate for the loss of the sigma. Thus: μένω, "I remain"; ἔμεινα, "I remained"; ἀποστέλλω, "I send"; ἀπέστειλα, "I sent"; κρίνω, "I judge"; ἔκρινα, "I judged" (in the latter the iota is long).

The aorist active of μένω, "I remain," is as follows:

Singular	Plural
1. ἔμεινα, I remained	1. ἐμείναμεν, we remained
2. ἔμεινας, you (sing.) remained	2. ἐμείνατε, you (pl.) remained
3. ἔμεινε(ν), he, she, or it remained	3. ἔμειναν, they remained

Some liquid verbs have second aorists (βάλλω, ἔβαλον) or irregular aorists (φέρω, ἤνεγκα), in which case the peculiarities of liquid aorists obviously would not apply. As always, principal parts are unpredictable.

157. Forms of Common Liquid Verbs

For your reference, here is a list of some of the most common verbs having liquid forms in one or more principal parts.

Present	Future	Aorist
αἴρω	ἀρῶ	ἦρα
ἀπαγγέλλω	ἀπαγγελῶ	ἀπήγγειλα
ἀποθνήσκω	ἀποθανοῦμαι	ἀπέθανον
ἀποκτείνω	ἀποκτενῶ	ἀπέκτεινα
ἀποστέλλω	ἀποστελῶ	ἀπέστειλα
βάλλω	βαλῶ	ἔβαλον
ἐγείρω	ἐγερῶ	ἤγειρα
κρίνω	κρινῶ	ἔκρινα
λέγω	ἐρῶ	εἶπον
μένω	μενῶ	ἔμεινα
σπείρω	σπερῶ	ἔσπειρα

(handwritten margin note: → ἔκρινον: NO LENGTHENING (CANT RE ALUS OI THIS ~/105A))

Finally, the verb πίπτω has the future πεσοῦμαι, which, though it does not have a stem ending in a liquid consonant, is conjugated like a liquid future.

158. Reciprocal Pronouns

The reciprocal pronoun is used when there is mutual interaction between members of a *plural* subject. By the nature of the word, there is no nominative. In biblical Greek the commonest forms are the following:

ἀλλήλων, of one another, each other
ἀλλήλοις, to or for one another, each other
ἀλλήλους, one another, each other

Examples: (1) ἔλεγον πρὸς ἀλλήλους, "They were talking to one another"; (2) ἐσθίομεν ἄρτον μετ' ἀλλήλων, "We are eating bread with one another"; (3) ἔχετε ἀγάπην ἀλλήλοις; "Do you have love for each other?" (Note: The three masculine forms given above are the *only* forms found in the NT. Feminine and neuter forms, e.g., ἀλλήλαις, ἄλληλα, sometimes occur in the LXX.)

159. Possessive Adjectives

The most common way of expressing possession in biblical Greek is by the genitive case of the personal pronouns: τὸ βιβλίον μου, "my book"; ὁ οἶκος αὐτῆς, "her house." But there were also possessive adjectives (for first and second person only) corresponding to English "my," "your" (sing.), "our," and "your" (pl.): ἐμός, σός, ἡμέτερος, and ὑμέτερος. These are declined like regular adjectives of the first and second declensions. They will agree with the nouns they modify in case number and gender. If the

(handwritten margin note at bottom: ἀ not ~/subject AS IN GENITIVE)

noun they modify has the article, they will stand in the attributive position. Examples: τὸ ἐμὸν βιβλίον, "my book"; τὰ πλοῖα τὰ ὑμέτερα, "your boats." The plural forms are relatively rare; the singular forms somewhat more common; but both occur much less frequently than the genitive of the personal pronoun.

160. Exercises

Practice and Review

1. ἐν ἐκείνῃ τῇ ἡμέρᾳ πῦρ πεσεῖται ἀπὸ τοῦ οὐρανοῦ καὶ ὁ ἄγγελος τοῦ φωτὸς ἀπαγγελεῖ τὸν λόγον σαρκὶ πάσῃ.

2. γινώσκομεν ὅτι ἀποθανούμεθα, ὅπου δὲ ἐλευσόμεθα; ἡμεῖς γὰρ οὐκ ἐτηρήσαμεν τὰς ἐντολὰς τοῦ θεοῦ.

3. κρινεῖ ὁ θεὸς ἕκαστον ἡμῶν ἐν τῇ ἡμέρᾳ τῇ ἐσχάτῃ, ὀφείλομεν οὖν πολλάκις παρακαλεῖν ἀλλήλους.

4. ὑμεῖς μὲν προσκυνεῖτε δαιμονίοις, ἡμεῖς δὲ προσκυνοῦμεν τῷ θεῷ τῷ ποιήσαντι τὸ ὕδωρ καὶ τὴν γῆν καὶ πάντα ἐν αὐτοῖς.

5. ὁ σπείρων βαλεῖ τὸ σπέρμα ἐπὶ τὴν γῆν, ἀλλὰ δοκοῦμεν ὅτι ὁ πονηρὸς ἐλεύσεται καὶ ἀρεῖ αὐτό.

6. εὑρήσομεν ἐκεῖνον τὸν ἄνθρωπον καὶ κρινοῦμεν αὐτὸν κατὰ τὸν ἡμέτερον νόμον· αὐτὸς γὰρ ἔλαβε τὰ σὰ βιβλία καὶ ἔφυγεν.

7. ἐρεῖτε τοὺς ἐμοὺς λόγους τοῖς ὄχλοις καὶ ἀποστελεῖτε τοὺς ὑμετέρους δούλους συναγαγεῖν τὰ τέκνα εἰς τὸ ἱερόν.

8. μενοῦμεν ἐν τῇ ἀληθείᾳ, ὁ θεὸς γὰρ ἀπέστειλεν τὸν ἅγιον προφήτην αὐτοῦ ἀπαγγέλλοντα ταῦτα.

9. τὸ ἔργον ἑκάστου κριθήσεται ἐν πυρί, καὶ ὁ κύριος αὐτὸς ἐγερεῖ ἡμᾶς ζῆν ἐν τῷ φωτὶ μετ' ἀλλήλων.

10. βαλεῖτε τὸν ὑμέτερον ἄρτον ἐπὶ τὸ ὕδωρ καὶ προσκυνήσετε τῷ υἱῷ τῆς δικαιοσύνης ἐν τούτῳ τῷ τόπῳ.

11. οἱ ἁμαρτωλοὶ ἐκεῖνοι δοκοῦσιν ὅτι τηροῦντες τὰς ἀνθρώπων ἐντολὰς εὑρήσουσι χάριν μετὰ θεοῦ.

12. ἐν τῷ σῷ ὀνόματι, κύριε, ἐσπείραμεν σπέρματα τῆς εἰρήνης, ἀλλὰ μενεῖ τὸ ἔργον τὸ ἡμέτερον;

13. ὁ κύριος ἀπέστειλεν τὴν ἐμὴν ἀδελφὴν ὅπου οὐκ ἔθελεν ἐλθεῖν, ἀλλ' ἔμεινεν ἐκεῖ καὶ ἀπήγγειλεν τὸ πᾶν θέλημα τοῦ θεοῦ.

14. οἱ δοκοῦντες ἔχειν τὸ πῦρ τοῦ πνεύματος ἦραν τὰς χεῖρας καὶ προσηύξαντο τῷ θεῷ.

LXX

1. ἐξῆλθεν δὲ Μωυσῆς εἰς συνάντησιν τῷ γαμβρῷ αὐτοῦ καὶ προσεκύνησεν αὐτῷ . . . καὶ ἠσπάσαντο ἀλλήλους· (Exod 18:7)

2. ὃς φυλάσσει ἐντολήν, τηρεῖ τὴν ἑαυτοῦ ψυχήν· (Prov 19:16)

3. εἶπεν δὲ Ιωσηφ πρὸς τοὺς ἀδελφοὺς αὐτοῦ . . . Ἀπαγγελῶ τῷ Φαραω καὶ ἐρῶ αὐτῷ, Οἱ ἀδελφοί μου . . . ἥκασιν πρός με· (Gen 46:31)

4. ἀλλὰ ἀποστελεῖ κύριος . . . εἰς τὴν σὴν τιμὴν ἀτιμίαν, . . . καὶ ἔσται τὸ φῶς τοῦ Ισραηλ εἰς πῦρ καὶ ἁγιάσει αὐτὸν ἐν πυρί . . . (Isa 10:16-17)

5. καὶ σπερῶ αὐτὴν ἐμαυτῷ ἐπὶ τῆς γῆς . . . καὶ ἐρῶ τῷ Οὐ-λαῷ-μου, Λαός μου εἶ σύ, καὶ αὐτὸς ἐρεῖ, Κύριος ὁ θεός μου εἶ σύ. (Hos 2:25, ET 2:23)

6. δός μοι, υἱέ, σὴν καρδίαν, οἱ δὲ σοὶ ὀφθαλμοὶ ἐμὰς ὁδοὺς τηρείτωσαν· (Prov 23:26)

7. καὶ εἶπεν αὐτῇ Σαμψων, Ἰδοὺ τῷ πατρί μου καὶ τῇ μητρί μου οὐκ ἀπήγγειλα αὐτό, καὶ σοὶ ἀπαγγελῶ; (Judg 14:16)

8. ἕκαστον κατὰ τὴν ὁδὸν αὐτοῦ κρινῶ ὑμᾶς, . . . λέγει κύριος· (Ezek 18:30)

9. οὐκ ἀποθανεῖται πᾶσα σὰρξ . . . ἀπὸ τοῦ ὕδατος τοῦ κατακλυσμοῦ (Gen 9:11)

10. καὶ πνεῦμα κυρίου ἀρεῖ σε εἰς γῆν . . . καὶ εἰσελεύσομαι ἀπαγγεῖλαι τῷ Αχααβ, καὶ ἀποκτενεῖ με· (3 Kgdms 18:12)

11. Οὐκ ἀποθανοῦνται πατέρες ὑπὲρ τέκνων, καὶ υἱοὶ οὐκ ἀποθανοῦνται ὑπὲρ πατέρων, ἀλλ᾽ ἢ ἕκαστος τῇ ἑαυτοῦ ἁμαρτίᾳ ἀποθανοῦνται. (2 Chr 25:4)

NT

1. ἐὰν δὲ ἐν τῷ φωτὶ περιπατῶμεν ὡς αὐτός ἐστιν ἐν τῷ φωτί, κοινωνίαν ἔχομεν μετ᾽ ἀλλήλων (1 John 1:7)

2. δοκεῖτε ὅτι εἰρήνην παρεγενόμην δοῦναι ἐν τῇ γῇ; οὐχί, λέγω (Luke 12:51)

3. ἀπεκρίνατο λέγων . . . ὁ Ἰωάννης, Ἐγὼ μὲν ὕδατι βαπτίζω ὑμᾶς· . . . αὐτὸς ὑμᾶς βαπτίσει ἐν πνεύματι ἁγίῳ καὶ πυρί· (Luke 3:16)

4. μείνατε ἐν τῇ ἀγάπῃ τῇ ἐμῇ. ἐὰν τὰς ἐντολάς μου τηρήσητε, μενεῖτε ἐν τῇ ἀγάπῃ μου, καθὼς ἐγὼ τὰς ἐντολὰς τοῦ πατρός μου τετήρηκα καὶ μένω αὐτοῦ ἐν τῇ ἀγάπῃ. (John 15:9-10)

5. ὃ ἑωράκαμεν καὶ ἀκηκόαμεν, ἀπαγγέλλομεν καὶ ὑμῖν, ἵνα καὶ ὑμεῖς κοινωνίαν ἔχητε μεθ᾽ ἡμῶν. καὶ ἡ κοινωνία δὲ ἡ ἡμετέρα μετὰ τοῦ πατρὸς καὶ μετὰ τοῦ υἱοῦ αὐτοῦ Ἰησοῦ Χριστοῦ. (1 John 1:3)

6. προσελθόντες δὲ οἱ δοῦλοι . . . εἶπον αὐτῷ, Κύριε, οὐχὶ καλὸν σπέρμα ἔσπειρας ἐν τῷ σῷ ἀγρῷ; (Matt 13:27)

7. οἱ πατέρες ἡμῶν ἐν τῷ ὄρει τούτῳ προσεκύνησαν καὶ ὑμεῖς λέγετε ὅτι ἐν Ἱεροσολύμοις ἐστὶν ὁ τόπος ὅπου προσκυνεῖν δεῖ. (John 4:20)

8. ἀποστελεῖ ὁ υἱὸς τοῦ ἀνθρώπου τοὺς ἀγγέλους αὐτοῦ, καὶ συλλέξουσιν ἐκ τῆς βασιλείας αὐτοῦ . . . τοὺς ποιοῦντας τὴν ἀνομίαν καὶ βαλοῦσιν αὐτοὺς εἰς τὴν κάμινον τοῦ πυρός· (Matt 13:41-42)

9. καὶ τὰ τέκνα αὐτῆς ἀποκτενῶ ἐν θανάτῳ. καὶ γνώσονται πᾶσαι αἱ ἐκκλησίαι ὅτι ἐγώ εἰμι ὁ ἐραυνῶν . . . καρδίας, καὶ δώσω ὑμῖν ἑκάστῳ κατὰ τὰ ἔργα ὑμῶν. (Rev 2:23)

10. εἰ ἐμὲ ἐδίωξαν, καὶ ὑμᾶς διώξουσιν· εἰ τὸν λόγον μου ἐτήρησαν, καὶ τὸν ὑμέτερον τηρήσουσιν. (John 15:20)

English to Greek

1. The demon will hurl fire upon your (pl.) houses and he will kill all the ones who do not bow down to him.
2. We observed the comandments of God and sowed peace in our land.
3. The woman exhorted us, announcing that God will judge those who do not walk in the light with one another.
4. We do not think that water will fall from heaven. So we are going to the lake where we will find it.
5. You (sing.) sent your slaves to take away my books, but my books will remain with me, each in its own place.

Vocabulary for LXX and NT Sentences

ἀγρός, field

ἀνομία, lawlessness, wickedness

ἀτιμία, dishonor

γαμβρός, father-in-law

δός, give! (imperative)

δοῦναι, to give

δώσω, I will give

ἐάν, (+ subjunctive) if

ἐραυνάω, search, examine

ἔχητε, you may have

ἤ, rather

ἥκω, have come

ἵνα, (+ subjunctive) in order that

καθώς, just as

κάμινος, furnace

κατακλυσμός, cataclysm, flood

κοινωνία, fellowship

μείνατε, aorist imperative

ὅ, (that) which

ὄρος, mountain

ὅς, (the one) who

οὐχί, no!, not

συλλέγω, gather

συνάντησις, meeting (with) + dat.

τηρείτωσαν, let them heed

τηρήσητε, you keep

τιμή, honor

φυλάσσω, obey, keep

ὡς, as

Lesson 23

161. Vocabulary

ἀγοράζω, I buy, redeem (agora)
ἄν, a particle that adds contingency;
    may add sense of "-ever"
γραφή, ἡ, writing, Scripture (graphic)
ἐάν, if (+ subj.; = εἰ + ἄν)
ἵνα, in order that, so that (+ subj.)
κώμη, ἡ, village

μηδέ, and not, nor, not even (+ subj.)
μηκέτι, no longer (+ subj.)
ὅπως, in order that, that (+ subj.)
ὅταν, whenever (usu. + subj.)
ὅτε, when (+ indic.)
οὐκέτι, no longer (+ indic.)
ὡς, as, how, that, about

162. Introduction to the Subjunctive Mood

So far all the verb conjugations to which you have been introduced belong to the indicative mood. (Sometimes the participle and the infinitive are considered moods, but they are more precisely described as a verbal adjective and a verbal noun respectively.) In this lesson you will learn the forms and functions of the subjunctive mood.

    The subjunctive mood is sometimes called the "mood of probability." This is a handy label, but like all such labels it does not convey the variety of meanings of which the mood is capable. The subjunctive conveys doubt, expectation, volition, intention, desire, and the like. Whereas the indicative asserts something as reality ("We see the child"), the subjunctive expresses action that is potential or contingent ("Let us see the child"; ". . . so that we may see the child"; "If we see the child . . ."; "Should we see the child?"). The various uses of the subjunctive frequently have the characteristic of futurity.

    The subjunctive occurs in the present, aorist, and perfect tenses. The perfect subjunctive is so rare that its forms will not be given. Because the precise meaning of the subjunctive is entirely dependent on its context, no translations will be given in the following paradigms. The negative for the subjunctive mood is μή.

163. Forms of the Subjunctive

The forms of the *present active* subjunctive are as follows:

	Singular		Plural
1.	λύω	1.	λύωμεν
2.	λύῃς	2.	λύητε
3.	λύῃ	3.	λύωσι(ν)

The forms of the *present middle/passive* subjunctive are as follows:

	Singular		Plural
1.	λύωμαι	1.	λυώμεθα
2.	λύῃ	2.	λύησθε
3.	λύηται	3.	λύωνται

The forms of the *aorist active* subjunctive are as follows:

	Singular		Plural
1.	λύσω	1.	λύσωμεν
2.	λύσῃς	2.	λύσητε
3.	λύσῃ	3.	λύσωσι(ν)

The forms of the *aorist middle* subjunctive are as follows:

	Singular		Plural
1.	λύσωμαι	1.	λυσώμεθα
2.	λύσῃ	2.	λύσησθε
3.	λύσηται	3.	λύσωνται

The forms of the *aorist passive* subjunctive are as follows:

	Singular		Plural
1.	λυθῶ	1.	λυθῶμεν
2.	λυθῇς	2.	λυθῆτε
3.	λυθῇ	3.	λυθῶσι(ν)

The chief characteristic of the forms of the subjunctive mood is the *long variable vowel* that connects the stem to the person number endings. Where the indicative used an omicron connecting vowel, the subjunctive uses an omega. Where the indicative used an epsilon, the subjunctive uses an eta. Note that certain third person plural forms make take movable ν.

The subjunctive uses *primary endings* throughout, even in the aorist, which is a secondary tense. The aorist active and middle subjunctive is built on the third principal part, the aorist passive on the sixth principal part. All aorist subjunctives lack the augment. Second aorist forms, which are not shown, are conjugated like the first aorist except that they are based on the second aorist stem, e.g., from λαμβάνω: λάβω, λάβῃς, λάβῃ, etc. Contrary to expectation, the aorist passive, in addition to having primary endings, has *active* endings! It is the stem, with the characteristic -θ (for the first aorist passive), that distinguishes these forms. Finally, the accent of the aorist passive subjunctive appears to be irregular, but is actually due to contraction between the tense suffix -θε and the endings.

164. Uses of the Subjunctive

The subjunctive mood is used both as the main verb of the sentence, that is, in *independent* clauses, and as a subordinate verb in *dependent* clauses. The first three uses described below are independent uses; the fourth and fifth are dependent. These are among the most common uses of the subjunctive. A few others will be introduced in later lessons.

(1) The first person plural subjunctive is used for exhortations. This is called the *hortatory subjunctive*. The speaker asks others to join in a particular action or state of being.

λέγωμεν πρὸς τὰ τέκνα καὶ παρακαλῶμεν αὐτά.
Let us speak to the children and (let us) comfort them.

ἔλθωμεν εἰς τὴν κώμην καὶ ἀγοράσωμεν ἄρτον.
Let us go into the village and (let us) buy bread.

(2) The *deliberative subjunctive* is used in questions of possibility, desirability, or necessity. Such questions ask what can, should, or must be done. They do not ask for information, but rather a course of action. Some deliberative questions are rhetorical and do not actually expect an answer, but others are genuine inquiries seeking a response. Deliberative questions may be direct or indirect. The first example below is a direct question; the second is an indirect question.

λάβωμεν ἄρτον ἀπὸ τῶν τέκνων ἡμῶν καὶ φάγωμεν αὐτόν;
Shall we take bread from our children and eat it?

ἔθελον γινώσκειν πῶς λαλήσωσι τῷ προφήτῃ.
They wanted to know how they might speak to the prophet.

(3) The subjunctive is used to assert strongly that something will not happen. This has been called the subjunctive of *emphatic negation*. This construction uses the double negative οὐ μή.

οὐ μὴ εἴπητε κακὰ περὶ τῆς μητρός μου.
You will never say bad things about my mother!

τὸν ζητοῦντα ὕδωρ οὐ μὴ πέμψω εἰς τὴν ἔρημον.
The one who seeks water I will never send into the desert.

(4) A very common use of the subjunctive is to express *purpose*. Such clauses will typically be introduced with ἵνα or ὅπως.

ἀναβαίνομεν πρὸς τὸ ἱερὸν ἵνα ἴδωμεν ταῦτα τὰ σημεῖα.
We are going up to the temple so that we may see these signs.

ἐζήτουν τὴν γυναῖκα ὅπως ἀκούσωσιν τὰ ῥήματα αὐτῆς.
They were seeking the woman so that they might hear her words.

(5) The subjunctive is used in *future or present general conditional clauses*. Biblical Greek uses several different types of conditional clauses. You are already familiar with the particle εἰ, which introduces simple conditions containing the indicative mood of a past or present verb in the protasis (the "if" clause) and a wide variety of possible moods and tenses in the apodosis (the "then" clause). In these conditions, the assumption in the protasis is expressed as a "real" case. The "if" in simple conditions sometimes borders on "because." Example: εἰ ὁ ἀνήρ ἐστιν ἐν τῷ ἁγίῳ τόπῳ, οὐ δύνασαι μετ᾽ αὐτοῦ λέγειν, "If the man is in the holy place, you cannot speak with him."

Future or present general conditions are introduced by the particle ἐάν (which is the combination of εἰ + ἄν) followed by the subjunctive mood in the protasis. Again, a variety of constructions occurs in the apodosis. These conditions express what can be expected to occur under certain circumstances, that is, conditions that are not yet actualized, but are likely. Conditions with ἐάν plus the subjunctive refer either to future time or to general circumstances in present time. The latter do *not* pertain to specific, "stated-as-actual" circumstances. They have more of a general, proverbial quality. Here are examples of a future and a present general condition, respectively:

ἐὰν δέξωμαι δῶρον ἀπ᾽ αὐτῶν, γράψω ὑμῖν.
"If I receive a gift from them, I will write to you."

ἐὰν ἁμαρτωλοὶ κράζωσιν τῷ κυρίῳ, ὁ κύριος ἀποκρίνεται.
"If sinners cry out to the Lord, the Lord answers."

Conditional clauses show great diversity. One sometimes finds mixed types and apparent exceptions to the "rules." But for now, this distinction should be learned: εἰ + the indicative mood for simple conditions (past or present); ἐάν + the subjunctive mood for future conditions and present general conditions. A third type will be discussed in a later lesson.

165. Tense and Time in the Subjunctive

As in the case of the participle, tense in the subjunctive has nothing to do with the time of action. An aorist subjunctive, for example, does not denote action in past time. Indeed, *all* tenses of the subjunctive denote potential action and, therefore, tend to refer to future time. As is usually the case outside the indicative, tense in the subjunctive pertains to *kind* of action. The distinction between a present and an aorist subjunctive cannot always be expressed in an English translation.

166. The Present Subjunctive of εἰμὶ

Singular	Plural
1. ὦ	1. ὦμεν
2. ᾖς	2. ἦτε
3. ᾖ	3. ὦσι(ν)

167. Exercises

Practice and Review

1. ὁ διδάσκαλος τῆς δικαιοσύνης ἀπέλυσεν τοὺς ὄχλους ἵνα ἀπελθόντες εἰς τὰς κώμας ἀγοράσωσιν ἑαυτοῖς ἄρτον.
2. συναγάγωμεν τὸν λαὸν εἰς τὸ ἱερὸν ἵνα διὰ τῶν γραφῶν παρακληθῶμεν.
3. ὅπου ἂν εἰσέλθητε εἰς οἶκον, ἐὰν εὕρητε ἐκεῖ τὸ βιβλίον τοῦ νόμου, γνώσεσθε ὅτι ἡ δόξα τοῦ θεοῦ μένει ἐν ἐκείνῳ τῷ τόπῳ.
4. μηκέτι οὖν ἀλλήλους κρίνωμεν, ὅτε γὰρ κρίνομεν τοὺς ἀδελφοὺς καὶ τὰς ἀδελφὰς ἡμῶν, οὐ πληροῦμεν τὸ τοῦ πνεύματος θέλημα.
5. πῶς ζήσωμεν ἐν τῷ κόσμῳ τούτῳ ὅπως ὁ λαὸς ἴδῃ τὸ φῶς τοῦ εὐαγγελίου;
6. ἐὰν μὴ ἀσπάσωμαι αὐτὴν πρὸς τὴν θύραν μηδὲ προσενέγκω ὕδωρ πίνειν, ἡ μήτηρ τῆς γυναικός μου οὐ πάλιν ὑποστρέψει εἰς τὸν οἶκον ἡμῶν.
7. τὸν ἐρχόμενον πρὸς ἐμὲ οὐ μὴ ἐκβάλω καὶ τὸν ζητοῦντα εἰρήνην οὐ μὴ ἀποστείλω εἰς τὴν ἔρημον.
8. ἐὰν μὴ ἁγιάσητε τὸν κύριον ἐν ταῖς καρδίαις ὑμῶν, πῶς προσκυνήσητε αὐτῷ εἰς τὸν αἰῶνα;
9. ὅταν προσεύχησθε οὐκ ἔσεσθε ὡς οἱ ἀγαπῶντες ἐν ταῖς ὁδοῖς προσεύχεσθαι, ὅπως οἱ ἄνθρωποι ἴδωσιν αὐτούς.
10. μηκέτι ἁμαρτάνωμεν εἰς τὸν οὐρανὸν ἀλλ' ἐργαζώμεθα τὸ ἀγαθὸν ἵνα ὦμεν τέκνα τῆς βασιλείας τοῦ θεοῦ.
11. οὐ μὴ πάλιν ἀγοράσωσιν ἄρτον ἐν ταύτῃ τῇ κώμῃ, πάντες οἱ γὰρ φαγόντες αὐτὸν οὐκέτι ζῶσιν.
12. ὅταν δὲ ἔλθῃ ὁ υἱὸς τοῦ ἀνθρώπου, αἱ γραφαὶ τῶν προφητῶν πληρωθήσονται.

13. ὅτε ἤμην μεθ' ὑμῶν ἔλεγον, Μὴ φοβώμεθα ἁμαρτίαν μηδὲ θάνατον, οὐκέτι γάρ ἐσμεν δοῦλοι τῆς σαρκός.

14. πίνωμεν οἶνον ἕως ἂν μὴ δυνώμεθα περιπατεῖν μηδὲ λαλεῖν;

LXX

1. καὶ εἶπεν ὁ θεός, Ποιήσωμεν ἄνθρωπον κατ' εἰκόνα ἡμετέραν (Gen 1:26)

2. νῦν οὖν ἐὰν δυνηθῇς τὴν γραφὴν ἀναγνῶναι . . . τρίτος ἐν τῇ βασιλείᾳ μου ἄρξεις. (Dan 5:16)

3. καὶ ἔσται σοι σημεῖον ἐπὶ τῆς χειρός σου . . . , ὅπως ἂν γένηται ὁ νόμος κυρίου ἐν τῷ στόματί σου· (Exod 13:9)

4. ἐὰν εἴπωμεν, Εἰσέλθωμεν εἰς τὴν πόλιν . . . ἀποθανούμεθα ἐκεῖ· καὶ ἐὰν καθίσωμεν ὧδε, καὶ ἀποθανούμεθα. (4 Kgdms 7:4)

5. πορευσώμεθα οὖν . . . εἰς τὴν ἔρημον, ἵνα θύσωμεν τῷ θεῷ ἡμῶν. (Exod 3:18)

6. ἐὰν . . . ἁμάρτῃ ἀνὴρ εἰς ἄνδρα . . . προσεύξονται ὑπὲρ αὐτοῦ πρὸς κύριον· καὶ ἐὰν τῷ κυρίῳ ἁμάρτῃ, τίς προσεύξεται ὑπὲρ αὐτοῦ; (1 Kgdms 2:25)

7. ἀδελφιδέ μου, ἐξέλθωμεν εἰς ἀγρόν, αὐλισθῶμεν ἐν κώμαις· (Cant 7:12, ET 7:11)

8. οὐ γὰρ μὴ προσκυνήσητε θεῷ ἑτέρῳ· ὁ γὰρ κύριος ὁ θεὸς . . . θεὸς ζηλωτής ἐστιν. (Exod 34:14)

9. Μωυσῆς . . . εἶπεν, Ἐὰν οὖν μὴ πιστεύσωσίν μοι μηδὲ εἰσακούσωσιν τῆς φωνῆς μου, ἐροῦσιν γὰρ . . . Οὐκ ὦπταί σοι ὁ θεός, τί ἐρῶ πρὸς αὐτούς; (Exod 4:1)

10. οὐ μὴ ἐξέλθητε . . . ἐὰν μὴ ὁ ἀδελφὸς ὑμῶν ὁ νεώτερος ἔλθῃ ὧδε. (Gen 42:15)

11. καὶ ζητήσετε ἐκεῖ κύριον τὸν θεὸν ὑμῶν καὶ εὑρήσετε, ὅταν ἐκζητήσητε αὐτὸν ἐξ ὅλης τῆς καρδίας σου (Deut 4:29)

12. καὶ ἀποστέλλουσιν καὶ συνάγουσιν τοὺς σατράπας . . . πρὸς αὐτοὺς καὶ λέγουσιν, Τί ποιήσωμεν κιβωτῷ θεοῦ Ισραηλ; (1 Kgdms 5:8)

NT

1. καὶ εἶπεν, Ἀμὴν λέγω ὑμῖν, ἐὰν μὴ . . . γένησθε ὡς τὰ παιδία, οὐ μὴ εἰσέλθητε εἰς τὴν βασιλείαν τῶν οὐρανῶν. (Matt 18:3)

2. πῶς δὲ πιστεύσωσιν οὗ οὐκ ἤκουσαν; πῶς δὲ ἀκούσωσιν χωρὶς κηρύσσοντος; πῶς δὲ κηρύξωσιν ἐὰν μὴ ἀποσταλῶσιν; (Rom 10:14-5)

3. εἶπον οὖν . . . Τί ποιῶμεν ἵνα ἐργαζώμεθα τὰ ἔργα τοῦ θεοῦ; (John 6:28)

4. ἐὰν πορευθῶ καὶ ἑτοιμάσω τόπον ὑμῖν, πάλιν ἔρχομαι καὶ παραλήμψομαι ὑμᾶς πρὸς ἐμαυτόν, ἵνα ὅπου εἰμὶ ἐγὼ καὶ ὑμεῖς ἦτε. (John 14:3)

5. Ἰησοῦς . . . λέγει . . . Πόθεν ἀγοράσωμεν ἄρτους ἵνα φάγωσιν οὗτοι; (John 6:5)

6. καὶ προσεύχεσθε ὑπὲρ τῶν διωκόντων ὑμᾶς, ὅπως γένησθε υἱοὶ τοῦ πατρὸς ὑμῶν τοῦ ἐν οὐρανοῖς (Matt 5:44-5)

7. τοῦτο δὲ . . . γέγονεν ἵνα πληρωθῶσιν αἱ γραφαὶ τῶν προφητῶν. (Matt 26:56)

8. εἰ νεκροὶ οὐκ ἐγείρονται, Φάγωμεν καὶ πίωμεν, αὔριον γὰρ ἀποθνῄσκομεν. (1 Cor 15:32)

9. καὶ ὑπὲρ πάντων ἀπέθανεν, ἵνα οἱ ζῶντες μηκέτι ἑαυτοῖς ζῶσιν ἀλλὰ τῷ ὑπὲρ αὐτῶν ἀποθανόντι καὶ ἐγερθέντι. (2 Cor 5:15)

10. προσερχώμεθα οὖν μετὰ παρρησίας τῷ θρόνῳ τῆς χάριτος, ἵνα λάβωμεν ἔλεος καὶ χάριν εὕρωμεν (Heb 4:16)

11. οὐκέτι οὐ μὴ πίω ἐκ τοῦ γενήματος τῆς ἀμπέλου ἕως τῆς ἡμέρας ἐκείνης ὅταν αὐτὸ πίνω καινὸν ἐν τῇ βασιλείᾳ τοῦ θεοῦ. (Mark 14:25)

12. ἀγαπῶμεν ἀλλήλους, ὅτι ἡ ἀγάπη ἐκ τοῦ θεοῦ ἐστιν (1 John 4:7-8)

English to Greek

1. Whenever we go into that village, we search for the prophet in order that we may hear all his words.

2. Let us no longer follow the man of sin nor do the deeds of the flesh.

3. If God opens the door of the prison, we will go out into the way. But if not, we will die, remaining faithful to the word.

4. Let us hear the voice of the Spirit in order that we may know the will of God and walk in the light.

5. The holy woman (absolutely) will not glorify the deeds of those who destroy the scriptures.

6. Shall I buy the whole kingdom in order that I might rule on the throne?

Vocabulary for LXX and NT Sentences

ἀγρός, field, country
ἀδελφιδός, beloved
ἄμπελος, grapevine
ἀναγνῶναι, to read
αὐλίζομαι, lodge, dwell
αὔριον, tomorrow
γενήμα, fruit, product
εἰκών, image
εἰσακούω, heed, obey
ἐκζητέω = ζητέω
ἔλεος, mercy
ζηλωτής, jealous
θύω, sacrifice
καινόν, new
κιβωτός, ark

νεώτερος, younger
οὗ, (the one) whom
παιδίον, (young) child, infant
παρρησία, boldness, confidence
Πόθεν, From where? Whence?
πόλις, city
προσεύχεσθε, here = imperative
σατράπης, satrap, governor
Τί, What?
τίς, who?
τρίτος, (as) third (most powerful)
χωρίς, without
ὧδε, here
ὦπται, has appeared (from ὁράω)

Lesson 24

168. Vocabulary

ἀγαπητός, ή, όν, beloved

ἀρχή, ή, beginning, ruler (archaic)

γλῶσσα, ή, tongue, language (glossary, glossolalia)

εἶναι, to be (infinitive of εἰμί)

ἔξεστι(ν), it is lawful (used only in the third person)

θεωρέω, I look at, behold (theory)

κελεύω, I command

μαρτυρέω, I witness, bear witness to, testify (martyr)

παιδίον, τό, infant, young child

παραβολή, ή, parable, proverb

πρό, (+ gen.) before (prologue)

σοφία, ή, wisdom (philosophy)

ὥστε, so that (often + inf.)

169. Introduction to the Infinitive

The forms of the infinitive were introduced with the corresponding conjugations of the indicative in earlier lessons. You have already seen some uses of the infinitive in the exercises and you are familiar with some verbs that take an infinitive to complete their meaning (δεῖ, δύναμαι, θέλω, μέλλω, ὀφείλω). In this lesson the forms of the infinitive are reviewed and a fuller description of its syntax is given.

Remember the basics: an infinitive is a *verbal noun*. As such it exhibits verbal qualities and nounlike qualities. As a verb, it has tense and voice (but not person and number). It may have a subject, a direct object, or an indirect object. It may have adverbial modifiers. Its function in the sentence may be to express purpose, result, time, or cause. As a noun, it may function as the subject of a sentence or as the direct object of a verb. The substantival nature of the infinitive is also seen in the fact that it may take a definite article and may even be the object of a preposition. In such constructions, the infinitive is treated as a *neuter* noun.

Tense in the infinitive pertains to kind of action, not time. A present tense infinitive denotes linear action; an aorist undefined action; a perfect completed action with a continuing result. It will not always be possible to express this difference in an English translation.

The subject of an infinitive is *in the accusative case*. This can be confusing because the direct object of an infinitive is also in the accusative. If an infinitive has both, only context will determine which is which. Here are examples of infinitives with a subject accusative, with a direct object accusative, and with both.

καλόν ἐστιν προσεύχεσθαι ἡμᾶς πολλάκις.
It is a good thing for *us* to pray often.

144

ὁ προφήτης ὀφείλει λαλεῖν λόγους τῆς εἰρήνης.
The prophet must speak *words* of peace.

ἐκεῖνος ὁ κακὸς ἀνὴρ οὐ θέλει ὑμᾶς γινώσκειν τὴν ἀλήθειαν.
That evil man does not want *you* to know the *truth*.

The negative particle μή is used with the infinitive.

170. Forms of the Infinitive

The forms of the infinitive are repeated here:

	Present	Aorist	Perfect
Act.	λύειν	λῦσαι	λελυκέναι
Mid.	λύεσθαι	λύσασθαι	λελύσθαι
Pass.	λύεσθαι	λυθῆναι	λελύσθαι

The present infinitives are based on the first principal part, the aorist active and middle infinitive on the third principal part, the aorist passive infinitive on the sixth principal part, the perfect active infinitive on the fourth principal part, and the perfect middle/passive infinitive on the fifth principal part. The accent of the aorist active, the aorist passive, and the perfect active will always be on the penult; that is, it is not recessive. The second aorist active infinitive is λαβεῖν; the second aorist middle infinitive is λαβέσθαι. Note the irregular accent of these forms as well. The present infinitive of εἰμί is εἶναι.

171. Syntax of the Infinitive

In addition to its complementary function with such verbs as δεῖ, δύναμαι, θέλω, μέλλω, etc., the infinitive has a variety of nounlike functions and verbal functions. Strictly speaking, the infinitive *always* acts as a noun, but its larger function in the sentence is sometimes more substantival, sometimes more verbal. Its nounlike functions include:

(1) The *subject* of the sentence:

καλόν ἐστιν τηρεῖν τὰς ἐντολὰς τοῦ θεοῦ.
It is good to keep the commandments of God.

(2) The *direct object* of a verb:

οἱ ἄνδρὲς οἱ πονηροὶ ἐζήτουν ἀποκτεῖναι τὸν προφήτην.
The evil men were seeking to kill the prophet.

The verbal aspects of the infinitive are seen in the following functions. These often involve constructions with the articular infinitive, sometimes as part of a prepositional phrase.

(3) To express *purpose*. This meaning is expressed in a number of ways, most often by the simple infinitive, the infinitive with the genitive article τοῦ, or the infinitive with the prepositions εἰς or πρός.

τὸ πνεῦμα ἀπέστειλέν σε κηρύσσειν τὸν λόγον τοῦ θεοῦ.
The Spirit sent you to preach the word of God.

ἐλήμφθησαν πρὸς τὰς ἐξουσίας εἰς τὸ σταυρωθῆναι.
They were taken to the authorities in order to be crucified.

(4) To express *result*. This meaning is expressed in various ways, commonly by the simple infinitive, the infinitive with the genitive article τοῦ, and the infinitive with ὥστε.

ἡ γυνὴ ἐθεράπευσεν τὸν τυφλόν, ὥστε τὸν ὄχλον θαυμάζειν.
The woman healed the blind man so that the crowd marveled.

ἀπέθανεν τὸ παιδίον τοῦ μὴ ἔχειν τὴν μητέρα αὐτοῦ εἰρηνην.
The infant died with the result that his mother had no peace.

(5) To express *time*. The infinitival clause may locate the action of the main verb in time relative to another action. The possible relations are threefold: prior, simultaneous, or subsequent. The most common constructions are the articular infinitive with πρό (prior), ἐν (simultaneous), or μετά (subsequent).

πρὸ τοῦ αὐτὸν εἰσελθεῖν εἰς τὸ ἱερὸν ἐλάλησα μετ' αὐτοῦ.
Before he entered the temple, I spoke with him.

ἐν τῷ προσεύχεσθαι αὐτοὺς ἐν τῇ ἐκκλησίᾳ τὸ παιδίον ἔκραξεν.
While they were praying in the assembly, the infant cried out.

μετὰ τὸ ἐκβληθῆναι τὰ δαιμόνια ὁ λαὸς ἐδόξασε τὸν κύριον.
After the demons had been cast out, the people glorified the Lord.

(6) To express *cause*. The most common infinitival construction to express cause is the articular infinitive with <u>διά</u>. *(MORE OFTEN THE SUBJUNCTIVE WOULD BE USED FOR THIS)*

ἔθελεν ὁ ἄρχων ἰδεῖν τὸν ἄνθρωπον διὰ τὸ ἀκοῦσαι περὶ αὐτοῦ.
The ruler wanted to see the man because (he) had heard about him.

172. Indirect Discourse

Indirect discourse is the reporting of speech (or thought, perception, etc.) in a dependent clause. English typically introduces indirect discourse with the conjunction "that." Suppose the original statement was "I see the man." This could be reported as *direct* discourse, using quotations marks: The woman says, "I see the man." As *indirect* discourse the original statement is subordinated to the main clause introducing it: The woman says *that* she sees the man. Biblical Greek often uses the same construction, introducing the discourse with ὅτι: ἡ γυνὴ λέγει ὅτι βλέπει τὸν ἄνθρωπον. You have already seen many examples of this in the exercises. Verbs such as ἀκούω, βλέπω, γινώσκω, λέγω, and πιστεύω may (with greater or lesser frequency) introduce indirect speech, thought, or perception with ὅτι.

But Greek has another way of introducing indirect discourse, one that has a partial, but less common parallel in English. If indirect discourse is introduced with the English word "consider," the construction may use the infinitive: "They consider him *to have* the best qualifications for the job." "I consider her *to be* the best in the field." This construction is limited in English, but somewhat more common in biblical Greek. Example: οὗτος ὁ ἄνθρωπος λέγει τὸν θεὸν μὴ εἶναι. "This man says that there is no God."

In one important respect, however, indirect discourse in Greek differs from indirect discourse in English. Whereas English will sometimes change the form of the original discourse when reporting it indirectly (chiefly when it is introduced with a past tense verb), Greek always retains the mood and tense of the original discourse. Examples:

	Original Discourse	**Indirect Discourse**
English	"I *see* the man."	She <u>says</u> that she *sees* the man.
Greek	βλέπω τὸν ἄνθρωπον.	αὐτὴ λέγει ὅτι *βλέπει* τὸν ἄνθρωπον.
English	"I *see* the man."	She <u>said</u> that she *saw (was seeing)* the man.
Greek	βλέπω τὸν ἄνθρωπον.	αὐτὴ εἶπεν ὅτι *βλέπει* τὸν ἄνθρωπον.
		STILL PRESENT, UNLIKE ENGLISH
English	"I *will see* the man."	She <u>said</u> that she *would see* the man.
Greek	ὄψομαι τὸν ἄνθρωπον.	αὐτὴ εἶπεν ὅτι *ὄψεται* τὸν ἄνθρωπον.
		STILL FUTURE
English	"I *saw* the man."	She <u>said</u> that she *had seen* the man.
Greek	εἶδον τὸν ἄνθρωπον.	αὐτὴ εἶπεν ὅτι *εἶδεν* τὸν ἄνθρωπον.

In the first example, where the indirect discourse is introduced with a present tense verb, English and Greek report the original discourse in the same way. But in the second example, English changes the tense of the original when the indirect discourse is introduced with a past tense. In the third example English changes the mood of an original future indicative to a subjunctive ("would see"). In the last example English changes the past tense of the original discourse to the past perfect. In none of these cases does Greek alter the original discourse (except for the necessary change to third person). This difference between English and Greek must be borne in mind when translating indirect discourse.

173. Exercises

Practice and Review

1. σὺ μὲν λέγεις, Οὐκ ἔξεστιν ἐργάζεσθαι ἐν σαββάτῳ οὐδὲ θεραπεῦσαι, ἡμεῖς δὲ θέλομεν ἀνοῖξαι τοὺς ὀφθαλμοὺς τῶν τυφλῶν.

2. ὁ ἄρχων ἐκέλευσε τὸν δοῦλον τὸν ἀγαπητὸν δέξασθαι τὰ καλὰ ἱμάτια ὡς δῶρα.

3. πρὸ τοῦ θεωρεῖν τὴν δόξαν τοῦ οὐρανοῦ δεῖ περιπατεῖν ἄνθρωπον ἐν ἀληθείᾳ ἐν τούτῳ τῷ κόσμῳ.

4. κακόν ἐστιν λαβεῖν παιδίον ἀπὸ τοῦ οἴκου τῆς μητρὸς αὐτοῦ.

5. διὰ τὸ μὴ λελυκέναι τὸν κύριον τὴν γλῶσσαν τοῦ ἀνδρός, οὐκ ἐδύνατο μαρτυρεῖν περὶ χάριτος τοῦ θεοῦ.

6. ἐλάλησε παραβολὴν κατ' αὐτῶν ὥστε ἆραι αὐτοὺς λίθους βαλεῖν ἐπ' αὐτόν.

7. ἐν τῷ ἀποθνήσκειν τὸν διδάσκαλον, εἶπεν ὁ υἱὸς αὐτοῦ ὅτι ἔχει τὴν σοφίαν τοῦ πατρὸς αὐτοῦ καὶ διδάξει ἐν τῷ τόπῳ αὐτοῦ.

8. ἡ ἀρχὴ τῆς σοφίας ἐστὶν τὸ φοβεῖσθαι τὸν κύριον καὶ προσκυνῆσαι αὐτῷ.

9. μετὰ τὸ ἀκοῦσαι τὴν παραβολὴν οἱ ἁμαρτωλοὶ ᾐτήσαντο τοὺς μαθητὰς ἀπελθεῖν ἀπὸ τῆς κώμης αὐτῶν.

10. εἰ ἡ γλῶσσα βούλεται ἄρχειν ὅλου τοῦ σώματος, ἡ κεφαλὴ ὀφείλει κελεύειν τὸ στόμα μὴ ἀνοῖξαι.

11. ἐληλύθαμεν ἰδεῖν τὴν ἀρχὴν τῶν ἐσχάτων ἡμερῶν πρὸ τοῦ ὀφθῆναι τὸν τοῦ θανάτου ἄγγελον.

12. ἔξεστιν οὕτως κράζειν ἐν τῷ ἱερῷ ὥστε λυθῆναι τὴν εἰρήνην καὶ μὴ δύνασθαι τὸν λαὸν ἀκοῦσαι τὰς γραφάς;

13. κακοὶ ἄνθρωποι ἐμαρτύρησαν κατὰ τοῦ ἀποστόλου εἰς τὸ κριθῆναι αὐτὸν καὶ ἐκβληθῆναι ἐκ τῆς συναγωγῆς.

14. ἐν τῷ θεωρεῖν ὑμᾶς τὸ παιδίον τὸ ἀγαπητὸν παρεγένοντο πᾶσαι αἱ ἅγιαι γυναῖκες λέγουσαι, Δεῖ βαπτισθῆναι αὐτήν.

15. ἐγινώσκετε τὸν προφήτην μὴ εἶναι πιστόν· εἴπετε οὖν ὅτι οὐκ ἀκολουθήσετε αὐτῷ εἰς τὴν ἔρημον, ἀλλὰ φεύξεσθε αὐτόν.

LXX

1. καὶ εἰσοίσεις [αὐτὸ] τῷ πατρί σου, καὶ φάγεται, ὅπως εὐλογήσῃ σε ὁ πατήρ σου πρὸ τοῦ ἀποθανεῖν αὐτόν. (Gen 27:10)

2. πάντα γὰρ ἦν διὰ χειρὸς Ιωσηφ διὰ τὸ τὸν κύριον μετ' αὐτοῦ εἶναι. (Gen 39:23)

3. καὶ νῦν υἱοὺς Ιουδα καὶ Ιερουσαλημ ὑμεῖς λέγετε κατακτήσεσθαι εἰς δούλους καὶ δούλας· οὐκ ἰδού εἰμι μεθ' ὑμῶν μαρτυρῆσαι κυρίῳ θεῷ ὑμῶν; (2 Chron 28:10)

4. καὶ ἐγένετο ἐν τῷ θεωρεῖν με . . . τὸ ὅραμα ἐζήτουν διανοηθῆναι (Dan 8:15)

5. οὐ πρέσβυς οὐδὲ ἄγγελος, ἀλλ' αὐτὸς κύριος ἔσωσεν αὐτοὺς διὰ τὸ ἀγαπᾶν αὐτούς (Isa 63:9)

6. Φυλάξω τὰς ὁδούς μου τοῦ μὴ ἁμαρτάνειν ἐν γλώσσῃ μου· (Ps 38:2, ET 39:1)

7. καὶ ἔπεσεν ἡ οἰκία ἐπὶ τὰ παιδία σου, καὶ ἐτελεύτησαν· ἐσώθην δὲ ἐγὼ μόνος καὶ ἦλθον τοῦ ἀπαγγεῖλαί σοι. (Job 1:19)

8. καὶ εἴπαμεν τῷ κυρίῳ, Οὐ δυνήσεται τὸ παιδίον καταλιπεῖν τὸν πατέρα· ἐὰν δὲ καταλίπῃ τὸν πατέρα, ἀποθανεῖται. (Gen 44:22)

9. ταῦτα ἀκούσας . . . Ἀντίοχος ἐκέλευσεν τὴν γλῶτταν αὐτοῦ ἐκτεμεῖν. (4 Macc 10:17)

10. καὶ ἔζησεν Μαθουσαλα μετὰ τὸ γεννῆσαι αὐτὸν τὸν Λαμεχ ὀκτακόσια δύο ἔτη καὶ ἐγέννησεν υἱοὺς καὶ θυγατέρας. (Gen 5:26)

11. ὁ δὲ Ααρων ὁ ἀδελφός σου λαλήσει πρὸς Φαραω ὥστε ἐξαποστεῖλαι τοὺς υἱοὺς Ισραηλ ἐκ τῆς γῆς αὐτοῦ (Exod 7:2)

NT

1. ἀποκριθεὶς δὲ αὐτῷ ὁ Πέτρος εἶπεν, Κύριε, εἰ σὺ εἶ, κέλευσόν με ἐλθεῖν πρὸς σὲ ἐπὶ τὰ ὕδατα. (Matt 14:28)

2. καὶ ἔρχονται πρὸς τὸν Ἰησοῦν καὶ θεωροῦσιν τὸν δαιμονιζόμενον . . . καὶ ἐφοβήθησαν. . . . καὶ ἤρξαντο παρακαλεῖν αὐτὸν ἀπελθεῖν ἀπὸ τῶν ὁρίων αὐτῶν. (Mark 5:15, 17)

3. ἔλεγεν γὰρ ὁ Ἰωάννης [τῷ Ἡρῴδῃ], Οὐκ ἔξεστίν σοι ἔχειν αὐτήν. καὶ θέλων αὐτὸν ἀποκτεῖναι ἐφοβήθη τὸν ὄχλον (Matt 14:4-5)

4. οἶδεν γὰρ ὁ πατὴρ ὑμῶν ὧν χρείαν ἔχετε πρὸ τοῦ ὑμᾶς αἰτῆσαι αὐτόν. (Matt 6:8)

5. καὶ ἔλεγεν αὐτῇ, . . . οὐ γὰρ ἐστιν καλὸν λαβεῖν τὸν ἄρτον τῶν τέκνων καὶ τοῖς κυναρίοις βαλεῖν. (Mark 7:27)

6. Ἐγένετο δὲ ἐν τῷ βαπτισθῆναι . . . τὸν λαὸν καὶ Ἰησοῦ βαπτισθέντος καὶ προσευχομένου ἀνεῳχθῆναι τὸν οὐρανὸν . . . φωνὴν ἐξ οὐρανοῦ γενέσθαι, Σὺ εἶ ὁ υἱός μου ὁ ἀγαπητός (Luke 3:21-22)

7. βασίλισσα νότου . . . ἦλθεν ἐκ τῶν περάτων τῆς γῆς ἀκοῦσαι τὴν σοφίαν Σολομῶνος (Luke 11:31)

8. φεῦγε εἰς Αἴγυπτον . . . μέλλει γὰρ Ἡρῴδης ζητεῖν τὸ παιδίον τοῦ ἀπολέσαι αὐτό. (Matt 2:13)

9. θέλω δὲ πάντας ὑμᾶς λαλεῖν γλώσσαις, μᾶλλον δὲ ἵνα προφητεύητε· μείζων δὲ ὁ προφητεύων ἢ ὁ λαλῶν γλώσσαις (1 Cor 14:5)
10. ἔθετο ὁ Παῦλος ἐν τῷ πνεύματι . . . πορεύεσθαι εἰς Ἱεροσόλυμα εἰπὼν . . . Μετὰ τὸ γενέσθαι με ἐκεῖ δεῖ με καὶ Ῥώμην ἰδεῖν. (Act 19:21)
11. Καὶ [Ἰησοῦς] ἔρχεται εἰς οἶκον· καὶ συνέρχεται πάλιν [ὁ] ὄχλος, ὥστε μὴ δύνασθαι αὐτοὺς μηδὲ ἄρτον φαγεῖν. (Mark 3:20)
12. οὐκ ἔχετε διὰ τὸ μὴ αἰτεῖσθαι ὑμᾶς (Jas 4:2)

English to Greek

1. Even the tongue of a young child is able to testify that we ought to love one another.
2. Before [he] told a parable to the crowd, the beloved teacher of wisdom commanded them to sit down by the sea.
3. In the beginning we wanted to behold the face of God, but now we hear that it is not lawful to see him.
4. Because I believe in the Lord, I do not fear the rulers of this earth.
5. You (pl.) came through the desert to bring bread to the young children, but they have gone to another place with the result that the bread is no longer good.

Vocabulary for LXX and NT Sentences

ἀνεῳχθῆναι, from ἀνοίγω
ἀπολέσαι, to destroy
βασίλισσα νότου, queen of the South
γλῶττα = γλῶσσα
δαιμονίζόμαι, be demon possessed
διανοέομαι, think, understand
δούλη, slave woman
ἔθετο, determined, resolved
εἷς, one
εἰσοίσεις, from ἐκφέρω
ἐκτέμνω, cut out
ἐξαποστεῖλαι, from ἐκ + ἀποστέλλω
εὐλογέω, bless
ἤ, than
θυγάτηρ, daughter
κατακτήσεσθαι, [that you will] take possession of

καταλείπω, abandon, leave behind
κέλευσον, imperative
κυνάριον, dog
μᾶλλον, more, rather
μείζων, greater
μόνος, alone
οἰκία = οἶκος
ὀκτακόσια δύο ἔτη, 802 years
ὅριον, territory, region
πέρας, ατος, end, boundary
πρέσβυς, elder, ambassador
συνέρχομαι, come together
τελευτάω, die
φεῦγε, imperative of φεύγω
φυλάσσω, keep, observe
χρεία, need
ὧν, (the things) of which

Lesson 25

174. Vocabulary

ἀληθής, ές, true

ἀρχιερεύς, έως, ὁ, chief priest

ἀσθενής, ές, weak, sick

βασιλεύς, έως, ὁ, king (Basil)

γένος, ους, τό, race, stock; people, descendants; kind (genus)

γραμματεύς, έως, ὁ, scribe (grammar)

δύναμις, εως, ἡ, power, strength; miracle (usu. plur.) (dynamite)

ἔθνος, ους, τό, nation; plur. τὰ ἔθνη, the nations, Gentiles (ethnic)

ἱερεύς, έως, ὁ, priest

κρίσις, εως, ἡ, judgment (crisis)

ὄρος, ους, τό, mountain (orology)

πίστις, εως, ἡ, faith, trust, belief

πλήρης, ες, full

πόλις, εως, ἡ, city (metropolis)

τέλος, ους, τό, end (teleology)

175. More Third Declension Noun Types

The third declension was introduced in Lesson 17. You may wish to review the basic endings and special characteristics of this declension in §117. In this lesson three new types of third declension nouns are given. The above vocabulary list contains three or four examples of each type. It happens that each of the three genders is represented.

176. Feminine Nouns in -ις, -εως

The declension of πόλις, πόλεως is as follows:

Singular		Plural	
Nom.	πόλις	Nom. Voc.	πόλεις
Gen.	πόλεως	Gen.	πόλεων
Dat.	πόλει	Dat.	πόλεσι(ν)
Acc.	πόλιν	Acc.	πόλεις
Voc.	πόλι		

The stem of πόλις is πόλι-, but the final iota often changes to epsilon. In addition, contraction sometimes occurs between the final stem vowel and the endings, so that it may be better simply to learn the endings as they occur rather than worry about their formation. The accent of genitive singular and plural is an exception to the rule found in §5 (3).

151

Lesson 25

177. Masculine Nouns in -ευς, -εως

Singular		Plural	
Nom.	βασιλεύς	Nom. Voc.	βασιλεῖς
Gen.	βασιλέως	Gen.	βασιλέων
Dat.	βασιλεῖ	Dat.	βασιλεῦσι(ν)
Acc.	βασιλέα	Acc.	βασιλεῖς
Voc.	βασιλεῦ		

The stem of βασιλεύς is βασιλευ-, but the final upsilon is dropped before endings beginning with a vowel. Again, due to contraction and other peculiarities, it is advisable to learn the endings as they occur and not to be overly concerned with their formation.

178. Neuter Nouns in -ος, -ους

Singular		Plural	
Nom. Voc.	γένος	Nom. Voc.	γένη
Gen.	γένους	Gen.	γενῶν
Dat.	γένει	Dat.	γένεσι(ν)
Acc.	γένος	Acc.	γένη

The stem of γένος is γένεσ-, but the final sigma is dropped in most forms, and contraction occurs between the epsilon and the endings. Like all neuter nouns, γένος has identical forms in the nominative, vocative, and accusative of each number.

179. Adjectives of the Third Declension

The adjectives you have learned up to this point are adjectives of the first and second declensions such as καλός, ή, όν. A smaller group of adjectives in biblical Greek is declined according to the third declension in all three genders. The most common type is illustrated by ἀληθής, "true."

	Singular			Plural	
	Masc. Fem.	Neut.		Masc. Fem.	Neut.
N.	ἀληθής	ἀληθές	N. V.	ἀληθεῖς	ἀληθῆ
G.	ἀληθοῦς	ἀληθοῦς	G.	ἀληθῶν	ἀληθῶν
D.	ἀληθεῖ	ἀληθεῖ	D.	ἀληθέσι(ν)	ἀληθέσι(ν)
A.	ἀληθῆ	ἀληθές	A.	ἀληθεῖς	ἀληθῆ
V.	ἀληθές	ἀληθές			

152

The stem of ἀληθής is ἀληθεσ-. The final sigma is dropped in most forms, and contraction occurs between the epsilon and the endings. Since third declension adjectives are not encountered as often as those of the first and second declensions, the student's chief aim should be recognition of these forms in context.

180. Exercises

Practice and Review

1. εἰ τὰ κηρυχθέντα ὑπὸ τῶν μαθητῶν ἀληθῆ ἐστιν, ἡ κρίσις τοῦ θεοῦ μέλλει πεσεῖν ἐπὶ τὴν πόλιν ἡμῶν.
2. οὖσαι πληρεῖς πίστεως καὶ δυνάμεως αἱ ἀδελφαὶ ὑμῶν οὐκ ἐφοβοῦντο τὸν βασιλέα.
3. ἀναβαινόντων εἰς τὸ ὄρος τῶν ἱερέων, ἄνθρωποι πονηροὶ εἰσῆλθον εἰς τὸ ἱερὸν λαβεῖν τὸ βιβλίον τοῦ νόμου.
4. ἐκεῖνοι οἱ ἄνδρες ἦσαν ἐκ γένους ἀρχιερέων· προσέφερον οὖν δῶρα ὑπὲρ ἁμαρτιῶν τοῦ ἔθνους.
5. τὸ ἔργον τοῦ γραμματέως ἐστὶν γράψαι τὰ ῥήματα τοῦ θεοῦ εἰς βιβλίον καὶ διδάσκειν αὐτὰ τῷ λαῷ.
6. ἀσθενὴς ἤμην καὶ ἐν φυλακῇ ἀλλ' οὐκ ἤλθετε ἰδεῖν με οὐδὲ προσηύξασθε ὑπὲρ ἐμοῦ.
7. ὁ μένων εἰς τὸ τέλος σωθήσεται καὶ γνώσεται τὴν ἀγάπην τοῦ κυρίου.
8. ὁ πέμψας με ἀληθής ἐστιν· ἐλεύσομαι οὖν καὶ ἀπαγγελῶ τὴν ἀλήθειαν αὐτοῦ εἰς τὰ ἔθνη.
9. ἔχωμεν πίστιν εἰς θεὸν ἵνα ὅταν ὁ υἱὸς τοῦ ἀνθρώπου ὑποστρέψῃ εὑρεθῶμεν πιστοὶ ἐν ἡμέρᾳ κρίσεως.
10. θεωροῦντες σημεῖα τε καὶ δυνάμεις γινομένας διὰ τῶν χειρῶν τοῦ προφήτου, οἱ ἀρχιερεῖς καὶ οἱ γραμματεῖς ἐθαύμασαν καὶ ἐδόξασαν τὸν βασιλέα τοῦ οὐρανοῦ.
11. ὢν ἀσθενὴς ἐν σώματι καὶ πνεύματι ἔτι θέλει ὁ τυφλὸς ἐξελθεῖν ἀπὸ τῆς πόλεως θεραπευθῆναι ὑπὸ τοῦ διδασκάλου ἐπὶ τὸ ὄρος.
12. γένος οὖν ὑπάρχοντες τοῦ θεοῦ οὐκ ὀφείλομεν δοκεῖν τὸν θεὸν εἶναι λίθον.
13. τὸ μὲν τέλος ἐκείνου τοῦ δικαίου δούλου ἔσται ἀληθὴς δόξα, τὸ δὲ τέλος τούτου τοῦ κακοῦ ἱερέως ἔσται κρίσις πυρός.
14. εἶπεν ὁ βασιλεὺς ὅτι ἡ πᾶσα πόλις ἐστὶν πλήρης αἵματος καὶ ὁ ἄγγελος τῆς κρίσεως ἐπ' αὐτὴν ἐλεύσεται.

LXX

1. οἱ δὲ ὀφθαλμοὶ Λείας ἀσθενεῖς, Ραχηλ δὲ καλὴ . . . ἠγάπησεν δὲ Ιακωβ τὴν Ραχηλ (Gen 29:17-18)
2. καὶ νῦν καθεστάκαμέν σε σήμερον ἀρχιερέα τοῦ ἔθνους σου καὶ φίλον βασιλέως καλεῖσθαί σε (1 Macc 10:20)

3. [Αβρααμ εἶπεν] ἐὰν ὦσιν πεντήκοντα δίκαιοι ἐν τῇ πόλει, ἀπολεῖς αὐτούς; . . .
   ὁ κρίνων πᾶσαν τὴν γῆν οὐ ποιήσεις κρίσιν; εἶπεν δὲ κύριος, Ἐὰν εὕρω ἐν
   Σοδομοις πεντήκοντα δικαίους ἐν τῇ πόλει, ἀφήσω πάντα τὸν τόπον δι'
   αὐτούς. (Gen 18:24-26)
4. Ἐγένετο δὲ μετὰ τὸ λαλῆσαι τὸν κύριον πάντα τὰ ῥήματα ταῦτα τῷ Ιωβ
   εἶπεν ὁ κύριος [τῷ] Ελιφας . . . Ἥμαρτες σὺ καὶ οἱ δύο φίλοι σου· οὐ γὰρ
   ἐλαλήσατε ἐνώπιόν μου ἀληθὲς (Job 42:7)
5. καὶ συνεκάλεσεν Ἰησοῦς . . . τοὺς υἱοὺς Ισραηλ . . . καὶ τοὺς ἄρχοντας αὐτῶν
   καὶ τοὺς γραμματεῖς αὐτῶν . . . καὶ εἶπεν πρὸς αὐτούς . . . ἑωράκατε ὅσα
   ἐποίησεν κύριος ὁ θεὸς ὑμῶν πᾶσιν τοῖς ἔθνεσιν τούτοις (Josh 23:2-3)
6. καὶ εἶπεν Σαφφαν ὁ γραμματεὺς πρὸς τὸν βασιλέα . . . Βιβλίον ἔδωκέν μοι
   Χελκιας ὁ ἱερεύς· . . . καὶ ἐγένετο ὡς ἤκουσεν ὁ βασιλεὺς τοὺς λόγους τοῦ
   βιβλίου τοῦ νόμου, καὶ διέρρηξεν τὰ ἱμάτια ἑαυτοῦ. (4 Kgdms 22:10-11)
7. πάντες οἱ ἀδελφοί μου καὶ οἱ ἐκ τοῦ γένους μου ἤσθιον ἐκ τῶν ἄρτων τῶν
   ἐθνῶν· (Tob 1:10)
8. καὶ διήνοιξεν κύριος τοὺς ὀφθαλμοὺς αὐτοῦ, καὶ εἶδεν, καὶ ἰδοὺ τὸ ὄρος
   πλῆρες ἵππων, καὶ ἄρμα πυρὸς περικύκλῳ Ελισαιε. (4 Kgdms 6:17)
9. ἐπιστρέψει κύριος ὁ θεὸς ἡμῶν τὸ ἔλεος αὐτοῦ ἐφ' ἡμᾶς, οὐ γὰρ ἐγκαταλείψει
   ἡμᾶς εἰς τέλος· (Judith 7:30)
10. καὶ εἶδεν ὁ λαὸς τὴν πίστιν τοῦ Σιμωνος καὶ τὴν δόξαν, ἣν ἐβουλεύσατο
    ποιῆσαι τῷ ἔθνει αὐτοῦ (1 Macc 14:35)
11. οἶδεν γὰρ πᾶσα φυλὴ λαοῦ μου ὅτι γυνὴ δυνάμεως εἶ σύ (Ruth 3:11)

NT

1. μήτε ἀρχὴν ἡμερῶν μήτε ζωῆς τέλος ἔχων, . . . μένει ἱερεὺς εἰς τὸ διηνεκές.
   (Heb 7:3)
2. Ὑμεῖς δὲ γένος ἐκλεκτόν, . . . ἔθνος ἅγιον, . . . ὅπως τὰς ἀρετὰς ἐξαγγείλητε
   τοῦ . . . ὑμᾶς καλέσαντος εἰς τὸ θαυμαστὸν αὐτοῦ φῶς· (1 Pet 2:9)
3. [Βαρναβᾶς] ἦν ἀνὴρ ἀγαθὸς καὶ πλήρης πνεύματος ἁγίου καὶ πίστεως. (Acts
   11:24)
4. ἐγενόμην τοῖς ἀσθενέσιν ἀσθενής, ἵνα τοὺς ἀσθενεῖς κερδήσω· τοῖς πᾶσιν
   γέγονα πάντα, ἵνα . . . τινὰς σώσω. (1 Cor 9:22)
5. καὶ ἤκουσαν οἱ ἀρχιερεῖς καὶ οἱ γραμματεῖς καὶ ἐζήτουν πῶς αὐτὸν
   ἀπολέσωσιν· ἐφοβοῦντο γὰρ αὐτόν (Mark 11:18)
6. καὶ ἐποίησεν ἡμᾶς βασιλείαν, ἱερεῖς τῷ θεῷ καὶ πατρὶ αὐτοῦ, αὐτῷ ἡ δόξα καὶ
   τὸ κράτος εἰς τοὺς αἰῶνας [τῶν αἰώνων]· ἀμήν. (Rev 1:6)
7. ἀλλὰ προσεληλύθατε Σιὼν ὄρει καὶ πόλει θεοῦ ζῶντος, Ἰερουσαλὴμ
   ἐπουρανίῳ (Heb 12:22)
8. Στέφανος δὲ πλήρης χάριτος καὶ δυνάμεως ἐποίει τέρατα καὶ σημεῖα μεγάλα
   ἐν τῷ λαῷ. (Acts 6:8)
9. Οὗτός ἐστιν ὁ μαθητὴς ὁ μαρτυρῶν περὶ τούτων καὶ ὁ γράψας ταῦτα, καὶ
   οἴδαμεν ὅτι ἀληθὴς αὐτοῦ ἡ μαρτυρία ἐστίν. (John 21:24)

10. καὶ ἔχει ἐπὶ τὸ ἱμάτιον καὶ ἐπὶ τὸν μηρὸν αὐτοῦ ὄνομα γεγραμμένον·
Βασιλεὺς βασιλέων καὶ κύριος κυρίων. (Rev 19:16)

English to Greek

1. A just king will heal the nation; his land will be full of peace unto the end.
2. A prophet can perform signs, but do priests and scribes have this kind of power?
3. The Gentiles said, "Let us go to the mountain of the Lord in order that we may find faith."
4. God has prepared a city for his people, and in the day of judgment all the weak will flee there and abide in love.

Vocabulary for LXX and NT Sentences

ἀπολεῖς, you will destroy
ἀπολέσωσιν, they might destroy
ἀρετή, virtue, praise
ἄρμα, chariot(s)
ἀφήσω, I will forgive
βουλεύομαι, determine, plan
διανοίγω = ἀνοίγω
διαρήσσω, tear, rend
(εἰς τὸ) διηνεκές = εἰς τὸν αἰῶνα
δύο, two
ἐγκαταλείπω, forsake, abandon
ἔδωκεν, gave
ἐκλεκτός, chosen
ἔλεος, mercy
ἐνώπιον, before, in the presence of
ἐξαγγέλλω, proclaim, declare
ἐπουράνιος, heavenly
ἥν, which

θαυμαστός, marvelous, wonderful
ἵππος, horse
καθεστάκαμεν, we have appointed
κερδαίνω, win, gain
κράτος, might, strength
μαρτυρία, testimony
μέγας, μεγάλη, μέγα, great
μηρός, thigh
οἶδα = γινώσκω
ὅσα, everything that
πεντήκοντα, fifty
περικύκλῳ, in a circle around
σήμερον, today
συν + καλέω, call together
τέρας, ατος, τό, wonder
τινάς, some
φίλος, friend
φυλή, tribe

Lesson 26

181. Vocabulary

ἀγρός, ὁ, field, country (agriculture)
αἰώνιος, ον, eternal (aeon)
ἐλεέω, I have mercy on, pity
ἐπερωτάω, I ask, question
ἐρωτάω, I ask, request, entreat
καρπός, ὁ, fruit

κρατέω, I seize, grasp, hold (to)
μετανοέω, I repent
οὖς, ὠτός, τό, ear (otology)
ὑπάγω, I go away, go
χαίρω, I rejoice
ὧδε, here, hither

182. Introduction to the Imperative

The imperative mood is used positively for commands and negatively for prohibitions. It chiefly uses the present and aorist tenses; the perfect imperative is rare in biblical Greek. The present imperative is constructed on the first principal part, the aorist active and middle imperatives on the third principal part, and the aorist passive imperative on the sixth. There is no first person imperative, only second and third. (The hortatory subjunctive is a kind of first person imperative.) The negative particle used with the imperative mood is μή.

183. Forms of the Present Imperative

The forms of the *present active* imperative are as follows:

Singular	Plural
2. λῦε, loosen!	2. λύετε, loosen!
3. λυέτω, let him/her/it loosen!	3. λυέτωσαν, let them loosen!

The forms of the *present middle/passive* imperative are as follows. (The translations given here are for the passive voice only.)

Singular	Plural
2. λύου, be loosened!	2. λύεσθε, be loosened!
3. λυέσθω, let him/her/it be loosened!	3. λυέσθωσαν, let them be loosened!

Note that the present imperative second person plural (in all voices) is identical in form to the corresponding present indicatives. Only context will determine which is intended.

184. Forms of the First Aorist Imperative

The forms of the *first aorist active* imperative are as follows:

Singular	Plural
2. λῦσον, loosen!	2. λύσατε, loosen!
3. λυσάτω, let him/her loosen!	3. λυσάτωσαν, let them loosen!

The forms of the *first aorist middle* imperative are as follows:

Singular	Plural
2. λῦσαι, loosen (for yourself)!	2. λύσασθε, loosen (for yourselves)!
3. λυσάσθω, let him/her loosen (for himself/herself)!	3. λυσάσθωσαν, let them loosen (for themselves)!

The forms of the *first aorist passive* imperative are as follows:

Singular	Plural
2. λύθητι, be loosened!	2. λύθητε, be loosened!
3. λυθήτω, let him/her be loosened!	3. λυθήτωσαν, let them be loosened!

Most forms of the first aorist active and middle imperative have the characteristic σα-. The passive has the characteristic -θη. All aorist imperatives naturally lack the augment.

185. Forms of the Second Aorist Imperative

The forms of the *second aorist active* imperative are as follows:

Singular	Plural
2. λάβε, take!	2. λάβετε, take!
3. λαβέτω, let him/her take!	3. λαβέτωσαν, let them take!

The forms of the *second aorist middle* imperative are as follows.

Singular	Plural
2. λαβοῦ, take (for yourself)!	2. λάβεσθε, take (for yourselves)!
3. λαβέσθω, let him/her take (for himself/herself)!	3. λαβέσθωσαν, let them take (for themselves)!

As usual, the second aorist has forms similar to the corresponding present tense forms except that the former are built on the third principal part of the verb. Note that the second aorist middle imperative second person singular, λαβοῦ, has an irregular accent. In addition, two common verbs have an irregular accent in the second aorist *active* imperative second person singular: εἰπέ, "say, tell!" and ἐλθέ, "go, come!"

186. Tense and Time in the Imperative

As is always the case outside the indicative, tense in the imperative mood does not pertain to time, but rather to *kind* of action. A present imperative usually implies that the action called for is to be prolonged or repeated, while the aorist does not carry this implication. This distinction is not always apparent, however, and it is particularly difficult to translate this nuance into English. Aorist and present tense imperatives will often be translated the same. Examples:

μετανοήσατε ἀπὸ τῶν ἁμαρτιῶν ὑμῶν καὶ πιστεύετε εἰς τὸν κύριον.
Repent of your sins and believe in the Lord!

μενέτω ἡ γυνὴ ἐν τῇ γῇ καὶ φαγέτωσαν τὸν καρπὸν τὰ τέκνα αὐτῆς.
Let the woman remain in the land, and let her children eat the fruit!

187. Prohibitions

Prohibitions are expressed in two ways in Greek: by μή with the *present imperative* or by μή with the *aorist subjunctive*. (Prohibitions with the aorist imperative are very rare.) The difference pertains to how the action is conceived. The present imperative with μή forbids the continuance of an action, often an action that is in progress: "Stop doing that!" The aorist subjunctive with μή is a categorical prohibition. It views the action as a whole and often forbids action that has not yet begun: "Do not (begin to) do that!" Examples:

ἄγγελος ὤφθη καὶ εἶπεν τῷ λαῷ, Μὴ φοβεῖσθε.
An angel appeared and said to the people, "Do not be afraid!"

μὴ εἰσέλθητε εἰς τὴν πόλιν μηδὲ εἴπητε τῷ βασιλεῖ.
Do not enter into the city nor speak to the king!

Lesson 26

188. Present Imperative of εἰμί

Singular	Plural
2. ἴσθι, be!	2. ἔστε, be!
3. ἔστω, let him, her, it be!	3. ἔστωσαν, let them be!

A less common form of the third person singular is ἤτω.

189. Exercises

Practice and Review

1. οἱ ἁμαρτωλοὶ ἔκραξαν, Κύριε, ἐλέησον ἡμᾶς καὶ μὴ πέμψῃς ἡμᾶς εἰς κρίσιν αἰώνιον.
2. εἶπεν ἡ γυνή, Κράτησον ἐκεῖνον τὸν ἄνθρωπον, αὐτὸς γὰρ ἔλαβεν καρπὸν ἐκ τῶν στομάτων τῶν παιδίων μου.
3. μὴ ἐρωτήσητε πῶς δύνανται οἱ νεκροὶ ἐγερθῆναι· πιστεύσατε καὶ χαίρετε ἐν τῇ δυνάμει τοῦ θεοῦ.
4. ὕπαγε εἰς τὸν σὸν οἶκον ἐν τῷ ἀγρῷ, εἶπεν ὁ πονηρὸς βασιλεύς. ἐλθὲ πάλιν πρὸς τὴν πόλιν ὅταν ἔχῃς δῶρα προσενέγκαι μοι.
5. οὐ γινώσκομεν πῶς ὁ προφήτης μὴ ἔχων πλοῖον διὰ τῆς θαλάσσης διῆλθεν· ἐπερώτησον αὐτόν, τότε ἐλθὲ ὧδε καὶ εἰπὲ ἡμῖν.
6. μετανόησον ἀπὸ τῶν ἔργων τῶν κακῶν καὶ βάλε τοὺς λόγους τοῦ πνεύματος εἰς τὰ ὦτά σου.
7. μὴ πίνετε οἶνον ἐν τῇ κώμῃ ἕως ἂν πέσητε ἐπὶ πρόσωπον ὑμῶν, ἀλλὰ πληροῦσθε ἐν πνεύματι.
8. μὴ ἀνοίξῃς τὰ ὦτά σου τοῖς ῥήμασιν τῶν δαιμονίων, ἀλλ' ἐρώτησον τὸν κύριον διδάσκειν σε σοφίαν.
9. μὴ χαίρετε ἐπὶ ταῖς βασιλείαις τοῦ κόσμου τούτου, ἀλλὰ δέξασθε τὸ φῶς τοῦ οὐρανοῦ καὶ κρατήσατε τὴν αἰώνιον ἀλήθειαν.
10. οἱ ἱερεῖς τῆς γῆς ἔστωσαν πιστοὶ καὶ ὁ ἄρχων ἐπὶ τοῦ θρόνου ἔστω δίκαιος.
11. ἐὰν ἡ καρδία ὑμῶν ᾖ πλήρης ἁμαρτίας, προσεύξασθε τῷ θεῷ, μετανοήσατε, καὶ ὑπάγετε ἐν εἰρήνῃ.
12. ἐκεῖναι αἱ γυναῖκες ἐλθέτωσαν ὧδε καὶ βαπτισθήτωσαν ὑπὸ τοῦ διδασκάλου.
13. ποιήσατε τὸν καρπὸν δικαιοσύνης καὶ ἐλεήσομεν ὑμᾶς, γέγραπται γάρ, Ἀπὸ τῶν καρπῶν αὐτῶν γνώσεσθε αὐτούς.
14. πορεύθητι εἰς τὸν ἀγρὸν καὶ ἐπερώτησον τοὺς δούλους τοὺς ἐργαζομένους ἐκεῖ εἰ τὸ τέλος τοῦ ἔργου ἐγγίζει.

LXX

1. καὶ εἶπεν ὁ θεός, Γενηθήτω φῶς. καὶ ἐγένετο φῶς. (Gen 1:3)

2. εἶπεν . . . ὁ πατὴρ αὐτῶν, Εἰ οὕτως ἐστίν, τοῦτο ποιήσατε· λάβετε ἀπὸ τῶν καρπῶν τῆς γῆς . . . καὶ καταγάγετε τῷ ἀνθρώπῳ δῶρα (Gen 43:11)

3. καὶ [Ρααβ] εἶπεν αὐτοῖς, Κατὰ τὸ ῥῆμα ὑμῶν οὕτως ἔστω· (Josh 2:21)

4. μὴ ἐκπορεύεσθε εἰς ἀγρὸν καὶ ἐν ταῖς ὁδοῖς μὴ βαδίζετε (Jer 6:25)

5. τάδε λέγει κύριος . . . ἐρωτήσατε τρίβους κυρίου αἰωνίους καὶ ἴδετε, ποία ἐστὶν ἡ ὁδὸς ἡ ἀγαθή, καὶ βαδίζετε ἐν αὐτῇ (Jer 6:16)

6. σῶσον τὸν δοῦλόν σου, ὁ θεός μου, τὸν ἐλπίζοντα ἐπὶ σέ. ἐλέησόν με, κύριε, ὅτι πρὸς σὲ κεκράξομαι ὅλην τὴν ἡμέραν. (Ps 85:2-3, ET 86:2-3. See §26, NT no. 2)

7. καὶ εἶπεν Ιωσαφατ βασιλεὺς Ιουδα πρὸς βασιλέα Ισραηλ, Ἐπερωτήσατε . . . σήμερον τὸν κύριον. (3 Kgdms 22:5)

8. καὶ ἐκάλεσεν ἄγγελος τοῦ θεοῦ τὴν Αγαρ ἐκ τοῦ οὐρανοῦ καὶ εἶπεν αὐτῇ . . . μὴ φοβοῦ· . . . ἀνάστηθι, λαβὲ τὸ παιδίον καὶ κράτησον τῇ χειρί σου αὐτό· εἰς γὰρ ἔθνος μέγα ποιήσω αὐτόν. (Gen 21:17-18)

9. καὶ εἶπα, Κύριε κύριε, ἵλεως γενοῦ . . . μετανόησον, κύριε, ἐπὶ τούτῳ. Καὶ τοῦτο οὐκ ἔσται, λέγει κύριος. (Amos 7:2-3)

10. μὴ χαῖρε ἐπὶ κακοποιοῖς μηδὲ ζήλου ἁμαρτωλούς· (Prov 24:19)

11. καὶ εἶδεν Αβιγαια τὸν Δαυιδ καὶ . . . προσεκύνησεν αὐτῷ ἐπὶ τὴν γῆν ἐπὶ τοὺς πόδας αὐτοῦ καὶ εἶπεν . . . λαλησάτω . . . ἡ δούλη σου εἰς τὰ ὦτά σου, καὶ ἄκουσον τῆς δούλης σου λόγον. (1 Kgdms 25:23-4)

12. καὶ [κύριος] εἶπεν, Μὴ ἐγγίσῃς ὧδε· λῦσαι τὸ ὑπόδημα ἐκ τῶν ποδῶν σου· ὁ γὰρ τόπος . . . γῆ ἁγία ἐστίν. (Exod 3:5)

NT

1. μὴ κρίνετε κατ᾽ ὄψιν, ἀλλὰ τὴν δικαίαν κρίσιν κρίνετε. (John 7:24)

2. καὶ ἰδοὺ γυνὴ Χαναναία . . . ἐξελθοῦσα ἔκραζεν λέγουσα, Ἐλέησόν με, κύριε υἱὸς Δαυίδ· (Matt 15:22)

3. ὁ ἐν τῷ ἀγρῷ μὴ ἐπιστρεψάτω ὀπίσω ἆραι τὸ ἱμάτιον αὐτοῦ. (Matt 24:18)

4. ὁ γὰρ θέλων ζωὴν ἀγαπᾶν καὶ ἰδεῖν ἡμέρας ἀγαθὰς . . . ποιησάτω ἀγαθόν, ζητησάτω εἰρήνην καὶ διωξάτω αὐτήν· (1 Pet 3:10-11)

5. Τότε ἐρεῖ . . . Πορεύεσθε ἀπ᾽ ἐμοῦ . . . εἰς τὸ πῦρ τὸ αἰώνιον τὸ ἡτοιμασμένον τῷ διαβόλῳ καὶ τοῖς ἀγγέλοις αὐτοῦ. (Matt 25:41)

6. καὶ γὰρ ἐγὼ ἄνθρωπός εἰμι ὑπὸ ἐξουσίαν, ἔχων ὑπ᾽ ἐμαυτὸν στρατιώτας, καὶ λέγω τούτῳ, Πορεύθητι, καὶ πορεύεται, καὶ ἄλλῳ, Ἔρχου, καὶ ἔρχεται, καὶ τῷ δούλῳ μου, Ποίησον τοῦτο, καὶ ποιεῖ. (Matt 8:9)

7. εἶπεν αὐτῇ, Θυγάτηρ, ἡ πίστις σου σέσωκέν σε· ὕπαγε εἰς εἰρήνην καὶ ἴσθι ὑγιὴς ἀπὸ τῆς μάστιγός σου. (Mark 5:34)

8. ἐν τούτῳ μὴ χαίρετε ὅτι τὰ πνεύματα ὑμῖν ὑποτάσσεται, χαίρετε δὲ ὅτι τὰ ὀνόματα ὑμῶν ἐγγέγραπται ἐν τοῖς οὐρανοῖς. (Luke 10:20)

9. Οὕτως . . . προσεύχεσθε . . . Πάτερ ἡμῶν ὁ ἐν τοῖς οὐρανοῖς, ἁγιασθήτω τὸ ὄνομά σου· ἐλθέτω ἡ βασιλεία σου· γενηθήτω τὸ θέλημά σου (Matt 6:9-10)

10. Πέτρος δὲ [λέγει] πρὸς αὐτούς, Μετανοήσατε . . . καὶ βαπτισθήτω ἕκαστος ὑμῶν ἐπὶ τῷ ὀνόματι Ἰησοῦ Χριστοῦ (Acts 2:38)

11. [Ἰούδας] ἔδωκεν αὐτοῖς σημεῖον λέγων, Ὃν ἂν φιλήσω αὐτός ἐστιν, κρατήσατε αὐτόν. (Matt 26:48)

12. ἀπεκρίθησαν οὖν οἱ γονεῖς αὐτοῦ καὶ εἶπαν, Οἴδαμεν ὅτι οὗτός ἐστιν ὁ υἱὸς ἡμῶν καὶ ὅτι τυφλὸς ἐγεννήθη· πῶς δὲ νῦν βλέπει οὐκ οἴδαμεν . . . αὐτὸν ἐρωτήσατε . . . αὐτὸς περὶ ἑαυτοῦ λαλήσει. ταῦτα εἶπαν οἱ γονεῖς αὐτοῦ ὅτι ἐφοβοῦντο τοὺς Ἰουδαίους· . . . διὰ τοῦτο οἱ γονεῖς αὐτοῦ εἶπαν . . . αὐτὸν ἐπερωτήσατε. (John 9:20)

English to Greek

1. Come here, children, and ask the teacher of righteousness how sinners are able to find eternal life.
2. Do not go away (sing.) into the field, but remain in the city and rejoice in the holy assembly.
3. Let the ones who have ears hear the good news of God and let them repent, saying, "We will hold fast to the truth."
4. Stop glorifying (pl.) those who kill, and do not send gifts of fruit to men having hands full of blood.

Vocabulary for LXX and NT Sentences

ἀνάστηθι, arise!
βαδίζω = περιπατέω
γονεῖς, parents
διάβολος, the Devil
δούλη, cf. δοῦλος
ἐγγέγραπται, from ἐν + γράφω
ἔδωκεν, gave
ζηλόω, admire, praise
ἵλεως, merciful
κακοποιός, evildoer
κατάγω, bring down, take down
κεκράξομαι, irreg. dep. fut. of κράζω
μάστιξ, ιγος, illness, disease
μέγα, great

οἶδα = γινώσκω
ὃν ἂν, the one whom
ὀπίσω, back
ὄψις, face, appearance
ποία, what? which?
σήμερον, today
στρατιώτης, soldier
τάδε, these things, thus
τρίβος, path
ὑγιής, well, cured
ὑπόδημα, sandal, shoe
ὑποτάσσω, subject, subordinate
φιλήσω, I kiss

Lesson 27

190. Vocabulary

ἐλπίς, ίδος, ἡ, hope

ἔξω, outside (sometimes + gen.)

θυγάτηρ, τρός, ἡ, daughter

καθώς, as, even as, just as

οἶδα, I know, understand

ὅς, ἥ, ὅ, who, which (relative pron.)

ὅσος, η, ον, as great as, as many as

ὅστις, ἥτις, ὅτι, whoever, whichever, whatever (indef. rel. pronoun)

ποῦ, where?

τίς, τί, who? which? what? (interrogative pronoun)

τις, τι, someone, something, a certain one, a certain thing (indef. pron.)

191. The Interrogative Pronoun and Adjective

The forms of the interrogative pronoun and adjective are as follows:

| | Singular | | | Plural | |
	Masc. Fem.	Neut.		Masc. Fem.	Neut.
N.	τίς	τί	N.	τίνες	τίνα
G.	τίνος	τίνος	G.	τίνων	τίνων
D.	τίνι	τίνι	D.	τίσι(ν)	τίσι(ν)
A.	τίνα	τί	A.	τίνας	τίνα

The interrogative is declined according to the third declension. Note one important peculiarity in its accentuation: the acute accent in τίς and τί never changes to the grave, even when another word follows immediately. Thus: τί λέγει ἡ γυνή; "What is the woman saying?"

The interrogative is usually used as a substantive, in which case it is an interrogative *pronoun;* less often it will modify a noun, in which case it is an interrogative *adjective.* Examples of the interrogative pronoun:

(1) τίς διδάσκει τὰ τέκνα; Who is teaching the children?

(2) τίνα ζητεῖτε ἐν τῷ ἱερῷ; Whom are you seeking in the temple?

(3) τίνι τῶν ἀνδρῶν ἐλάλησας; To which of the men did you speak?

(4) τί ἐποίησεν ἡ μήτηρ σου; What did your mother do?

Examples of the interrogative adjective:

(5) τί βιβλίον θέλει ἡ γυνή; What book does the woman want?

162

(6) τίς βασιλεὺς οὐ θέλει δύναμιν; What king does not want power?

(7) τίνα καρπὸν ἔχετε; What (sort of) fruit do you have?

The interrogative pronoun is also used in indirect questions. These are questions reported in a dependent clause, normally by someone other than the original questioner. Unlike direct questions, they are not punctuated with a question mark in English or in Greek. See §172. Thus: οὐ γινώσκομεν τί ποιοῦσι τὰ τέκνα. "We do not know what the children are doing."

Finally, the accusative singular neuter (τί) is also used adverbially with the meaning *Why?* Thus: τί λέγεις τοῦτο; "Why do you say this?"

192. The Indefinite Pronoun and Adjective

The forms of the indefinite pronoun and adjective are as follows:

	Singular			Plural	
	Masc. Fem.	Neut.		Masc. Fem.	Neut.
N.	τις	τι	N.	τινές	τινά
G.	τινός	τινός	G.	τινῶν	τινῶν
D.	τινί	τινί	D.	τισί(ν)	τισί(ν)
A.	τινά	τι	A.	τινάς	τινά

The forms of the indefinite pronoun and adjective are exactly like those of the interrogative except for accent. All forms of the indefinite pronoun and adjective are enclitic. They receive the accents shown above only when required by the rules of enclitic accenting (§42). Context will normally make it clear whether the interrogative or the indefinite is being used, but it will be helpful to pay attention to accent as well.

The indefinite pronoun can also be used either alone as a substantive or with a noun as an adjective. Examples of the indefinite as a pronoun:

(1) ἐάν τις εἴπῃ, ὑμεῖς ἀκούσετε. If someone speaks, you will listen.

(2) οὐκ ἔχουσι τι κατὰ σοῦ. They do not have anything against you.

(3) τινὲς τῶν ἱερέων ἐπίστευσαν. Some of the priests believed.

Examples of the indefinite as an adjective:

(1) ἀνήρ τις ἦλθε πρὸς τὸν ἱερόν. A certain man went to the temple.

(2) αἱ ἀδελφαὶ ἦλθον ἐπί τι ὕδωρ. The sisters came upon some water.

(3) ἱερεύς τις ἦ ἔν τινι πόλει. A certain priest was in a certain city.

193. The Relative Pronoun

The declension of the relative pronoun is as follows:

	Singular				Plural		
	Masc.	Fem.	Neut.		Masc.	Fem.	Neut.
N.	ὅς	ἥ	ὅ	N.	οἵ	αἵ	ἅ
G.	οὗ	ἧς	οὗ	G.	ὧν	ὧν	ὧν
D.	ᾧ	ᾗ	ᾧ	D.	οἷς	αἷς	οἷς
A.	ὅν	ἥν	ὅ	A.	οὕς	ἅς	ἅ

The relative pronoun is declined according to the first and second declensions. In particular, its endings are similar to those of αὐτός. Note that some of the nominative forms are very similar to the corresponding forms of the definite article. This is another instance when accent marks will help in distinguishing similar forms.

A relative pronoun agrees with its antecedent in number and gender, but normally takes the case required by the syntax of its own clause. Examples: (1) ὁ ἀνὴρ ὃς ἦλθεν ἀπὸ τῆς κώμης ἐκήρυξε τὸν λόγον, "The man who came from the village preached the word"; (2) ἡ γυνὴ ἣν εἴδομεν θέλει ἀγοράσαι τὸ βιβλίον, "The woman whom we saw wants to buy the book"; (3) ὁ θεὸς ᾧ προσκυνεῖτέ ἐστι θεὸς λίθου, "The god whom you worship is a god of stone"; (4) ἤδη ἀκηκόαμεν ταῦτα ἃ λέγετε. "We have already heard these things which you are saying."

An important and fairly common exception to the above occurs when the antecedent of the relative pronoun is in the genitive or dative case and the relative itself would normally be in the accusative case as the object of a verb in the relative clause. In such cases the relative pronoun is usually *attracted to the case of its antecedent*. Examples: (1) ἀκούομεν τῶν λόγων ὧν ἡ θυγάτηρ σου λέγει, "We hear the words which your daughter speaks"; (2) ἐγγίζουσι τῷ ἀγρῷ ᾧ ὁ βασιλεὺς ἠγόρασεν, "They are drawing near to the field which the king bought." In the first example ὧν would have been οὕς (as the direct object of λέγει) had it not been attracted to the case of its antecedent; in the second example ᾧ would have been ὅν (as the direct object of ἠγόρασεν) apart from attraction.

Finally, the antecedent of a relative pronoun is sometimes omitted. The English translation may need to supply a word to complete the sense. Thus, ὅς may be translated not simply "who" but "he who" or "the one who." Similarly, ἥ may be translated "she who", ὅ may be translated "that which," and the like. Examples: (1) ποιεῖς ὃ οὐκ ἔξεστιν ποιεῖν ἐν τῷ σαββάτῳ, "You are doing that which is not lawful to do on the Sabbath"; (2) ὃς ἀκούει τῆς φωνῆς τοῦ πνεύματος γνώσεται τὸ θέλημα τοῦ θεοῦ, "The one who hears the voice of the Spirit will know the will of God."

194. Conditional Relative Clauses

Relative pronouns (and a few other words) are sometimes followed by conditional particles (ἐάν or ἄν), thus introducing conditional relative clauses. Remember that the particle ἄν tends to add indefiniteness, sometimes translatable by the suffix "-ever." These clauses, therefore, are introduced in English with the words "whoever," "whichever," "whatever," "wherever," "whenever," and the like. Since these clauses contain the particle ἐάν or ἄν, the verb will normally be in the subjunctive mood. Examples:

ὃς ἐὰν εἴπῃ κατὰ τοῦ πνεύματος ἐλεύσεται εἰς κρίσιν.
Whoever speaks against the Spirit will come into judgment.

ὃ ἐάν με αἰτήσητε πέμψω ὑμῖν.
Whatever you ask of me I will send to you.

ὅπου ἐὰν κηρυχθῇ οὗτος ὁ λόγος ἁμαρτωλοὶ σωθήσονται.
Wherever this word is preached, sinners will be saved.

ὅταν ἔλθῃ ὁ προφήτης πρὸς τὴν θάλασσαν βαπτισθησόμεθα.
Whenever the prophet comes to the lake, we will be baptized.

(In the last example, remember that ὅταν = ὅτε + ἄν.)

195. The Indefinite Relative Pronoun

The indefinite relative pronoun, ὅστις, ἥτις, ὅτι, is the combination of the relative pronoun ὅς and the indefinite pronoun τις. Both parts of the word are declined. For example, the nominative plural forms are: οἵτινες, αἵτινες, ἅτινα. Its meaning, "whoever," "whichever," "whatever," is very similar to the meaning of the relative pronoun with ἐάν or ἄν discussed above. Moreover, ὅστις itself may be accompanied by ἐάν or ἄν, in which case it will normally be followed by a verb in the subjunctive mood. In some cases, ὅστις may be equivalent to the simple relative ὅς. Unlike the simple relative ὅς, the indefinite relative pronoun occurs almost exclusively in the nominative case. Examples:

ὅστις θέλει ἀκολουθεῖν μοι ὀφείλει πιστεύειν.
Whoever wishes to follow me must believe.

ὅστις ἂν ποιήσῃ τὸ θέλημα τοῦ θεοῦ ἀδελφός μου καὶ ἀδελφή ἐστιν.
Whoever does the will of God is my brother and sister.

οὐκ ἐπίστευσα τῷ ἀνθρώπῳ ὅστις ἐλάλει πρός με.
I did not trust the man who was speaking to me

196. The Verb οἶδα

This verb is actually the perfect tense of the stem εἰδ- (cf. εἶδον, the functional third principal part of ὁράω or βλέπω). This word came to denote mental rather than visual perception and is used with a present tense meaning, "I know." It is roughly synonymous, therefore, with γινώσκω. As a second perfect οἶδα lacks the characteristic kappa, but its conjugation is otherwise regular: οἶδα, οἶδας, οἶδε(ν), οἴδαμεν, etc. The pluperfect of οἶδα is ᾔδειν, ᾔδεις, ᾔδει, ᾔδειμεν, etc. It is used as an imperfect: "I knew." The subjunctive of οἶδα is εἰδῶ, εἰδῇς, εἰδῇ, εἰδῶμεν, etc. The infinitive is εἰδέναι. For the full conjugation of οἶδα, see §338.

197. Exercises

Practice and Review

1. Ποῦ ὑπάγεις, διδάσκαλε, τί διδάσκεις καὶ τίς ἀκολουθεῖ σοι ἐν τῇ ὁδῷ τῆς ἀληθείας;
2. κηρύσσομεν τὸ εὐαγγέλιον ἐν τούτῳ τῷ κόσμῳ ἵνα εἰδῆτε τίς ἐστιν ἡ ἐλπὶς ἡμῶν.
3. γυνὴ ἥτις ἦν ἐν τῷ ὄχλῳ παρεκάλεσε τὴν θυγατέρα αὐτῆς μαρτυρῆσαι περὶ τῆς πίστεως.
4. ἰδόντες τὰ σημεῖα ταῦτα ὀφείλομεν ἀπαγγεῖλαι ἃ ἐθεωρήσαμεν καὶ ἠκούσαμεν.
5. ἀνήρ τις εἰσῆλθεν εἰς τὴν πόλιν καὶ ἠρώτησεν, Ποῦ ἐστιν ὁ υἱὸς τοῦ βασιλέως καὶ τί ἐστιν τὸ ὄνομα αὐτοῦ;
6. ὁ ἄγγελος τῆς εἰρήνης ἐλεύσεται καὶ λύσει ὑμᾶς ἐκ τῆς φυλακῆς ἐν ὥρᾳ ᾗ οὐ γινώσκετε.
7. οἴδαμεν ὅτι ὅστις λαμβάνει τὸν σὸν οἶνον καὶ πίνει αὐτὸν βληθήσεται εἰς τὴν φυλακήν.
8. τίς οὖν ἔσται ἡμῶν ἡ ἐλπὶς καὶ ἡ δόξα ἐν τῇ ἡμέρᾳ τῆς κρίσεως; ἰδοὺ ὑμεῖς ἐστε ἡ δόξα ἡμῶν καὶ ἡ ἐλπίς.
9. καθὼς γέγραπται ἐν τῷ βιβλίῳ τοῦ νόμου, εἴ τις θέλει πρῶτος εἶναι ἔστω ὡς παιδίον καὶ ποιείτω ἔργα δικαιοσύνης ἄλλοις.
10. ἀναβαίνοντες ἀπὸ τῆς θαλάσσης ἐπεριπατήσαμεν εἰς τὴν κώμην ἵνα ἀγοράσωμεν παρὰ τῶν ἀνθρώπων πλοῖα ὅσα εἶχον.
11. ὃς ἐὰν θέλῃ τὴν ζωὴν εὑρεῖν ἐγγισάτω τῷ θρόνῳ τῆς χάριτος καὶ κραζέτω τῷ ποιήσαντι οὐρανὸν καὶ γῆν.
12. ἡ θυγάτηρ σου ἣν ὁ πιστὸς προφήτης ἤγειρεν ἐκ τῶν νεκρῶν οἶδε τὴν δύναμιν τοῦ θεοῦ.
13. τινὲς ἄνδρες ἐλήλυθαν εἰς τὴν συναγωγὴν λαλοῦντες πονηρά. ἀλλὰ ὅσα λέγουσι καὶ ὅσα διδάσκουσι μὴ πιστεύσητε, τὰ γὰρ ῥήματα αὐτῶν οὐκ ἔστιν ἀληθῆ.
14. οἱ τυφλοὶ οὓς ἐθεράπευσεν ὁ ἀπόστολος ἐν τῷ ἱερῷ ἐν σαββάτῳ ἐξεβλήθησαν ἔξω ὑπὸ τῶν ἐξουσίων.

LXX

1. καὶ ἐν νεκροῖς αἱ ἐλπίδες αὐτῶν, οἵτινες ἐκάλεσαν θεοὺς ἔργα χειρῶν ἀνθρώπων (Wis 13:10)

2. καὶ εἶπαν πρὸς Σαμψων, Οὐκ οἶδας ὅτι ἄρχουσιν ἡμῶν οἱ ἀλλόφυλοι, καὶ ἵνα τί ταῦτα ἐποίησας ἡμῖν; καὶ εἶπεν αὐτοῖς Σαμψων, Καθὼς ἐποίησαν ἡμῖν, οὕτως ἐποίησα αὐτοῖς. (Judg 15:11)

3. Ἐπικατάρατος ὁ ἄνθρωπος, ὃς τὴν ἐλπίδα ἔχει ἐπ' ἄνθρωπον . . . καὶ εὐλογημένος ὁ ἄνθρωπος, ὃς πέποιθεν ἐπὶ τῷ κυρίῳ, καὶ ἔσται κύριος ἐλπὶς αὐτοῦ· (Jer 17:5, 7)

4. Ἐὰν δὲ εὑρεθῇ ἐν σοὶ ἐν μιᾷ τῶν πόλεών σου, ὧν κύριος ὁ θεός σου δίδωσίν σοι, ἀνὴρ ἢ γυνή, ὅστις ποιήσει τὸ πονηρὸν ἐναντίον κυρίου τοῦ θεοῦ σου . . . καὶ ἐξάξεις τὸν ἄνθρωπον ἐκεῖνον ἢ τὴν γυναῖκα ἐκείνην καὶ λιθοβολήσετε αὐτοὺς ἐν λίθοις (Deut 17:2, 5)

5. ὅσα ἐὰν λαλήσῃ ὁ προφήτης ἐπὶ τῷ ὀνόματι κυρίου, καὶ μὴ γένηται τὸ ῥῆμα . . . τοῦτο τὸ ῥῆμα, ὃ οὐκ ἐλάλησεν κύριος· (Deut 18:22)

6. ἐάν τις ἔλθῃ πρὸς σὲ καὶ ἐρωτήσῃ σε καὶ εἴπῃ σοι, Ἔστιν ἐνταῦθα ἀνήρ; καὶ ἐρεῖς, Οὐκ ἔστιν· (Judg 4:20)

7. τί γὰρ οἶδας, ὃ οὐκ οἴδαμεν; ἢ τί συνίεις, ὃ οὐχὶ καὶ ἡμεῖς; (Job 15:9)

8. καὶ ἠρώτησα αὐτὴν καὶ εἶπα, Τίνος εἶ θυγάτηρ; ἡ δὲ ἔφη, Θυγάτηρ Βαθουηλ εἰμὶ τοῦ υἱοῦ Ναχωρ (Gen 24:47)

9. οὐαὶ οἱ ἐν κρυφῇ βουλὴν ποιοῦντες . . . καὶ ἐροῦσιν, Τίς ἡμᾶς ἑώρακεν καὶ τίς ἡμᾶς γνώσεται ἢ ἃ ἡμεῖς ποιοῦμεν; (Isa 29:15)

10. εἰσὶ δέ τινες ἄνδρες Ιουδαῖοι . . . οἱ ἄνθρωποι ἐκεῖνοι οὐκ ἐφοβήθησάν σου τὴν ἐντολὴν . . . καὶ τῇ εἰκόνι σου . . . οὐ προσεκύνησαν. (Dan 3:12)

11. καὶ ὁ ἄνθρωπος, ὃς ἐὰν μὴ ἀκούσῃ ὅσα ἐὰν λαλήσῃ ὁ προφήτης ἐπὶ τῷ ὀνόματί μου, ἐγὼ ἐκδικήσω ἐξ αὐτοῦ. . . . καὶ ὃς ἂν λαλήσῃ ἐπ' ὀνόματι θεῶν ἑτέρων, ἀποθανεῖται ὁ προφήτης ἐκεῖνος. (Deut 18:19-20)

NT

1. Λέγει αὐτῷ Θωμᾶς, Κύριε, οὐκ οἴδαμεν ποῦ ὑπάγεις· πῶς δυνάμεθα τὴν ὁδὸν εἰδέναι; (John 14:5)

2. ταύτην δὲ θυγατέρα Ἀβραὰμ οὖσαν, ἣν ἔδησεν ὁ Σατανᾶς . . . οὐκ ἔδει λυθῆναι ἀπὸ τοῦ δεσμοῦ τούτου τῇ ἡμέρᾳ τοῦ σαββάτου; (Luke 13:16)

3. Ἀκούσας δέ τις . . . ταῦτα εἶπεν αὐτῷ, Μακάριος ὅστις φάγεται ἄρτον ἐν τῇ βασιλείᾳ τοῦ θεοῦ. (Luke 14:15)

4. Τί τὸ ὄφελος, ἀδελφοί μου, ἐὰν πίστιν λέγῃ τις ἔχειν ἔργα δὲ μὴ ἔχῃ; μὴ δύναται ἡ πίστις σῶσαι αὐτόν; (Jas 2:14)

5. ἠθέλησεν ὁ θεὸς γνωρίσαι τί τὸ πλοῦτος τῆς δόξης τοῦ μυστηρίου τούτου ἐν τοῖς ἔθνεσιν, ὅ ἐστιν Χριστὸς ἐν ὑμῖν, ἡ ἐλπὶς τῆς δόξης· (Col 1:27)

6. Ἦσαν δὲ ἐκεῖ γυναῖκες . . . ἀπὸ μακρόθεν θεωροῦσαι, αἵτινες ἠκολούθησαν τῷ Ἰησοῦ ἀπὸ τῆς Γαλιλαίας διακονοῦσαι αὐτῷ· (Matt 27:55)

7. ὅσοι γὰρ πνεύματι θεοῦ ἄγονται, οὗτοι υἱοὶ θεοῦ εἰσιν. (Rom 8:14)

8. ἀλλὰ καθὼς γέγραπται, Ἃ ὀφθαλμὸς οὐκ εἶδεν καὶ οὖς οὐκ ἤκουσεν . . . ἃ ἡτοίμασεν ὁ θεὸς τοῖς ἀγαπῶσιν αὐτόν. (1 Cor 2:9)

9. τί γάρ μοι τοὺς ἔξω κρίνειν; οὐχὶ τοὺς ἔσω ὑμεῖς κρίνετε; τοὺς δὲ ἔξω ὁ θεὸς κρινεῖ. (1 Cor 5:12-13)

10. καὶ ἐάν τις ὑμῖν εἴπῃ, Τί ποιεῖτε τοῦτο; εἴπατε, Ὁ κύριος αὐτοῦ χρείαν ἔχει (Mark 11:3)

11. Ὃς ἐὰν δέξηται τοῦτο τὸ παιδίον ἐπὶ τῷ ὀνόματί μου, ἐμὲ δέχεται· καὶ ὃς ἂν ἐμὲ δέξηται, δέχεται τὸν ἀποστείλαντά με· (Luke 9:48)

12. Καὶ πορευομένων αὐτῶν ἐν τῇ ὁδῷ εἶπέν τις πρὸς αὐτόν, Ἀκολουθήσω σοι ὅπου ἐὰν ἀπέρχῃ. (Luke 9:57)

English to Greek

1. The woman who preaches words of hope in the synagogue led your (sing.) daughter outside.

2. We do not know who is teaching the children, and you (pl.) do not know where they are being taught.

3. A certain priest entered the temple and said, "Whoever wishes to know God must walk in the path of truth just as the teacher of righteousness taught."

4. Take as many gifts as you (pl.) have and present them to the king. Who knows what the king will do for the servants whom he loves?

5. Whoever seeks glory does not do the Lord's work, and whoever desires anything more than God does not have a true heart.

Vocabulary for LXX and NT Sentences

ἀλλόφυλος, foreigner, Philistine
βουλή, plan
δεσμός, chain, bond
διακονέω, serve, minister to
δίδωσι, gives
ἔδει, impf. of δεῖ
ἔδησεν, bound
εἰκών, όνος, image
ἐκδικέω, exact vengeance, punish
ἐναντίον, before, in the presence of
ἐνταῦθα, here
ἐξάξεις, from ἐκ + ἄγω
ἐπικατάρατος, cursed
ἔσω, inside, within
εὐλογημένος, blessed

ἔφη = εἶπεν
ἤ, or
ἵνα τί, why? (common in LXX)
κρυφῇ, secret
λιθοβολέω, throw stones at
μακάριος, blessed, happy
μακρόθεν, from a distance, afar
μιά, one
μυστήριον, mystery
οὐαί, woe!
οὐχί, strengthened form of οὐ
ὄφελος, benefit, gain
πλοῦτος, wealth, riches
συνίω, understand
χρεία, need

Lesson 28

198. Vocabulary

ἀποδίδωμι, I give back, render, reward
δίδωμι, I give, grant (antidote, dose)
ἔτος, ους, τό, year (etesian)
εὐθύς, immediately, at once, then
μέγας, μεγάλη, μέγα, large, great
   (megaphone, megabyte)
παραδίδωμι, I hand over, betray

πολύς, πολλή, πολύ, much, many
   (polytheism, polygamy)
πρεσβύτερος, α, ον, older, elder
   (presbyter)
χαρά, ἡ, joy, delight
χρόνος, ὁ, time (chronology)

199. Introduction to μι Verbs

All verbs that you have learned up to this point (with the exception of εἰμί) belong to the omega conjugation, so called because the present active indicative first person singular form (the lexical form) ends with that letter. There is a second class of verbs in Greek called the μι conjugation because its lexical form ends with -μι. This group is relatively small in number, but not in importance. Several very common verbs are part of the μι conjugation, and these, together with numerous compound forms, account for thousands of word occurrences in biblical Greek. Μι verbs have been postponed so that the full verbal system could be presented first, using the omega conjugation. Μι verbs differ from omega verbs only in the present and second aorist systems.

200. Principal Parts of δίδωμι

δίδωμι is the most common of all the μι verbs. Its principal parts are:

   1. δίδωμι 2. δώσω 3. ἔδωκα 4. δέδωκα 5. δέδομαι 6. ἐδόθην

   The stem of δίδωμι is δο-. This stem is variously modified in the principal parts. (1) In the first principal part the stem is lengthened to ω and a *present system* reduplication, δι-, is prefixed. The present system reduplication follows most of the rules of perfect tense reduplication except that the reduplicated syllable has iota rather than epsilon. Since this is a present *system* reduplication, the δι- will appear on *all* forms based on this principal part, including the imperfect indicative. (2) The second principal part (future active indicative) also shows a lengthening of the stem and the regular sigma suffix. There is no reduplication. (3) The third principal part (aorist active in-

169

dicative) has the lengthened stem, an epsilon augment, and a κα suffix rather than the usual σα for the first aorist. (4) The fourth principal part (perfect active indicative) has the lengthened stem, perfect tense reduplication, and the characteristic κα suffix. (5) The fifth principal part (perfect middle/passive indicative) does *not* lengthen the stem vowel. It has the perfect tense reduplication and the regular endings. (6) The sixth principal part (aorist passive indicative) also has the short stem vowel. It is augmented and has the characteristic θη suffix. The conjugation of these principal parts requires no special comment except for the present and second aorist systems.

201. The Present System of δίδωμι

The reduplication δι- is the sign of the present system. If a form of δίδωμι has this syllable, it must be either a present or imperfect form. The *present active indicative* is as follows:

Singular	Plural
1. δίδωμι, I give	1. δίδομεν, we give
2. δίδως, you (sing.) give	2. δίδοτε, you (pl.) give
3. δίδωσι(ν), he, she, or it gives	3. διδόασι(ν), they give

Note that the stem vowel is lengthened in the singular but not in the plural. The endings (-μι, -ς, -σι, -μεν, -τε, -ασι) are added directly to the stem. In the present middle/passive the stem vowel remains short throughout and the endings -μαι, -σαι, -ται, -μεθα, -σθε, -νται are added. In most forms of the imperfect the stem vowel remains short; occasionally it is lengthened to ου. The regular secondary endings for active and middle/passive are added. The imperfect of δίδωμι will always have the δι- reduplication *and* the augment. See the full conjugation of the present system in §300-305.

The forms of the *present active subjunctive* are the following. (The stem vowel contracts with the endings, producing the irregular accent.)

Singular	Plural
1. διδῶ	1. διδῶμεν
2. διδῷς	2. διδῶτε
3. διδῷ	3. διδῶσι(ν)

The forms of the *present active imperative* are the following:

Singular	Plural
2. δίδου, give!	2. δίδοτε, give!
3. διδότω, let him/her/it give!	3. διδότωσαν, let them give!

The forms of the *present active participle* are the following:

διδούς	διδοῦσα	διδόν
διδόντος	διδούσης	διδόντος
διδόντι	διδούσῃ	διδόντι
etc.	etc.	etc.

The *present active infinitive* is διδόναι, "to give." Note the irregular (non-recessive) accent in both the infinitive and the participle.

202. The Aorist Active System of δίδωμι

The *aorist active indicative* of δίδωμι is formed quite regularly except for the substitution of κα for σα.

Singular	Plural
1. ἔδωκα, I gave	1. ἐδώκαμεν, we gave
2. ἔδωκας, you (sing.) gave	2. ἐδώκατε, you (pl.) gave
3. ἔδωκε(ν), he, she, or it gave	3. ἔδωκαν, they gave

The remainder of the aorist active system, however, uses *second aorist* forms which lack the characteristic κα of the above indicative forms. The forms of the *aorist active subjunctive* are as follows:

Singular	Plural
1. δῶ	1. δῶμεν
2. δῷς	2. δῶτε
3. δῷ	3. δῶσι(ν)

Note that this conjugation is identical to that of the present active subjunctive except for the lack of the present system reduplication δι-. Similarly, the forms of the *aorist active imperative* are:

	Singular		Plural
2. δός, give!		2. δότε, give!	
3. δότω, let him, her, it give!		3. δότωσαν, let them give!	

The forms of the *aorist active participle* are:

δούς	δοῦσα	δόν
δόντος	δούσης	δόντος
δόντι	δούσῃ	δόντι
etc.	etc.	etc.

The *aorist active infinitive* is δοῦναι, "to give."

The aorist imperative, participle, and infinitive closely resemble the corresponding forms of the present tense except for the lack of the present system reduplication δι-. These are the most helpful clues in identifying a form of δίδωμι: If it has the prefix δι-, it must be present or imperfect. If it has the prefix δε-, it must be perfect or pluperfect. If it has neither, it must be aorist or future. If it has neither *and* is not indicative, it is almost certainly aorist. For the full conjugation of the aorist active and middle, see §306-11.

δίδωμι, along with its compound forms, occurs over 3,000 times in biblical Greek. The ability to recognize at least its more common forms is essential to gaining a working knowledge of the language.

203. Irregular Adjectives

Three very common adjectives that have a few irregular forms are πᾶς, πολύς, and μέγας. You have already been introduced to πᾶς (§150-51). πολύς and μέγας are similar in that a few of their forms are shortened, by a letter in the case of πολύς, by a syllable in the case of μέγας. Shortened forms occur in the nominative and accusative cases of both the masculine singular and the neuter singular. Otherwise, these adjectives pose no special problems. Apart from the shortened forms, πολύς and μέγας are declined like adjectives of the first and second declension.

204. The Declension of πολύς

Singular

	Masculine	Feminine	Neuter
Nom.	πολύς	πολλή	πολύ
Gen.	πολλοῦ	πολλῆς	πολλοῦ
Dat.	πολλῷ	πολλῇ	πολλῷ
Acc.	πολύν	πολλήν	πολύ

Plural

	Masculine	Feminine	Neuter
Nom.	πολλοί	πολλαί	πολλά
Gen.	πολλῶν	πολλῶν	πολλῶν
Dat.	πολλοῖς	πολλαῖς	πολλοῖς
Acc.	πολλούς	πολλάς	πολλά

205. The Declension of μέγας

Singular

	Masculine	Feminine	Neuter
Nom.	μέγας	μεγάλη	μέγα
Gen.	μεγάλου	μεγάλης	μεγάλου
Dat.	μεγάλῳ	μεγάλῃ	μεγάλῳ
Acc.	μέγαν	μεγάλην	μέγα
Voc.	μεγάλε	μεγάλη	μέγα

Plural

	Masculine	Feminine	Neuter
Nom. Voc.	μεγάλοι	μεγάλαι	μεγάλα
Gen.	μεγάλων	μεγάλων	μεγάλων
Dat.	μεγάλοις	μεγάλαις	μεγάλοις
Acc.	μεγάλους	μεγάλας	μεγάλα

206. Exercises

Practice and Review

1. ἐν τῇ ἐσχάτῃ ἡμέρᾳ ἀποδώσει ὁ κύριος πᾶσιν ἀνθρώποις μεγάλοις καὶ μικροῖς κατὰ τὰ ἔργα αὐτῶν.
2. ἦν δὲ ὁ υἱος ὁ πρεσβύτερος ἐν τῷ ἀγρῷ· καὶ ὡς ἤγγισεν τῷ οἴκῳ ἤκουσε τῆς φωνῆς χαρᾶς μεγάλης.

3. ἐν ἐκείνῳ τῷ ἔτει ἀδελφὸς παρέδωκεν ἀδελφὴν εἰς θάνατον καὶ θυγάτηρ παρέδωκεν πατέρα εἰς φυλακήν.

4. οὐ πᾶς ὁ διδοὺς μεγάλα δῶρα τῷ ἱερῷ εἰσελεύσεται εἰς τὴν βασιλείαν τῶν οὐρανῶν, ἀλλ᾽ ὁ διδοὺς καὶ ἰδίαν καρδίαν καὶ ὑπάρχοντα τῷ θεῷ.

5. οἱ δοῦλοι τοῦ ἀγροῦ εἶπον, Τοῦτο τὸ ἔτος ἐργαζώμεθα τὴν γῆν καὶ ὀψόμεθα ἐν τῷ ἐρχομένῳ ἔτει εἰ δίδωσι καρπόν.

6. μετὰ δὲ πολὺν χρόνον αἱ πισταὶ ἀδελφαὶ συνήγαγον τοὺς πρεσβυτέρους τῆς ἐκκλησίας προσεύχεσθαι.

7. ὁ βασιλεὺς ἐκέλευσε τὸ σῶμα τοῦ προφήτου τοῦ σταυρωθέντος ἀποδοθῆναι εὐθὺς τοῖς μαθηταῖς αὐτοῦ.

8. τὸ πνεῦμα ἔδωκεν ἡμῖν ἐξουσίαν τέκνα θεοῦ γενέσθαι καὶ ἡμεῖς δίδομεν τὴν αὐτὴν ἐξουσίαν ἄλλοις.

9. ὁ θεὸς δέδωκεν ἁμαρτωλοῖς χρόνον ἵνα μετανοήσωσιν, ἀλλά τινες οὐ θέλουσι μετανοῆσαι ἐκ τῆς ἁμαρτίας αὐτῶν.

10. ἐγένετο δὲ πολλὴ χαρὰ ἐν ἐκείνῃ τῇ πόλει, οἱ γὰρ λύσαντες τὸν οἶκον τοῦ ἀρχιερέως παρεδόθησαν τοῖς πρεσβυτέροις τοῦ λαοῦ.

11. ἐκείνη ἡ γυνὴ οὕτως ἠγάπησεν τὸ ἔθνος αὐτῆς ὥστε ἔδωκε τὴν ψυχὴν αὐτῆς ἵνα μὴ παραδῷ τοὺς ἱερεῖς τῷ κακῷ βασιλεῖ.

12. μὴ δῶτε μέγα βιβλίον τοῖς μὴ βουλομένοις ποιῆσαι πολὺ ἔργον, ἀποδώσουσιν γὰρ εὐθὺς τὸ βιβλίον βάλλοντες αὐτὸ ἐπὶ τὴν γῆν.

13. θέλω ἐλθεῖν πρὸς ὑμᾶς καὶ χρόνον τινὰ μεῖναι ἐν τῇ κώμῃ ὑμῶν· ὁ γὰρ κύριος ἀνέῳγε τῷ εὐαγγελίῳ μεγάλην θύραν.

14. πάντων οἱ ὀφθαλμοὶ ἐν τῇ συναγωγῇ ἐθεώρουν αὐτὸν καὶ πάντων τὰ ὦτα ἤκουον, καὶ πάντες οἱ πιστεύοντες ἔκραξαν λέγοντες, Πᾶν τὸ ῥῆμα ἐκ τοῦ στόματος αὐτοῦ ἀληθές ἐστιν καὶ ἐδόθη αὐτῷ ὑπὸ θεοῦ.

LXX

1. καὶ ἤρξαντο τὰ ἑπτὰ ἔτη τοῦ λιμοῦ ἔρχεσθαι, καθὰ εἶπεν Ιωσηφ. καὶ ἐγένετο λιμὸς ἐν πάσῃ τῇ γῇ, ἐν δὲ πάσῃ γῇ Αἰγύπτου ἦσαν ἄρτοι. (Gen 41:54)

2. εἶπεν δὲ Λαβαν, Οὐκ ἔστιν οὕτως ἐν τῷ τόπῳ ἡμῶν, δοῦναι τὴν νεωτέραν πρὶν ἢ τὴν πρεσβυτέραν· (Gen 29:26)

3. ἁμαρτάνοντι ἀνδρὶ μεγάλη παγίς, δίκαιος δὲ ἐν χαρᾷ καὶ ἐν εὐφροσύνῃ ἔσται. (Prov 29:6)

4. εἶπα δὲ ὅτι Ὁ χρόνος ἐστὶν ὁ λαλῶν, ἐν πολλοῖς δὲ ἔτεσιν οἴδασιν σοφίαν. (Job 32:7)

5. [ὁ θεὸς εἶπεν τῷ Αβιμελεχ] νῦν δὲ ἀπόδος τὴν γυναῖκα τῷ ἀνθρώπῳ, ὅτι προφήτης ἐστὶν καὶ προσεύξεται περὶ σοῦ καὶ ζήσῃ· εἰ δὲ μὴ ἀποδίδως, γνῶθι ὅτι ἀποθανῇ σὺ καὶ πάντα τὰ σά. (Gen 20:7)

6. [Μελχισεδεκ εἶπεν] εὐλογητὸς ὁ θεὸς ὁ ὕψιστος, ὃς παρέδωκεν τοὺς ἐχθρούς σου ὑποχειρίους σοι. καὶ ἔδωκεν αὐτῷ δεκάτην ἀπὸ πάντων. (Gen 14:20)

7. καὶ δώσω σοι καὶ τῷ σπέρματί σου μετὰ σὲ τὴν γῆν, ἣν παροικεῖς, πᾶσαν τὴν γῆν Χανααν (Gen 17:8)

8. ἐν ἐκείνῃ τῇ ἡμέρᾳ ηὔξησεν κύριος τὸν Ἰησοῦν ἐναντίον παντὸς τοῦ γένους Ισραηλ, καὶ ἐφοβοῦντο αὐτὸν . . . ὅσον χρόνον ἔζη. (Josh 4:14)

9. ἐδούλευσεν ὁ λαὸς τῷ κυρίῳ πάσας τὰς ἡμέρας Ἰησοῦ καὶ πάσας τὰς ἡμέρας τῶν πρεσβυτέρων . . . ὅσοι ἔγνωσαν πᾶν τὸ ἔργον κυρίου τὸ μέγα (Judg 2:7)

10. καὶ εἶπεν κύριος πρὸς Μωυσῆν, Μὴ φοβηθῇς αὐτόν, ὅτι εἰς τὰς χεῖράς σου παραδέδωκα αὐτὸν καὶ πάντα τὸν λαὸν αὐτοῦ καὶ πᾶσαν τὴν γῆν αὐτοῦ (Num 21:34)

11. Αβρααμ δὲ . . . ἔσται εἰς ἔθνος μέγα καὶ πολύ, καὶ ἐνευλογηθήσονται ἐν αὐτῷ πάντα τὰ ἔθνη τῆς γῆς. (Gen 18:18)

12. καὶ ἡ γῆ οὐ δώσει τὸν καρπὸν αὐτῆς, καὶ ἀπολεῖσθε ἐν τάχει ἀπὸ τῆς γῆς τῆς ἀγαθῆς, ἧς ἔδωκεν ὁ κύριος ὑμῖν. (Deut 11:17)

13. ἰδοὺ πεποίηκα κατὰ τὸ ῥῆμά σου· ἰδοὺ δέδωκά σοι καρδίαν . . . σοφήν . . . καὶ ἃ οὐκ ᾐτήσω, δέδωκά σοι, καὶ πλοῦτον καὶ δόξαν (3 Kgdms 3:12-13)

NT

1. καὶ εἶπεν αὐτοῖς ὁ ἄγγελος, Μὴ φοβεῖσθε, ἰδοὺ γὰρ εὐαγγελίζομαι ὑμῖν χαρὰν μεγάλην ἥτις ἔσται παντὶ τῷ λαῷ (Luke 2:10)

2. [Ἰησοῦς] εἶπεν . . . , Δότε αὐτοῖς . . . φαγεῖν. καὶ λέγουσιν αὐτῷ, Ἀπελθόντες ἀγοράσωμεν . . . ἄρτους καὶ δώσομεν αὐτοῖς φαγεῖν; (Mark 6:37)

3. λέγει ὁ κύριος τοῦ ἀμπελῶνος . . . Κάλεσον τοὺς ἐργάτας καὶ ἀπόδος αὐτοῖς τὸν μισθὸν ἀρξάμενος ἀπὸ τῶν ἐσχάτων ἕως τῶν πρώτων. (Matt 20:8)

4. εἶπεν οὖν ὁ Ἰησοῦς, Ἔτι χρόνον μικρὸν μεθ᾽ ὑμῶν εἰμι καὶ ὑπάγω πρὸς τὸν πέμψαντά με. (John 7:33)

5. καὶ δυνάμει μεγάλῃ ἀπεδίδουν τὸ μαρτύριον οἱ ἀπόστολοι τῆς ἀναστάσεως τοῦ κυρίου Ἰησοῦ, χάρις τε μεγάλη ἦν ἐπὶ πάντας αὐτούς. (Acts 4:33)

6. καὶ εἶπεν αὐτῷ, Ταῦτά σοι πάντα δώσω, ἐὰν πεσὼν προσκυνήσῃς μοι. τότε λέγει αὐτῷ ὁ Ἰησοῦς, Ὕπαγε, Σατανᾶ· (Matt 4:9-10)

7. καὶ ἐρῶ τῇ ψυχῇ μου, Ψυχή, ἔχεις πολλὰ ἀγαθὰ κείμενα εἰς ἔτη πολλά· (Luke 12:29)

8. συγκακοπάθησον τῷ εὐαγγελίῳ κατὰ δύναμιν θεοῦ, τοῦ σώσαντος ἡμᾶς καὶ καλέσαντος . . . οὐ κατὰ τὰ ἔργα ἡμῶν ἀλλὰ κατὰ ἰδίαν . . . χάριν, τὴν δοθεῖσαν ἡμῖν ἐν Χριστῷ Ἰησοῦ πρὸ χρόνων αἰωνίων (2 Tim 1:8-9)

9. Ἰδοὺ ἀναβαίνομεν εἰς Ἱεροσόλυμα, καὶ ὁ υἱὸς τοῦ ἀνθρώπου παραδοθήσεται τοῖς ἀρχιερεῦσιν καὶ γραμματεῦσιν (Matt 20:18)

10. Καὶ ἀπήγαγον τὸν Ἰησοῦν πρὸς τὸν ἀρχιερέα, καὶ συνέρχονται πάντες οἱ ἀρχιερεῖς καὶ οἱ πρεσβύτεροι καὶ οἱ γραμματεῖς. (Mark 14:53)

11. ὁ νόμος διὰ Μωϋσέως ἐδόθη, ἡ χάρις καὶ ἡ ἀλήθεια διὰ Ἰησοῦ Χριστοῦ ἐγένετο. (John 1:17)

12. καὶ εὐθὺς ἀναβαίνων ἐκ τοῦ ὕδατος εἶδεν σχιζομένους τοὺς οὐρανοὺς καὶ τὸ πνεῦμα ὡς περιστερὰν καταβαῖνον εἰς αὐτόν· (Mark 1:10)

English to Greek

1. In the time of the great prophet, men and women were not willing to give glory to God, and the land did not give back its fruit.
2. After many years under an evil king, all the elders of the people said, "Let us no longer sin against the Lord."
3. Everyone who announces words of hope to sinners will be loved by God and will know much joy.
4. You (pl.) handed over the evil messenger to the authorities, and immediately he was thrown into prison.
5. All things were created by the Lord; therefore, if the people of the Lord have many things, let them give to the children who do not have much.

Vocabulary for LXX and NT Sentences

ἀμπελών, ῶνος, vineyard
ἀναστάσις, resurrection
ἀπάγω, lead away
ἀπολεῖσθε, you will perish
αὐξάνω, increase, exalt, strengthen
γνῶθι, know! (2 aor. impv.)
δεκάτη, tenth part, tithe
δουλεύω, serve
ἔγνωσαν, knew (2 aor. indic.)
ἐναντίον, before, in the presence of
ἐνευλογέω, bless
ἑπτά, seven
ἐργάτης, worker
εὐλογητός, blessed
εὐφροσύνη, gladness, joy
ἐχθρός, enemy
καθὰ = καθώς

κεῖμαι, lay away, store up
λιμός, famine
μαρτύριον, testimony
μισθός, pay, wages, reward
νεωτέρος, younger
παγίς, snare, trap
παροικέω, live in, inhabit
περιστερά, dove
πλοῦτος, wealth, riches
πρὶν ἤ, before
σοφός, wise
συγκακοπαθέω, accept one's share of suffering, join in suffering
σχίζω, divide
ἐν τάχει, with speed, quickly
ὑποχείριος, subject
ὕψιστος, most high

Lesson 29

207. Vocabulary

ἀπόλλυμι or ἀπολλύω, I destroy, lose;
(mid. voice) perish, be ruined
(Apollyon; see Rev 9:11)

ἀφίημι, I let go, forgive, leave, permit

δείκνυμι and δεικνύω, I show, point
out; explain, prove (deictic)

εἷς, μία, ἕν, one, a, an, single
(henotheism, hendiadys)

ἐπιτίθημι, I place upon, lay upon
(epithet)

λοιπός, ή, όν, remaining, rest; (subst.)
the rest, the others; (adv.)
henceforth, finally

μηδείς, μηδεμία, μηδέν, no one,
nothing, no (= μηδέ + εἷς)

οὐδείς, οὐδεμία, οὐδέν, no one,
nothing, no (= οὐδέ + εἷς)

προστίθημι, I add (to), increase;
continue (prosthesis)

τίθημι, I place, put, appoint (thesis)

208. Principal Parts of τίθημι

Τίθημι is another very common μι verb. Its principal parts are the following:

    1. τίθημι 2. θήσω 3. ἔθηκα 4. τέθεικα 5. τέθειμαι 6. ἐτέθην

The stem of τίθημι is θε-. This stem is variously modified in the principal parts. (1) In the first principal part the stem is lengthened to η and the *present system* reduplication, τι-, is prefixed. This reduplication appears on *all* forms of the present and the imperfect. (2) The second principal part (future active indicative) also shows a lengthening of the stem and the regular σ suffix. There is no reduplication. (3) The third principal part (aorist active indicative) has the lengthened stem, an epsilon augment, and a κα suffix. (4) In the fourth principal part (perfect active indicative) the stem lengthens to ει rather than η. There is perfect tense reduplication and the characteristic κα suffix. (5) The fifth principal part (perfect middle/passive indicative) also lengthens the stem vowel to ει. It has the perfect tense reduplication and the regular endings. (6) The stem of τίθημι undergoes an unusual change in the sixth principal part (aorist passive indicative). If the tense suffix -θη were attached to the stem θε, an awkward succession of two syllables beginning with θ would result. To avoid this, the stem is changed from θε to τε (the stem vowel remaining short). The regular aorist augment and the θη suffix are then added. The conjugation of these principal parts is regular except for the present and second aorist systems.

209. The Present System of τίθημι

The *present active indicative* of τίθημι is as follows:

Singular	Plural
1. τίθημι, I place	1. τίθεμεν, we place
2. τίθης, you (sing.) place	2. τίθετε, you (pl.) place
3. τίθησι(ν), he, she or it places	3. τιθέασι(ν), they place

The *present middle/passive indicative* of τίθημι is as follows:

Singular	Plural
1. τίθεμαι, I am placed	1. τιθέμεθα, we are placed
2. τίθεσαι, you (sing.) are placed	2. τίθεσθε, you (pl.) are placed
3. τίθεται, he, she or it is placed	3. τίθενται, they are placed

The forms of the imperfect of τίθημι should cause little difficulty. As part of the present system, they will have the present reduplication τι- and, as past tense forms, they will have the temporal augment. Thus, the imperfect active: ἐτίθην, ἐτίθεις, ἐτίθει, etc. The imperfect middle/passive: ἐτιθέμην, ἐτίθεσο, ἐτίθετο, etc. See the full conjugation in §§312-17.

The forms of the *present active subjunctive* are as follows:

Singular	Plural
1. τιθῶ	1. τιθῶμεν
2. τιθῇς	2. τιθῆτε
3. τιθῇ	3. τιθῶσι(ν)

The forms of the *present active imperative* are the following:

Singular	Plural
2. τίθει, place!	2. τίθετε, place!
3. τιθέτω, let him, her, it place!	3. τιθέτωσαν, let them place!

The forms of the *present active participle* are the following:

τιθείς	τιθεῖσα	τιθέν
τιθέντος	τιθείσης	τιθέντος
τιθέντι	τιθείσῃ	τιθέντι
etc.	etc.	etc.

The *present active infinitive* is τιθέναι, "to place."

210. The Aorist Active System of τίθημι

The *aorist active indicative* of τίθημι is formed quite regularly except for the substitution of κα for σα.

Singular	Plural
1. ἔθηκα, I placed	1. ἐθήκαμεν, we placed
2. ἔθηκας, you (sing.) placed	2. ἐθήκατε, you (pl.) placed
3. ἔθηκε(ν), he, she, or it placed	3. ἔθηκαν, they placed

The remainder of the aorist active system, like that of δίδωμι, uses *second aorist* forms which lack the κα of the above conjugation. The forms of the aorist active and middle subjunctive, imperative, participle, and infinitive can be found in §§318-23. The most helpful clues in identifying these forms are to remember that (1) the stem of τίθημι is θε, which remains short in some cases, lengthens (to θη or θει) in others, or, in the case of the subjunctive mood, contracts with the endings; and (2) no form of the aorist will have the present system reduplication τι-. The second aorist forms of τίθημι are often identical to the corresponding present tense forms except for the lack of the present system reduplication. Thus, the aorist active subjunctive is θῶ, θῇς, θῇ, etc. The aorist active imperative is θές, θέτω, θέτε, θέτωσαν. The aorist active participle is θείς, θεῖσα, θέν. The aorist active infinitive is θεῖναι. A comparison of these forms with those in §209 shows the importance of the prefix τι- in distinguishing nonindicative forms.

211. The Verb ἀφίημι

The verb ἀφίημι is a compound of the preposition ἀπό and the verb ἵημι. (The final vowel of the preposition is dropped and the π is aspirated before the rough breathing.) Its principal parts are: ἀφίημι, ἀφήσω, ἀφῆκα, ἀφεῖκα, ἀφεῖμαι, and ἀφέθην. The stem of ἀφίημι is ἑ, which is lengthened to η or ει in the first five principal parts. The present system reduplication is ἱ-. Again, the presence or absence of this reduplication is one of the best aids in identifying forms of this verb, especially nonindicative forms. If additional help is needed, a reference lexicon should provide it.

212. The Verbs ἀπόλλυμι/ἀπολλύω and δείκνυμι/δεικνύω

The peculiarity about these two words is that they have some μι forms and some ω forms in the present system. In the μι forms, the endings attach directly to the stem, whereas the ω forms use a connecting vowel. Thus, a form ending in -υται is a μι form, whereas one ending in -υεται is an ω form. There is no particular system determining when one form will be used rather than the other. During the Hellenistic period the μι conjugation was in decline. These two verbs illustrate the transition toward a more uniform verbal system, that is, one lacking the μι endings. The following information should enable the student to identify most forms. Additional help can be found in a reference lexicon.

Principal Parts of ἀπόλλυμι/ἀπολλύω:
(1) Present: ἀπόλλυμι/ἀπολλύω (2) Future: ἀπολέσω/ἀπολῶ (3) Aorist active and middle: ἀπώλεσα/ἀπωλόμην (4) Second perfect: ἀπόλωλα (the participle, ἀπολωλώς, has a middle meaning) The fifth and sixth parts do not occur.

Principal Parts of δείκνυμι/δεικνύω:
(1) Present: δείκνυμι/δεικνύω (2) Future: δείξω (3) Aorist Active: ἔδειξα (4) Perfect: δέδειχα (5) Perfect M/P: δέδειγμαι (6) Aorist Pass.: ἐδείχθην

213. The Number One and Related Words

The declension of the number one is as follows:

	Masc.	Fem.	Neut.
Nom.	εἷς	μία	ἕν
Gen.	ἑνός	μιᾶς	ἑνός
Dat.	ἑνί	μιᾷ	ἑνί
Acc.	ἕνα	μίαν	ἕν

The Greek words οὐδείς and μηδείς are compounds of the number "one" with the negatives οὐδέ and μηδέ. They are generally used with the indicative and nonindicative moods respectively. Their declensions are like that of the number "one."

214. Exercises

Practice and Review

1. ὁ πονηρὸς βασιλεὺς εἶπεν ὅτι θέλει προσενεγκεῖν δῶρα τῷ παιδίῳ, ἐν δὲ τῇ καρδίᾳ αὐτοῦ ἤθελεν ἀπολέσαι αὐτό.
2. ἡ γυνὴ οὐκ ἐβούλετο ἀφιέναι τὰ τέκνα αὐτῆς ἐν τῷ ἀγρῷ, ἀλλὰ ὅτε εἶπεν ὁ δοῦλος ὅτι οἴσει αὐτὰ εἰς τὴν κώμην τότε εἶπεν, Ἀφήσω αὐτά.
3. οὐ δύνασθε προσθεῖναι ἓν ἔτος τῇ ζωῇ ὑμῶν· ὀφείλετε οὖν ζῆν τὰ ἔτη τὰ λοιπὰ ἐν εἰρήνῃ καὶ ἐλπίδι.
4. ἡ μήτηρ οὐ δύναται εὑρεῖν τὸν τόπον ὅπου ἡ μικρὰ θυγάτηρ αὐτῆς ἔθηκεν τὸ βιβλίον καὶ ἡ μικρὰ θυγάτηρ οὐ θέλει τὸν ὁδὸν δεικνύειν αὐτῇ.

5. ὁ δίκαιος γραμματεὺς ἀπέθανεν ἀλλ᾽ οὐδεὶς τῶν λοιπῶν γραμματέων ἐθεώρησε ποῦ τὸ σῶμα αὐτοῦ ἐτέθη ὑπὸ τῶν ἐξουσιῶν.

6. οὐδεὶς ἠθέλησε τὰ λοιπὰ ἱμάτια· ἐπεθήκαμεν οὖν αὐτὰ ἐπὶ τοῦ λίθου ἐν τῷ ἱερῷ ἵνα δοθῶσιν ἀνθρώποις ἐν φυλακῇ.

7. θεράπευσας τὸν τυφλὸν εἶπεν αὐτῷ ὁ προφήτης, Εἰπὲ μηδενί, πορεύου δὲ καὶ σεαυτὸν δεῖξον τῷ ἱερεῖ.

8. νῦν ἀφίενταί σου αἱ ἁμαρτίαι, ἀλλ᾽ ἐὰν λαλήσῃς κατὰ τῶν ἁγίων γραφῶν οὐκ ἀφεθήσεταί σοι.

9. ἐκήρυξεν ὁ ἀπόστολος ἐν δυνάμει καὶ πνεύματι ὥστε πολλαὶ ψυχαὶ ἐβαπτίσθησαν καὶ προσετέθησαν τῇ ἐκκλησίᾳ ἐν μιᾷ ἡμέρᾳ.

10. ὁ ἄγγελος τοῦ κυρίου ἔδειξεν τοῖς μαθηταῖς ἐν τῷ πλοίῳ ὅτι οὐδεὶς ἐξ αὐτῶν ἀπολεῖται ἐν τῇ θαλάσσῃ.

11. μηδεὶς θέτω τὸ βιβλίον τοῦ νόμου εἰς τὸ πῦρ μηδὲ εἰς τὸ ὕδωρ, ὁ γὰρ ἀπόλεσας τὰ ῥήματα τοῦ θεοῦ οὐκ ἐλεηθήσεται ἐν τῇ κρίσει.

12. καταβαίνων ἀπὸ τῆς μεγάλης πόλεως ὁ διδάσκαλος ἠρώτησεν, Τίνες εἰσιν ἐν τούτῳ τῷ τόπῳ οἳ οὐκ ἔχουσιν τὸ πνεῦμα; ἐπιθήσω τὰς χεῖρας ἐπ᾽ αὐτῶν.

13. ἐθήκαμεν ἕνα λίθον μέγαν παρὰ τὴν συναγωγὴν καὶ ἐκεῖ συνερχόμεθα καὶ ἐσθίομεν.

14. Τὸ λοιπόν, ἀδελφοί μου καὶ ἀδελφαί, χαίρετε ἐν τῷ κυρίῳ καὶ τίθετε ἐν ταῖς καρδίαις ὑμῶν ἀκολουθεῖν αὐτῷ.

LXX

1. [Αβρααμ εἶπεν] ἐὰν ὦσιν πεντήκοντα δίκαιοι ἐν τῇ πόλει, ἀπολεῖς αὐτούς; . . . εἶπεν δὲ κύριος, Ἐὰν εὕρω ἐν Σοδομοις πεντήκοντα δικαίους ἐν τῇ πόλει, ἀφήσω πάντα τὸν τόπον δι᾽ αὐτούς . . . καὶ προσέθηκεν ἔτι λαλῆσαι πρὸς αὐτὸν καὶ εἶπεν, Ἐὰν δὲ εὑρεθῶσιν ἐκεῖ τεσσαράκοντα; καὶ εἶπεν, Οὐ μὴ ἀπολέσω ἕνεκεν τῶν τεσσαράκοντα. (Gen 18:24, 26, 29)

2. τίς ἔδειξεν αὐτῷ κρίσιν; ἢ ὁδὸν συνέσεως τίς ἔδειξεν αὐτῷ; (Isa 40:14)

3. Οὐχὶ θεὸς εἷς ἔκτισεν ὑμᾶς; οὐχὶ πατὴρ εἷς πάντων ὑμῶν; (Mal 2:10)

4. τούτῳ γὰρ τῷ τρόπῳ πολὺν ζήσεις χρόνον, καὶ προστεθήσεταί σοι ἔτη ζωῆς σου. (Prov 9:11)

5. καὶ ἔλαβεν Θημαρ σποδὸν καὶ ἐπέθηκεν ἐπὶ τὴν κεφαλὴν αὐτῆς . . . καὶ ἐπέθηκεν τὰς χεῖρας αὐτῆς ἐπὶ τὴν κεφαλὴν αὐτῆς καὶ ἐπορεύθη πορευομένη καὶ κράζουσα. (2 Kgdms 13:19)

6. καὶ Ιουδας ἔπεσεν, καὶ οἱ λοιποὶ ἔφυγον. καὶ ἦρεν Ιωναθαν καὶ Σιμων Ιουδαν τὸν ἀδελφὸν αὐτῶν καὶ ἔθαψαν αὐτόν (1 Macc 9:18-19)

7. καὶ οὐ μὴ κακοποιήσωσιν οὐδὲ μὴ δύνωνται ἀπολέσαι οὐδένα ἐπὶ τὸ ὄρος τὸ ἅγιόν μου (Isa 11:9)

8. καὶ ἐξιλάσεται περὶ αὐτοῦ ὁ ἱερεὺς περὶ τῆς ἁμαρτίας αὐτοῦ, ἧς ἥμαρτεν, καὶ ἀφεθήσεται αὐτῷ ἡ ἁμαρτία. (Lev 5:6)

9. καθήσεσθε ἕκαστος εἰς τοὺς οἴκους ὑμῶν, μηδεὶς ἐκπορευέσθω ἐκ τοῦ τόπου αὐτοῦ τῇ ἡμέρᾳ τῇ ἑβδόμῃ. (Exod 16:29)

10. Ἐν οἴνῳ μὴ ἀνδρίζου· πολλοὺς γὰρ ἀπώλεσεν ὁ οἶνος. (Sir 31:25)

11. [Μανασσης ὁ βασιλεὺς Ιουδα] ἔθηκεν τὸ γλυπτὸν . . . ἐν τῷ οἴκῳ, ᾧ εἶπεν κύριος πρὸς Δαυιδ καὶ πρὸς Σαλωμων τὸν υἱὸν αὐτοῦ, Ἐν τῷ οἴκῳ τούτῳ . . . θήσω τὸ ὄνομά μου ἐκεῖ εἰς τὸν αἰῶνα (4 Kgdms 21:7)

NT

1. μία ἡμέρα παρὰ κυρίῳ ὡς χίλια ἔτη καὶ χίλια ἔτη ὡς ἡμέρα μία. (2 Pet 3:8)

2. οἱ δὲ ἀρχιερεῖς καὶ οἱ πρεσβύτεροι ἔπεισαν τοὺς ὄχλους ἵνα αἰτήσωνται τὸν Βαραββᾶν, τὸν δὲ Ἰησοῦν ἀπολέσωσιν. (Matt 27:20)

3. ζητεῖτε δὲ πρῶτον τὴν βασιλείαν [τοῦ θεοῦ] καὶ τὴν δικαιοσύνην αὐτοῦ, καὶ ταῦτα πάντα προστεθήσεται ὑμῖν. (Matt 6:33)

4. Πάλιν παραλαμβάνει αὐτὸν ὁ διάβολος εἰς ὄρος . . . καὶ δείκνυσιν αὐτῷ πάσας τὰς βασιλείας τοῦ κόσμου καὶ τὴν δόξαν αὐτῶν (Matt 4:8)

5. ἀλλὰ ἔχω κατὰ σοῦ ὅτι τὴν ἀγάπην σου τὴν πρώτην ἀφῆκες. (Rev 2:4)

6. Ταῦτα αὐτοῦ λαλοῦντος αὐτοῖς ἰδοὺ ἄρχων εἷς ἐλθὼν προσεκύνει αὐτῷ λέγων ὅτι Ἡ θυγάτηρ μου ἄρτι ἐτελεύτησεν· ἀλλὰ ἐλθὼν ἐπίθες τὴν χεῖρά σου ἐπ᾽ αὐτήν, καὶ ζήσεται. (Matt 9:18)

7. [αἱ γυναῖκες] ὑποστρέψασαι ἀπὸ τοῦ μνημείου ἀπήγγειλαν ταῦτα πάντα τοῖς ἕνδεκα καὶ πᾶσιν τοῖς λοιποῖς. ἦσαν δὲ ἡ Μαγδαληνὴ Μαρία καὶ Ἰωάννα καὶ Μαρία ἡ Ἰακώβου καὶ αἱ λοιπαὶ σὺν αὐταῖς. (Luke 24:9-10)

8. ὁ εὑρὼν τὴν ψυχὴν αὐτοῦ ἀπολέσει αὐτήν, καὶ ὁ ἀπολέσας τὴν ψυχὴν αὐτοῦ ἕνεκεν ἐμοῦ εὑρήσει αὐτήν. (Matt 10:39)

9. ἐρεῖ τις, Σὺ πίστιν ἔχεις, κἀγὼ ἔργα ἔχω· δεῖξόν μοι τὴν πίστιν σου χωρὶς τῶν ἔργων, κἀγώ σοι δείξω ἐκ τῶν ἔργων μου τὴν πίστιν. (James 2:18)

10. καθὼς γινώσκει με ὁ πατὴρ κἀγὼ γινώσκω τὸν πατέρα, καὶ τὴν ψυχήν μου τίθημι ὑπὲρ τῶν προβάτων. . . . διὰ τοῦτό με ὁ πατὴρ ἀγαπᾷ ὅτι ἐγὼ τίθημι τὴν ψυχήν μου, ἵνα πάλιν λάβω αὐτήν. οὐδεὶς αἴρει αὐτὴν ἀπ᾽ ἐμοῦ, ἀλλ᾽ ἐγὼ τίθημι αὐτὴν ἀπ᾽ ἐμαυτοῦ. ἐξουσίαν ἔχω θεῖναι αὐτήν, καὶ ἐξουσίαν ἔχω πάλιν λαβεῖν αὐτήν· (John 10:15, 17-18)

11. ἓν σῶμα καὶ ἓν πνεῦμα, καθὼς καὶ ἐκλήθητε ἐν μιᾷ ἐλπίδι τῆς κλήσεως ὑμῶν· εἷς κύριος, μία πίστις, ἓν βάπτισμα, εἷς θεὸς καὶ πατὴρ πάντων, ὁ ἐπὶ πάντων καὶ διὰ πάντων καὶ ἐν πᾶσιν. (Eph 4:4)

English to Greek

1. Behold, the Lord is appointing a messenger in the city of blood. Let no one lay hands on him.

2. This woman has one brother, one sister, and one infant. The remaining children in the house do not live here.

3. You (pl.) were about to perish in your sins, for no one showed you the way of righteousness.

4. This great sin will be forgiven (to) the king, but if he adds to his sins again, he will come into judgment.

Vocabulary for LXX and NT Sentences

ἀνδρίζομαι, act manly, act tough

ἄρτι, now, just now

βάπτισμα, baptism

γλυπτόν, carved image

διάβολος, devil

ἕβδομος, η, ον, seventh

ἕνδεκα, eleven

ἕνεκεν, because of, for the sake of

ἐξιλάσεται, he will make atonement

ἤ, or

θάπτω, bury

κἀγώ = καὶ ἐγώ

κακοποιέω, do harm

κλῆσις, calling

μνημεῖον, tomb

οὐχί, stronger form of οὐ

πεντήκοντα, fifty

πρόβατον, sheep

πρῶτον, first (adverb)

σποδός, ashes

συνέσις, understanding

τελευτάω, die

τεσσαράκοντα, forty

τρόπος, way

χίλια, one thousand

χωρίς, without

Lesson 30

215. Vocabulary

ἀνίστημι, I arise, cause to rise
δέκα, ten (decagon)
δύο, δυσί(ν) dative pl., two (dual)
δώδεκα, twelve (dodecagon)
ἐπιγινώσκω, I recognize, know,
    understand, perceive
ἑπτά, seven (heptagon)

ἵστημι, I stand, stand firm, appear;
    cause to stand, set, establish
πέντε, five (Pentateuch, pentagon)
τέσσαρες, τέσσαρα, four (Diatessaron)
τρεῖς, τρία, three (trio)
φημί, I say (emphasis)

216. Principal Parts of ἵστημι

ἵστημι is a very common μι verb with a large number of compound forms. Its principal parts are:

    1. ἵστημι   2. στήσω   3. ἔστησα or ἔστην   4. ἕστηκα   5. ἕσταμαι   6. ἐστάθην

    The stem of ἵστημι is στα-. This stem is variously modified in the principal parts. (1) In the first principal part the stem vowel is lengthened to η and the present system reduplication, ἱ- (note the rough breathing), is prefixed. This reduplication appears on *all* forms of the present and the imperfect. (2) The second principal part (future active indicative) also shows a lengthening of the stem vowel and the regular σ suffix. There is no reduplication. (3) The third principal part introduces a special feature of this verb. Ἵστημι has *both* a complete first *and* a complete second aorist (unlike δίδωμι and τίθημι, which had first aorist forms in the indicative only and second aorist forms elsewhere). The first aorist, ἔστησα, has the lengthened stem and the regular σα suffix. Its meaning is transitive: "I cause to stand, establish, etc." The second aorist, ἔστην, has the lengthened stem in most moods and modes but lacks the σα of the first aorist. Its meaning is intransitive: "I stand, stand firm, etc." (4) In the fourth principal part (perfect active indicative) the stem vowel lengthens to η. There is perfect tense reduplication, ἑ- (again, note the rough breathing) and the κα suffix. (5) In the fifth principal part (perfect middle/passive indicative) the stem vowel remains short. It has perfect tense reduplication and the regular endings. (6) The stem vowel also remains short in the sixth principal part (aorist passive indicative). The regular augment and -θη suffix complete the form.

217. Conjugation of ἵστημι

ἵστημι is the most complex of the μι verbs due to the diversity of its forms and the variation between the transitive and intransitive meanings. In addition to having both first and second aorist systems, ἵστημι has a first perfect and second perfect. The first perfect is found in various moods and modes; the second perfect chiefly in the participle. The first perfect participle is ἑστηκώς; the second perfect is ἑστώς. The meaning of both is "having come to stand" or simply "standing."

The choice between transitive and intransitive meanings is usually made clear by context, but the following division may also be helpful. The *transitive* meaning, "cause to stand, establish," is expressed by the present, imperfect, future active, and first aorist active. The *intransitive* meaning, "stand, stand firm, appear," is expressed by the future middle and passive, the second aorist, the first aorist passive, both perfects, and the pluperfect.

Since certain tenses of ἵστημι are relatively uncommon in biblical Greek (such as the present), only selected aorist and perfect forms are given below. For a more complete conjugation, see §§324-35. When trying to identify forms, remember the basics. Present and imperfect forms will have the ἱ- reduplication. Perfect forms will be reduplicated with ἑ-. First aorist forms will have the suffix σα; second aorist forms will lack it. (An exception here is the third person plural form ἔστησαν. Because *the ending itself* is -σαν, this form could be either first or second aorist. Context must decide.)

The *second aorist active indicative* of ἵστημι is as follows:

Singular	Plural
1. ἔστην, I stood	1. ἔστημεν, we stood
2. ἔστης, you (sing.) stood	2. ἔστητε, you (pl.) stood
3. ἔστη, he, she, it stood	3. ἔστησαν, they stood

The *second aorist active imperative* is as follows:

Singular	Plural
2. στῆθι, stand!	2. στῆτε, stand!
3. στήτω, let him, her, it stand!	3. στήτωσαν, let them stand!

The *first perfect active participle,* "standing," is as follows:

Masc. — ἑστηκώς, ἑστηκότος, ἑστηκότι, ἑστηκότα, ἑστηκότες, etc.

Fem. — ἑστηκυῖα, ἑστηκυίας, ἑστηκυίᾳ, ἑστηκυῖαν, ἑστηκυῖαι, etc.

Neut. — ἑστηκός, ἑστηκότος, ἑστηκότι, ἑστηκός, ἑστηκότα, etc.

The *second perfect active participle,* "standing," is as follows:

Masc. — ἑστώς, ἑστῶτος, ἑστῶτι, ἑστῶτα, ἑστῶτες, ἑστώτων, etc.
Fem. — ἑστῶσα, ἑστώσης, ἑστώσῃ, ἑστῶσαν, ἑστῶσαι, ἑστωσῶν, etc.
Neut. — ἑστός, ἑστῶτος, ἑστῶτι, ἑστός, ἑστῶτα, ἑστώτων, etc.

Here are examples of the transitive and intransitive uses of ἵστημι.

Transitive — "cause to stand, set, place, establish."

(1) ἔστησα τὸ παιδίον ἐπὶ λίθον. "I set the child on a rock."
(2) ὁ κύριος στήσει ἡμέραν. "The Lord will establish a day."
(3) δυνάμεθα στῆσαι τὸν νόμον; "Can we establish the Law?"

Intransitive — "stand, stand firm."

(1) εἶδές με ἑστῶτα ἐν τῷ ἱερῷ. "You saw me standing in the temple."
(2) σταθήσεται ἡ βασιλεία ἡ πονηρά; "Will the evil kingdom stand?"
(3) ἡ γυνὴ ἔστη ἐν τῷ ἀγρῷ. "The woman stood in the field."
(4) ἕστηκας ἐπὶ γῇ ἁγίᾳ. "You are standing on holy ground."

218. The Verb φημί

This verb is roughly synonymous with λέγω. Its forms include the present third singular φησίν, "he, she says," the present third plural φασίν, "they say," and the very common imperfect third singular ἔφη, "he/she said." φημί normally introduces *direct* discourse, much less often indirect discourse with ὅτι or the accusative and infinitive (see §172).

219. Second Aorist of βαίνω and γινώσκω

These two verbs are unusual in that they belong to the ω conjugation but have aorists of the μι type. βαίνω is rare in its simple form (four times in the LXX, none in the NT), but quite common in compounds: ἀναβαίνω, καταβαίνω, etc. The second aorist stem of βαίνω is βα-, usually lengthened to βη-. Its (uncompounded) forms are:

	Singular		Plural
1.	ἔβην, I went	1.	ἔβημεν, we went
2.	ἔβης, you (sing.) went	2.	ἔβητε, you (pl.) went
3.	ἔβη, he, she, or it went	3.	ἔβησαν, they went

The infinitive is βῆναι.
The subjunctive is βῶ, βῇς, βῇ, etc.
The imperative is βῆθι (or βα), βάτω, βάτε, βάτωσαν.
The participle is βάς, βᾶσα, βάν.

The second aorist stem of γινώσκω is γνο-, usually lengthened to γνω-. Its forms are:

	Singular		Plural
1.	ἔγνων, I knew	1.	ἔγνωμεν, we knew
2.	ἔγνως, you (sing.) knew	2.	ἔγνωτε, you (pl.) knew
3.	ἔγνω, he, she, or it knew	3.	ἔγνωσαν, they knew

The infinitive is γνῶναι.
The subjunctive is γνῶ, γνῷς, γνῷ, etc.
The imperative is γνῶθι, γνώτω, γνῶτε, γνώτωσαν.
The participle is γνούς, γνοῦσα, γνόν.

220. Numbers

The number "one" was introduced in §213. The number "two" is not declined except for the dative plural form δυσί(ν). The numbers "three" and "four" are declined as follows:

	Masc. Fem.	Neut.		Masc. Fem.	Neut.
N.	τρεῖς	τρία	N. V.	τέσσαρες	τέσσαρα
G.	τριῶν	τριῶν	G.	τεσσάρων	τεσσάρων
D.	τρισί(ν)	τρισί(ν)	D.	τέσσαρσι(ν)	τέσσαρσι(ν)
A.	τρεῖς	τρία	A.	τέσσαρας	τέσσαρα

Cardinal numbers from 5 to 199 are not declined.

221. The Article Before μέν and δέ

The article is occasionally found before μέν and δέ with no noun, participle, or other substantive following. In such cases it has the force of a pronoun. This is simply a way to continue a narrative, and it sometimes seems to mark a shift in the subject of the verb. Example:

ὁ διδάσκαλος ἀπέλυσεν τοὺς μαθητάς. οἱ δὲ ἀπῆλθον εἰς τὴν πόλιν.
The teacher dismissed the disciples. And they went away into the city.

222. Exercises

Practice and Review

1. ἐκεῖνος ὁ προφήτης ἀγαπᾷ ἑστὼς ἐν τῷ ἱερῷ λαλῆσαι περὶ τῶν ἑπτὰ πνευμάτων τοῦ θεοῦ.

2. Δέκα δοῦλοι, ἔφη ἡ γυνή, ἀνέβησαν πρὸς τὴν πόλιν φέροντες δύο λίθους μεγάλους εἰς τὴν συναγωγήν.

3. εὐθὺς ἐπιγνοῦσα ὅτι τις ἀνοίγει τὴν θύραν, ἡ θυγάτηρ ὑμῶν ἠρώτησεν, Τίς ἐστιν ἐκεῖ;

4. αἱ δέκα ἐντολαὶ ἐδόθησαν ἡμῖν ἵνα περιπατήσωμεν ἐν εἰρήνῃ μετ' ἀλλήλων, ἀλλὰ ὁ πᾶς νόμος πληροῦται ἐν δυσὶ λόγοις, θεὸν ἀγαπήσεις καὶ ἄλλους ἀγαπήσεις.

5. τὰ ἔθνη ἔλεγον πρὸς ἀλλήλους, Γνῶθι σεαυτόν, ἀλλὰ τὸ ἀγαπητὸν γένος ἡμῶν βούλεται προσθεῖναι, Γνῶθι τὸν κύριον.

6. πῶς σταθήσεται ἡ βασιλεία εἰ τρεῖς βασιλεῖς θέλουσιν τὴν δύναμιν κρατῆσαι;

7. ἀνάβηθι εἰς τὸ ὄρος καὶ εἰπὲ πρὸς τοὺς μαθητὰς τοὺς προσκυνοῦντας ἐκεῖ, Κατάβατε νῦν εἰς τὴν πόλιν καὶ ποιήσατε ἔργα δικαιωσύνης.

8. λαβόμενος παιδίον ὁ διδάσκαλος ἔστησεν αὐτὸ πρὸ τοῦ ὄχλου καὶ εἶπεν, Τοῦτο τὸ παιδίον ἐπέγνω τὰ δώδεκα βιβλία τῶν προφητῶν.

9. ὅτε κατέβη ὁ λαὸς πρὸς τὴν θάλασσαν ἀνέστη ἑπτὰ δαιμόνια ἐκ τοῦ ὕδατος.

10. εὕρομεν πέντε ἄνδρας ἑστῶτας ἐν τῇ κώμῃ ζητοῦντας ἔργον. ἐλθέτωσαν εἰς τὸν ἀγρόν.

11. ὁ ἱερεὺς φησίν, Τὸ ῥῆμα τοῦ κυρίου ἀναστήσει τοὺς νεκροὺς ἐν τῇ ἐσχάτῃ ἡμέρᾳ, ἀλλὰ πολλοὶ φεύξεται ἀπὸ τοῦ προσώπου τοῦ κυρίου.

12. ἡ ἀδελφή σου ἐθεράπευσε τὸν τυφλὸν ὥστε ἐπιγνῶναι αὐτὸν πολλοὺς ἀνθρώπους ἑστῶτας ἐν τῇ συναγωγῇ.

13. τινὲς τῶν ἑστηκότων ὧδε ὄψονται τοὺς τέσσαρας ἀγγέλους τοῦ οὐρανοῦ καταβαίνοντας εἰς τὴν γῆν.

14. ἀναστὰς ὁ υἱὸς ἠκολούθησεν τῇ μητρὶ αὐτοῦ εἰς τὸν οἶκον. ἡ δὲ οὐκ ἔγνω ὅτι αὐτὸς ἐγγίζει.

LXX

1. ἠγάπησεν δὲ Ιακωβ τὴν Ραχηλ καὶ εἶπεν, Δουλεύσω σοι ἑπτὰ ἔτη περὶ Ραχηλ τῆς θυγατρός σου τῆς νεωτέρας. (Gen 29:18)

2. Ἰδοὺ ἡμέραι ἔρχονται, φησὶν κύριος, καὶ διαθήσομαι τῷ οἴκῳ Ισραηλ καὶ τῷ οἴκῳ Ιουδα διαθήκην καινήν. (Jer 38:31, ET 31:31)

3. προφήτην ἐκ τῶν ἀδελφῶν σου ὡς ἐμὲ ἀναστήσει σοι κύριος ὁ θεός σου, αὐτοῦ ἀκούσεσθε. (Deut 18:15)

4. ἤγγισεν δὲ Ιακωβ πρὸς Ισαακ τὸν πατέρα αὐτοῦ, καὶ ἐψηλάφησεν αὐτὸν καὶ εἶπεν, Ἡ μὲν φωνὴ φωνὴ Ιακωβ, αἱ δὲ χεῖρες χεῖρες Ησαυ. καὶ οὐκ ἐπέγνω αὐτόν· (Gen 27:22-23)

5. Λαβόντες δὲ οἱ ἄνδρες τὰ δῶρα ταῦτα . . . ἔλαβον ἐν ταῖς χερσὶν αὐτῶν καὶ τὸν Βενιαμιν καὶ ἀναστάντες κατέβησαν εἰς Αἴγυπτον καὶ ἔστησαν ἐναντίον Ιωσηφ. (Gen 43:15)

6. καὶ ἐγένετο λόγος κυρίου πρὸς Ησαιαν λέγων, Πορεύθητι καὶ εἰπὸν [τῷ] Εζεκια, Τάδε λέγει κύριος ὁ θεὸς . . . ἰδοὺ προστίθημι πρὸς τὸν χρόνον σου ἔτη δέκα πέντε· (Isa 38:4-5)

7. Ταῦτα τὰ θηρία τὰ μεγάλα εἰσὶ τέσσαρες βασιλεῖαι, αἳ ἀπολοῦνται ἀπὸ τῆς γῆς· (Dan 7:17)

8. ἐπέγνω δὲ Ιωσηφ τοὺς ἀδελφοὺς αὐτοῦ, αὐτοὶ δὲ οὐκ ἐπέγνωσαν αὐτόν. (Gen 42:8)

9. εἶπεν δὲ Μωυσῆς πρὸς τὸν λαόν, Θαρσεῖτε· στῆτε καὶ ὁρᾶτε τὴν σωτηρίαν τὴν παρὰ τοῦ θεοῦ, ἣν ποιήσει ἡμῖν σήμερον· (Exod 14:13)

10. καὶ ἦν Ιωνας ἐν τῇ κοιλίᾳ τοῦ κήτους τρεῖς ἡμέρας καὶ τρεῖς νύκτας. καὶ προσηύξατο Ιωνας πρὸς κύριον τὸν θεὸν αὐτοῦ ἐκ τῆς κοιλίας τοῦ κήτους (Jon 2:1-2, ET 1:17–2:1)

11. οἱ δὲ εἶπαν, Δώδεκά ἐσμεν οἱ παῖδές σου ἀδελφοὶ . . . καὶ ἰδοὺ ὁ νεώτερος μετὰ τοῦ πατρὸς ἡμῶν σήμερον, ὁ δὲ ἕτερος οὐχ ὑπάρχει. (Gen 42:13)

NT

1. καὶ προαγαγὼν αὐτοὺς ἔξω ἔφη, Κύριοι, τί με δεῖ ποιεῖν ἵνα σωθῶ; οἱ δὲ εἶπαν, Πίστευσον ἐπὶ τὸν κύριον Ἰησοῦν καὶ σωθήσῃ (Acts 16:30-31)

2. λαβὼν παιδίον ἔστησεν αὐτὸ ἐν μέσῳ αὐτῶν καὶ . . . εἶπεν αὐτοῖς, Ὃς ἂν ἓν τῶν . . . παιδίων δέξηται ἐπὶ τῷ ὀνόματί μου, ἐμὲ δέχεται· (Mark 9:36-37)

3. ὥσπερ γὰρ ἦν Ἰωνᾶς ἐν τῇ κοιλίᾳ τοῦ κήτους τρεῖς ἡμέρας καὶ τρεῖς νύκτας, οὕτως ἔσται ὁ υἱὸς τοῦ ἀνθρώπου ἐν τῇ καρδίᾳ τῆς γῆς τρεῖς ἡμέρας καὶ τρεῖς νύκτας. (Matt 12:40)

4. ἐὰν δὲ [ὁ ἀδελφός σου] μὴ ἀκούσῃ, παράλαβε μετὰ σοῦ ἔτι ἕνα ἢ δύο, ἵνα ἐπὶ στόματος δύο μαρτύρων ἢ τριῶν σταθῇ πᾶν ῥῆμα· (Matt 18:16)

5. εἶπεν δὲ τῷ ἀνδρὶ . . . Ἔγειρε καὶ στῆθι εἰς τὸ μέσον· καὶ ἀναστὰς ἔστη. (Luke 6:8)

6. ἄρτι γινώσκω ἐκ μέρους, τότε δὲ ἐπιγνώσομαι καθὼς καὶ ἐπεγνώσθην. (1 Cor 13:12)

7. Καὶ εἶδον ἐκ τῆς θαλάσσης θηρίον ἀναβαῖνον, ἔχον κέρατα δέκα καὶ κεφαλὰς ἑπτά καὶ ἐπὶ τῶν κεράτων αὐτοῦ δέκα διαδήματα (Rev 13:1)

8. Μετὰ τοῦτο εἶδον τέσσαρας ἀγγέλους ἑστῶτας ἐπὶ τὰς τέσσαρας γωνίας τῆς γῆς, κρατοῦντας τοὺς τέσσαρας ἀνέμους τῆς γῆς (Rev 7:1)

9. οἱ δὲ λέγουσιν αὐτῷ, Οὐκ ἔχομεν ὧδε εἰ μὴ πέντε ἄρτους καὶ δύο ἰχθύας. ὁ δὲ εἶπεν, Φέρετέ μοι ὧδε αὐτούς. (Matt 14:17-18)

10. ἐκβαλὼν δὲ ἔξω πάντας ὁ Πέτρος . . . προσηύξατο καὶ ἐπιστρέψας πρὸς τὸ σῶμα εἶπεν, Ταβιθά, ἀνάστηθι. ἡ δὲ ἤνοιξεν τοὺς ὀφθαλμοὺς αὐτῆς, καὶ ἰδοῦσα τὸν Πέτρον ἀνεκάθισεν. δοὺς δὲ αὐτῇ χεῖρα ἀνέστησεν αὐτήν· (Acts 9:40-41)

11. καὶ καθίσας ἐφώνησεν τοὺς δώδεκα καὶ λέγει αὐτοῖς, Εἴ τις θέλει πρῶτος εἶναι, ἔσται πάντων ἔσχατος καὶ πάντων διάκονος. (Mark 9:35)

English to Greek

1. We recognized five men standing beside the sea and three women sitting on a rock.
2. If the twelve apostles exhort everyone to seek the will of God, they will establish the law of love.
3. But the ruler said to his slave, "Stand up, and let us go down to see the prophet, for my three children are dying, but he can heal them."
4. Ten slaves were working in my two fields, and after seven hours they approached me asking for water and bread.

Vocabulary for LXX and NT Sentences

ἀνακαθίζω, sit up (ἀνά = up)
ἄνεμος, wind
ἀπολοῦνται, future mid. of ἀπόλλυμι
ἄρτι = νῦν
γωνία, corner
διάδημα, crown, diadem
διάκονος, servant
διαθήκη, covenant
διαθήσομαι, I will make (a covenant)
δουλεύω, serve
εἰ μή, except
ἤ, or
θαρσέω, take courage
θηρίον, beast
ἰχθύς, -ύος, fish

καινός, new
κέρας, -ατος, horn
κῆτος, -ους, sea creature, whale
κοιλία, belly
μάρτυς, witness
[ἐκ] μέρους, in part
μέσος, midst, middle
νεώτερος, younger
προάγω, lead forth, bring out
σήμερον, today
τάδε, these things, thus
φωνέω, call
ψηλαφάω, feel, touch
ὥσπερ, just as

Lesson 31

223. Vocabulary

διό, therefore, for this reason

ἔμπροσθεν, before, in front of (+ gen.)

ἐνώπιον, before, in the sight of, in the presence of (+ gen.)

ἐπαγγελία, ἡ, promise

ἤ, or, than

ἰσχυρός, ά, όν, strong, mighty

κρείσσων (or κρείττων), ον, better compar. of ἀγαθός

μακάριος, α, ον, blessed, happy

μᾶλλον, more, rather

μείζων, ον, greater; comparative of μέγας, also used as superlative

μόνος, η, ον, only, alone (monorail) neut. μόνον as adv.

οὐχί, not (strengthened form of οὐ)

πλείων, ον, more, larger; compar. of πολύς (pleonasm)

224. Comparative Adjectives

Adjectives have three degrees: positive, comparative, and superlative. (1) The *positive* degree of an adjective is its simple, dictionary form, such as καλός or ἰσχυρός. (2) The *comparative*, formed in English with -er or the word "more," has in Greek either the suffix -τερος, α, ον, declined according to the first and second declension, or the suffix -(ι)ων, -(ι)ον, declined according to the third declension. (3) The *superlative*, formed in English with -est or the word "most," has in Greek either the suffix -τατος, η, ον, or the suffix -ιστος, η, ον, both declined according to the first and second declensions.

Most adjectives in English that form the comparative and superlative degrees with the above-mentioned suffixes do so simply by adding those suffixes to the dictionary form of the adjective. Thus: "strong, stronger, strongest." Many Greek adjectives do the same: ἰσχυρός "strong," ἰσχυρότερος "stronger," ἰσχυρότατος "strongest." But, as in English, the comparative and superlative forms of Greek adjectives are sometimes irregular. Examples: μέγας "great," μείζων "greater," μέγιστος "greatest"; ἀγαθός "good," κρείσσων "better," ἄριστος "best" (not in NT and rare in LXX).

The tendency in biblical Greek is to make one of the degrees do duty for two. The superlative degree, for example, is rare in biblical Greek and the comparative often substitutes for it. In certain expressions, the positive degree may substitute for the comparative.

225. Forms of Certain Comparative Adjectives

The declension of πλείων, ονος "more" is as follows:

| | Singular | | | Plural | |
	Masc. Fem.	Neut		Masc. Fem.	Neut.
N.	πλείων	πλεῖον	N. V.	πλείονες	πλείονα
G.	πλείονος	πλείονος	G.	πλειόνων	πλειόνων
D.	πλείονι	πλείονι	D.	πλείοσι(ν)	πλείοσι(ν)
A.	πλείονα	πλεῖον	A.	πλείονας	πλείονα

The forms of κρείσσων/κρείττων, ον and μείζων, ον are similar. Two contracted forms also occur: πλείω for πλείονα (acc. sing. M/F, and nom. and acc. plur. neut.), and πλείους for πλείονες and πλείονας (nom. plur. M/F and acc. plur. M/F respectively).

226. Comparisons in Greek

In Greek there are two ways to express comparison. (1) A word in the genitive case may follow the comparative adjective. Example: ἡ χάρις τοῦ θεοῦ ἐστιν μείζων τῆς δυνάμεως τῆς ἁμαρτίας. "The grace of God is greater than the power of sin." This case function is called the *genitive of comparison*. (2) The conjunction ἤ may be used, followed by a noun in the same case as the first member of the comparison. Example: ὁ διώκων δικαιοσύνην ἐστὶν κρείττων ἢ ὁ διώκων δόξαν. "The one who pursues righteousness is better than the one who pursues glory."

227. Adverbs

Some adverbs are closely related to adjectives. One way this relation can be seen is to remove the final ν from the genitive plural form of the adjective and put a ς in its place. Thus: καλός "good" . . . καλῶν (gen. plur.) . . . καλῶς "well." Similarly, κακῶς "badly, wrongly"; ἄλλως "otherwise"; ἑτέρως "differently"; and πάντως "in every way, by all means." Adverbs are formed in a variety of ways, however, some of them unpredictable.

Adverbs that derive from adjectives may also have comparative and superlative degrees, though these are not common in biblical Greek. When they occur, the comparative form of the adverb is the same as the neuter accusative singular form of the comparative adjective. The superlative form of the adverb is the same as the neuter accusative plural form of the superlative adjective. It is nearly impossible to find a common adjective whose related adverb occurs in both comparative and superlative forms *in biblical Greek*. For the sake of illustration only, σοφός "wise" may be used. The adverb = σοφῶς "wisely"; the comparative adverb = σοφώτερον "more wisely"; and the superlative adverb = σοφώτατα "most wisely."

228. Questions Expecting a "Yes" or "No" Answer

Questions in biblical Greek sometimes are expressed in a way that anticipates a "yes" or "no" answer. In English, this is indicated by voice intonation or by appending a short interrogative phrase to a declarative statement (see below). In Greek, this is indicated by adding a negative to the question. Questions expecting the answer "no" contain the negative μή; questions expecting the answer "yes" have the negative οὐ (οὐκ, οὐχ, οὐχί).

> μὴ ἐφάγετε τὸν ἄρτον τῶν τέκνων;
> You didn't eat the children's bread, did you?
>> Expected answer: No, we did not!

> ἐκείνη ἡ γυνὴ οὐκ ἔστιν ἡ μήτηρ τοῦ βασιλέως;
> That woman is the mother of the king, isn't she?
>> Expected answer: Yes, she is!

229. Contrary to Fact Conditions

In addition to the simple conditions, future conditions, and present general conditions discussed in §164 (5), another type of condition is found in biblical Greek: the contrary to fact condition. In this type of condition, an *unreal* circumstance is assumed in the protasis (the "if" clause). The apodosis (the "then" clause) expresses what *would have* occurred if that circumstance had truly existed. The protasis of a contrary to fact condition is introduced with the particle εἰ. The apodosis usually contains ἄν, though ἄν is sometimes omitted. Both clauses use past tense verbs of the indicative mood. If the verb in the protasis is negated, it will take the negative μή. The negative used in the apodosis is οὐ.

In the following two examples, note that there are two general types of contrary to fact conditions: present and past. The present type uses the imperfect tense: "If X were (now) the case, Y would not be happening." The past type usually uses the aorist tense: "If X had (at some point in the past) been the case, Y would not have happened." But mixed types occur, for example, with the verb εἰμί, since it has no aorist tense.

> εἰ ἐκείνη ἡ γυνὴ ἦν νεκρά, οὐκ ἂν ἐπεριπάτει ἐν τῇ κώμῃ.
> If that woman were dead, she would not be walking around in the village.

εἰ ὁ ἀνὴρ οὗτος μὴ ἠγάπησεν ἑτέραν, ἡ γυνὴ αὐτοῦ οὐκ ἂν ἐσταύρωσεν αὐτόν.
If this man had not loved another (woman), his wife would not have crucified
him.

230. Exercises

Practice and Review

1. ὁ λαβὼν τὴν ἐπαγγελίαν τοῦ πνεύματος τοῦ ἁγίου μείζων ἐστὶν τοῦ ἑστηκότος
   ἔμπροσθεν ἀρχόντων.
2. ἐὰν γὰρ μόνον ἀγαπήσητε τοὺς ἀγαπῶντας ὑμᾶς, τίνα δόξαν δέξεσθε; οὐχὶ
   καὶ οἱ ἁμαρτωλοὶ ποιοῦσιν τοῦτο;
3. εἰ ὁ δοῦλος τοῦ ἀνδρὸς ἐκείνου ἦν μακάριος, οὐκ ἂν ἀπῆλθεν ἵνα ζητήσῃ
   κρείττονα ζωήν.
4. ποῦ εἰσιν τὰ βιβλία μου; τέκνα, μὴ ἐβάλετε τὰ βιβλία μου εἰς τὴν θάλασσαν;
5. ὁ υἱὸς ἔφη, Πάλιν ἥμαρτον εἰς οὐρανὸν καὶ ἐνώπιόν σου. διὸ εἰμι
   πονηρότερος πάντων τῶν ἀδελφῶν μου.
6. καλόν ἐστι διὰ δικαιοσύνην διωχθῆναι ἢ μαρτυρεῖν μηδὲν καὶ δέξασθαι
   δῶρα.
7. ἡ πόλις ἡμῶν ἐστι ἡ μικρότερα πασῶν τῶν πόλεων ἐν τῇ γῇ, ἀλλ' ἐγεννήσαμεν
   ἱερεῖς καὶ προφήτας πλείονας ἢ αὐτῶν.
8. λέγεις ὅτι ἔχεις πλείονα παιδία τοῦ μεγίστου βασιλέως. μὴ σὺ μείζων εἶ τῆς
   μητρὸς ἡμῶν, ἥτις ἔχει δώδεκα παιδία;
9. προσκυνήσωμεν ἐνώπιον τοῦ θρόνου τοῦ θεοῦ μᾶλλον ἢ τοῦ θρόνου τῶν
   βασιλέων.
10. εἰ ἐποίεις σημεῖα πλείονα καὶ μείζονα τῶν σημείων τοῦ διδασκάλου ἡμῶν,
    ἠκολουθοῦμεν ἄν σοι.
11. αἱ χεῖρές μου ἀσθενέστεραι ἢ οἱ πόδες μου. διὸ δύναμαι περιπατεῖν μετὰ σοῦ
    ἀλλ' οὐ δύναμαι φέρειν πλεῖον ἢ ἕνα λίθον.
12. μακάριοι οἱ ἰσχυροὶ ἐν πίστει. οὐχὶ συναχθήσονται ἔμπροσθεν τοῦ κυρίου καὶ
    εὑρήσουσι χάριν;
13. μόνος οὐκ εἰμί, οἱ γὰρ ἄγγελοι τοῦ πατρός μού εἰσιν ὧδε καὶ ἔχουσι δύναμιν
    πλείονα τῶν ἐξουσίων τοῦ κόσμου τούτου.
14. εἰ ἔδωκας ἡμῖν ἐπαγγελίαν κρείττονα καὶ ἐλπίδα ἰσχυροτέραν, οὐκ ἂν
    ἐγενόμεθα μαθηταὶ τοῦ κηρύξαντος εἰρήνην.

LXX

1. [ὁ λαὸς εἶπεν πρὸς Μωυσῆν] τί τοῦτο ἐποίησας ἡμῖν ἐξαγαγὼν ἐξ Αἰγύπτου; .
   . . κρεῖσσον γὰρ ἡμᾶς δουλεύειν τοῖς Αἰγυπτίοις ἢ ἀποθανεῖν ἐν τῇ ἐρήμῳ
   ταύτῃ. (Exod 14:11-12)
2. καὶ ἐκβαλεῖ κύριος πάντα τὰ ἔθνη ταῦτα . . . καὶ κληρονομήσετε ἔθνη μεγάλα
   καὶ ἰσχυρότερα μᾶλλον ἢ ὑμεῖς. (Deut 11:23)

3. καὶ ἐγένοντο πλείους οἱ ἀποθανόντες διὰ τοὺς λίθους τῆς χαλάζης ἢ οὓς ἀπέκτειναν οἱ υἱοὶ Ισραηλ μαχαίρᾳ ἐν τῷ πολέμῳ. (Josh 10:11)

4. εἶπεν δὲ Ραχηλ τῇ Λεια, Δός μοι τῶν μανδραγορῶν τοῦ υἱοῦ σου. εἶπεν δὲ Λεια, Οὐχ ἱκανόν σοι ὅτι ἔλαβες τὸν ἄνδρα μου; μὴ καὶ τοὺς μανδραγόρας τοῦ υἱοῦ μου λήμψῃ; (Gen 30:14-15)

5. Μακάριοι πάντες οἱ φοβούμενοι τὸν κύριον οἱ πορευόμενοι ἐν ταῖς ὁδοῖς αὐτοῦ. τοὺς πόνους τῶν καρπῶν σου φάγεσαι· μακάριος εἶ, καὶ καλῶς σοι ἔσται. (Ps 127:1-2, ET 128:1-2)

6. καὶ εἶπεν ὁ θεὸς πρὸς Καιν, Ποῦ ἐστιν Αβελ ὁ ἀδελφός σου; ὁ δὲ εἶπεν, Οὐ γινώσκω· μὴ φύλαξ τοῦ ἀδελφοῦ μού εἰμι ἐγώ; (Gen 4:9)

7. καὶ ποῦ ἐστιν πάντα τὰ θαυμάσια αὐτοῦ, ὅσα διηγήσαντο ἡμῖν οἱ πατέρες ἡμῶν λέγοντες, Οὐχὶ ἐξ Αἰγύπτου ἀνήγαγεν ἡμᾶς κύριος; (Judg 6:13)

8. μεγιστὰν καὶ κριτὴς καὶ δυνάστης δοξασθήσεται, καὶ οὐκ ἔστιν αὐτῶν τις μείζων τοῦ φοβουμένου τὸν κύριον. (Sir 10:24)

9. καὶ εἶπεν Ελισαιε, Μὴ φοβοῦ, ὅτι πλείους οἱ μεθ' ἡμῶν ὑπὲρ τοὺς μετ' αὐτῶν. (4 Kgdms 6:16)

10. ἡ ἁμαρτία μου ἐνώπιόν μού ἐστιν διὰ παντός. σοὶ μόνῳ ἥμαρτον καὶ τὸ πονηρὸν ἐνώπιόν σου ἐποίησα (Ps 50:5-6, ET 51:4-5)

11. καὶ νῦν ὁ λαός σου . . . εἰ μὴ ἐφαύλισάν με, οὐκ ἂν ἦρα τὸ δόρυ μου ἐπ' αὐτούς· ἀλλὰ αὐτοὶ ἑαυτοῖς ἐποίησαν ταῦτα. (Judith 11:2)

12. οὐχ οὗτοι οἱ λόγοι εἰσίν, οὓς ἐλάλησεν κύριος ἐν χερσὶν τῶν προφητῶν τῶν ἔμπροσθεν . . . ; (Zech 7:7)

NT

1. ὁ γὰρ πατὴρ φιλεῖ τὸν υἱὸν καὶ πάντα δείκνυσιν αὐτῷ ἃ αὐτὸς ποιεῖ, καὶ μείζονα τούτων δείξει αὐτῷ ἔργα, ἵνα ὑμεῖς θαυμάζητε. (John 5:20)

2. εἰ γὰρ ἐπιστεύετε Μωϋσεῖ, ἐπιστεύετε ἂν ἐμοί· περὶ γὰρ ἐμοῦ ἐκεῖνος ἔγραψεν. (John 5:46)

3. μὴ σὺ μείζων εἶ τοῦ πατρὸς ἡμῶν Ἰακώβ, ὃς ἔδωκεν ἡμῖν τὸ φρέαρ καὶ αὐτὸς ἐξ αὐτοῦ ἔπιεν καὶ οἱ υἱοὶ αὐτοῦ (John 4:12)

4. καὶ κρείττονός ἐστιν διαθήκης μεσίτης, ἥτις ἐπὶ κρείττοσιν ἐπαγγελίαις νενομοθέτηται. (Heb 8:6)

5. ὅτι τὸ μωρὸν τοῦ θεοῦ σοφώτερον τῶν ἀνθρώπων ἐστίν καὶ τὸ ἀσθενὲς τοῦ θεοῦ ἰσχυρότερον τῶν ἀνθρώπων. (1 Cor 1:25)

6. Πέτρος καὶ Ἰωάννης ἀποκριθέντες εἶπον πρὸς αὐτούς, Εἰ δίκαιόν ἐστιν ἐνώπιον τοῦ θεοῦ ὑμῶν ἀκούειν μᾶλλον ἢ τοῦ θεοῦ, κρίνατε· (Acts 4:19)

7. ἔχοντες . . . τὸ αὐτὸ πνεῦμα τῆς πίστεως κατὰ τὸ γεγραμμένον, Ἐπίστευσα, διὸ ἐλάλησα, καὶ ἡμεῖς πιστεύομεν, διὸ καὶ λαλοῦμεν (2 Cor 4:13)

8. εἶπεν οὖν ἡ Μάρθα πρὸς τὸν Ἰησοῦν, Κύριε, εἰ ἦς ὧδε οὐκ ἂν ἀπέθανεν ὁ ἀδελφός μου· (John 11:21)

9. [μνημονεύετε] τῶν λόγων τοῦ κυρίου Ἰησοῦ ὅτι αὐτὸς εἶπεν, Μακάριόν ἐστιν μᾶλλον διδόναι ἢ λαμβάνειν. (Acts 20:35)

10. Διὰ τοῦτο λέγω ὑμῖν, μὴ μεριμνᾶτε τῇ ψυχῇ ὑμῶν τί φάγητε [ἢ τί πίητε,] μηδὲ τῷ σώματι ὑμῶν τί ἐνδύσησθε. οὐχὶ ἡ ψυχὴ πλεῖόν ἐστιν τῆς τροφῆς καὶ τὸ σῶμα τοῦ ἐνδύματος; (Matt 6:25)

11. ὅστις δ' ἂν ἀρνήσηταί με ἔμπροσθεν τῶν ἀνθρώπων, ἀρνήσομαι κἀγὼ αὐτὸν ἔμπροσθεν τοῦ πατρός μου τοῦ ἐν [τοῖς] οὐρανοῖς. (Matt 10:33)

12. καὶ ἐὰν ἀσπάσησθε τοὺς ἀδελφοὺς ὑμῶν μόνον, τί περισσὸν ποιεῖτε; οὐχὶ καὶ οἱ ἐθνικοὶ τὸ αὐτὸ ποιοῦσιν; (Matt 5:47)

English to Greek

1. The mighty promises of God are better than the words of a king, are they not?
2. There is no joy in the city; therefore, let us drink water rather than the better wine.
3. If your (sing.) daughter were happy, she would not be sitting alone in front of your house crying out and asking for more bread.
4. You are not greater than the high priest who stands in the sight of God, are you?
5. Our sister is smaller than all the women in the village, but she has more faith than the scribes.

Vocabulary for LXX and NT Sentences

ἀνήγαγεν, from ἀνά (up) + ἀγώ
ἀρνέομαι, deny
διαθήκη, covenant
διὰ παντός, through all (time), always
διηγέομαι, tell, relate
δόρυ, spear
δουλεύω, serve (as a δοῦλος)
δυνάστης, ruler, official
ἐθνικός, pagan, Gentile
ἐνδύμα, clothing
ἐνδύω, (mid.) wear, put on
ἐξαγαγών, from ἐξάγω
θαυμάσιον, wonderful (deed)
ἱκανόν, enough
κἀγώ = καὶ ἐγώ
κληρονομέω, inherit
κριτής, judge

μανδραγόρας, mandrake (a plant with alleged magical powers)
μάχαιρα, sword
μεγιστάν, ὁ, magnate, great man
μεριμνάω, worry, be anxious
μεσίτης, ὁ, mediator
μνημονεύω, remember (+ gen.)
μωρόν, foolishness
νομοθετέομαι, enact (as law)
περισσόν = πλεῖον
πόλεμος, war
πόνος, labor
τροφή, food, nourishment
φαυλίζω, slight, snub, scorn
φρέαρ, well
φύλαξ, keeper
χάλαζα, hail

Lesson 32

231. Vocabulary

ἄχρι, ἄχρις, as far as, up to (+ gen.)

δεξιός, ά, όν, right (dexterity)

καιρός, ὁ, time, season

μέσος, η, ον, middle, in the midst

ὅμοιος, α, ον, like, similar (+ dat.)

σωτηρία, ἡ, salvation (soteriology)

τοιοῦτος, αὕτη, οὗτον or οὗτο, such

φανερόω, I make known, reveal

φόβος, ὁ, fear; reverence (phobia)

χρεία, ἡ, need, necessity, lack

232. Proper Names

In the LXX and NT sentences you have encountered many proper names of persons, nations, and geographical entities. As in English, they are capitalized, but unlike English they are sometimes accompanied by the definite article. Sometimes the article is used to mark the second mention of a name when the first mention lacked the article. Thus, Saul is Σαῦλος in Acts 8:3 but ὁ Σαῦλος in Acts 9:1. (See also Ἰησοῦς in Mark 1:9 but ὁ Ἰησοῦς in 1:14.) Other times the article may add slight emphasis to a proper name. Lastly, many names are indeclinable, and the article may be used with them to reveal the case of the name and thus its function in the sentence. But many instances of the article with names cannot be reduced to a rule. The article must, of course, be omitted in the translation.

Some names in biblical Greek are declined regularly. Examples: "Paul" (Παῦλος, Παύλου, Παύλῳ, Παῦλον, Παῦλε), "Peter" (Πέτρος, Πέτρου, Πέτρῳ, Πέτρον, Πέτρε), "James" (Ἰάκωβος, Ἰακώβου, Ἰακώβῳ, Ἰάκωβον), "Saul" (Σαῦλος, Σαύλου, Σαύλῳ, Σαῦλον), and "Mary" (Μαρία, Μαρίας, Μαρίᾳ, Μαρίαν). But there are also indeclinable Hebrew forms of the last two names (Σαούλ, Μαριάμ). Other biblical names use only indeclinable forms: Abraham (Ἀβραάμ), Isaac (Ἰσαάκ), Jacob (Ἰακώβ), and David (Δαυ[ε]ίδ).

Because of their special importance and peculiarities, the declensions of "Jesus," "John," and "Moses" are given here in full.

Nom.	Ἰησοῦς	Nom.	Ἰωάν(ν)ης	Nom.	Μω(υ)σῆς
Gen.	Ἰησοῦ	Gen.	Ἰωάν(ν)ου	Gen.	Μωυσέως
Dat.	Ἰησοῦ	Dat.	Ἰωάν(ν)ει	Dat.	Μωυσεῖ or -ῇ
Acc.	Ἰησοῦν	Acc.	Ἰωάν(ν)ην	Acc.	Μωυσῆν or -έα
Voc.	Ἰησοῦ	Voc.	Ἰωάν(ν)η	Voc.	Μωυσῆ

233. Some Special Uses of the Cases

The basic case functions were introduced in §17. The dative of means was discussed in §59, the genitive absolute in §135, the accusative as the subject of an infinitive in §169, and the genitive of comparison in §226. The cases have several other functions. Many of these functions can be made more explicit by the use of a preposition, but since the case alone often conveys the idea, you should be familiar with some of the common uses.

(1) *Genitive of Time.* The genitive indicates the time *within which* or "kind" of time at which some action occurs. Example: προσεύχομαι ἡμέρας καὶ νυκτὸς ὑπὲρ τῶν τέκνων μου, "I pray day and night for my children."

(2) *Subjective and Objective Genitive.* When the noun modified by the genitive is a noun of action (i.e., is closely related to a verb), the word in the genitive may denote either the subject or object of that action. Examples: (subjective) θαυμάζομεν τὴν ἀγάπην τοῦ θεοῦ, "We marvel at the love of God"; (objective) οὐκ ἔχομεν τὸν φόβον τοῦ θανάτου, "We do not have the fear of death."

(3) *Genitive of Apposition.* The word in the genitive may refer to the same person or thing as the word it modifies. The genitive simply identifies that person or thing more precisely. Example: ἤγαγον ὑμᾶς εἰς τὴν γῆν Αἰγύπτου, "I led you into the land of Egypt."

(4) *Dative of Reference (or Respect).* The dative indicates the thing with reference to which something is true. Example: μακάριοι οἱ ἀληθεῖς τῇ καρδίᾳ, αὐτοὶ γὰρ τῆς φωνῆς τοῦ θεοῦ ἀκούσουσιν, "Blessed are the true in (reference to the) heart, for they will hear the voice of God."

(5) *Dative of Time.* The dative indicates the time *at which* the action of the verb occurred. Example: λέγω ὑμῖν ὅτι ταύτῃ τῇ νυκτὶ εὑρήσετε τὴν εἰρήνην ἣν ζητεῖτε, "I tell you that on this night you will find the peace that you are seeking."

(6) *Dative of Advantage or Disadvantage.* The dative may indicate the person to whose benefit or detriment something is done. Examples: (Advantage) ἀνοίξω τὴν θύραν τοῖς τέκνοις, "I will open the door for the children"; (disadvantage) μαρτυρεῖτε ἑαυτοῖς ὅτι ἁμαρτωλοί ἐστε, "You are testifying against yourselves that you are sinners."

(7) *Accusative of Extent (or Measure).* The accusative may denote the *extent* of time or space *over which* some action occurred. Example: αἱ γυναῖκες προσεκύνουν ἐν τῷ ἱερῷ ὅλην τὴν ἡμέραν, "The women worshipped in the temple the entire day."

(8) *Accusative of Reference (or Respect).* This use of the accusative is similar to the dative of reference but less common. Example: ἐγώ εἰμι ἱερεὺς πιστὸς τὰ ἅγια, "I am a faithful priest with respect to holy things."

234. Optative Mood

Biblical Greek has another mood: the optative. If the subjunctive is the "mood of probability," the optative might be called the "mood of possibility." It is a sort of weakened subjunctive. During the Hellenistic period the optative fell into disuse; its functions were replaced by the subjunctive, the imperative, and the future indicative. In biblical Greek it is relatively rare, occurring mostly in stereotyped phrases with certain verbs.

Most optative forms can be identified by the morpheme οι or αι. The most common use of the optative in biblical Greek is to express a wish. It also occurs in certain indirect questions and conditional clauses. Because of its infrequency, the forms of the optative will not be given. However, two specific words that are among the most common occurrences of the optative are γένοιτο and εἴη, the aorist optative of γίνομαι and the present optative of εἰμί respectively. γένοιτο is the standard translation in the LXX of the Hebrew word "amen," meaning "May it be!" With the particle μή it is used as a negative wish, common in Paul's epistles: μὴ γένοιτο, "May it not be!" The form εἴη is found in wishes and indirect questions: ἠρώτησα τίς εἴη ὁ μέλλων ποιῆσαι τοῦτο, "I asked who could be the one who would do this."

235. The Article in Various Constructions

The Greek definite article has the power to make a substantive out of almost any part of speech. You have seen attributive and/or predicate constructions involving adjectives, participles, the demonstrative pronoun, and αὐτός. You have seen the article with infinitives. The article may also be used in attributive and substantive constructions with prepositional phrases, expressions involving the genitive, and even adverbs. Most of these constructions are readily understandable. If one remembers that the article makes a substantive of whatever follows it, then it is no longer necessary for a noun to appear in that position. Context will determine what noun, if any, needs to be supplied in the translation. Examples:

οἱ ἐν τῇ κώμῃ ἡμῶν οὐ φοβοῦνται τὸν βασιλέα.
"The people/men in our village do not fear the king."

οἱ τοῦ προφήτου παρεκάλουν ἡμᾶς προσκυνεῖν θεῷ.
"The sons/followers of the prophet exhorted us to worship God."

βλέποντες εἰς τὰ ἔμπροσθεν ἔχομεν ἐλπίδα ἐν τῷ θεῷ.
"Looking to the things that lie ahead, we have hope in God."

236. Connectives and Style in Biblical Greek

If you have done many of the LXX and NT exercises in this book, you have translated a fair amount of biblical Greek. You should now be able to work through many passages in the Bible using a lexicon and a grammar. One discovery you will make in working with continuous Greek prose is that Greek often has lengthy and complex paragraphs. Sentences in biblical Greek are seldom joined without some kind of connective, but the way in which they are joined can vary.

Classical Greek used subordination extensively; it was chiefly a *hypotactic* language (ὑπό "under" and τάσσω "order, arrange"). NT Greek does this to a degree, but less extensively than classical Greek. The LXX, being for the most part a translation from Hebrew rather than an original Greek composition, has a Semitic quality that removes it even farther from the classical style. The LXX is chiefly *paratactic* (παρά "alongside" + τάσσω) in that it often links sentences without indicating their logical relationship to one another. In the LXX clause after clause is connected to what follows by καί, reflecting the ubiquitous Hebrew conjunction *waw* in the original. The NT likewise uses connectives, but with greater variety: ἀλλά, γάρ, δέ, καί, μέν, οὖν, οὕτως, τε, τότε, etc. One particularly striking example is the μέν . . . δέ construction, which is well represented in several NT books, but rare in the LXX (except for those few books that were originally composed in Greek).

As you read biblical Greek you will encounter different styles with respect to parataxis, hypotaxis, and many other factors. The many authors (and translators) behind the Greek Bible worked under widely varying circumstances and had varying degrees of literary finesse. Their diction is sometimes stilted, sometimes sublime. Their messages are full of power, inspiration, challenge, and hope.

237. Exercises

Practice and Review

1. ἐδεξάμεθα τὴν ἐλπίδα τῆς σωτηρίας καὶ περιπατοῦμεν ἐν τῇ ἀληθείᾳ ἀπὸ τῆς πρώτης ἡμέρας ἄχρι τοῦ νῦν.
2. καὶ τὰ τέκνα ἐφοβήθησαν φόβον μέγαν καὶ ἔλεγον πρὸς ἀλλήλους, Τῆς μητρὸς ἡμῶν ἔχομεν χρείαν.
3. καὶ εἶπον, Ἰδοὺ θεωρῶ τοὺς οὐρανοὺς ἠνοιγμένους καὶ τὸν υἱὸν τοῦ ἀνθρώπου ἑστῶτα ἐκ δεξιῶν τοῦ θεοῦ ἐν μέσῳ τῶν ἁγίων ἀγγέλων.
4. οἱ ποιήσαντες τοιαῦτα οὐκ εἰσελεύσονται τὴν βασιλείαν τῆς αἰωνίου εἰρήνης οὐδὲ ὄψονται τὸ φῶς τῆς σωτηρίας.
5. ἐν ἐκείνῳ τῷ καιρῷ ἔπεσεν φόβος μέγας ἐπὶ πάντας τοὺς ἐν τῇ πόλει. οὐκ ἐδυνάμεθα ἰδεῖν τὴν σωτηρίαν ἡμῶν, ἐφύγομεν οὖν εἰς τὰ ὄρη.
6. οἱ τοῦ ἀποστόλου ἐπέθηκαν τὰς χεῖρας ἐφ᾽ ἡμᾶς καὶ ἐξήλθομεν κηρύσσοντες ἡμέρας καὶ νυκτός.

7. καὶ ἦν ἀνὴρ ἐν τῇ συναγωγῇ οὗ ἡ δεξιὰ χεὶρ ἦν ἀσθενής, ἀναστὰς δὲ ὁ προφήτης ἐν μέσῳ τοῦ ὄχλου ἐθεράπευσεν αὐτήν.

8. οὐ χρείαν ἔχετε ἵνα τις διδάσκῃ ὑμᾶς, ὁ γὰρ κύριος αὐτὸς ἐφανέρωσεν ὑμῖν πάντα.

9. οἱ μαθηταί μου ὀφείλουσιν εἶναι ὅμοιοι παιδίοις, τῶν γὰρ τοιούτων ἐστὶν ἡ βασιλεία.

10. οἱ ἰσχυροὶ τῇ πίστει διδάξουσιν ἐν τῷ ἱερῷ ὅλον τὸ ἔτος καὶ πᾶς ὁ λαὸς ἐλεύσεται ἀκούειν.

11. τῇ ἐσχάτῃ ἡμέρᾳ τοῦ ἔτους ὁ γραμματεὺς μὴ δυνάμενος εὑρεῖν τὰ βιβλία αὐτοῦ ἔκραξεν τῇ γυναικί, Μὴ γένοιτο.

12. γενώμεθα πιστοὶ ἄχρι θανάτου καὶ μὴ ἔχωμεν φόβον τῶν ἀποκτεινόντων τὸ σῶμα.

13. αἱ γυναῖκες ἐθαύμαζον καὶ ἐπηρώτων ἀλλήλας τίς εἴη οὗτος ὁ τυφλός.

14. ἦν καιρὸς ὅτε ἐδοκοῦμεν τὸν θεὸν εἶναι ὅμοιον ἀνθρώπῳ, νῦν δὲ ἡ ἀλήθεια τοῦ θεοῦ πεφανέρωται ἡμῖν.

LXX

1. καὶ εἶπεν Σαουλ, Οὐκ ἀποθανεῖται οὐδεὶς ἐν τῇ ἡμέρᾳ ταύτῃ, ὅτι σήμερον κύριος ἐποίησεν σωτηρίαν ἐν Ισραηλ. (1 Kgdms 11:13)

2. ἐγὼ διὰ παντὸς μετὰ σοῦ, ἐκράτησας τῆς χειρὸς τῆς δεξιᾶς μου (Ps 72:23, ET 73:23)

3. Καὶ εἶπεν Μωυσῆς, Τάδε λέγει κύριος, Περὶ μέσας νύκτας ἐγὼ εἰσπορεύομαι εἰς μέσον Αἰγύπτου καὶ τελευτήσει πᾶν πρωτότοκον (Exod 11:4-5)

4. Ἐγένετο δὲ ἐν τῷ καιρῷ ἐκείνῳ καὶ εἶπεν Αβιμελεχ . . . πρὸς Αβρααμ λέγων, Ὁ θεὸς μετὰ σοῦ ἐν πᾶσιν, οἷς ἐὰν ποιῇς· (Gen 21:22)

5. καὶ εἶπεν, Κύριε ὁ θεὸς Ισραηλ, οὐκ ἔστιν ὅμοιός σοι θεὸς ἐν οὐρανῷ καὶ ἐπὶ τῆς γῆς (2 Chron 6:14)

6. μὴ ζηλούτω ἡ καρδία σου ἁμαρτωλούς, ἀλλὰ ἐν φόβῳ κυρίου ἴσθι ὅλην τὴν ἡμέραν· (Prov 23:17)

7. εἶπα τῷ κυρίῳ, Κύριός μου εἶ σύ, ὅτι τῶν ἀγαθῶν μου οὐ χρείαν ἔχεις (Ps 15:2, ET 16:2)

8. καὶ εἶπεν αὐτῷ, Εὐλογία σοι γένοιτο, ἄδελφε. καὶ ἐκάλεσεν τὸν υἱὸν αὐτοῦ καὶ εἶπεν αὐτῷ, Παιδίον, ἑτοίμασον τὰ πρὸς τὴν ὁδόν (Tob 5:17)

9. εἴη τὸ ὄνομα κυρίου εὐλογημένον ἀπὸ τοῦ νῦν καὶ ἕως τοῦ αἰῶνος· (Ps 112:2, ET 113:2)

10. τὸ στόμα μου ἐξαγγελεῖ τὴν δικαιοσύνην σου, ὅλην τὴν ἡμέραν τὴν σωτηρίαν σου (Ps 70:15, ET 71:15)

11. εἶπεν Φαραω πᾶσιν τοῖς παισὶν αὐτοῦ, Μὴ εὑρήσομεν ἄνθρωπον τοιοῦτον, ὃς ἔχει πνεῦμα θεοῦ ἐν αὐτῷ; (Gen 41:38)

NT

1. φόβος οὐκ ἔστιν ἐν τῇ ἀγάπῃ ἀλλ' ἡ τελεία ἀγάπη ἔξω βάλλει τὸν φόβον, ὅτι ὁ φόβος κόλασιν ἔχει, ὁ δὲ φοβούμενος οὐ τετελείωται ἐν τῇ ἀγάπῃ. (1 John 4:18)

2. ἐν παντὶ τόπῳ ἡ πίστις ὑμῶν ἡ πρὸς τὸν θεὸν ἐξελήλυθεν, ὥστε μὴ χρείαν ἔχειν ἡμᾶς λαλεῖν τι. (1 Thess 1:8)

3. οὗτος ἦλθεν πρὸς αὐτὸν νυκτὸς καὶ εἶπεν αὐτῷ, Ῥαββί, οἴδαμεν ὅτι ἀπὸ θεοῦ ἐλήλυθας διδάσκαλος· (John 3:2)

4. καὶ νῦν ἰδοὺ χεὶρ κυρίου ἐπὶ σέ καὶ ἔσῃ τυφλὸς μὴ βλέπων τὸν ἥλιον ἄχρι καιροῦ. (Acts 13:11)

5. τότε ἐρεῖ ὁ βασιλεὺς τοῖς ἐκ δεξιῶν αὐτοῦ, Δεῦτε οἱ εὐλογημένοι τοῦ πατρός μου, κληρονομήσατε τὴν ἡτοιμασμένην ὑμῖν βασιλείαν (Matt 25:34)

6. Τί οὖν; ἁμαρτήσωμεν, ὅτι οὐκ ἐσμὲν ὑπὸ νόμον ἀλλὰ ὑπὸ χάριν; μὴ γένοιτο. (Rom 6:15)

7. Μακάριοι οἱ πτωχοὶ τῷ πνεύματι, ὅτι αὐτῶν ἐστιν ἡ βασιλεία τῶν οὐρανῶν. (Matt 5:3)

8. Ἀγαπητοί νῦν τέκνα θεοῦ ἐσμεν, καὶ οὔπω ἐφανερώθη τί ἐσόμεθα. οἴδαμεν ὅτι ἐὰν φανερωθῇ, ὅμοιοι αὐτῷ ἐσόμεθα, ὅτι ὀψόμεθα αὐτὸν καθώς ἐστιν. (1 John 3:2)

9. Ἐπηρώτων δὲ αὐτὸν οἱ μαθηταὶ αὐτοῦ τίς αὕτη εἴη ἡ παραβολή. (Luke 8:9)

10. ὑμεῖς προσκυνεῖτε ὃ οὐκ οἴδατε· ἡμεῖς προσκυνοῦμεν ὃ οἴδαμεν, ὅτι ἡ σωτηρία ἐκ τῶν Ἰουδαίων ἐστίν. (John 4:22)

11. καὶ λαβὼν παιδίον ἔστησεν αὐτὸ ἐν μέσῳ αὐτῶν καὶ . . . εἶπεν αὐτοῖς, Ὃς ἂν ἓν τῶν τοιούτων παιδίων δέξηται ἐπὶ τῷ ὀνόματί μου, ἐμὲ δέχεται· (Mark 9:36-37)

English to Greek

1. Not knowing the fear of the Lord, the evil king said to Peter and Paul that he did not have need of eternal salvation.

2. While we were praying, the voice of Moses came from heaven and revealed to us the time of judgment.

3. Those who do not sin with respect to the tongue will sit at the right hand of God like the Lord Jesus and his servant, John.

4. On the one hand, the (people) in the city cried out, "May such things not happen!" But the (people) in the field said, "Let us be faithful even until death."

Vocabulary for LXX and NT Sentences

δεῦτε, come!
διὰ παντὸς, through all time, always
ἐξαγγέλλω, proclaim, declare
εὐλογέω, bless
εὐλογία, blessing
ζηλόω, admire, show zeal for
ἥλιος, sun
κληρονομέω, inherit

κόλασις, punishment
παῖς, παιδός, servant
πρωτότοκον, firstborn
σήμερον, today
τάδε, these things, thus
τελείος, α, ον, perfect, complete
τελειόω, make perfect
τελευτάω = ἀποθνήσκω

Paradigms

THE FIRST DECLENSION

238. First Declension Feminine Nouns

Singular		Plural	
Nom. Voc.	ὥρα	Nom. Voc.	ὧραι
Gen.	ὥρας	Gen.	ὡρῶν
Dat.	ὥρᾳ	Dat.	ὥραις
Acc.	ὥραν	Acc.	ὥρας
Nom. Voc.	ἀλήθεια	Nom. Voc.	ἀλήθειαι
Gen.	ἀληθείας	Gen.	ἀληθειῶν
Dat.	ἀληθείᾳ	Dat.	ἀληθείαις
Acc.	ἀλήθειαν	Acc.	ἀληθείας
Nom. Voc.	φωνή	Nom. Voc.	φωναί
Gen.	φωνῆς	Gen.	φωνῶν
Dat.	φωνῇ	Dat.	φωναῖς
Acc.	φωνήν	Acc.	φωνάς
Nom. Voc.	δόξα	Nom. Voc.	δόξαι
Gen.	δόξης	Gen.	δοξῶν
Dat.	δόξῃ	Dat.	δόξαις
Acc.	δόξαν	Acc.	δόξας

239. First Declension Masculine Nouns

	Singular		Plural
Nom.	προφήτης	Nom. Voc.	προφῆται
Gen.	προφήτου	Gen.	προφητῶν
Dat.	προφήτῃ	Dat.	προφήταις
Acc.	προφήτην	Acc.	προφήτας
Voc.	προφῆτα		

Nom.	μαθητής	Nom. Voc.	μαθηταί
Gen.	μαθητοῦ	Gen.	μαθητῶν
Dat.	μαθητῇ	Dat.	μαθηταῖς
Acc.	μαθητήν	Acc.	μαθητάς
Voc.	μαθητά		

THE SECOND DECLENSION

240. Second Declension Masculine/Feminine Nouns

	Singular		Plural
Nom.	λόγος	Nom.	λόγοι
Gen.	λόγου	Gen.	λόγων
Dat.	λόγῳ	Dat.	λόγοις
Acc.	λόγον	Acc.	λόγους
Voc.	λόγε	Voc.	λόγοι

Nom.	ἀδελφός	Nom.	ἀδελφοί
Gen.	ἀδελφοῦ	Gen.	ἀδελφῶν
Dat.	ἀδελφῷ	Dat.	ἀδελφοῖς
Acc.	ἀδελφόν	Acc.	ἀδελφούς
Voc.	ἀδελφέ	Voc.	ἀδελφοί

Nom.	ἄνθρωπος	Nom.	ἄνθρωποι
Gen.	ἀνθρώπου	Gen.	ἀνθρώπων
Dat.	ἀνθρώπῳ	Dat.	ἀνθρώποις
Acc.	ἄνθρωπον	Acc.	ἀνθρώπους
Voc.	ἄνθρωπε	Voc.	ἄνθρωποι

Nom.	ὁδός	Nom.	ὁδοί
Gen.	ὁδοῦ	Gen.	ὁδῶν
Dat.	ὁδῷ	Dat.	ὁδοῖς
Acc.	ὁδόν	Acc.	ὁδούς
Voc.	ὁδέ	Voc.	ὁδοί

241. Second Declension Neuter Nouns

Singular		Plural	
Nom.	ἔργον	Nom.	ἔργα
Gen.	ἔργου	Gen.	ἔργων
Dat.	ἔργῳ	Dat.	ἔργοις
Acc.	ἔργον	Acc.	ἔργα
Voc.	ἔργον	Voc.	ἔργα

Nom.	τέκνον	Nom.	τέκνα
Gen.	τέκνου	Gen.	τέκνων
Dat.	τέκνῳ	Dat.	τέκνοις
Acc.	τέκνον	Acc.	τέκνα
Voc.	τέκνον	Voc.	τέκνα

THE THIRD DECLENSION

242. Third Declension Nouns

Singular		Plural	
Nom.	ἄρχων	Nom.	ἄρχοντες
Gen.	ἄρχοντος	Gen.	ἀρχόντων
Dat.	ἄρχοντι	Dat.	ἄρχουσι(ν)
Acc.	ἄρχοντα	Acc.	ἄρχοντας
Voc.	ἄρχων	Voc.	ἄρχοντες

Singular		Plural	
Nom.	σάρξ	Nom.	σάρκες
Gen.	σαρκός	Gen.	σαρκῶν
Dat.	σαρκί	Dat.	σαρξί(ν)
Acc.	σάρκα	Acc.	σάρκας
Voc.	σάρξ	Voc.	σάρκες

	Singular		Plural
Nom.	σῶμα	Nom.	σώματα
Gen.	σώματος	Gen.	σωμάτων
Dat.	σώματι	Dat.	σώμασι(ν)
Acc.	σῶμα	Acc.	σώματα
Voc.	σῶμα	Voc.	σώματα

	Singular		Plural
Nom.	πόλις	N. V.	πόλεις
Gen.	πόλεως	Gen.	πόλεων
Dat.	πόλει	Dat.	πόλεσι(ν)
Acc.	πόλιν	Acc.	πόλεις
Voc.	πόλι		

	Singular		Plural
Nom.	βασιλεύς	N. V.	βασιλεῖς
Gen.	βασιλέως	Gen.	βασιλέων
Dat.	βασιλεῖ	Dat.	βασιλεῦσι(ν)
Acc.	βασιλέα	Acc.	βασιλεῖς
Voc.	βασιλεῦ		

	Singular		Plural
N. V.	γένος	N. V.	γένη
Gen.	γένους	Gen.	γενῶν
Dat.	γένει	Dat.	γένεσι(ν)
Acc.	γένος	Acc.	γένη

ARTICLE, ADJECTIVES, AND PARTICIPLES

243. The Definite Article

	Singular				Plural		
	Masc.	Fem.	Neut.		Masc.	Fem.	Neut.
N.	ὁ	ἡ	τό	N.	οἱ	αἱ	τά
G.	τοῦ	τῆς	τοῦ	G.	τῶν	τῶν	τῶν
D.	τῷ	τῇ	τῷ	D.	τοῖς	ταῖς	τοῖς
A.	τόν	τήν	τό	A.	τούς	τάς	τά

244. First and Second Declension Adjectives

	Singular				Plural		
	Masc.	Fem.	Neut.		Masc.	Fem.	Neut.
N.	καλός	καλή	καλόν	N.V.	καλοί	καλαί	καλά
G.	καλοῦ	καλῆς	καλοῦ	G.	καλῶν	καλῶν	καλῶν
D.	καλῷ	καλῇ	καλῷ	D.	καλοῖς	καλαῖς	καλοῖς
A.	καλόν	καλήν	καλόν	A.	καλούς	καλάς	καλά
V.	καλέ	καλή	καλόν				

	Singular				Plural		
	Masc.	Fem.	Neut.		Masc.	Fem.	Neut.
N.	μικρός	μικρά	μικρόν	N.V.	μικροί	μικραί	μικρά
G.	μικροῦ	μικρᾶς	μικροῦ	G.	μικρῶν	μικρῶν	μικρῶν
D.	μικρῷ	μικρᾷ	μικρῷ	D.	μικροῖς	μικραῖς	μικροῖς
A.	μικρόν	μικράν	μικρόν	A.	μικρούς	μικράς	μικρά
V.	μικρέ	μικρά	μικρόν				

245. Adjectives of the Third Declension

	Singular			Plural	
	Masc. Fem.	Neut.		Masc. Fem.	Neut.
N.	ἀληθής	ἀληθές	N. V.	ἀληθεῖς	ἀληθῆ
G.	ἀληθοῦς	ἀληθοῦς	G.	ἀληθῶν	ἀληθῶν
D.	ἀληθεῖ	ἀληθεῖ	D.	ἀληθέσι(ν)	ἀληθέσι(ν)
A.	ἀληθῆ	ἀληθές	A.	ἀληθεῖς	ἀληθῆ
V.	ἀληθές	ἀληθές			

246. Irregular Adjectives

	Singular		
	Masculine	Feminine	Neuter
Nom.	πᾶς	πᾶσα	πᾶν
Gen.	παντός	πάσης	παντός
Dat.	παντί	πάσῃ	παντί
Acc.	πάντα	πᾶσαν	πᾶν

Paradigms

Plural

	Masculine	Feminine	Neuter
Nom.	πάντες	πᾶσαι	πάντα
Gen.	πάντων	πασῶν	πάντων
Dat.	πᾶσι(ν)	πάσαις	πᾶσι(ν)
Acc.	πάντας	πάσας	πάντα

Singular

	Masculine	Feminine	Neuter
Nom.	πολύς	πολλή	πολύ
Gen.	πολλοῦ	πολλῆς	πολλοῦ
Dat.	πολλῷ	πολλῇ	πολλῷ
Acc.	πολύν	πολλήν	πολύ

Plural

	Masculine	Feminine	Neuter
Nom.	πολλοί	πολλαί	πολλά
Gen.	πολλῶν	πολλῶν	πολλῶν
Dat.	πολλοῖς	πολλαῖς	πολλοῖς
Acc.	πολλούς	πολλάς	πολλά

Singular

	Masculine	Feminine	Neuter
Nom.	μέγας	μεγάλη	μέγα
Gen.	μεγάλου	μεγάλης	μεγάλου
Dat.	μεγάλῳ	μεγάλη	μεγάλῳ
Acc.	μέγαν	μεγάλην	μέγα
Voc.	μεγάλε	μεγάλη	μέγα

Plural

	Masculine	Feminine	Neuter
Nom. Voc.	μεγάλοι	μεγάλαι	μεγάλα
Gen.	μεγάλων	μεγάλων	μεγάλων
Dat.	μεγάλοις	μεγάλαις	μεγάλοις
Acc.	μεγάλους	μεγάλας	μεγάλα

247. Irregular Comparative Adjectives

	Singular				Plural	
	Masc. Fem.	Neut.			Masc. Fem.	Neut.
N.	πλείων	πλεῖον		N. V.	πλείονες	πλείονα
G.	πλείονος	πλείονος		G.	πλειόνων	πλειόνων
D.	πλείονι	πλείονι		D.	πλείοσι(ν)	πλείοσι(ν)
A.	πλείονα	πλεῖον		A.	πλείονας	πλείονα

248. Present Active Participle

Singular

	Masculine	Feminine	Neuter
Nom. Voc.	λύων	λύουσα	λῦον
Gen.	λύοντος	λυούσης	λύοντος
Dat.	λύοντι	λυούσῃ	λύοντι
Acc.	λύοντα	λύουσαν	λῦον

Plural

	Masculine	Feminine	Neuter
Nom. Voc.	λύοντες	λύουσαι	λύοντα
Gen.	λυόντων	λυουσῶν	λυόντων
Dat.	λύουσι(ν)	λυούσαις	λύουσι(ν)
Acc.	λύοντας	λυούσας	λύοντα

249. Present Middle/Passive Participle

Singular

	Masculine	Feminine	Neuter
Nom. Voc.	λυόμενος	λυομένη	λυόμενον
Gen.	λυομένου	λυομένης	λυομένου
Dat.	λυομένῳ	λυομένῃ	λυομένῳ
Acc.	λυόμενον	λυομένην	λυόμενον

Plural

	Masculine	Feminine	Neuter
Nom. Voc.	λυόμενοι	λυόμεναι	λυόμενα
Gen.	λυομένων	λυομένων	λυομένων
Dat.	λυομένοις	λυομέναις	λυομένοις
Acc.	λυομένους	λυομένας	λυόμενα

250. Aorist Active Participles

Singular

	Masculine	Feminine	Neuter
Nom. Voc.	λύσας	λύσασα	λῦσαν
Gen.	λύσαντος	λυσάσης	λύσαντος
Dat.	λύσαντι	λυσάσῃ	λύσαντι
Acc.	λύσαντα	λύσασαν	λῦσαν

Plural

	Masculine	Feminine	Neuter
Nom. Voc.	λύσαντες	λύσασαι	λύσαντα
Gen.	λυσάντων	λυσασῶν	λυσάντων
Dat.	λύσασι(ν)	λυσάσαις	λύσασι(ν)
Acc.	λύσαντας	λυσάσας	λύσαντα

251. Aorist Middle Participles

Singular

	Masculine	Feminine	Neuter
Nom. Voc.	λυσάμενος	λυσαμένη	λυσάμενον
Gen.	λυσαμένου	λυσαμένης	λυσαμένου
Dat.	λυσαμένῳ	λυσαμένῃ	λυσαμένῳ
Acc.	λυσάμενον	λυσαμένην	λυσάμενον

Plural

	Masculine	Feminine	Neuter
Nom. Voc.	λυσάμενοι	λυσάμεναι	λυσάμενα
Gen.	λυσαμένων	λυσαμένων	λυσαμένων
Dat.	λυσαμένοις	λυσαμέναις	λυσαμένοις
Acc.	λυσαμένους	λυσαμένας	λυσάμενα

252. Second Aorist Active Participles

Singular

	Masculine	Feminine	Neuter
Nom. Voc.	ἰδών	ἰδοῦσα	ἰδόν
Gen.	ἰδόντος	ἰδούσης	ἰδόντος
Dat.	ἰδόντι	ἰδούσῃ	ἰδόντι
Acc.	ἰδόντα	ἰδοῦσαν	ἰδόν

	Masculine	Plural Feminine	Neuter
Nom. Voc.	ἰδόντες	ἰδοῦσαι	ἰδόντα
Gen.	ἰδόντων	ἰδουσῶν	ἰδόντων
Dat.	ἰδοῦσι(ν)	ἰδούσαις	ἰδοῦσι(ν)
Acc.	ἰδόντας	ἰδούσας	ἰδόντα

253. Second Aorist Middle Participles

	Masculine	Singular Feminine	Neuter
Nom. Voc.	γενόμενος	γενομένη	γενόμενον
Gen.	γενομένου	γενομένης	γενομένου
Dat.	γενομένῳ	γενομένῃ	γενομένῳ
Acc.	γενόμενον	γενομένην	γενόμενον

	Masculine	Plural Feminine	Neuter
Nom. Voc.	γενόμενοι	γενόμεναι	γενόμενα
Gen.	γενομένων	γενομένων	γενομένων
Dat.	γενομένοις	γενομέναις	γενομένοις
Acc.	γενομένους	γενομένας	γενόμενα

254. Aorist Passive Participles

	Masculine	Singular Feminine	Neuter
Nom. Voc.	λυθείς	λυθεῖσα	λυθέν
Gen.	λυθέντος	λυθείσης	λυθέντος
Dat.	λυθέντι	λυθείσῃ	λυθέντι
Acc.	λυθέντα	λυθεῖσαν	λυθέν

	Masculine	Plural Feminine	Neuter
Nom. Voc.	λυθέντες	λυθεῖσαι	λυθέντα
Gen.	λυθέντων	λυθεισῶν	λυθέντων
Dat.	λυθεῖσι(ν)	λυθείσαις	λυθεῖσι(ν)
Acc.	λυθέντας	λυθείσας	λυθέντα

255. Perfect Active Participles

	Singular Masculine	Feminine	Neuter
Nom. Voc.	λελυκώς	λελυκυῖα	λελυκός
Gen.	λελυκότος	λελυκυίας	λελυκότος
Dat.	λελυκότι	λελυκυίᾳ	λελυκότι
Acc.	λελυκότα	λελυκυῖαν	λελυκός

	Plural Masculine	Feminine	Neuter
Nom. Voc.	λελυκότες	λελυκυῖαι	λελυκότα
Gen.	λελυκότων	λελυκυιῶν	λελυκότων
Dat.	λελυκόσι(ν)	λελυκυίαις	λελυκόσι(ν)
Acc.	λελυκότας	λελυκυίας	λελυκότα

256. Perfect Middle/Passive Participles

	Singular Masculine	Feminine	Neuter
Nom. Voc.	λελυμένος	λελυμένη	λελυμένον
Gen.	λελυμένου	λελυμένης	λελυμένου
Dat.	λελυμένῳ	λελυμένῃ	λελυμένῳ
Acc.	λελυμένον	λελυμένην	λελυμένον

	Plural Masculine	Feminine	Neuter
Nom. Voc.	λελυμένοι	λελυμέναι	λελυμένα
Gen.	λελυμένων	λελυμένων	λελυμένων
Dat.	λελυμένοις	λελυμέναις	λελυμένοις
Acc.	λελυμένους	λελυμένας	λελυμένα

PRONOUNS

257. Personal Pronouns

First Person

Singular			Plural	
Nom.	ἐγώ, I		Nom.	ἡμεῖς, we
Gen.	ἐμοῦ or μου, of me		Gen.	ἡμῶν, of us
Dat.	ἐμοί or μοι, to/for me		Dat.	ἡμῖν, to/for us
Acc.	ἐμέ or με, me		Acc.	ἡμᾶς, us

Second Person

Singular			Plural	
Nom.	σύ, you		Nom.	ὑμεῖς, you
Gen.	σοῦ or σου, of you		Gen.	ὑμῶν, of you
Dat.	σοί or σοι, to/for you		Dat.	ὑμῖν, to/for you
Acc.	σέ or σε, you		Acc.	ὑμᾶς, you

Third Person

	Singular		
	Masc.	Fem.	Neut.
N.	αὐτός, he	αὐτή, she	αὐτό, it
G.	αὐτοῦ, of him	αὐτῆς, of her	αὐτοῦ, of it
D.	αὐτῷ, to/for him	αὐτῇ, to/for her	αὐτῷ, to/for it
A.	αὐτόν, him	αὐτήν, her	αὐτό, it

	Plural		
	Masc.	Fem.	Neut.
N.	αὐτοί, they	αὐταί, they	αὐτά, they
G.	αὐτῶν, of them	αὐτῶν, of them	αὐτῶν, of them
D.	αὐτοῖς, to/for them	αὐταῖς, to/for them	αὐτοῖς, to/for them
A.	αὐτούς, them	αὐτάς, them	αὐτά, them

258. The Relative Pronoun

	Singular					Plural		
	Masc.	Fem.	Neut.			Masc.	Fem.	Neut.
N.	ὅς	ἥ	ὅ		N.	οἵ	αἵ	ἅ
G.	οὗ	ἧς	οὗ		G.	ὧν	ὧν	ὧν
D.	ᾧ	ᾗ	ᾧ		D.	οἷς	αἷς	οἷς
A.	ὅν	ἥν	ὅ		A.	οὕς	ἅς	ἅ

259. Reflexive Pronouns

First Person

	Singular				Plural	
	Masc.	Fem.			Masc.	Fem.
G.	ἐμαυτοῦ	ἐμαυτῆς		G.	ἑαυτῶν	ἑαυτῶν
D.	ἐμαυτῷ	ἐμαυτῇ		D.	ἑαυτοῖς	ἑαυταῖς
A.	ἐμαυτόν	ἐμαυτήν		A.	ἑαυτούς	ἑαυτάς

Second Person

	Singular				Plural	
	Masc.	Fem.			Masc.	Fem.
G.	σεαυτοῦ	σεαυτῆς		G.	ἑαυτῶν	ἑαυτῶν
D.	σεαυτῷ	σεαυτῇ		D.	ἑαυτοῖς	ἑαυταῖς
A.	σεαυτόν	σεαυτήν		A.	ἑαυτούς	ἑαυτάς

Third Person

	Singular					Plural		
	Masc.	Fem.	Neut.			Masc.	Fem.	Neut.
G.	ἑαυτοῦ	ἑαυτῆς	ἑαυτοῦ		G.	ἑαυτῶν	ἑαυτῶν	ἑαυτῶν
D.	ἑαυτῷ	ἑαυτῇ	ἑαυτῷ		D.	ἑαυτοῖς	ἑαυταῖς	ἑαυτοῖς
A.	ἑαυτόν	ἑαυτήν	ἑαυτό		A.	ἑαυτούς	ἑαυτάς	ἑαυτά

260. Demonstrative Pronouns (and Adjectives)

Singular

	Masc.	Fem.	Neut.
N.	οὗτος	αὕτη	τοῦτο
G.	τούτου	ταύτης	τούτου
D.	τούτῳ	ταύτῃ	τούτῳ
A.	τοῦτον	ταύτην	τοῦτο

Plural

	Masc.	Fem.	Neut.
N.	οὗτοι	αὗται	ταῦτα
G.	τούτων	τούτων	τούτων
D.	τούτοις	ταύταις	τούτοις
A.	τούτους	ταύτας	ταῦτα

Singular

	Masc.	Fem.	Neut.
N.	ἐκεῖνος	ἐκείνη	ἐκεῖνο
G.	ἐκείνου	ἐκείνης	ἐκείνου
D.	ἐκείνῳ	ἐκείνῃ	ἐκείνῳ
A.	ἐκεῖνον	ἐκείνην	ἐκεῖνο

Plural

	Masc.	Fem.	Neut.
N.	ἐκεῖνοι	ἐκεῖναι	ἐκεῖνα
G.	ἐκείνων	ἐκείνων	ἐκείνων
D.	ἐκείνοις	ἐκείναις	ἐκείνοις
A.	ἐκείνους	ἐκείνας	ἐκεῖνα

261. Interrogative Pronoun (and Adjective)

	Singular Masc. Fem.	Neut.		Plural Masc. Fem.	Neut.
N.	τίς	τί	N.	τίνες	τίνα
G.	τίνος	τίνος	G.	τίνων	τίνων
D.	τίνι	τίνι	D.	τίσι(ν)	τίσι(ν)
A.	τίνα	τί	A.	τίνας	τίνα

262. The Indefinite Pronoun (and Adjective)

	Singular				Plural	
	Masc. Fem.	Neut.			Masc. Fem.	Neut.
N.	τις	τι		N.	τινές	τινά
G.	τινός	τινός		G.	τινῶν	τινῶν
D.	τινί	τινί		D.	τισί(ν)	τισί(ν)
A.	τινά	τι		A.	τινάς	τινά

NUMBERS

263. Numbers — One

	Masc.	Fem.	Neut.
Nom.	εἷς	μία	ἕν
Gen.	ἑνός	μιᾶς	ἑνός
Dat.	ἑνί	μιᾷ	ἑνί
Acc.	ἕνα	μίαν	ἕν

264. Numbers — Three and Four

	Masc. Fem.	Neut.			Masc. Fem.	Neut.
N.	τρεῖς	τρία		N. V.	τέσσαρες	τέσσαρα
G.	τριῶν	τριῶν		G.	τεσσάρων	τεσσάρων
D.	τρισί(ν)	τρισί(ν)		D.	τέσσαρσι(ν)	τέσσαρσι(ν)
A.	τρεῖς	τρία		A.	τέσσαρας	τέσσαρα

THE REGULAR VERB — INDICATIVE

265. The Present Active Indicative

Singular	Plural
1. λύω	1. λύομεν
2. λύεις	2. λύετε
3. λύει	3. λύουσι(ν)

266. Present Middle/Passive Indicative

Singular	Plural
1. λύομαι	1. λυόμεθα
2. λύῃ	2. λύεσθε
3. λύεται	3. λύονται

267. Imperfect Active Indicative

Singular	Plural
1. ἔλυον	1. ἐλύομεν
2. ἔλυες	2. ἐλύετε
3. ἔλυε(ν)	3. ἔλυον

268. Imperfect Middle/Passive Indicative

Singular	Plural
1. ἐλυόμην	1. ἐλυόμεθα
2. ἐλύου	2. ἐλύεσθε
3. ἐλύετο	3. ἐλύοντο

269. Future Active Indicative

Singular	Plural
1. λύσω	1. λύσομεν
2. λύσεις	2. λύσετε
3. λύσει	3. λύσουσι(ν)

270. Future Middle Indicative

Singular	Plural
1. λύσομαι	1. λυσόμεθα
2. λύσῃ	2. λύσεσθε
3. λύσεται	3. λύσονται

271. First Aorist Active Indicative

Singular
1. ἔλυσα
2. ἔλυσας
3. ἔλυσε(ν)

Plural
1. ἐλύσαμεν
2. ἐλύσατε
3. ἔλυσαν

272. First Aorist Middle Indicative

Singular
1. ἐλύσαμην
2. ἐλύσω
3. ἐλύσατο

Plural
1. ἐλυσάμεθα
2. ἐλύσασθε
3. ἐλύσαντο

273. Second Aorist Active Indicative

Singular
1. ἔλαβον
2. ἔλαβες
3. ἔλαβε(ν)

Plural
1. ἐλάβομεν
2. ἐλάβετε
3. ἔλαβον

274. Second Aorist Middle Indicative

Singular
1. ἐλαβόμην
2. ἐλάβου
3. ἐλάβετο

Plural
1. ἐλαβόμεθα
2. ἐλάβεσθε
3. ἐλάβοντο

275. Perfect Active Indicative

Singular
1. λέλυκα
2. λέλυκας
3. λέλυκε(ν)

Plural
1. λελύκαμεν
2. λελύκατε
3. λελύκασι(ν) or -καν

276. Perfect Middle/Passive Indicative

Singular
1. λέλυμαι
2. λέλυσαι
3. λέλυται

Plural
1. λελύμεθα
2. λέλυσθε
3. λέλυνται

277. The Pluperfect Active Indicative

Singular
1. ἐλελύκειν
2. ἐλελύκεις
3. ἐλελύκει

Plural
1. ἐλελύκειμεν
2. ἐλελύκειτε
3. ἐλελύκεισαν

278. Aorist Passive Indicative

Singular
1. ἐλύθην
2. ἐλύθης
3. ἐλύθη

Plural
1. ἐλύθημεν
2. ἐλύθητε
3. ἐλύθησαν

279. Future Passive Indicative

Singular
1. λυθήσομαι
2. λυθήσῃ
3. λυθήσεται

Plural
1. λυθησόμεθα
2. λυθήσεσθε
3. λυθήσονται

THE REGULAR VERB — SUBJUNCTIVE

280. Present Active Subjunctive

Singular
1. λύω
2. λύῃς
3. λύῃ

Plural
1. λύωμεν
2. λύητε
3. λύωσι(ν)

281. Present Middle/Passive Subjunctive

Singular | Plural
1. λύωμαι | 1. λυώμεθα
2. λύῃ | 2. λύησθε
3. λύηται | 3. λύωνται

282. Aorist Active Subjunctive

Singular | Plural
1. λύσω | 1. λύσωμεν
2. λύσῃς | 2. λύσητε
3. λύσῃ | 3. λύσωσι(ν)

283. Aorist Middle Subjunctive

Singular | Plural
1. λύσωμαι | 1. λυσώμεθα
2. λύσῃ | 2. λύσησθε
3. λύσηται | 3. λύσωνται

284. Aorist Passive Subjunctive

Singular | Plural
1. λυθῶ | 1. λυθῶμεν
2. λυθῇς | 2. λυθῆτε
3. λυθῇ | 3. λυθῶσι(ν)

THE REGULAR VERB — INFINITIVE AND IMPERATIVE

285. Infinitive

	Present	Aorist	Perfect
Act.	λύειν	λῦσαι	λελυκέναι
Mid.	λύεσθαι	λύσασθαι	λελύσθαι
Pass.	λύεσθαι	λυθῆναι	λελύσθαι

286. Present Active Imperative

Singular	Plural
2. λῦε	2. λύετε
3. λυέτω	3. λυέτωσαν

287. Present Middle/Passive Imperative

Singular	Plural
2. λύου	2. λύεσθε
3. λυέσθω	3. λυέσθωσαν

288. Aorist Active Imperative

Singular	Plural
2. λῦσον	2. λύσατε
3. λυσάτω	3. λυσάτωσαν

289. Aorist Middle Imperative

Singular	Plural
2. λῦσαι	2. λύσασθε
3. λυσάσθω	3. λυσάσθωσαν

290. Aorist Passive Imperative

Singular	Plural
2. λύθητι	2. λύθητε
3. λυθήτω	3. λυθήτωσαν

291. Second Aorist Active Imperative

Singular	Plural
2. λάβε	2. λάβετε
3. λαβέτω	3. λαβέτωσαν

292. Second Aorist Middle Imperative

Singular	Plural
2. λαβοῦ	2. λάβεσθε
3. λαβέσθω	3. λαβέσθωσαν

THE VERB εἰμί

293. Present Indicative of εἰμί

Singular	Plural
1. εἰμί	1. ἐσμέν
2. εἶ	2. ἐστέ
3. ἐστί(ν)	3. εἰσί(ν)

294. Imperfect Indicative of εἰμί

Singular	Plural
1. ἤμην	1. ἦμεν (or ἤμεθα)
2. ἦς (or ἦσθα)	2. ἦτε
3. ἦν	3. ἦσαν

295. Future Indicative of εἰμί

Singular	Plural
1. ἔσομαι	1. ἐσόμεθα
2. ἔσῃ	2. ἔσεσθε
3. ἔσται	3. ἔσονται

296. Subjunctive of εἰμί

Singular	Plural
1. ὦ	1. ὦμεν
2. ᾖς	2. ἦτε
3. ᾖ	3. ὦσι(ν)

297. Imperative of εἰμί

Singular	Plural
2. ἴσθι	2. ἔστε
3. ἔστω (or ἤτω)	3. ἔστωσαν

298. Infinitive of εἰμί

εἶναι

299. Present Participle of εἰμί

	Singular		
	Masculine	Feminine	Neuter
Nom. Voc.	ὤν	οὖσα	ὄν
Gen.	ὄντος	οὔσης	ὄντος
Dat.	ὄντι	οὔσῃ	ὄντι
Acc.	ὄντα	οὖσαν	ὄν

	Plural		
	Masculine	Feminine	Neuter
Nom. Voc.	ὄντες	οὖσαι	ὄντα
Gen.	ὄντων	οὐσῶν	ὄντων
Dat.	οὖσι(ν)	οὔσαις	οὖσι(ν)
Acc.	ὄντας	οὔσας	ὄντα

PRESENT SYSTEM OF δίδωμι

300. Indicative

		Present Active	Impf. Active	Present M/P	Impf. M/P
Sing.	1.	δίδωμι	ἐδίδουν	δίδομαι	ἐδιδόμην
	2.	δίδως	ἐδίδους	δίδοσαι	ἐδίδοσο
	3.	δίδωσι(ν)	ἐδίδου	δίδοται	ἐδίδοτο
Plur.	1.	δίδομεν	ἐδίδομεν	διδόμεθα	ἐδιδόμεθα
	2.	δίδοτε	ἐδίδοτε	δίδοσθε	ἐδίδοσθε
	3.	διδόασι(ν)	ἐδίδοσαν	δίδονται	ἐδίδοντο

301. Present Subjunctive

	Present Active	Present M/P
Sing.	1. διδῶ	1. διδῶμαι
	2. διδῷς	2. διδῷ
	3. διδῷ	3. διδῶται
Plur.	1. διδῶμεν	1. διδώμεθα
	2. διδῶτε	2. διδῶσθε
	3. διδῶσι(ν)	3. διδῶνται

302. Present Imperative

	Present Active	Present Mid./Pass.
Sing.	2. δίδου	2. δίδοσο
	3. διδότω	3. διδόσθω
Plur.	2. δίδοτε	2. δίδοσθε
	3. διδότωσαν	3. διδόσθωσαν

303. Present Infinitive

Present Active	Present Mid./Pass.
διδόναι	δίδοσθαι

304. Present Active Participle

διδούς	διδοῦσα	διδόν
διδόντος	διδούσης	διδόντος
διδόντι	διδούσῃ	διδόντι
διδόντα	διδοῦσαν	διδόν
διδόντες	διδοῦσαι	διδόντα
διδόντων	διδουσῶν	διδόντων
διδοῦσι(ν)	διδούσαις	διδοῦσι(ν)
διδόντας	διδούσας	διδόντα

305. Present Middle/Passive Participle

διδόμενος	διδομένη	διδόμενον
διδομένου	διδομένης	διδομένου
διδομένῳ	διδομένῃ	διδομένῳ
διδόμενον	διδομένην	διδόμενον
διδόμενοι	διδόμεναι	διδόμενα
διδομένων	διδομένων	διδομένων
διδομένοις	διδομέναις	διδομένοις
διδομένους	διδομένας	διδόμενα

AORIST ACTIVE AND MIDDLE OF δίδωμι

306. Aorist Active and Middle Indicative

		Aorist Active	Aorist Middle
Sing.	1.	ἔδωκα	1. ἐδόμην
	2.	ἔδωκας	2. ἔδου
	3.	ἔδωκε(ν)	3. ἔδοτο
Plur.	1.	ἐδώκαμεν	1. ἐδόμεθα
	2.	ἐδώκατε	2. ἔδοσθε
	3.	ἔδωκαν	3. ἔδοντο

307. Aorist Active and Middle Subjunctive

		Aorist Active	Aorist Middle
Sing.	1.	δῶ	1. δῶμαι
	2.	δῷς	2. δῷ
	3.	δῷ	3. δῶται
Plur.	1.	δῶμεν	1. δώμεθα
	2.	δῶτε	2. δῶσθε
	3.	δῶσι(ν)	3. δῶνται

308. Aorist Active and Middle Imperative

	Aorist Active	Aorist Middle
Sing.	2. δός	2. δοῦ
	3. δότω	3. δόσθω
Plur.	2. δότε	2. δόσθε
	3. δότωσαν	3. δόσθωσαν

309. Aorist Active and Middle Infinitive

Aorist Active	Aorist Middle
δοῦναι	δόσθαι

310. Aorist Active Participle

δούς	δοῦσα	δόν
δόντος	δούσης	δόντος
δόντι	δούσῃ	δόντι
δόντα	δοῦσαν	δόν
δόντες	δοῦσαι	δόντα
δόντων	δουσῶν	δόντων
δοῦσι(ν)	δούσαις	δοῦσι(ν)
δόντας	δούσας	δόντα

311. Aorist Middle Participle

δόμενος	δομένη	δόμενον
δομένου	δομένης	δομένου
δομένῳ	δομένῃ	δομένῳ
δόμενον	δομένην	δόμενον
δόμενοι	δόμεναι	δόμενα
δομένων	δομένων	δομένων
δομένοις	δομέναις	δομένοις
δομένους	δομένας	δόμενα

PRESENT SYSTEM OF τίθημι

312. Indicative

		Present Active	Impf. Active	Present M/P	Impf. M/P
Sing.	1.	τίθημι	ἐτίθην	τίθεμαι	ἐτιθέμην
	2.	τίθης	ἐτίθεις	τίθεσαι	ἐτίθεσο
	3.	τίθησι(ν)	ἐτίθει	τίθεται	ἐτίθετο
Plur.	1.	τίθεμεν	ἐτίθεμεν	τιθέμεθα	ἐτιθέμεθα
	2.	τίθετε	ἐτίθετε	τίθεσθε	ἐτίθεσθε
	3.	τιθέασι(ν)	ἐτίθεσαν	τίθενται	ἐτίθεντο

313. Present Subjunctive

		Present Active	Present M/P
Sing.	1.	τιθῶ	τιθῶμαι
	2.	τιθῇς	τιθῇ
	3.	τιθῇ	τιθῆται
Plur.	1.	τιθῶμεν	τιθώμεθα
	2.	τιθῆτε	τιθῆσθε
	3.	τιθῶσι(ν)	τιθῶνται

314. Present Imperative

		Present Active	Present M/P
Sing.	2.	τίθει	τίθεσο
	3.	τιθέτω	τιθέσθω
Plur.	2.	τίθετε	τίθεσθε
	3.	τιθέτωσαν	τιθέσθωσαν

315. Present Infinitive

Present Active	Present M/P
τιθέναι	τίθεσθαι

316. Present Active Participle

τιθείς	τιθεῖσα	τιθέν
τιθέντος	τιθείσης	τιθέντος
τιθέντι	τιθείσῃ	τιθέντι
τιθέντα	τιθεῖσαν	τιθέν
τιθέντες	τιθεῖσαι	τιθέντα
τιθέντων	τιθεισῶν	τιθέντων
τιθεῖσι(ν)	τιθείσαις	τιθεῖσι(ν)
τιθέντας	τιθείσας	τιθέντα

317. Present Middle/Passive Participle

τιθέμενος	τιθεμένη	τιθέμενον
τιθεμένου	τιθεμένης	τιθεμένου
τιθεμένῳ	τιθεμένῃ	τιθεμένῳ
τιθέμενον	τιθεμένην	τιθέμενον
τιθέμενοι	τιθέμεναι	τιθέμενα
τιθεμένων	τιθεμένων	τιθεμένων
τιθεμένοις	τιθεμέναις	τιθεμένοις
τιθεμένους	τιθεμένας	τιθέμενα

AORIST ACTIVE AND MIDDLE OF τίθημι

318. Aorist Active and Middle Indicative

		Aorist Active	Aorist Middle
Sing.	1.	ἔθηκα	1. ἐθέμην
	2.	ἔθηκας	2. ἔθου
	3.	ἔθηκε(ν)	3. ἔθετο
Plur.	1.	ἐθήκαμεν	1. ἐθέμεθα
	2.	ἐθήκατε	2. ἔθεσθε
	3.	ἔθηκαν	3. ἔθεντο

319. Aorist Active and Middle Subjunctive

		Aorist Active		Aorist Middle
Sing.	1.	θῶ	1.	θῶμαι
	2.	θῇς	2.	θῇ
	3.	θῇ	3.	θῆται
Plur.	1.	θῶμεν	1.	θώμεθα
	2.	θῆτε	2.	θῆσθε
	3.	θῶσι(ν)	3.	θῶνται

320. Aorist Active and Middle Imperative

		Aorist Active		Aorist Middle
Sing.	2.	θές	2.	θοῦ
	3.	θέτω	3.	θέσθω
Plur.	2.	θέτε	2.	θέσθε
	3.	θέτωσαν	3.	θέσθωσαν

321. Aorist Active and Middle Infinitive

Aorist Active	Aorist Middle
θεῖναι	θέσθαι

322. Aorist Active Participle

θείς	θεῖσα	θέν
θέντος	θείσης	θέντος
θέντι	θείσῃ	θέντι
θέντα	θεῖσαν	θέν
θέντες	θεῖσαι	θέντα
θέντων	θεισῶν	θέντων
θεῖσι(ν)	θείσαις	θεῖσι(ν)
θέντας	θείσας	θέντα

323. Aorist Middle Participle

θέμενος	θεμένη	θέμενον
θεμένου	θεμένης	θεμένου
θεμένῳ	θεμένῃ	θεμένῳ
θέμενον	θεμένην	θέμενον

θέμενοι	θέμεναι	θέμενα
θεμένων	θεμένων	θεμένων
θεμένοις	θεμέναις	θεμένοις
θεμένους	θεμένας	θέμενα

PRESENT SYSTEM OF ἵστημι

324. Indicative

		Present Active	Impf. Active	Present M/P	Impf. M/P
Sing.	1.	ἵστημι	ἵστην	ἵσταμαι	ἱστάμην
	2.	ἵστης	ἵστης	ἵστασαι	ἵστασο
	3.	ἵστησι(ν)	ἵστη	ἵσταται	ἵστατο
Plur.	1.	ἵσταμεν	ἵσταμεν	ἱστάμεθα	ἱστάμεθα
	2.	ἵστατε	ἵστατε	ἵστασθε	ἵστασθε
	3.	ἵστᾶσι(ν)	ἵστασαν	ἵστανται	ἵσταντο

325. Present Subjunctive

		Present Active	Present M/P
Sing.	1.	ἱστῶ	1. ἱστῶμαι
	2.	ἱστῇς	2. ἱστῇ
	3.	ἱστῇ	3. ἱστῆται
Plur.	1.	ἱστῶμεν	1. ἱστώμεθα
	2.	ἱστῆτε	2. ἱστῆσθε
	3.	ἱστῶσι(ν)	3. ἱστῶνται

326. Present Imperative

	Present Active	Present M/P
Sing.	2. ἵστη	2. ἵστασο
	3. ἱστάτω	3. ἱστάσθω
Plur.	2. ἵστατε	2. ἵστασθε
	3. ἱστάτωσαν	3. ἱστάσθωσαν

327. Present Infinitive

Present Active	Present M/P
ἱστάναι	ἵστασθαι

328. Present Active Participle

ἱστάς	ἱστᾶσα	ἱστάν
ἱστάντος	ἱστάσης	ἱστάντος
ἱστάντι	ἱστάσῃ	ἱστάντι
ἱστάντα	ἱστᾶσαν	ἱστάν
ἱστάντες	ἱστᾶσαι	ἱστάντα
ἱστάντων	ἱστασῶν	ἱστάντων
ἱστᾶσι(ν)	ἱστάσαις	ἱστᾶσι(ν)
ἱστάντας	ἱστάσας	ἱστάντα

329. Present Middle/Passive Participle

ἱστάμενος	ἱσταμένη	ἱστάμενον
ἱσταμένου	ἱσταμένης	ἱσταμένου
ἱσταμένῳ	ἱσταμένῃ	ἱσταμένῳ
ἱστάμενον	ἱσταμένην	ἱστάμενον
ἱστάμενοι	ἱστάμεναι	ἱστάμενα
ἱσταμένων	ἱσταμένων	ἱσταμένων
ἱσταμένοις	ἱσταμέναις	ἱσταμένοις
ἱσταμένους	ἱσταμένας	ἱστάμενα

FIRST AND SECOND AORIST ACTIVE OF ἵστημι

330. Aorist Active Indicative

		1st Aorist Active	2nd Aorist Active
Sing.	1.	ἔστησα	1. ἔστην
	2.	ἔστησας	2. ἔστης
	3.	ἔστησε(ν)	3. ἔστη
Plur.	1.	ἐστήσαμεν	1. ἔστημεν
	2.	ἐστήσατε	2. ἔστητε
	3.	ἔστησαν	3. ἔστησαν

331. Aorist Active Subjunctive

		1st Aorist Active	2nd Aorist Active
Sing.	1.	στήσω	1. στῶ
	2.	στήσῃς	2. στῇς
	3.	στήσῃ	3. στῇ
Plur.	1.	στήσωμεν	1. στῶμεν
	2.	στήσητε	2. στῆτε
	3.	στήσωσι(ν)	3. στῶσι(ν)

332. Aorist Active Imperative

		1st Aorist Active	2nd Aorist Active
Sing.	2.	στῆσον	2. στῆθι
	3.	στησάτω	3. στήτω
Plur.	2.	στήσατε	2. στῆτε
	3.	στησάτωσαν	3. στήτωσαν

333. Aorist Active Infinitive

1st Aorist Active   2nd Aorist Active
   στῆσαι   στῆναι

334. First Aorist Active Participle

στήσας	στήσασα	στῆσαν
στήσαντος	στησάσης	στήσαντος
στήσαντι	στησάσῃ	στήσαντι
στήσαντα	στήσασαν	στῆσαν
στήσαντες	στήσασαι	στήσαντα
στησάντων	στησασῶν	στησάντων
στήσασι(ν)	στησάσαις	στήσασι(ν)
στήσαντας	στησάσας	στήσαντα

335. Second Aorist Active Participle

στάς	στᾶσα	στάν
στάντος	στάσης	στάντος
στάντι	στάσῃ	στάντι
στάντα	στᾶσαν	στάν
στάντες	στᾶσαι	στάντα
στάντων	στασῶν	στάντων
στᾶσι(ν)	στάσαις	στᾶσι(ν)
στάντας	στάσας	στάντα

SECOND AORIST OF βαίνω AND γινώσκω

336. Second Aorist of βαίνω

(Note: In biblical Greek βαίνω occurs almost exclusively in compound forms.)

Second Aorist Indicative

Singular	Plural
1. ἔβην	1. ἔβημεν
2. ἔβης	2. ἔβητε
3. ἔβη	3. ἔβησαν

Second Aorist Subjunctive

Singular	Plural
1. βῶ	1. βῶμεν
2. βῇς	2. βῆτε
3. βῇ	3. βῶσι(ν)

Second Aorist Imperative

Singular	Plural
2. βῆθι (or βα)	2. βάτε
3. βάτω	3. βάτωσαν

Second Aorist Infinitive

βῆναι

Second Aorist Participle

βάς	βᾶσα	βάν
βάντος	βάσης	βάντος
βάντι	βάσῃ	βάντι
βάντα	βᾶσαν	βάν
βάντες	βᾶσαι	βάντα
βάντων	βασῶν	βάντων
βᾶσι(ν)	βάσαις	βᾶσι(ν)
βάντας	βάσας	βάντα

337. Second Aorist of γινώσκω

Second Aorist Indicative

Singular	Plural
1. ἔγνων	1. ἔγνωμεν
2. ἔγνως	2. ἔγνωτε
3. ἔγνω	3. ἔγνωσαν

Second Aorist Subjunctive

Singular	Plural
1. γνῶ	1. γνῶμεν
2. γνῷς	2. γνῶτε
3. γνῷ (or γνοῖ)	3. γνῶσι(ν)

Second Aorist Imperative

Singular	Plural
2. γνῶθι	2. γνῶτε
3. γνώτω	3. γνώτωσαν

Second Aorist Infinitive
γνῶναι

Second Aorist Participle

γνούς	γνοῦσα	γνόν
γνόντος	γνούσης	γνόντος
γνόντι	γνούσῃ	γνόντι
γνόντα	γνοῦσαν	γνόν
γνόντες	γνοῦσαι	γνόντα
γνόντων	γνουσῶν	γνόντων
γνοῦσι(ν)	γνούσαις	γνοῦσι(ν)
γνόντας	γνούσας	γνόντα

CONJUGATION OF οἶδα

338. Second Perfect and Pluperfect of οἶδα

Perfect Indicative

Singular	Plural
1. οἶδα	1. οἴδαμεν
2. οἶδας	2. οἴδατε
3. οἶδε(ν)	3. οἴδασι(ν)

Pluperfect Indicative

Singular	Plural
1. ᾔδειν	1. ᾔδειμεν
2. ᾔδεις	2. ᾔδειτε
3. ᾔδει	3. ᾔδεισαν

Perfect Subjunctive

Singular	Plural
1. εἰδῶ	1. εἰδῶμεν
2. εἰδῇς	2. εἰδῆτε
3. εἰδῇ	3. εἰδῶσι(ν)

Perfect Imperative

Singular	Plural
2. ἴσθι	2. ἴστε
3. ἴστω	3. ἴστωσαν

Perfect Infinitive

εἰδέναι

Perfect Participle

εἰδώς	εἰδυῖα	εἰδός
εἰδότος	εἰδυίας	εἰδότος
εἰδότι	εἰδυίᾳ	εἰδότι
εἰδότα	εἰδυῖαν	εἰδός
εἰδότες	εἰδυῖαι	εἰδότα
εἰδότων	εἰδυιῶν	εἰδότων
εἰδόσι(ν)	εἰδυίαις	εἰδόσι(ν)
εἰδότας	εἰδυίας	εἰδότα

SECOND AORIST ACTIVE AND MIDDLE (λαμβάνω)

339. Second Aorist Indicative

	Active	Middle
Sing.	1. ἔλαβον	1. ἐλαβόμην
	2. ἔλαβες	2. ἐλάβου
	3. ἔλαβε(ν)	3. ἐλάβετο
Plur.	1. ἐλάβομεν	1. ἐλαβόμεθα
	2. ἐλάβετε	2. ἐλάβεσθε
	3. ἔλαβον	3. ἐλάβοντο

340. Second Aorist Subjunctive

	Active	Middle
Sing.	1. λάβω	1. λάβωμαι
	2. λάβῃς	2. λάβῃ
	3. λάβῃ	3. λάβηται
Plur.	1. λάβωμεν	1. λαβώμεθα
	2. λάβητε	2. λάβησθε
	3. λάβωσι(ν)	3. λάβωνται

341. Second Aorist Imperative

	Active	Middle
Sing.	2. λάβε	2. λαβοῦ
	3. λαβέτω	3. λαβέσθω
Plur.	2. λάβετε	2. λάβεσθε
	3. λαβέτωσαν	3. λαβέσθωσαν

342. Second Aorist Infinitive

Active	Middle
λαβεῖν	λαβέσθαι

343. Second Aorist Participles

Active	Middle
λαβών, λαβοῦσα, λαβόν	λαβόμενος, η, ον

(For a complete paradigm of 2nd aorist participles, see §§252-53 above.)

FUTURE AND AORIST OF LIQUID VERBS (μένω)

344. Future Indicative

	Active	Middle
Sing.	1. μενῶ	1. μενοῦμαι
	2. μενεῖς	2. μενῇ
	3. μενεῖ	3. μενεῖται
Plur.	1. μενοῦμεν	1. μενοῦμεθα
	2. μενεῖτε	2. μενεῖσθε
	3. μενοῦσι(ν)	3. μενοῦνται

345. Aorist Indicative

	Active	Middle
Sing.	1. ἔμεινα	1. ἐμεινάμην
	2. ἔμεινας	2. ἐμείνω
	3. ἔμεινε(ν)	3. ἐμείνατο
Plur.	1. ἐμείναμεν	1. ἐμεινάμεθα
	2. ἐμείνατε	2. ἐμείνασθε
	3. ἔμειναν	3. ἐμείναντο

346. Aorist Subjunctive

	Active	Middle
Sing.	1. μείνω	1. μείνωμαι
	2. μείνῃς	2. μείνῃ
	3. μείνῃ	3. μείνηται
Plur.	1. μείνωμεν	1. μεινώμεθα
	2. μείνητε	2. μείνησθε
	3. μείνωσι(ν)	3. μείνωνται

347. Aorist Imperative

	Active	Middle
Sing.	2. μεῖνον	2. μεῖναι
	3. μεινηάτω	3. μεινάσθω
Plur.	2. μείνατε	2. μείνασθε
	3. μεινάτωσαν	3. μεινάσθωσαν

348. Aorist Infinitive

Active	Middle
μεῖναι	μείνασθαι

349. Aorist Participle

Active	Middle
μείνας, μείνασα, μεῖναν	μεινάμενος, -η, -ον

CONTRACT VERBS

350. πληρόω (Shown in uncontracted and contracted form.)

	Present Active	Imperfect Active	Present Mid./Pass.	Imperfect Mid./Pass.
Indic.				
Sing. 1.	(πληρόω) πληρῶ	(ἐπλήροον) ἐπλήρουν	(πληρόομαι) πληροῦμαι	(ἐπληροόμην) ἐπληρούμην
2.	(πληρόεις) πληροῖς	(ἐπλήροες) ἐπλήρους	(πληρόῃ) πληροῖ	(ἐπληρόου) ἐπληροῦ
3.	(πληρόει) πληροῖ	(ἐπλήροε) ἐπλήρου	(πληρόεται) πληροῦται	(ἐπληρόετο) ἐπληροῦτο
Plur. 1.	(πληρόομεν) πληροῦμεν	(ἐπληρόομεν) ἐπληροῦμεν	(πληροόμεθα) πληρούμεθα	(ἐπληροόμεθα) ἐπληρούμεθα
2.	(πληρόετε) πληροῦτε	(ἐπληρόετε) ἐπληροῦτε	(πληρόεσθε) πληροῦσθε	(ἐπληρόεσθε) ἐπληροῦσθε
3.	(πληρόουσι) πληροῦσι(ν)	(ἐπλήροον) ἐπλήρουν	(πληρόονται) πληροῦνται	(ἐπληρόοντο) ἐπληροῦντο
Subj.				
Sing. 1.	(πληρόω) πληρῶ		(πληρόωμαι) πληρῶμαι	
2.	(πληρόῃς) πληροῖς		(πληρόῃ) πληροῖ	
3.	(πληρόῃ) πληροῖ		(πληρόηται) πληρῶται	
Plur. 1.	(πληρόωμεν) πληρῶμεν		(πληροώμεθα) πληρώμεθα	
2.	(πληρόητε) πληρῶτε		(πληρόησθε) πληρῶσθε	
3.	(πληρόωσι) πληρῶσι(ν)		(πληρόωνται) πληρῶνται	
Impv.				
Sing. 2.	(πλήροε) πλήρου		(πληρόου) πληροῦ	
3.	(πληροέτω) πληρούτω		(πληροέσθω) πληρούσθω	
Plur. 2.	(πληρόετε) πληροῦτε		(πληρόεσθε) πληροῦσθε	
3.	(πληροέτωσαν) πληρούτωσαν		(πληροέσθωσαν) πληρούσθωσαν	
Inf.	(πληρόειν) πληροῦν		(πληρόεσθαι) πληροῦσθαι	
Part.				
Masc.	(πληρόων) πληρῶν		(πληροόμενος) πληρούμενος	
Fem.	(πληρόουσα) πληροῦσα		(πληροομένη) πληρουμένη	
Neut.	(πληρόον) πληροῦν		(πληροόμενον) πληρούμενον	

CONTRACT VERBS

351. ποιέω (Shown in uncontracted and contracted form.)

		Present Active	Imperf. Active	Present Mid./Pass.	Imperf. Mid./Pass.
Indic.					
Sing.	1.	(ποιέω) ποιῶ	(ἐποίεον) ἐποίουν	(ποιέομαι) ποιοῦμαι	(ἐποιεόμην) ἐποιούμην
	2.	(ποιέεις) ποιεῖς	(ἐποίεες) ἐποίεις	(ποιέῃ) ποιῇ	(ἐποιέου) ἐποιοῦ
	3.	(ποιέει) ποιεῖ	(ἐποίεε) ἐποίει	(ποιέεται) ποιεῖται	(ἐποιέετο) ἐποιεῖτο
Plur.	1.	(ποιέομεν) ποιοῦμεν	(ἐποιέομεν) ἐποιοῦμεν	(ποιεόμεθα) ποιούμεθα	(ἐποιεόμεθα) ἐποιούμεθα
	2.	(ποιέετε) ποιεῖτε	(ἐποιέετε) ἐποιεῖτε	(ποιέεσθε) ποιεῖσθε	(ἐποιέεσθε) ἐποιεῖσθε
	3.	(ποιέουσι) ποιοῦσι(ν)	(ἐποίεον) ἐποίουν	(ποιέονται) ποιοῦνται	(ἐποιέοντο) ἐποιοῦντο
Subj.					
Sing.	1.	(ποιέω) ποιῶ		(ποιέωμαι) ποιῶμαι	
	2.	(ποιέῃς) ποιῇς		(ποιέῃ) ποιῇ	
	3.	(ποιέῃ) ποιῇ		(ποιέηται) ποιῆται	
Plur.	1.	(ποιέωμεν) ποιῶμεν		(ποιεώμεθα) ποιώμεθα	
	2.	(ποιέητε) ποιῆτε		(ποιέησθε) ποιῆσθε	
	3.	(ποιέωσι) ποιῶσι(ν)		(ποιέωνται) ποιῶνται	
Impv.					
Sing.	2.	(ποίεε) ποίει		(ποιέου) ποιοῦ	
	3.	(ποιεέτω) ποιείτω		(ποιεέσθω) ποιείσθω	
Plur.	2.	(ποιέετε) ποιεῖτε		(ποιέεσθε) ποιεῖσθε	
	3.	(ποιεέτωσαν) ποιείτωσαν		(ποιεέσθωσαν) ποιείσθωσαν	
Inf.		(ποιέειν) ποιεῖν		(ποιέεσθαι) ποιεῖσθαι	
Part.					
Masc.		(ποιέων) ποιῶν		(ποιεόμενος) ποιούμενος	
Fem.		(ποιέουσα) ποιοῦσα		(ποιεομένη) ποιουμένη	
Neut.		(ποιέον) ποιοῦν		(ποιεόμενον) ποιούμενον	

CONTRACT VERBS

352. ἀγαπάω (Shown in uncontracted and contracted form.)

	Present Active	Imperf. Active	Present Mid./Pass.	Imperf. Mid./Pass.
Indic.				
Sing. 1.	(ἀγαπάω) ἀγαπῶ	(ἠγάπαον) ἠγάπων	(ἀγαπάομαι) ἀγαπῶμαι	(ἠγαπαόμην) ἠγαπώμην
2.	(ἀγαπάεις) ἀγαπᾷς	(ἠγάπαες) ἠγάπας	(ἀγαπάῃ) ἀγαπᾷ	(ἠγαπάου) ἠγαπῶ
3.	(ἀγαπάει) ἀγαπᾷ	(ἠγάπαε) ἠγάπα	(ἀγαπάεται) ἀγαπᾶται	(ἠγαπάετο) ἠγαπᾶτο
Plur. 1.	(ἀγαπάομεν) ἀγαπῶμεν	(ἠγαπάομεν) ἠγαπῶμεν	(ἀγαπαόμεθα) ἀγαπώμεθα	(ἠγαπαόμεθα) ἠγαπώμεθα
2.	(ἀγαπάετε) ἀγαπᾶτε	(ἠγαπάετε) ἠγαπᾶτε	(ἀγαπάεσθε) ἀγαπᾶσθε	(ἠγαπάεσθε) ἠγαπᾶσθε
3.	(ἀγαπάουσι) ἀγαπῶσι(ν)	(ἠγάπαον) ἠγάπων	(ἀγαπάονται) ἀγαπῶνται	(ἠγαπάοντο) ἠγαπῶντο
Subj.				
Sing. 1.	(ἀγαπάω) ἀγαπῶ		(ἀγαπάωμαι) ἀγαπῶμαι	
2.	(ἀγαπάῃς) ἀγαπᾷς		(ἀγαπάῃ) ἀγαπᾷ	
3.	(ἀγαπάῃ) ἀγαπᾷ		(ἀγαπάηται) ἀγαπᾶται	
Plur. 1.	(ἀγαπάωμεν) ἀγαπῶμεν		(ἀγαπαώμεθα) ἀγαπώμεθα	
2.	(ἀγαπάητε) ἀγαπᾶτε		(ἀγαπάησθε) ἀγαπᾶσθε	
3.	(ἀγαπάωσι) ἀγαπῶσι(ν)		(ἀγαπάωνται) ἀγαπῶνται	
Impv.				
Sing. 2.	(ἀγάπαε) ἀγάπα		(ἀγαπάου) ἀγαπῶ	
3.	(ἀγαπαέτω) ἀγαπάτω		(ἀγαπαέσθω) ἀγαπάσθω	
Plur. 2.	(ἀγαπάετε) ἀγαπᾶτε		(ἀγαπάεσθε) ἀγαπᾶσθε	
3.	(ἀγαπαέτωσαν) ἀγαπάτωσαν		(ἀγαπαέσθωσαν) ἀγαπάσθωσαν	
Inf.	(ἀγαπάειν) ἀγαπᾶν		(ἀγαπάεσθαι) ἀγαπᾶσθαι	
Part.				
Masc.	(ἀγαπάων) ἀγαπῶν		(ἀγαπαόμενος) ἀγαπώμενος	
Fem.	(ἀγαπάουσα) ἀγαπῶσα		(ἀγαπαομένη) ἀγαπωμένη	
Neut.	(ἀγαπάον) ἀγαπῶν		(ἀγαπαόμενον) ἀγαπώμενον	

Greek to English Vocabulary

Principal parts of certain common and/or irregular verbs are included. In some cases these are functional principal parts that do not, in fact, derive from the same verb as the present tense. The number in parentheses after the definition refers to the lesson in which the word was introduced.

ἀγαθός, -ή, -όν, good, noble (5)

ἀγαπάω, ἀγαπήσω, ἠγάπησα, ἠγάπηκα, ἠγάπημαι, ἠγαπήθην, I love (21)

ἀγάπη, ἡ, love (7)

ἀγαπητός, -ή, -όν, beloved (24)

ἄγγελος, ὁ, angel, messenger (6)

ἁγιάζω, I sanctify, consecrate (20)

ἅγιος, -α, -ον, holy, consecrated (5)

ἀγοράζω, I buy, redeem (23)

ἀγρός, ὁ, field, country (26)

ἄγω, ἄξω, ἤγαγον, ἦχα, ἦγμαι, ἤχθην, I lead (10)

ἀδελφή, ἡ, sister (3)

ἀδελφός, ὁ, brother (4)

αἷμα, -ατος, τό, blood (17)

αἴρω, ἀρῶ, ἦρα, ἦρκα, ἦρμαι, ἤρθην, I take up, take away, lift up (10)

αἰτέω, αἰτήσω, ᾔτησα, ᾔτηκα, ᾔτημαι, ᾐτήθην, I ask, request (often uses middle) (21)

αἰών, αἰῶνος, ὁ, age, world (17)

αἰώνιος, -ον, eternal (26)

ἀκήκοα, I have heard (perfect of ἀκούω) (15)

ἀκολουθέω, I follow (+ dat.) (21)

ἀκούω, ἀκούσω, ἤκουσα, ἀκήκοα, ἤκουσμαι, ἠκούσθην, I hear (2)

ἀλήθεια, ἡ, truth (3)

ἀληθής, -ές, true (25)

ἀλλά, but (4)

ἀλλήλων, each other, one another (22)

ἄλλος, -η, -ο, other (8)

ἁμαρτάνω, I sin (18)

ἁμαρτία, ἡ, sin (7)

ἁμαρτωλός, ὁ, sinner (9)

ἀμήν, amen, truly (11)

ἄν, particle that adds contingency; may add sense of "-ever" (23)

ἀναβαίνω, I go up (10)

ἀνήρ, ἀνδρός, ὁ, man, husband (17)

ἄνθρωπος, ὁ, human being, person, man (4)

ἀνίστημι, I arise, cause to rise (30)

ἀνοίγω, ἀνοίξω, ἀνέῳξα or ἤνοιξα or

ἠνέῳξα, ἀνέῳγα, ἀνέῳγμαι or
ἠνέῳγμαι or ἤνοιγμαι, ἀνεῴχθην or
ἠνοίχθην or ἠνεῴχθην, I open (12)

ἀπαγγέλλω, I report, announce, declare
(22)

ἀπέρχομαι, I depart, go away, go (10)

ἀπεστάλην, I was sent (2nd aorist passive of ἀποστέλλω) (16)

ἀπό, (+ gen.) from (6)

ἀποδίδωμι, I give back, render, reward
(28)

ἀποθνῄσκω, ἀποθανοῦμαι, ἀπέθανον, I
die (10)

ἀποκρίνομαι, ἀποκρινοῦμαι,
ἀπεκρινάμην, ἀποκέκριμαι, —,
ἀπεκρίθην, I answer (+ dat.) (9)

ἀποκτείνω, I kill (10)

ἀπόλλυμι or ἀπολλύω, ἀπολέσω or
ἀπολῶ, ἀπώλεσα or ἀπωλόμην,
ἀπόλωλα, —, —, I destroy, lose;
(mid. voice) perish, be ruined (29)

ἀπολύω, I release, dismiss (13)

ἀποστέλλω, ἀποστελῶ, ἀπέστειλα,
ἀπέσταλκα, ἀπέσταλμαι, ἀπεστάλην,
I send (8)

ἀπόστολος, ὁ, apostle (10)

ἄρτος, ὁ, bread, loaf (7)

ἀρχή, ἡ, beginning, ruler (24)

ἀρχιερεύς, -έως, ὁ, chief priest (25)

ἄρχω, ἄρξω, ἦρξα, (active) I rule
(+ gen.); (middle) I begin (9)

ἄρχων, ἄρχοντος, ὁ, ruler (17)

ἀσθενής, -ές, weak, sick (25)

ἀσπάζομαι, I greet, salute (19)

αὐτός, -ή, -ό, he, she, it (7); same; -self
(8)

ἀφίημι, ἀφήσω, ἀφῆκα, ἀφεῖκα,
ἀφεῖμαι, ἀφέθην, I let go, leave, forgive, permit (29)

ἄχρι, ἄχρις, as far as, up to (+ gen.)
(32)

βαίνω, βήσομαι, ἔβην, βέβηκα, —, —, I
go (only in compound forms; simple form not in NT, rare in LXX)
(cf. Lesson 10 and §336)

βάλλω, βαλῶ, ἔβαλον, βέβληκα,
βέβλημαι, ἐβλήθην, I throw, put,
place, cast (6)

βαπτίζω, I baptize (8)

βασιλεία, ἡ, kingdom, reign, rule (3)

βασιλεύς, -έως, ὁ, king (25)

βιβλίον, τό, book (11)

βλέπω, βλέψω, ἔβλεψα, I see (2)

βούλομαι, (dep.) I wish, want (18)

γάρ, for (postpositive) (5)

γέγονα, I have become (perfect of
γίνομαι) (15)

γενήσομαι, I will become (dep. fut. of
γίνομαι) (12)

γεννάω, I beget, bear (21)

γένος, -ους, τό, race, stock; people, descendants; kind (25)

γῆ, ἡ, earth, soil, land (3)

γίνομαι, γενήσομαι, ἐγενόμην, γέγονα,
γεγένημαι, ἐγενήθην, become, be,
happen, arise, come, appear
(+ nom.) (9)

γινώσκω, γνώσομαι, ἔγνων, ἔγνωκα,
ἔγνωσμαι, ἐγνώσθην, I know (2)

γλῶσσα, ἡ, tongue, language (24)

γνωρίζω, I make known, reveal (20)

γνώσομαι, I will know (dep. fut. of
γινώσκω) (12)

γραμματεύς, -έως, ὁ, scribe (25)

γραφή, ἡ, writing, Scripture (23)

γράφω, γράψω, ἔγραψα, γέγραφα,
γέγραμμαι, ἐγράφην, I write (2)

γυνή, γυναικός, ἡ, woman, wife (17)

δαιμόνιον, τό, demon (11)

δέ, but, and (4)

δεῖ, it is necessary (+ inf.) (13)

δείκνυμι and δεικνύω, δείξω, ἔδειξα, δέδειχα, δέδειγμαι, ἐδείχθην, I show, point out; explain, prove (29)

δέκα, ten (30)

δεξιός, -ά, -όν, right (32)

δέχομαι, δέξομαι, ἐδεξάμην, —, δέδεγμαι, ἐδέχθην, I receive, accept (11)

διά, (+ gen.) through; (+ acc.) for the sake of, because of (6)

διδάσκαλος, ὁ, teacher (12)

διδάσκω, I teach (2)

δίδωμι, δώσω, ἔδωκα, δέδωκα, δέδομαι, ἐδόθην, I give, grant (28)

διέρχομαι, I go through (9)

δίκαιος, -α, -ον, righteous, just (5)

δικαιοσύνη, ἡ, righteousness (13)

διό, therefore, for this reason (31)

διώκω, διώξω, ἐδίωξα, δεδίωκα, δεδίωγμαι, ἐδιώχθην, I pursue, persecute (18)

δοκέω, think, seem, seem good (22)

δόξα, ἡ, glory, honor (3)

δοξάζω, I glorify (12)

δοῦλος, ὁ, slave, servant (4)

δύναμαι, I can, am able (9)

δύναμις, -εως, ἡ, power, strength; miracle (usu. plural) (25)

δύο, two (30)

δώδεκα, twelve (30)

δῶρον, τό, gift (7)

ἐάν, if (+ subj.) (23)

ἑαυτοῦ, of himself, herself, etc. (21)

ἐβλήθην, I was thrown (aorist passive of βάλλω) (16)

ἐγγίζω, I draw near (15)

ἐγείρω, ἐγερῶ, ἤγειρα, —, ἐγήγερμαι, ἠγέρθην, I raise up (8)

ἐγενήθην, I became (aorist pass. of γίνομαι) (16)

ἐγήγερμαι, I have been raised, am risen (perf. pass. of ἐγείρω) (15)

ἔγνωκα, I have come to know (perfect of γινώσκω) (15)

ἐγνώσθην, I was known (aorist passive of γινώσκω) (16)

ἐγράφην, I was written (2nd aorist passive of γράφω) (16)

ἐγώ, I (7)

ἔθνος, -ους, τό, nation; plur. τὰ ἔθνη, the nations, Gentiles (25)

εἰ, if, whether (usu. followed by an indicative mood verb) (12)

εἶδον, I saw (serves as the 2nd aorist of βλέπω) (14)

εἰμί, I am (7)

εἶναι, to be (infinitive of εἰμί) (24)

εἶπον, I said (serves as the 2nd aorist of λέγω) (14)

εἴρηκα, I have said (serves as the perfect of λέγω) (15)

εἰρήνη, ἡ, peace (8)

εἰς, (+ acc.) into, to, against (6)

εἷς, μία, ἕν, one, a, an, single (29)

εἰσέρχομαι, I go in, I enter (9)

ἐκ, ἐξ, (+ gen.) out of, by (6)

ἕκαστος, -η, -ον, each, every (22)

ἐκβάλλω, I cast out (16)

ἐκεῖ, there, to that place (13)

ἐκεῖνος, -η, -ο, that (8)

ἐκκλησία, ἡ, assembly, church (3)

ἐλεέω, I have mercy on, pity (26)

ἐλεύσομαι, I will come (dep. fut. of ἔρχομαι) (12)

ἐλήλυθα, I have come (serves as the perfect of ἔρχομαι) (15)

ἐλήμφθην, I was taken (aorist passive of λαμβάνω) (16)

ἐλπίς, -ίδος, ἡ, hope (27)

ἐμαυτοῦ, of myself (21)

ἐμός, ἐμή, ἐμόν, my, mine (22)

ἔμπροσθεν, before, in front of (+ gen.)
(31)

ἐν, (+ dat.) in (6)

ἐντολή, ἡ, commandment (22)

ἐνώπιον, before, in the sight of, in the
presence of (+ gen.) (31)

ἐξέρχομαι, I go out (9)

ἔξεστι(ν), it is lawful (used only in the
third person) (24)

ἐξουσία, ἡ, authority (8)

ἔξω, outside (sometimes + gen.) (27)

ἐπαγγελία, ἡ, promise (31)

ἐπερωτάω, I ask, question (26)

ἐπί, (+ gen.) on, upon, over; (+ dat.)
on, at, in addition to; (+ acc.) on,
over, toward, for (11)

ἐπιγινώσκω, I recognize, know, understand, perceive (30)

ἐπιστρέφω, ἐπιστρέψω, ἐπέστρεψα,
ἐπέστροφα, ἐπέστραμμαι,
ἐπεστράφην, I turn, return (13)

ἐπιτίθημι, I place upon, lay upon (29)

ἑπτά, seven (30)

ἐργάζομαι, (dep.) I work, do (18)

ἔργον, τό, deed, work (4)

ἔρημος, ἡ, desert (6)

ἔρχομαι, ἐλεύσομαι, ἦλθον, ἐλήλυθα, —,
—, I come, I go (9)

ἐρωτάω, I ask, request, entreat (26)

ἐσθίω, φάγομαι, ἔφαγον, —, —, —, I
eat (7)

ἔσχατος, -η, -ον, last (5)

ἕτερος, -α, -ον, other, different (15)

ἔτι, yet, still (11)

ἑτοιμάζω, I prepare (13)

ἔτος, -ους, τό, year (28)

εὐαγγελίζομαι, (usu. dep.) I bring good
news, preach (18)

εὐαγγέλιον, τό, good news, Gospel (20)

εὐθύς, immediately, at once, then (28)

εὑρέθην, I was found (aorist passive of
εὑρίσκω) (16)

εὑρίσκω, εὑρήσω, εὗρον, εὕρηκα,
εὕρημαι, εὑρέθην, I find (8)

ἔφαγον, I ate (2nd aor. of ἐσθίω) (14)

ἔχω, ἕξω, ἔσχον, ἔσχηκα, —, —, I have
(3)

ἑώρακα, I have seen (serves as the perfect of βλέπω) (15)

ἕως, until; (+ gen.) as far as (17)

ζάω, I live (conjugated with η rather
than α in the present tense) (21)

ζητέω, I seek, ask for, deliberate (21)

ζωή, ἡ, life (3)

ἤ, or, than (31)

ἠγέρθην, I was raised (aorist passive of
ἐγείρω) (16)

ἤδη, already (13)

ἦλθον, I came, went (serves as the 2nd
aorist of ἔρχομαι) (14)

ἡμέρα, ἡ, day (3)

ἡμέτερος, -α, -ον, our (22)

ἤνεγκα, I brought, bore, carried (irregular 1st aorist of φέρω, conjugated
with -κα) (14)

ἠνέχθην, I was brought (serves as the
aorist passive of φέρω) (16)

ἤχθην, I was led (aor. pass. of ἄγω)
(16)

θάλασσα, ἡ, sea, lake (3)

θάνατος, ὁ, death (4)

θαυμάζω, I marvel, wonder (12)

θέλημα, -ατος, τό, will (17)

θέλω, I wish, will, desire (2)

θεός, ὁ, God, god (4)

θεραπεύω, I heal, serve (11)

θεωρέω, I look at, behold (24)

θρόνος, ὁ, a throne (13)

θυγάτηρ, -τρός, ἡ, daughter (27)

θύρα, ἡ, door (20)

ἴδιος, -α, -ον, one's own (13)

ἰδού, behold!, see! (11)

ἱερεύς, έως, ὁ, priest (25)

ἱερόν, τό, temple (10)

ἱμάτιον, τό, garment (13)

ἵνα, in order that, so that (+ subj.) (23)

ἵστημι, στήσω, ἔστησα or ἔστην, ἔστηκα, ἔσταμαι, ἐστάθην, (intransitive) I stand, stand firm, appear; (transitive) cause to stand, set, establish (30)

ἰσχυρός, -ά, -όν, strong, mighty (31)

κάθημαι, (dep.) I sit, live, stay (18)

καθίζω, I sit; seat (trans.) (19)

καθώς, as, even as, just as (27)

καί, and (2)

καιρός, ὁ, time, season (32)

κακός, -ή, -όν, bad, evil (5)

καλέω, I call, name, invite (21)

καλός, -ή, -όν, good, beautiful (5)

καρδία, ἡ, heart (3)

καρπός, ὁ, fruit (26)

κατά, (+ gen.) against; (+ acc.) according to (7)

καταβαίνω, I go down (10)

κεφαλή, ἡ, head (13)

κελεύω, I command (24)

κηρύσσω, κηρύξω, ἐκήρυξα, κεκήρυχα, κεκήρυγμαι, ἐκηρύχθην, I preach, proclaim (12)

κόσμος, ὁ, world (6)

κράζω, I cry out, call out (13)

κρατέω, I seize, grasp, hold (to) (26)

κρείσσων (or κρείττων), -ον, better compar. of ἀγαθός (31)

κρίνω, κρινῶ, ἔκρινα, κέκρικα, κέκριμαι, ἐκρίθην, I judge (8)

κρίσις, -εως, ἡ, judgment (25)

κτίζω, I create (20)

κύριος, ὁ, Lord, master, owner (4)

κώμη, ἡ, village (23)

λαλέω, I speak (21)

λαμβάνω, λήμψομαι, ἔλαβον, εἴληφα, εἴλημμαι, ἐλήμφθην, I take, receive (5)

λαός, ὁ, a people (8)

λέγω, ἐρῶ, εἶπον, εἴρηκα, εἴρημαι, ἐρρέθην, I say, speak, tell (2)

λήμψομαι, I will take, receive (dep. fut. of λαμβάνω) (12)

λίθος, ὁ, stone (6)

λογίζομαι, (dep.) I reckon, consider (18)

λόγος, ὁ, word (4)

λοιπός, -ή, -όν, remaining, rest; (subst.) the rest, the others; (adv.) henceforth, finally (29)

λύω, λύσω, ἔλυσα, λέλυκα, λέλυμαι, ἐλύθην, I loosen, destroy (2)

μαθητής, ὁ, disciple (6)

μακάριος, -α, -ον, blessed, happy (31)

μᾶλλον, more, rather (31)

μαρτυρέω, I witness, testify (24)

μέγας, μεγάλη, μέγα, large, great (28)

μείζων, -ον, greater; compar. of μέγας (31)

μέλλω, I am about to, am going to (10)

μέν . . . δέ, on the one hand . . . on the other; but (11)

μένω, I remain, stay, abide (6)

μέσος, -η, -ον, middle, in the midst (32)

μετά, (+ gen.) with; (+ acc.) after, behind (6)

μετανοέω, I repent (26)

μή, not (the usual negative for non-indicative moods) (18)

μηδέ, and not, nor, not even (+ subj.) (23)

μηδείς, μηδεμία, μηδέν, no one, nothing, no (= μηδέ + εἷς) (29)

μηκέτι, no longer (+ subj.) (23)

μήτηρ, μητρός, ἡ, mother (19)

μικρός, -ά, -όν, small, little (5)

μόνος, -η, -ον, only, alone, neut. μόνον as adv. (31)

νεκρός, -ά, -όν, dead (5)

νόμος, ὁ, a law (4)

νῦν, now (12)

νύξ, νυκτός, ἡ, night (17)

ὁ, ἡ, τό, the (5)

ὁδός, ἡ, way, road (6)

οἶδα, I know, understand (27)

οἶκος, ὁ, house (4)

οἶνος, ὁ, wine (14)

ὅλος, -η, -ον, whole (predicate position) (13)

ὅμοιος, -α, -ον, like, similar (+ dat.) (32)

ὄνομα, -ατος, τό, name (17)

ὅπου, where, whither (22)

ὅπως, in order that, that (+ subj.) (23)

ὁράω, ὄψομαι, εἶδον, ἑώρακα, ὦμμαι, ὤφθην, I see (21)

ὄρος, -ους, τό, mountain (25)

ὅς, ἥ, ὅ, who, which (relative pron.) (27)

ὅσος, -η, -ον, as great as, as many as (27)

ὅστις, ἥτις, ὅτι, whoever, whichever, whatever (indef. rel. pronoun) (27)

ὅταν, whenever (usu. + subj.) (23)

ὅτε, when (+ indic.) (23)

ὅτι, that, because (2)

οὐ, οὐκ, οὐχ, not (2)

οὐδέ, and not, nor, not even (9)

οὐδείς, οὐδεμία, οὐδέν, no one, nothing, no (= οὐδέ + εἷς) (29)

οὐκέτι, no longer (+ indic.) (23)

οὖν, therefore, consequently (8)

οὔπω, not yet (15)

οὐρανός, ὁ, heaven, sky (4)

οὖς, ὠτός, τό, ear (26)

οὔτε, neither, nor (11)

οὗτος, αὕτη, τοῦτο, this (8)

οὕτως, thus, so (8)

οὐχί, not (strengthened form of οὐ) (postpositive) (31)

ὀφείλω, I owe, ought, must (10)

ὀφθαλμός, ὁ, eye (11)

ὄχλος, ὁ, crowd (7)

ὄψομαι, I will see (serves as the dep. future of βλέπω) (14)

παιδίον, τό, infant, young child (24)

πάλιν, again (11)

παρά, (+ gen.) from; (+ dat.) beside, with, among; (+ acc.) by, along (10)

παραβολή, ἡ, parable, proverb (24)

παραγίνομαι, I come, arrive (19)

παραδίδωμι, I hand over, betray (28)

παρακαλέω, I exhort, encourage, comfort (21)

παραλαμβάνω, I receive, take along (19)

πᾶς, πᾶσα, πᾶν, all, every; entire, whole (21)

πατήρ, πατρός, ὁ, father (19)

πείθω, πείσω, ἔπεισα, πέποιθα, πέπεισμαι, ἐπείσθην, I persuade (13)

πέμπω, πέμψω, ἔπεμψα, πέπομφα, πέπεμμαι, ἐπέμφθην, I send (6)

πέντε, five (30)

πέποιθα, I depend on, trust in (perfect active of πείθω) (15)

περί, (+ gen.) about, concerning; (+ acc.) around (6)

περιπατέω, I walk, live (21)

πεσοῦμαι, I will fall (fut. of πίπτω) (22)

πίνω, πίομαι, ἔπιον, πέπωκα, πέπομαι, ἐπόθην, I drink (14)

πίπτω, πεσοῦμαι, ἔπεσον, πέπτωκα, —, —, I fall (14)

πιστεύω, I believe (2)

πίστις, -εως, ἡ, faith, trust, belief (25)

πιστός, -ή, -όν, faithful, believing (5)

πλείων, -ον, more, larger; comparative of πολύς (31)

πλήρης, -ες, full (25)

πληρόω, πληρώσω, ἐπλήρωσα, πεπλήρωκα, πεπλήρωμαι, ἐπληρώθην, I fill, make full of, fulfill (21)

πλοῖον, τό, boat, multitude (7)

πνεῦμα, -ατος, τό, spirit, Spirit (17)

ποιέω, ποιήσω, ἐποίησα, πεποίηκα, πεποίημαι, ἐποιήθην, I do, make (21)

πόλις, -εως, ἡ, city (25)

πολλάκις, often, many times (15)

πολύς, πολλή, πολύ, much, many (28)

πονηρός, -ά, -όν, wicked, evil (5)

πορεύομαι, πορεύσομαι, ἐπορευσάμην, —, πεπόρευμαι, ἐπορεύθην, I go, walk, live (9)

ποῦ, where? (27)

πούς, ποδός, ὁ, foot (19)

πρεσβύτερος, -α, -ον, older, elder (28)

πρό, (+ gen.) before (24)

πρός, (+ acc.) to, toward, with (6)

προσέρχομαι, I come to, approach (14)

προσεύχομαι, I pray (12)

προσκυνέω, I worship, bow down to (usu. + dat, less often + acc.) (22)

προστίθημι, I add (to), increase; continue (29)

προσφέρω, I offer, present (14)

πρόσωπον, τό, a face (8)

προφήτης, ὁ, prophet (6)

πρῶτος, -η, -ον, first (5)

πῦρ, πυρός, τό, fire (22)

πῶς, how? (16)

ῥῆμα, -ατος, τό, word (17)

σάββατον, τό, Sabbath (19)

σάρξ, σαρκός, ἡ, flesh (17)

σεαυτοῦ, of yourself (21)

σημεῖον, τό, sign, miracle, portent (14)

σός, σή, σόν, your (sing.) (22)

σοφία, ἡ, wisdom (24)

σπείρω, σπερῶ, ἔσπειρα, —, ἔσπαρμαι, ἐσπάρην, I sow (22)

σπέρμα, -ατος, τό, seed (17)

σταυρόω, I crucify (21)

στόμα, -ατος, τό, mouth (17)

σύ, you (sing.) (7)

σύν, (+ dat.) with (9)

συνάγω, I gather together (10)

συναγωγή, ἡ, synagogue, gathering (19)

σῴζω, σώσω, ἔσωσα, σέσωκα, σέσωμαι or σέσωσμαι, ἐσώθην, I save (7)

σῶμα, -ατος, τό, body (17)

σωτηρία, ἡ, salvation (32)

τέ, and (a weak conjunction, often correlated with τέ or καί) (11)

τέθνηκα, I have died, I am dead (perfect of θνῄσκω) (15)

τέκνον, τό, child (4)

τέλος, -ους, τό, end (25)

τέσσαρες, τέσσαρα, four (30)

τηρέω, I keep, observe, obey (22)

τίθημι, θήσω, ἔθηκα, τέθεικα, τέθειμαι, ἐτέθην, I place, put, appoint (29)

τίς, τί, who? which? what? (interrogative) (27)

τις, τι, someone, something, a certain one, a certain thing (indefinite) (27)

τοιοῦτος, -αύτη, -οῦτον or -οῦτο, such (32)

τόπος, ὁ, place (11)

τότε, then (11)

τρεῖς, τρία, three (30)

τυφλός, -ή, -όν, blind, blind person (20)

ὕδωρ, ὕδατος, τό, water (22)

υἱός, ὁ, son (4)

ὑμέτερος, -α, -ον, your (pl.) (22)

ὑπάγω, I go away, go (26)

ὑπάρχω, I am, exist (τὰ ὑπάρχοντα, possessions, belongings) (18)

ὑπέρ, (+ gen.) in behalf of; (+ acc.) above (10)

ὑπό, (+ gen.) by; (+ acc.) under (9)

ὑποστρέφω, I return (13)

φάγομαι, I will eat (dep. fut. of ἐσθίω) (14)

φανερόω, I make known, reveal (32)

φέρω, οἴσω, ἤνεγκα, ἐνήνοχα, ἐνήνεγμαι, ἠνέχθην, I bring, bear, carry (12)

φεύγω, φεύξομαι, ἔφυγον, I flee (14)

φημί, I say (30)

φοβέομαι, I fear (21)

φόβος, ὁ, fear; reverence (32)

φυλακή, ἡ, prison, watch, guard (20)

φωνή, ἡ, voice, sound (3)

φῶς, φωτός, τό, light (22)

χαίρω, I rejoice (26)

χαρά, ἡ, joy, delight (28)

χαρίζομαι, I graciously give, forgive (20)

χάρις, χάριτος, ἡ, grace, favor (20)

χείρ, χειρός, ἡ, hand (19)

χρεία, ἡ, need, necessity, lack (32)

χρόνος, ὁ, time (28)

ψυχή, ἡ, soul, life (7)

ὧδε, here, hither (26)

ὤν, οὖσα, ὄν, being (present participle of εἰμί) (18)

ὥρα, ἡ, hour, time (3)

ὡς, as, how, that, about (23)

ὥστε, so that (often + inf.) (24)

ὤφθην, I was seen (serves as the aorist passive of βλέπω) (16)

English to Greek Vocabulary

abide, μένω

about, περί (+ gen.), ὡς

above, ὑπέρ (+ acc.)

accept, δέχομαι

according to, κατά (+ acc.)

after, μετά (+ acc.)

again, πάλιν

against, κατά (+ gen.)

age, αἰών

all, πᾶς

alone, μόνος

along, παρά (+ acc.)

already, ἤδη

am able, δύναμαι

am, εἰμί, γίνομαι, ὑπάρχω

amen, ἀμήν

among, παρά (+ dat.)

and not, μηδέ (+ subj.); οὐδέ (+ indic.)

and, καί, δέ, τέ

angel, ἄγγελος

announce, ἀπαγγέλλω

answer, (verb) ἀποκρίνομαι (+ dat.)

apostle, ἀπόστολος

appear, γίνομαι, ἵστημι

appoint, τίθημι

approach, προσέρχομαι

arise, ἀνίστημι, γίνομαι

around, περί (+ acc.)

arrive, παραγίνομαι

as far as, ἄχρι (+ gen.), ἕως (+ gen.)

as great as, ὅσος

as many as, ὅσος

as, ὡς, καθώς

ask for, ζητέω

ask, αἰτέω, ἐρωτάω, ἐπερωτάω

assembly, ἐκκλησία

at once, εὐθύς

at, ἐπί (+ dat.)

authority, ἐξουσία

bad, κακός

baptize, βαπτίζω

be about to, μέλλω

be going to, μέλλω

be, εἰμί, γίνομαι, ὑπάρχω

bear, φέρω

bear (a child), γεννάω

beautiful, καλός

because of, διά (+ acc.)

because, ὅτι

become, γίνομαι

before, ἐνώπιον, ἔμπροσθεν, πρό (all + gen.)

beget, γεννάω

begin, ἄρχω (middle voice)

beginning, ἀρχή

behind, μετά (+ acc.)

behold!, (interjection) ἰδού

behold, θεωρέω

being, ὤν, οὖσα, ὄν

belief, πίστις

believe, πιστεύω

believing, πιστός

belongings, τὰ ὑπάρχοντα

beloved, ἀγαπητός

beside, παρά (+ dat.)

betray, παραδίδωμι

better, κρείσσων

blessed, μακάριος

blind, blind person, τυφλός

blood, αἷμα

boat, πλοῖον

body, σῶμα

book, βιβλίον

bow down to, προσκυνέω (usu. + dat.)

bread, ἄρτος

bring good news, εὐαγγελίζομαι

bring, φέρω

brother, ἀδελφός

but, δέ, ἀλλά, μέν . . . δέ

buy, ἀγοράζω

by, ὑπό (+ gen.), παρά (+ acc.)

call out, κράζω

call, καλέω

can, δύναμαι

carry, φέρω

cast out, ἐκβάλλω

cause to stand, ἵστημι

certain one, certain thing, τις, τι

chief priest, ἀρχιερεύς

child, παιδίον, τέκνον

church, ἐκκλησία

city, πόλις

come, ἔρχομαι, γίνομαι, παραγίνομαι

come to, προσέρχομαι

comfort, παρακαλέω

command, (verb) κελεύω

commandment, ἐντολή

concerning, περί (+ gen.)

consecrate, ἁγιάζω

consecrated, ἅγιος

consequently, οὖν

consider, λογίζομαι

continue, προστίθημι

country, ἀγρός

create, κτίζω

crowd, ὄχλος

crucify, σταυρόω

cry out, κράζω

daughter, θυγάτηρ

day, ἡμέρα

dead, νεκρός

death, θάνατος

deed, ἔργον

deliberate, ζητέω

delight, χαρά

demon, δαιμόνιον

depart, ἀπέρχομαι

depend on, πέποιθα (perf. of πείθω)

descendants, γένος

desert, ἔρημος

desire, (verb) θέλω

destroy, λύω, ἀπόλλυμι, ἀπολλύω

die, ἀποθνήσκω

different, ἕτερος

disciple, μαθητής

dismiss, ἀπολύω

do, ποιέω, ἐργάζομαι

door, θύρα

draw near, ἐγγίζω

drink, πίνω

each other, ἀλλήλων

each, ἕκαστος

ear, οὖς

earth, γῆ

eat, ἐσθίω

elder, πρεσβύτερος

encourage, παρακαλέω

end, τέλος

enter, εἰσέρχομαι

entire, πᾶς

entreat, ἐρωτάω

establish, ἵστημι

eternal, αἰώνιος

even as, καθώς

every, πᾶς, ἕκαστος

evil, κακός, πονηρός

exhort, παρακαλέω

exist, ὑπάρχω

explain, δείκνυμι, δεικνύω

eye, ὀφθαλμός

face, πρόσωπον

faith, πίστις

faithful, πιστός

fall, πίπτω

father, πατήρ

favor, χάρις

fear, (noun) φόβος

field, ἀγρός

fill, πληρόω

finally, (τό) λοιπός

find, εὑρίσκω

fire, πῦρ

first, πρῶτος

five, πέντε

flesh, σάρξ

follow, ἀκολουθέω

foot, πούς

for the sake of, διά (+ acc.)

for this reason, διό

for, (preposition) ἐπί (+ acc.)

for, (conjunction) γάρ (postpositive)

forgive, ἀφίημι, χαρίζομαι

four, τέσσαρες

from, ἀπό, (+ gen.), παρά (+ gen.)

fruit, καρπός

fulfill, πληρόω

full, πλήρης

garment, ἱμάτιον

gather together, συνάγω

gathering, συναγωγή

Gentiles, ἔθνος (plur.)

gift, δῶρον

give back, ἀποδίδωμι

give, δίδωμι

glorify, δοξάζω

glory, δόξα

go away, ἀπέρχομαι, ὑπάγω

go down, καταβαίνω

go in, εἰσέρχομαι

go out, ἐξέρχομαι

go through, διέρχομαι

go up, ἀναβαίνω

go, ἔρχομαι, πορεύομαι, ὑπάγω

God, god, θεός

good news, εὐαγγέλιον

good, ἀγαθός, καλός

Gospel, εὐαγγέλιον

grace, χάρις

graciously give, χαρίζομαι

grant, δίδωμι

grasp, κρατέω

great, μέγας

greater, μείζων

greet, ἀσπάζομαι

guard, φυλακή

hand over, παραδίδωμι

hand, χείρ

happen, γίνομαι

happy, μακάριος

have mercy on, ἐλεέω

have, ἔχω

he, αὐτός

head, κεφαλή

heal, θεραπεύω

hear, ἀκούω

heart, καρδία
heaven, οὐρανός
henceforth, (τό) λοιπός
here, ὧδε
herself, ἑαυτῆς
himself, ἑαυτοῦ
hither, ὧδε
hold (to), κρατέω
holy, ἅγιος
honor, δόξα
hope, (noun) ἐλπίς
hour, ὥρα
house, οἶκος
how, ὡς
how?, πῶς
human being, ἄνθρωπος
husband, ἀνήρ

I, ἐγώ
if, εἰ (usu. with indic.); ἐάν (+ subj.)
immediately, εὐθύς
in addition to, ἐπί (+ dat.)
in behalf of, ὑπέρ (+ gen.);
in front of, ἔμπροσθεν (+ gen.)
in order that, ἵνα (+ subj.), ὅπως
   (+ subj.)
in the midst, μέσος
in the presence of, ἐνώπιον (+ gen.)
in the sight of, ἐνώπιον (+ gen.)
in, ἐν (+ dat.)
increase, προστίθημι
infant, παιδίον
into, εἰς (+ acc.)
invite, καλέω
it, αὐτό
itself, ἑαυτοῦ

joy, χαρά
judge, κρίνω
judgment, κρίσις
just as, καθώς
just, δίκαιος

keep, τηρέω
kill, ἀποκτείνω
kind, (noun) γένος
king, βασιλεύς
kingdom, βασιλεία
know, γινώσκω, οἶδα, ἐπιγινώσκω

lack, χρεία
lake, θάλασσα
land, γῆ
language, γλῶσσα
large, μέγας
larger, μείζων, πλείων
last, ἔσχατος
law, νόμος
(it is) lawful, ἔξεστι(ν)
lay upon, ἐπιτίθημι
lead, ἄγω
leave, ἀφίημι
let go, ἀφίημι
life, ψυχή, ζωή
lift up, αἴρω
light, φῶς
like, ὅμοιος (+ dat.)
little, μικρός
live, ζάω, περιπατέω, κάθημαι,
   πορεύομαι
loaf, ἄρτος
look at, θεωρέω
loosen, λύω
Lord, κύριος
lose, ἀπόλλυμι, ἀπολλύω
love, (noun) ἀγάπη
love, (verb) ἀγαπάω

make full of, πληρόω
make known, φανερόω, γνωρίζω
make, ποιέω
man, ἀνήρ, ἄνθρωπος
many, πολύς
many times, πολλάκις
marvel, θαυμάζω

master, κύριος

messenger, ἄγγελος

middle, μέσος

mighty, ἰσχυρός

mine, ἐμός

miracle, σημεῖον, δύναμις (usu. plur.)

more, μᾶλλον, πλείων

mother, μητήρ

mountain, ὄρος

mouth, στόμα

much, πολύς

multitude, ὄχλος

must, ὀφείλω

my, ἐμός

myself, ἐμαυτοῦ

name, (verb) καλέω

name, (noun) ὄνομα

nation, ἔθνος

(it is) necessary, δεῖ (+ inf.)

necessity, χρεία

need, χρεία

neither, οὔτε

night, νύξ

no longer, οὐκέτι (+ indic.); μηκέτι
  (+ subj.)

no one, οὐδείς (+ indic.); μηδείς
  (+ subj.)

noble, ἀγαθός

nor, οὔτε, οὐδέ (+ indic.); μηδέ
  (+ subj.)

not even, οὐδέ (+ indic.); μηδέ
  (+ subj.)

not yet, οὔπω

not, μή (nonindicative)

not, οὐ, οὐκ, οὐχ (indicative)

not, (strong form) οὐχί

nothing, οὐδέ (+ indic.); μηδέ (+ subj.)

now, νῦν

obey, τηρέω

observe, τηρέω

often, πολλάκις

older, πρεσβύτερος

on the one hand . . . on the other, μέν
  . . . δέ

on, ἐπί (+ dat., gen., or acc.)

one another, ἀλλήλων

one's own, ἴδιος

one, εἷς, μία, ἕν

only, μόνος

open, ἀνοίγω

or, ἤ

other, ἄλλος, ἕτερος, λοιπός

ought, ὀφείλω

our, ἡμέτερος

out of, ἐκ (+ gen.)

outside, ἔξω (sometimes + gen.)

over, ἐπί (+ gen. or acc.)

owe, ὀφείλω

owner, κύριος

parable, παραβολή

peace, εἰρήνη

people, λαός, γένος

perish, ἀπόλλυμι, ἀπολλύω (mid. voice)

permit, ἀφίημι

persecute, διώκω

person, ἄνθρωπος

persuade, πείθω

pity, ἐλεέω

place upon, ἐπιτίθημι

place, (verb) βάλλω, τίθημι

place, (noun) τόπος

point out, δείκνυμι, δεικνύω

portent, σημεῖον

possessions, τὰ ὑπάρχοντα

power, δύναμις

pray, προσεύχομαι

preach, κηρύσσω, εὐαγγελίζομαι

prepare, ἑτοιμάζω

present, προσφέρω

priest, ἱερεύς

prison, φυλακή

proclaim, κηρύσσω
promise, (noun) ἐπαγγελία
prophet, προφήτης
prove, δείκνυμι, δεικνύω
proverb, παραβολή
pursue, διώκω
put, βάλλω, τίθημι

question, (verb) ἐπερωτάω

race, γένος
raise up, ἐγείρω
raise, ἀνίστημι
rather, μᾶλλον
receive, δέχομαι, λαμβάνω,
   παραλαμβάνω
reckon, λογίζομαι
recognize, ἐπιγινώσκω
redeem, ἀγοράζω
reign, βασιλεία
rejoice, χαίρω
release, ἀπολύω
remain, μένω
remaining, λοιπός
render, ἀποδίδωμι
repent, μετανοέω
report, ἀπαγγέλλω
request, αἰτέω, ἐρωτάω
rest, λοιπός
return, ἐπιστρέφω, ὑποστρέφω
reveal, φανερόω, γνωρίζω
reverence, φόβος
reward, ἀποδίδωμι
right, δεξιός
righteous, δίκαιος
righteousness, δικαιοσύνη
road, ὁδός
rule, (verb) ἄρχω (+ gen.)
rule, (noun) βασιλεία
ruler, ἀρχή, ἄρχων

Sabbath, σάββατον

salute, ἀσπάζομαι
salvation, σωτηρία
same, αὐτός (attrib. position)
sanctify, ἁγιάζω
save, σώζω
say, λέγω, φημί
scribe, γραμματεύς
Scripture, γραφή
sea, θάλασσα
season, καιρός
seat, (transitive) καθίζω
see!, (interjection) ἰδού
see, βλέπω, ὁράω
seed, σπέρμα
seek, ζητέω
seem, seem good, δοκέω
seize, κρατέω
-self, αὐτός (pred. position)
send, πέμπω, ἀποστέλλω
servant, δοῦλος
serve, θεραπεύω
set, set up, ἵστημι
seven, ἑπτά
she, αὐτή
show, δείκνυμι, δεικνύω
sick, ἀσθενής
sign, σημεῖον
similar, ὅμοιος (+ dat.)
sin, (noun) ἁμαρτία
sin, (verb) ἁμαρτάνω
single, εἷς, μία, ἕν
sinner, ἁμαρτωλός
sister, ἀδελφή
sit, καθίζω, κάθημαι
sky, οὐρανός
slave, δοῦλος
small, μικρός
so that, ἵνα (+ subj.); ὥστε (often +
   inf.)
so, οὕτως
soil, γῆ
someone, something, τις, τι

son, υἱός

soul, ψυχή

sound, φωνή

sow, σπείρω

speak, λαλέω, λέγω

spirit, Spirit, πνεῦμα

stand, stand firm, ἵστημι

stay, μένω, κάθημαι

still, ἔτι

stock, γένος

stone, λίθος

strength, δύναμις

strong, ἰσχυρός

such, τοιοῦτος

synagogue, συναγωγή

take along, παραλαμβάνω

take up, take away, αἴρω

take, λαμβάνω

teach, διδάσκω

teacher, διδάσκαλος

tell, λέγω

temple, ἱερόν

ten, δέκα

testify, μαρτυρέω

than, ἤ

that, (demonstrative) ἐκεῖνος

that, (conjunction) ὅπως (+ subj.)

that, (introducing discourse) ὅτι, ὡς

the, ὁ, ἡ, τό

then, τότε, εὐθύς

there, ἐκεῖ

therefore, οὖν, διό

think, δοκέω

this, οὗτος

three, τρεῖς

throne, θρόνος

through, διά (+ gen.)

throw, βάλλω

thus, οὕτως

time, καιρός, χρόνος, ὥρα

to, εἰς (+ acc.), πρός (+ acc.)

tongue, γλῶσσα

toward, ἐπί (+ acc.), πρός (+ acc.)

true, ἀληθής

truly, ἀμήν

trust in, πέποιθα (perf. of πείθω)

trust, (noun) πίστις

truth, ἀλήθεια

turn, ἐπιστρέφω

twelve, δώδεκα

two, δύο

under, ὑπό (+ acc.)

understand, ἐπιγινώσκω, οἶδα

until, ἕως

up to, ἄχρι (+ gen.)

upon, ἐπί (+ gen.)

village, κώμη

voice, φωνή

walk, περιπατέω, πορεύομαι

want, βούλομαι

watch, (noun) φυλακή

water, ὕδωρ

way, ὁδός

weak, ἀσθενής

what?, τίς, τί

whatever, ὅστις

when, ὅτε (+ indic.)

whenever, ὅταν (usu. + subj.)

where, ὅπου

where?, ποῦ

whether, εἰ (usu. + indic.)

which, ὅς, ἥ, ὅ

which?, τίς, τί

whichever, ὅστις

whither, ὅπου

who, ὅς, ἥ, ὅ

who?, τίς, τί

whoever, ὅστις

whole, πᾶς, ὅλος

why?, τί

wicked, πονηρός
wife, γυνή
will, (noun) θέλημα
will, (verb) θέλω
wine, οἶνος
wisdom, σοφία
wish, (verb) θέλω, βούλομαι
with, μετά (+ gen.), παρά (+ dat.),
   πρός (+ acc.), σύν (+ dat.)
witness, (verb) μαρτυρέω
woman, γυνή
wonder, θαυμάζω
word, λόγος, ῥῆμα

work, (noun) ἔργον
work, (verb) ἐργάζομαι
world, κόσμος, αἰών
worship, προσκυνέω (usu. + dat.)
write, γράφω
writing, γραφή

year, ἔτος
yet, ἔτι
you, σύ
your, σός, σή, σόν (sing.); ὑμέτερος
   (plural)
yourself, σεαυτοῦ

Bibliography for Further Study

Several works are available for the student who wishes to pursue the study of Biblical Greek. Some tools for lexical and grammatical study are listed below.

GREEK LEXICONS AND RELATED TOOLS

Alsop, J. R. *An Index to the Bauer-Arndt-Gingrich Lexicon.* 2nd ed., Grand Rapids: Zondervan, 1981. Enables the student to locate New Testament citations quickly; especially helpful with common words whose entries in Bauer (see next entry) are lengthy.

Bauer, W., William F. Arndt, F. Wilbur Gingrich, and Frederick W. Danker. *A Greek-English Lexicon of the New Testament and Other Early Christian Literature.* Chicago: University of Chicago Press, 1979. The standard lexicon for New Testament study.

Kubo, S. *A Reader's Greek Lexicon of the New Testament.* Grand Rapids: Zondervan, 1975. Very useful for the intermediate student. Not a reference lexicon; arranged canonically, not alphabetically, to facilitate reading the NT text. Contains word frequency statistics.

Liddell, H. G. and R. Scott. *A Greek-English Lexicon.* 9th ed. Revised and augmented by H. S. Jones. Oxford: Clarendon, 1940. Supplement added in 1968. The standard Greek lexicon for classical Greek, but contains many Hellenistic, LXX, and NT references.

Louw, J. P. and E. A. Nida. *Greek-English Lexicon of the New Testament Based on Semantic Domains.* 2 vols. New York: American Bible Society, 1988. The product of recent linguistic study. Arranged by semantic domains (i.e., clusters of words with similar meanings), not alphabetically.

Lust, J., E. Eynikel, and K. Hauspie, eds. *A Greek-English Lexicon of the Septuagint.* 2

vols. Deutsche Bibelgesellschaft, 1992-96. The first complete lexicon of the LXX in over 100 years. Includes a helpful introduction and bibliography.

GREEK GRAMMARS

Blass, F. and A. Debrunner. *A Greek Grammar of the New Testament and Other Early Christian Literature.* Translated and edited by Robert W. Funk. Chicago: University of Chicago Press, 1961. A standard text. Valuable, but not always coherent in its arrangement.

Brooks, J. A. and C. L. Winbury. *Syntax of New Testament Greek.* Washington: University Press of America, 1979. A handbook-sized grammar, not a reference book. Very useful, arranged well, amply illustrated with NT examples.

Burton, Ernest DeWitt. *Syntax of the Moods and Tenses in New Testament Greek.* Chicago: University of Chicago Press, 1900. Reprinted by Kregel, 1976. Old, but still one of the best treatments of the verbal system.

Conybeare, F. C. and St. George Stock. *Grammar of Septuagint Greek. With Selected Readings, Vocabularies, and Updated Indexes.* Originally published by Ginn and Company, 1905. Peabody, MA: Hendrickson, 1995. Contains an introduction and major sections covering word formation and syntax.

Dana, H. E. and Julius R. Mantey. *A Manual Grammar of the Greek New Testament.* Toronto, Ontario: Macmillan, 1955. An older but still useful handbook; indebted to the work of A. T. Robertson.

Moulton, James Hope, et al. *A Grammar of New Testament Greek.* Edinburgh: T. & T. Clark, 1908-1976. See esp. vol. 3: *Syntax,* by Nigel Turner, 1963, and vol. 4: *Style,* by Nigel Turner, 1976. A thorough treatment by British scholars.

Robertson, A. T. *A Grammar of the Greek New Testament in the Light of Historical Research.* Nashville: Broadman Press, 1934. A massive work (1400+ pages) by a very capable scholar; loaded with NT references; theologically sensitive but sometimes overreaching.

Smyth, Herbert W. *Greek Grammar.* Cambridge, MA: Harvard University Press, 1920. The best classical Greek grammar in English. Must be used with care by students of biblical Greek since the latter often diverges from classical usage.

Wallace, Daniel B. *Greek Grammar beyond the Basics.* Grand Rapids: Zondervan, 1997. A comprehensive, advanced grammar that attempts to bridge the gap between the study of syntax and theological exegesis.

Zerwick, Maximilian. *Biblical Greek Illustrated by Examples.* 4th ed. Adapted by Joseph Smith from the 4th Latin ed. Rome: Pontifical Biblical Institute, 1963. A useful, handbook-sized treatment by a Jesuit scholar.

Index

Numbers refer to sections. Subpoints within sections are indicated by decimals. Greek words are alphabetized according to their English transliterations.

Index

Index